Intercultural Communication

Intercultural Communication

A Contextual Approach

Second Edition

James W. Neuliep
St. Norbert College

Houghton Mifflin Company   BOSTON   NEW YORK

Editor-in-Chief: Charles Hartford
Sponsoring Editor: Adam Forrand
Associate Editor: Kristen Desmond-LeFevre
Editorial Associate: Brigitte Maser
Associate Project Editor: Kristin Penta
Editorial Assistant: May Jawdat
Senior Production/Design Coordinator: Jodi O'Rourke
Senior Manufacturing Coordinator: Jane Spelman
Marketing Manager: Barbara LeBuhn

Cover Art: Harold Burch, New York City

Printed in the U.S.A.

Library of Congress Control Number: 2001133316

ISBN: 0-618-21854-8

1 2 3 4 5 6 7 8 9–CS–06 05 04 03 02

To Jan, forever . . .

Preface

Intercultural Communication: A Contextual Approach, 2/e is designed for college level students taking their first course in intercultural communication. The purpose of the book is to introduce students to some of the fundamental topics, theories, concepts, and themes that are the center of the study of intercultural communication.

The overall organizational scheme of this book is based on a *contextual model of intercultural communication.* Presented in Chapter One, this model represents intercultural communication as the exchange of verbal messages and nonverbal messages that occur within the cultural, microcultural, environmental, sociorelational, and perceptual contexts of the participants.

This is a new edition of *Intercultural Communication: A Contextual Approach.* The organizational scheme of this new edition remains essentially unchanged from the first edition, but many substantive revisions have been incorporated into each chapter, and a new chapter has been added.

Chapter One alerts students to the importance and necessity of intercultural communication as we enter the dawn of the twenty-first century. Data from the 2000 census is reviewed and points to the growing diversity of the U.S. population, focusing on the growth of the Hispanic population. The chapter continues with extended discussions of the nature of human communication and culture. Chapter One also includes the addition of the Personal Report of Communication Apprehension (PRCA-24) and the Generalized Ethnocentrism scale. The Personal Report of Intercultural Communication Apprehension (PRICA), included in the first edition, remains a part of the chapter. Finally, a delineation of three fundamental assumptions of intercultural communication has been included.

In Chapter Two, culture is defined as an accumulated pattern of values, beliefs, and behaviors that are shared by an identifiable group of people with a common history and verbal and nonverbal code systems. The outer circle of the model of intercultural communication represents the cultural context. This is the largest circle because culture permeates every aspect of the communicative exchange, even the physical geography. All communicative exchanges between persons occur within culture. The cultural context is the focus of Chapter Two. Well-recognized topics such as individualism-collectivism, high-low context, weak-strong uncertainty avoidance, value orientations, and high-low power distance are discussed. Self-report scales measuring each of these topics are included in this chapter.

The focus of Chapter Three is the microcultural context. Within most cultures, there are groups of people who differ in some significant way from the general "macro" culture. These groups are sometimes called minorities, subcultures, or cocultures. In this book, the term "microculture" is used to refer to those identifiable groups of people who share a set of values, beliefs and behaviors and who possess a common history and verbal and nonverbal symbol system that is similar to but systematically varies from the larger, often dominant cultural milieu. Microcultures can be different from the larger culture in a variety of ways, most often because of race, ethnicity, language, religion, or even because of their behavioral practices. Often times such microcultures develop their own language for communicating outside of the dominant or majority culture's context or value system. A new feature of Chapter Three is an extended discussion of the Hispanic microculture in the United States. Thus, in the revised Chapter Three, four U.S. microcultures are highlighted, including Hispanics, African Americans, Amish, and Hmong.

Chapter Four focuses on the environmental context. While culture prescribes the overall rules for communication, the environmental context prescribes when and what specific rules apply. The environmental context includes the physical geography, architecture, landscape design, housing, perceptions of privacy, time orientation, and even the climate of a particular culture. These environmental factors play a key role in how people communicate. In this chapter, students are given the opportunity to assess their privacy preferences and their monochronic/polychronic orientations. The revised Chapter Four includes coverage of the nature of privacy in the U.S., with a special focus on the perceptions of privacy among U.S. students.

Chapter Five focuses on the perceptual contexts of the participants. The perceptual context refers to the individual characteristics of the participants, including their cognitions, attitudes, dispositions, and motivations. How an individual gathers, stores, and retrieves information is uniquely human but also culturally influenced. An individual's attitudes about others, including stereotypes, are culturally influenced. In this chapter, students can assess their stereotypes of African Americans and Jews and compare their results with those of other students, both past and present. A new component of Chapter Five is a discussion of American racism as a parallel to ethnocentrism.

The sociorelational context is the focus of Chapter Six. Whenever two people come together and interact, they establish some sort of social relationship based upon their group memberships. Within such relationships each person assumes a role. Roles prescribe *with whom, about what, and how* to communicate. Roles vary from culture to culture. For example, in just about every culture there are student and teacher role relationships. How student/teacher roles are defined varies significantly from culture to culture. For example, the U.S. American definition of a student varies significantly from the Japanese definition of a student. What it means to be a mother or a father varies considerably from one culture to another. One's roles prescribe the types of verbal and nonverbal symbols that are exchanged. Chapter Six contains a completely revised and updated discussion of family groups and sex and gender groups. In addition, the contextual model of intercultural communication represents the sociorelational context as defined by verbal and nonverbal codes.

Chapter Seven focuses on the verbal code, human language. Throughout much of this text, cultural *differences* are highlighted. In Chapter Seven, however, language is characterized as essentially *human* rather than cultural. Based on the ideas of Noam Chomsky and other contemporary linguists, Chapter Seven points out that regardless of culture, people are born with the capacity for language. Humans are born with universal grammar and—through culture—are exposed to a subset of it, which constitutes their particular culture's language (e.g., English, French, etcetera). The language of a particular culture is simply a subset of universal language. To be sure, however, culture certainly affects how we use language. Thus, Chapter Seven outlines several styles of language and how they vary across cultures.

Chapter Eight focuses on nonverbal language. After a discussion of the relationship between verbal and nonverbal codes, seven channels of nonverbal communication are discussed, including kinesics, paralanguage, proxemics, haptics, olfactics, physical appearance and dress, and chronemics.

In the discussion of kinesics, the use of gestures across cultures and an extended discussion of affect displays across cultures are discussed. In the coverage of paralanguage, cultural uses of silence and tonal languages are discussed. Cultural variations of space are covered in the section on proxemics. High and low contact cultures are the focus of the section on haptics. An extended discussion of olfactics across cultures is presented and students can assess their perception of smell by completing the Personal Report of Olfactic Perception and Sensitivity (PROPS) scale. The discussion of physical appearance and dress looks at cultural variations in Muslim cultures and Japan, among others. The discussion of chronemics reviews Hall's monochronic/polychronic distinction in addition to a treatment of the use of calendars across cultures. Finally, the chapter closes with a cross-cultural application of Nonverbal Expectancy Violations Theory.

Chapter Nine discusses the development of intercultural relationships. Five factors that affect relationships are the focus of this chapter, including uncertainty reduction, intercultural communication apprehension, sociocommunicative style, empathy, and similarity. Each factor is discussed with an emphasis on intercultural relationships. The chapter also includes a completely revised discussion of relationship differences among Eastern and Western cultures, marital relationships across cultures, interracial and intercultural relationships, arranged marriages, mate selection practices across cultures, and divorce. In this chapter, students can complete the Factors in Choosing a Mate instrument and compare their preferences with other cultures.

Chapter Ten focuses on intercultural communication in organizations. In this chapter, all of the contexts presented earlier are applied to the organizational context. Organizational examples from the cultural, microcultural, environmental, perceptual, and sociorelational contexts have been updated. Because they are three of our largest trade partners, management perspectives in Japan, Germany, and Mexico are highlighted. The section on management practices in Mexico is completely new. A model of intercultural conflict, with an emphasis on organizations, has also been added to this edition.

The previous Chapter Eleven has now been divided into two different chapters. In this edition, the focus of Chapter Eleven is acculturation and culture shock. A new chapter Twelve focuses on intercultural competence.

The central theme of Chapter Eleven includes the practical aspects of traveling or moving to a new culture. A new model of assimilation/acculturation is presented along with factors that influence the acculturation process, such as perceived similarity and host culture attitudes. A four stage "U" model of culture shock is outlined. In addition, the chapter now includes a discussion of the "W" curve model of culture shock. The chapter also includes a variety of self-report inventories to help students prepare for their journeys abroad.

A new Chapter Twelve has been added, and this chapter focuses on intercultural competence. This model represents intercultural competence as four interdependent components: knowledge, affective, psychomotor, and situational features components. A new self-assessment instrument has been included so that students can assess the knowledge component of the competence model. In addition to the model, a completely new section on intercultural training has been incorporated.

This new edition contains several new graphic features, including Recap boxes, Self-Assessment boxes, Intercultural Conversation boxes, and Intercultural Communication boxes. Recap boxes serve to review and quickly summarize concepts discussed throughout the core text paragraphs. Most chapters contain a number of Self-Assessment boxes. These are self-report instruments for students to complete; they are designed so that students can learn about themselves as they learn about important concepts in intercultural communication. The instruments included throughout have documented validity and reliability. As in the first edition, most of the chapters in this revised edition contain intercultural conversations. These boxes include hypothetical scripts that illustrate how the various concepts discussed in the chapters manifest themselves in human interaction. Although hypothetical, these dialogues are based on naturally occurring human interaction and are modeled from a variety of sources, including Craig Storti's book *Cross Cultural Dialogues* (Intercultural Press, 1994), Andrew Murphy's *Cultural Encounters in the USA: Cross-Cultural Dialogues and Mini-Dramas* (National Textbook Company, 1991), and the *Going International* film series, especially part three, *Managing the Overseas Assignment* (Copeland Griggs, 1983). Intercultural Communication in Practice boxes detail examples of intercultural communication as it works in the real world. Each chapter also includes a summary, a glossary of terms, and an extensive reference list.

New to this edition is a Student Workbook. This workbook is designed to accompany the text. Instructors should encourage their students to use this workbook, as it includes a number of study guides, sample test questions, and exercises all designed to facilitate the comprehension and application of the material in the text.

A number of people have been instrumental in the revision of this book. As in the first edition, this book has been strongly influenced by the writing and research of William B. Gudykunst. His influence can be seen throughout this text. Gudykunst's substantial contributions to the field remain a strong influence on the way we write and teach about intercultural communication. The editorial and production staff at Houghton Mifflin deserves much of the credit for what is good in this book. They have been incredibly patient with me and I wish to express my gratitude publicly. My Sponsoring Editor, Adam Forrand, has been extremely supportive of this project. I truly appreciate Adam's conceptual contributions to this revision. Very special thanks to my Associate Editor, Kristen Desmond-LeFevre, and my Editorial Associate, Brigitte Maser. Kristen and Brigitte have been unbelievably tolerant and merciful of my numerous missed deadlines and "off-the-wall" sense of humor. Brigitte especially kept me on track throughout the entire editorial and production process. Thanks also to Senior Project Editor Rachel D'Angelo Wimberly, Associate Project Editor Kristin Penta, and Editorial Assistant May Jawdat, who each spent countless hours on the production of the book. Special thanks also go out to Dr. Corwin King, Central Washington University; Dr. Radda Hegde, Rutgers University; Professor Henry Tkachuk, Concordia College; and Professor Tina Kistler, Santa Barbara City College; the reviewers of this book, whose suggestions were incorporated into the revision. I appreciate very much your constructive comments and recommendations.

Personally, I am blessed with many friends who supported me throughout the writing process. Thanks to Ken Zahorski and the Office of Faculty Development at St. Norbert College who helped this project with a summer grant so that I could write the Instructor's Resource Manual and Student Workbook. Special thanks to Jeff Zahn, Dan Ryan, Gary and Karen Wyman, Josephine, Roxanne, Kevin and Donna Hutchinson, and my best friend, Jan. A very special and sincere thank you goes to my students, from whom I have learned a great deal about culture and life. This book has always been about and for you.

J. W. N.
DePere, WI

The Necessity of Intercultural Communication

> *... the history of our planet has been in great part the history of the mixing of peoples.*
>
> —Arthur M. Schlesinger Jr.[1]

CHAPTER OBJECTIVES

After reading this chapter you should be able to:

- List and discuss the benefits of intercultural communication.
- Recognize the increasing racial and ethnic diversity in the U.S. population.
- Identify and discuss the eight dimensions of communication.
- Assess your degree of communication apprehension.
- Define and discuss the nature of culture.
- Identify and discuss the five contexts of intercultural communication.
- Discuss the relationship between intercultural communication, uncertainty, and anxiety.
- Assess your degree of intercultural communication apprehension.
- Identify and discuss the three fundamental assumptions of intercultural communication.
- Assess your degree of ethnocentrism.

At the dawn of the twenty-first century, Marshall McLuhan's vision of a global village is no longer considered an abstract idea but a virtual certainty. Technological and sociopolitical changes have made the world a smaller planet. Telecommunication systems link the world via satellites and fiber optics. The ability of the mass media to bring events from across the globe into our homes, businesses, and schools dramatically reduces the distance between peoples of different cultures and societies. Supersonic jets carry people from one country to another faster than the speed of sound. Mass migrations force interaction between people of different races, nationalities, and ethnicities.

Noted historian and Pulitzer Prize winner Arthur Schlesinger warns us that history tells an ugly story of what happens when people of diverse cultural, ethnic, religious, or linguistic backgrounds converge in one place. Witness the war in the former Yugoslavia. As the stranglehold of ideological repression in Eastern Europe was released, ethnic groups that once lived peacefully within their geopolitical borders now clash and kill one another by the thousands in the name of nationalism and ethnic cleansing. The hostility of one group of people against another, *different* group of people is among the most instinctive of human drives. Schlesinger contends that unless a common goal binds diverse people together, tribal hostilities will drive them apart. By replacing the conflict of political ideologies that dominated in the twentieth century, ethnic and racial strife will usher in the new millennium as *the* explosive issue.[2]

The Need for Intercultural Communication

International tensions in the Middle East, Northern Ireland, and Eastern Europe are striking examples of the need for effective and competent intercultural communication. Although political in origin, such conflicts are fueled by ethnic and religious differences. Indeed, national conflicts within our own borders, often ignited by racial and ethnic tensions, underscore the necessity for skillful intercultural communication. An international incident with potentially global consequences occurred relatively recently, stressing the need for intercultural communication. The incident began on April 1, 2001, when a United States Navy plane collided with a Chinese fighter jet in international airspace over the South China Sea. As a result of the collision, the U.S. plane, an EP-3 electronic warfare and surveillance aircraft, was damaged and nearly crashed. However, due to heroic efforts on the part of the crew, the plane landed safely at a Chinese air base. China reported that its plane was missing and its pilot presumed dead. The twenty-four crew members of the U.S. plane were detained by the Chinese military. China and the United States disagreed as to the cause of the collision, each side blaming the other.[3]

In the days and weeks following the incident, contentious negotiations took place between Chinese and American officials over the release of the crew. For their release, China demanded that the United States accept responsibility and apologize for the collision. The United States refused, arguing that the collision was the fault of the Chinese pilot. In the meantime, public pressure was mounting on President Bush to gain the release of the crew. On April 4, Secretary of State Colin Powell expressed "regret" over the collision and the disappearance of the Chinese jet pilot. Although Chinese officials acknowledged Powell's statement as a move in the right direction, they insisted that the United States apologize for the incident. On April 8, Vice President Dick Cheney and Colin Powell rejected China's demands for an apology but expressed "sorrow" about the disappearance of the Chinese pilot. They also drafted a letter of sympathy to the pilot's wife.

The Chinese continued to demand an apology. On April 10, American officials said that President Bush would be willing to offer the Chinese a letter expressing regret over the incident, including a statement admitting that the U.S. aircraft had landed in Chinese territory without seeking permission. The Chinese continued to demand an apology. Finally, on April 11, the United States issued a letter to the Chinese Foreign Minister asking him to "convey to the Chinese people and to the family of pilot Wang Wei that we are very sorry for their loss." The letter continued, "We are very sorry the entering of China's airspace and the landing did not have verbal clearance." To be sure, the word *apology* did not appear in the letter. But in their announcement of the letter to the Chinese people, Chinese officials chose to translate the double "very sorry" as "shenbiao qianyi," which means a deep expression of apology or regret and is an expression not used unless one is admitting wrongdoing and accepting responsibility for it. On the basis of that letter and the subsequent translation, China agreed to release the American crew. John Pomfret of the Washington Post Foreign Service asserted, "In the end, it was a matter of what the United States chose to say and what China chose to hear." Apparently such delicacies in communication are common during United States-China negotiations. According to Bates Gill, director of the Center for Northeast Asian Policy Studies at the Brookings Institution, U.S. negotiators often use words, such as *acknowledge,* that when translated into Chinese mean "admit" or "recognize"—so that the Chinese can interpret such wording as an admission of U.S. guilt.[4]

THE BENEFITS OF INTERCULTURAL COMMUNICATION

Although the challenges of an increasingly diverse world are great, the benefits are even greater. Communicating and establishing relationships with people from different cultures can lead to a host of benefits, including healthier communities; increased international, national, and local commerce; reduced conflict; and personal growth through increased tolerance. Joan England argues that genuine community is a condition of togetherness in which people have lowered their defenses and have learned to accept and celebrate their differences. England contends that we can no longer define equality as "sameness" but instead must value our differences with others, whether they be differences of race, gender, ethnicity, lifestyle, occupation, or professional discipline.[5] Healthy communities are made up of individuals working collectively for the benefit of everyone, not just their own group. Through open and honest intercultural communication people can work together to achieve goals that benefit everyone, regardless of group or cultural orientation. According to M. Scott Peck, the overall mission of human communication is (or should be) reconciliation. He argues that effective communication can ultimately lower or remove the walls and barriers of misunderstanding that separate human beings from one another. Peck states that the rules for community building are the same as the rules for effective communication. Communication is the foundation of all human relationships. Moreover, argues Peck, the principles of community are applicable to any situation in which two people are gathered together, including the global community, the home, business, or neighborhood. Healthy communities support all community members and strive to understand, appreciate, and acknowledge each member.[6]

Our ability to interact with persons from different cultures both within and outside our borders has immense economic benefits. According to the United States Department of Commerce, the markets that hold the greatest potential for dramatic increases in U.S. exports are Argentina, Brazil, China, India, Mexico, Poland, South Africa, South Korea, Turkey, and ASEAN (the Association of Southeast Asian Nations, which includes Brunei, Indonesia, Malaysia, the Philippines, Singapore, Thailand, and Vietnam). India, for example, is the fifth largest economy in the world (ranking above France, Italy, the United Kingdom, and Russia) and one of the few world markets that offer immense prospects for growth and earning potential in practically all areas of business, especially for small and medium-sized businesses. Only through successful intercultural communication can such business potentials be realized.[7]

Intercultural conflict is inevitable; we will never be able to avoid it entirely. We can, however, through cooperative intercultural communication, reduce and manage it. Often conflict stems from our inability to see another person's point of view, especially if that person is from a different culture. We develop blatant, and often incorrect, generalizations about people from other cultures that lead us to mistrust them. Mistrust leads to defensive behavior, which fosters conflict. However, by thinking and acting cooperatively, and by communicating assertively (not aggressively) and responsively, we can learn to effectively manage and reduce intercultural conflict.

RECAP

Benefits of Intercultural Communication

1. Healthier communities

2. Increased commerce

3. Reduced conflict

4. Personal growth through tolerance

Common Stereotypes

. . . about blacks	**. . . about whites**	**. . . about Asians**
"They're lazy."	"They think they know everything."	"They're sneaky."
"All of them are on welfare."	"Most of them are arrogant."	"They are hard to figure out."
"They like to dance."	"They're all rich."	"They are really good at math."
"They do drugs."	"They are really materialistic."	"I wouldn't trust them."

As you communicate with people from different cultures, you learn more about them and their way of life, including their values, history, habits, and the substance of their personality. As your relationships with people from other cultures develop, you start to understand them better, perhaps even empathizing with them. One of the things you will learn eventually is that although your cultures are different, you have much in common. As humans we all have the same basic needs and desires—we just have different ways of achieving them. As we learn that our way is not the only way, we develop a tolerance for difference.

DIVERSITY IN THE UNITED STATES

One need not travel to faraway countries to understand the need for, and experience the benefits of, intercultural communication. Largely because of immigration trends, cultural and ethnic diversity in the United States is a fact of life. Immigrants in record numbers are crossing U.S. borders. If the current immigration trend continues, by 2025 whites will make up 62 percent of the population, and by 2050 nearly half of the U.S. population will be nonwhite. Americans of European descent, who were 90 percent of the population in 1960, will then be a minority of less than 50 percent.[8]

Every ten years, at the beginning of a new decade, the United States Department of Commerce conducts a census. The results of the 2000 census profile the remarkable racial and ethnic diversity that has been a hallmark of American society. According to 2000 census data, whites numbered 211 million, constituting 75 percent of the total population. The 35 million Hispanics or Latinos (of any race) living in the United States constitute 12.5 percent of the population and are now considered the second largest nonwhite group in the United States. The Hispanic population increased nearly 60 percent from 1990 to 2000. By 2025 Hispanics will account for 18 percent of the total population, while the percentage of the white population will drop considerably (see Figure 1-1).[9]

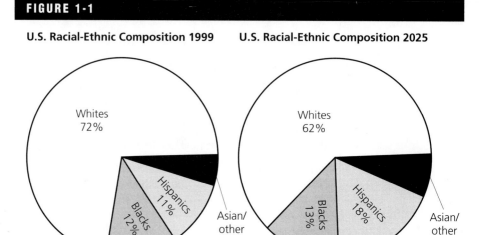

FIGURE 1-1

U.S. Racial-Ethnic Composition 1999   U.S. Racial-Ethnic Composition 2025

The federal government uses the terms *Hispanic* and *Latino* interchangeably and classifies Hispanics/Latinos as an ethnic group but not as a racial group. According to the U.S. Bureau of the Census, Hispanics are a heterogeneous group comprised of Mexicans, Cubans, Puerto Ricans, persons from Central and South America, and persons of other Spanish descent. Nearly 80 percent of all Hispanics/Latinos live in southern or western areas of the United States. In fact, half of all Hispanics in the United States live in two states, California and Texas. But that trend is likely to change in the next decade as the Hispanic population expands geographically. For example, from 1990 to 2000 the Hispanic population of Green Bay, Wisconsin, grew 470 percent.[10]

Blacks, or African Americans, now the second largest nonwhite group, make up just over 12 percent of the total population. Whereas the Hispanic population is projected to grow considerably in the next 25 years, the black population is projected to remain relatively stable and increase only 1 percentage point (to 13 percent of the population) by the year 2025. Over half of all blacks live in the South and over half of all blacks live inside central metropolitan cities. Persons of Asian descent make up about 4 percent of the population and include persons of Asian Indian, Chinese, Filipino, Japanese, Korean, Vietnamese, and other Asian origins. American Indians and Alaskan natives comprise less than 1 percent of the total U.S. population. Although the United States is growing in ethnic and racial diversity, some parts of the country are more diverse than others. For example, nearly 30 percent of the persons living in New York City, 46 percent of the persons living in Los Angeles, and 26 percent of the persons living in Chicago are Hispanic.[11]

In addition to the rapid growth of nonwhite populations in the United States, another trend is emerging: an increasing number of groups are revitalizing their ethnic traditions and promoting their cultural and ethnic uniqueness through language. Language is a vital part of maintaining one's cultural heritage. Over 32 million people in the United States speak languages other than English at home. Over 90 percent of the people in Laredo, Texas, speak Spanish at home. Almost half of the population in Monterey Park, California, speak an Asian language at home. One-third of the population of Chicago speak a language other than English at home. Fifty percent of the homes in Miami and Los Angeles use a language other than English.[12]

Although the United States prides itself as a nation of immigrants, there is a growing sense of uncertainty, fear, and distrust between different cultural, ethnic, and linguistic groups. These feelings create anxiety that can foster separatism rather than unity. Arthur Schlesinger alerts us that

> a cult of ethnicity has arisen both among non-Anglo whites and among nonwhite minorities to denounce the idea of a melting pot, to challenge the concept of "one people," and to protect, promote, and perpetuate separate ethnic and racial communities.[13]

Many Americans are frustrated, confused, and uncertain. Only through intercultural communication can such uncertainty be reduced. Only when diverse people come together and interact can they unify rather than separate. Unity is impossible without communication. Intercultural communication is a necessity.

HUMAN COMMUNICATION

Communication is everywhere. Everywhere, every day, people are communicating. Even when they are alone, people are bombarded with communication. Communication professor Charles Larson estimates that Americans are exposed to over 5,000 persuasive messages every day.[14] To imagine life without the ability to communicate is difficult, perhaps even impossible. Most people would be miserable if they were not allowed to communicate with others. Indeed, solitary confinement is perhaps the worst form of punishment inflicted on humans. Human communication—that is, the ability to symbolize and use language—separates humans from animals. Communication with others is the essence of what it means to be human.

Communication has a profound effect on humans. Through communication, people conduct their lives. People define themselves via their communication with others. Communication is the vehicle by which people initiate, maintain, and terminate their relationships with others. Communication is the means by which people influence and persuade others. Through communication, local, regional, national, and international conflicts are managed and resolved.

Ironically, however, communication, and particularly one's style of communication, can be the source of many problems. Marriage counselors indicate that a breakdown in communication is the most frequently cited reason for relational dissolution in the United States.[15] A specific kind of communication—that is, public speaking—is one of people's most frequently cited fears, even more than the fear of death.

This textbook is about the ubiquitous subject labeled *communication*. Specifically, this is a book about *intercultural communication*—that is, communication between people of different cultures and ethnicities. Throughout the course of this book, you will be introduced to concepts and theories that explain the process of people of differing cultural backgrounds coming together and exchanging verbal and nonverbal messages. Chapter 1 is designed as an introductory chapter. The first part of the chapter outlines and discusses the nature of communication and examines communication variables that apply to everyone, regardless of cultural background. The second part outlines and discusses the nature of culture. Culture is seen as a paradox—that is, culture is simultaneously both a very subtle and a clearly defined influence on human thought processes and behavior. The last part of the chapter presents a model of intercultural communication that will serve as the organizing scheme of the rest of this book.

The Nature of Human Communication

Because of its ubiquitous nature communication is very difficult to define. Nearly thirty-five years ago, Frank Dance compiled a list of 98 different definitions of communication.[16] A few years later, Dance and Carl Larson presented a listing of over 125 definitions of communication.[17] If you were to go to your university library and select ten different introductory communication texts, the probability is that each would offer a different definition of communication.[18] Although there are many definitions of communication, these definitions are important because the way people define communication influences how they think and theorize about communication.

Although there is no universally agreed-upon definition of communication, there are certain properties of communication that most communication scholars agree describe its nature. Table 1-1 outlines eight of these properties, along with eight definitions of communication. These definitions come from a variety of scholars with diverse backgrounds in the communication field.

DIMENSION 1: PROCESS

Almost all communication scholars concur that communication is a process. A process is anything that is ongoing, ever-changing, and continuous. A process does not have a specific beginning or ending point. A process is not static or at rest; it is always moving. The human body is a process; it is always aging. Communication is always developing; it is never still or motionless. There is no exact beginning or ending point of a communication exchange. Although individual *verbal* messages have definite beginning and ending points, the overall process of communication does not. For example, José and Juan meet in the hallway and greet each other. José says, "What's up, Juan!" and Juan says, "Not much, man." Both José's and Juan's verbal messages have exact beginning and ending points. But to determine exactly when and where their *nonverbal* communication begins and ends is virtually impossible. They may not be verbally communicating with each other,

TABLE 1-1 Eight Properties and Definitions of Communication	
1. Process	"Communication theory reflects a process point of view . . . you cannot talk about the beginning or the end of communication. . . ." (Berlo)[1]
2. Dynamic	"Communication is a transaction among symbol users in which meanings are dynamic, changing as a function of earlier usages and of changes in perceptions and metaperceptions. Common to both meanings is the notion that communication is time-bound and irreversible." (Bowers & Bradac)[2]
3. Interactive/Transactive	"Communication occurs when two or more people interact through the exchange of messages." (Goss)[3]
4. Symbolic	". . . all the symbols of the mind, together with the means of conveying them through space and preserving them in time." (Cooley)[4]
5. Intentional	". . . communication has as its central interest those behavioral situations in which source transmits a message to a receivers(s) with conscious intent to affect the latter's behavior." (Miller)[5]
6. Contextual	"Communication always and inevitably occurs within some context." (Fisher)[6]
7. Ubiquitous	". . . communication is the discriminatory response of an organism to a stimulus." (Stevens)[7]
8. Cultural	". . . culture is communication . . . communication is culture." (Hall)[8]

1. *D. K. Berlo,* The Process of Communication *(New York: Holt, Rinehart & Winston, 1960), p. 24.*
2. *J. W. Bowers and J. J. Bradac, "Issues in Communication Theory: A Metatheoretical Analysis," in* Communication Yearbook, *no. 5, ed. M. Burgoon (New Brunswick: Transaction Books, 1982), p. 3.*
3. *B. Goss,* Communication in Everyday Life *(Belmont, Calif.: Wadsworth, 1983).*
4. *C. Cooley,* Social Organization *(New York: Scribner, 1909), p. 61.*
5. *G. R. Miller, "On Defining Communication: Another Stab,"* Journal of Communication, *16, nos. 88–89 (1966), 92.*
6. *B. A. Fisher,* Interpersonal Communication: Pragmatics of Human Relationships *(New York: Random House, 1987), p. 22.*
7. *S. S. Stevens, "Introduction: A Definition of Communication,"* The Journal of the Acoustical Society of America, *22 (1950), 689.*
8. *E. T. Hall,* The Silent Language *(New York: Doubleday, 1959).*

but they are still communicating nonverbally. Even if they walk away from each other, they are communicating that they are no longer talking with each other. A process is something that continues to develop and change; it does not stop, nor can it reverse itself. Because communication is irreversible, it affects future communication. How José and Juan interact with each other today is very much influenced by how they interacted yesterday, last week, or even years ago. Think about your own relationships with your friends and how what you have said to each other in the past influences what you say today. Imagine the last time you had an argument with your boyfriend or girlfriend, for example. You may have said some things you now regret. Such interaction influences your relationships and how you interact today.

DIMENSION 2: DYNAMIC

Inextricably bound to the notion that communication is a process is the fact that communication is dynamic. The terms *process* and *dynamic* are closely related. Part of what makes communication a process is its dynamic nature. Something that is dynamic is active and/or forceful. Unfortunately, communication is typically discussed as if it were some physical entity or "thing" that people can hold or touch. Because communication is a dynamic process, it is impossible to capture its essence in a written definition or graphic model. This problem is not unlike the problem faced by a photographer who tries to capture the dynamic essence of a running horse with a photograph. Certainly the photograph can be very informative about the horse, but the camera cannot make a complete reproduction of the object photographed. The relationship between the forward and hind legs, the beautiful "dynamic" muscular motions, cannot be truly represented in a photograph. Any discussion of communication as a dynamic process is subject to similar limitations.[19] To fully appreciate the process, one must be a part of it or witness it in motion. As a dynamic process, communication is flexible, adaptive, and fluid; it is impossible to replicate it completely in a picture, drawing, or model.

DIMENSION 3: INTERACTIVE/TRANSACTIVE

Communication is interactive and transactive because it occurs between people. While some might argue that people can communicate with themselves (what is called *intrapersonal communication*), most scholars believe that interaction between people is a fundamental dimension of communication. Communication requires the *active participation* of two people sending and receiving messages. Active participation means that people are *consciously directing* their messages to someone else.[20] This means that communication is a two-way process: interactive. Likewise, to say that communication is transactional means that while José is sending messages to Juan, Juan is *simultaneously* sending messages to José. Juan's eye contact, facial expression, and body language are nonverbal messages to José informing him how his message is being received. Each person in an interactional setting simultaneously sends (encodes) and receives (decodes) messages. For example, when you listen to your friends talk about the great party they went to last night, it is obvious to you that they are sending you messages. At the same time as they describe the party to you, you are sending messages to them, too. Your eye contact, smiles, and other nonverbal reactions are communicating to them your interest in their story. Hence, both you and your friends are sending and receiving messages at the same time.

DIMENSION 4: SYMBOLIC

That communication is symbolic is another fundamental assumption guiding most communication scholars. A symbol is an arbitrarily selected and learned stimulus that represents something else. Symbols can be verbal or nonverbal.

Symbols are the vehicle by which the thoughts and ideas of one person can be communicated to another person. Messages are constructed with verbal and non-verbal symbols. Through symbols meanings are transferred between people.

Symbols (that is, words) have no natural relationship with what they represent (they are arbitrarily selected and learned). The verbal symbols "C A T" have no natural connection with cute fuzzy animals that purr and like to be scratched. The symbols "C A T" have no meaning in other languages (see Figure 1-2).

Nonverbal symbols are arbitrary also. Showing someone your upright middle finger may not communicate much in some cultures. Verbal and nonverbal symbols are meaningful only to people who have learned to associate them with what they represent. People can have just about any symbols they choose represent whatever they want them to. You and your friends probably communicate with each other using private symbols that no one else understands. You have your own secret code. You have words, phrases, gestures, and handshakes that only you and your friends know, understand, and use. This allows you to communicate with each other with your own "foreign" language. Drug dealers and users have an elaborate and highly ruled language that allows them to communicate about their illegal activities—for example, "blow a splif" is symbolic code for "smoke a marijuana cigarette."

Any verbal language (English, Chinese, Russian) is a code made up of symbols. The letters of the English alphabet (A, B, C, . . .) are a set of symbols that represent sounds. When we combine the individual symbols (for example, C + A + T) they become meaningful. By using symbols, people can represent their thoughts and ideas through writing or speaking. Once an idea has been encoded with symbols, it becomes a message. During communication, people encode their thoughts and send them to someone else. The other person listens to the message and translates it—that is, decodes it. When José saw Juan, he encoded a greeting. Juan decoded (that is, translated) the message and encoded a response. Interaction, then, is the process of encoding and decoding messages. People who speak different languages are simply using different codes.

FIGURE 1-2 Symbols Representing "Cat" in Six Languages

chat (French)

neiko (Japanese)

gato (Spanish)

Katze (German)

paka (Swahili)

koska (Russian)

DIMENSION 5: INTENTIONAL

Perhaps one of the most debated issues regarding the communication process centers around intentionality. On one side of the debate are those who argue that communication is intentional. On the other side are those who insist that communication can occur unintentionally. Intentional communication exists whenever two or more people consciously engage in interaction with some purpose.[21] For example, if Kyoko says to Akira, "Hey, do you want to go out to eat tonight?" and Akira responds by saying, "Yeah, that sounds like a good idea!" intentional communication has surely taken place.

Unintentional communication may exist, however. For example, at a party, Kyoko thinks that Akira is consciously ignoring her because he interacts with several other people. Kyoko senses that Akira is consciously sending her a message when, in fact, Akira's intention is simply to talk with new friends. Akira is not intentionally ignoring Kyoko, but she thinks that he is indeed sending her a message (that is, a nonverbal message). Since a response has been elicited in Kyoko, some communication scholars argue that communication has occurred.

There are three interpretations that can be drawn from the above discussion. To many communication scholars intentionality is a central property of the communication process. Others insist that any message interpreted by a person qualifies as communication whether or not the message was intentionally sent. Still others insist that all behavior, intentional or not, is informative and meaningful, thus is communicative. Thus, whenever a person (for example, Kyoko) responds to some stimulus (Akira talking with other people), communication has occurred. This textbook focuses on intentional communication and takes the position that intentional communication, either verbal or nonverbal, is more informative than unintentional communication.

DIMENSION 6: CONTEXTUAL

Communication is dependent on the context in which it occurs. The effects and outcomes, styles and fashions, and the resulting meaning are all dependent on the context in which the communication occurs. In this textbook, a *context* is the cultural, physical, relational, and perceptual environment in which communication occurs. In many ways the context defines the meaning of any messages. For example, the context of the classroom defines the kind of communication that will occur. Most students sit quietly while the professor psychologically stimulates them with a brilliant lecture.

There are essentially five different kinds of context that influence the process of communication: (1) the cultural environment, (2) the microcultural environment, (3) the physical environment, (4) the sociorelational environment, and (5) the perceptual environment. The cultural context includes all of the factors and influences that make up one's culture and will be discussed in detail in the section The Nature of Culture of this chapter. The physical context is the actual geographical space or territory in which the communication takes place. For example, communication between Juan and José will be different when they are interacting on a busy street in a big city compared with when they are in their university library. The sociorelational context refers to social roles and group memberships (for example, demographics). Sex, age, religious affiliation, educational level, and economic status affect how one communicates with and relates to others. Finally, the perceptual context includes all of the motivations, intentions, and personality traits people bring to the communication event. When you are interacting with your professor about an examination that you just failed, you have a very different set of motivations and intentions than when you are asking someone out on a date.

DIMENSION 7: UBIQUITOUS

That communication is ubiquitous simply means that communication is everywhere, done by everyone, all of the time. Humans are constantly bombarded with verbal and nonverbal messages. Wherever one goes, there is some communication happening. In fact, some scholars in the field of communication argue that it is impossible to *not* communicate. Paul Watzlawick, Janet Beavin, and Don Jackson have argued that *one cannot not communicate.* The logic of their argument is that (1) behavior has no opposite—one cannot not behave; (2) in an interactional setting, all behavior has informational value and/or message value—it is informative; (3) since behavior is informative, it is communicative; and (4) if behavior is communicative and one cannot not behave, then one cannot not communicate.[22]

DIMENSION 8: CULTURAL

Culture shapes communication, and communication is culture bound. People from different cultures communicate differently. The verbal and nonverbal

---

Australian Colloquialisms

Amber fluid = beer

Bag of fruit = men's clothing

Barbi = barbeque

Bickie = cookie

Bottler = person who performs well

Off = used to describe rotten food

Tucker = food

Culture influences nonverbal communication, such as the perception and use of personal space. In some cultures, people stand or sit very close to one another when they interact. *(Marcello Bertinetti/Photo Researchers)*

symbols we use to communicate with our friends and families are strongly influenced by our culture. Perhaps the most obvious verbal communication difference between two cultures is language. Even cultures speaking the same language have different meanings for different symbols, however. For example, although English is the dominant language spoken in the United States and in England, many words and phrases have different meanings in these two cultures. In England, to "bomb" an examination is to perform very well. To have "intercourse" with someone is simply to talk with him or her. When in London, do not bother to ask for directions to the nearest bathroom or restroom. In England, it is called the "water closet" or the "WC." Australians also speak English but have a variety of colloquialisms not well understood by persons from the United States.

Culture also has a dramatic affect on nonverbal communication. Nonverbal symbols, gestures, and perceptions of personal space and time vary significantly from culture to culture. In the United States, for example, people generally stand about two-and-a-half feet, or an arm's length, away from others when communicating. In many Middle Eastern cultures, people stand very close to one another when interacting, especially men, in order to smell each other's breath. In Saudi Arabia, two men walking together are likely to be holding hands as a sign of trust.

Communication, then, is the dynamic process of encoding and decoding verbal and nonverbal messages within a defined cultural, physical, sociorelational, and perceptual environment. Although many of our messages are sent intentionally, many others, perhaps our nonverbal messages, can unintentionally influence others.

Human Communication Apprehension

Although communication is difficult to define, we know that people begin to communicate at birth and continue communicating throughout their lives. We also know that many people experience fear and anxiety when communicating with others, particularly in situations such as public speaking, class presentations, a first date, or a job interview. The fear or anxiety people experience when communicating with others is called *communication apprehension (CA)*. In the past thirty-five years a substantial body of research has accumulated regarding the nature and prevalence of CA. Jim McCroskey, considered the father of the CA concept, finds that nearly everyone experiences some kind of CA sometimes, but that roughly one in five adults in the United States suffers from CA virtually whenever that person communicates with others. He argues that experiencing CA is "normal"—that is, all of us experience it occasionally, but that it can be a problem for us.

McCroskey concludes that there are four types of CA, including *traitlike CA, context-based CA, audience-based CA,* and *situational CA.* Traitlike CA is an enduring general personality predisposition where an individual experiences CA most of the time across most communication situations. Twenty percent of adults in the United States experience traitlike CA. Context-based CA is restricted to a certain generalized context, such as public speaking, group meetings, or job interviews. Persons with context-based CA experience anxiety only in particular contexts and not in others. Audience-based CA is triggered not by the specific context, but by the specific person or audience with whom one is communicating. Hence, persons with audience-based CA experience anxiety when communicating with, for instance, strangers or their superiors. College students with audience-based CA may experience anxiety when communicating with professors, but not when communicating with other students. Finally, situational-based CA, experienced by virtually everyone, occurs with the combination of a specific context and a specific audience. For example, students may feel anxious interacting with professors only if they are alone with the professor in the professor's office. At other times, perhaps in the hallways or in the classroom, interacting with the professor may not be a problem.[23] To repeat, virtually everyone experiences CA at some time. To experience CA does not mean that you are abnormal or sick. Following is the Personal Report of Communication Apprehension (PRCA-24), a scale designed to measure your degree of CA. Take a few moments and complete the scale.

Self-Assessment 1-1

This instrument is composed of 24 statements concerning your feelings about communicating with other people. Please indicate in the space provided the degree to which each statement applies to you by marking whether you (1) strongly agree, (2) agree, (3) are undecided, (4) disagree, or (5) strongly disagree with each statement. There are no right or wrong answers. Many of the statements are similar to other statements. Do not be concerned about this. Work quickly; just record your first impressions.

1. _____ I dislike participating in group discussions.

2. _____ Generally, I am comfortable while participating in group discussions.

3. _____ I am tense and nervous while participating in group discussions.

4. _____ I like to get involved in group discussions.

5. _____ Engaging in group discussions with new people makes me tense and nervous.

6. _____ I am calm and relaxed while participating in group discussions.

7. _____ Generally, I am nervous when I have to participate in group discussions.

8. _____ Usually I am calm and relaxed while participating in meetings.

9. _____ I am very calm and relaxed when I am called upon to express an opinion at a meeting.

10. _____ I am afraid to express myself at meetings.

11. _____ Communicating at meetings usually makes me uncomfortable.

12. _____ I am very relaxed when answering questions at a meeting.

13. _____ While participating in a conversation with a new acquaintance, I feel very nervous.

14. _____ I have no fear of speaking up in conversations.

15. _____ Ordinarily I am very tense and nervous in conversations.

16. _____ Ordinarily I am very calm and relaxed in conversations.

17. _____ When conversing with a new acquaintance, I feel very relaxed.

18. _____ I am afraid to speak up in conversations.

19. _____ I have no fear of giving a speech.

20. _____ Certain parts of my body feel very tense and rigid while I am giving a speech.

—Continued

21. _____ I feel relaxed while giving a speech.

22. _____ My thoughts become confused and jumbled when I am giving a speech.

23. _____ I face the prospect of giving a speech with confidence.

24. _____ While giving a speech, I get so nervous I forget facts I really know.

SCORING: The PRCA-24 allows you to compute a total score and four subscores. The total score represents your degree of traitlike CA. Total scores may range from 24 to 120. McCroskey argues that any score above 72 indicates general CA. Scores above 80 indicate a very high level of CA. Scores below 59 indicate a very low level of CA.

Total PRCA Score:
Step 1. Add what you marked for scale items 1, 3, 5, 7, 10, 11, 13, 15, 18, 20, 22, and 24.
Step 2. Add what you marked for scale items 2, 4, 6, 8, 9, 12, 14, 16, 17, 19, 21, and 23.
Step 3. Subtract the score from step 1 from 84 (i.e., 84 minus the score of step 1). Then add the score of step 2 to that total. The sum is your PRCA score.

The subscores indicate your degree of CA across four common contexts, including group discussions, meetings, interpersonal conversations, and public speaking. For these scales, a score above 18 is high and a score above 23 is very high.

Subscores for Contexts:
Group Subscore: 18 + scores for items 2, 4, and 6, minus scores for items 1, 3, and 5.
Meeting Subscore: 18 + scores for items 8, 9, and 10, minus scores for items 7, 10, and 11.
Interpersonal Subscore: 18 + scores for items 14, 16, and 17, minus scores for items 13, 15, and 18.
Public Speaking Subscore: 18 + scores for items 19, 21, and 23, minus scores for items 20, 22, and 24.

Copyright James C. McCroskey. Scales used with permission of James C. McCroskey.
SOURCE: McCroskey, J. C. (1982). _An Introduction to Rhetorical Communication_, 4th ed. Englewood Cliffs, NJ: Prentice-Hall.

The Nature of Culture

Like communication, culture is ubiquitous and has a profound effect on humans. Culture is simultaneously invisible and pervasive. As we go about our daily lives, we are not overtly conscious of our culture's influence on us. How often have you sat in your dorm room or classroom and consciously thought about what it means to be an American? As you stand in the lunch line, do you say to yourself, "_I am acting like an American_"? As you sit in your classroom, do you say to yourself, "_The professor is really acting like an American_"? Yet most of your thoughts, emotions, and behaviors are culturally driven. One need only step into a culture different from one's own to feel the immense impact of culture.

Culture has a direct influence on the physical, relational, and perceptual environment. The next time you enter your communication classroom, consider how the room is arranged *physically,* including where you sit and where the professor teaches, the location of the chalkboard, windows, and so forth. Does the professor lecture from behind a podium? Do the students sit facing the professor? Is the chalkboard used? Next, think about your *relationship* with the professor and the other students in your class. Is the relationship formal or informal? Do you interact with the professor and students about topics other than class material? Would you consider the relationship personal or impersonal? Finally, think about your *perceptual disposition*—that is, your attitudes, motivations, and emotions about the class. Are you happy to be in the class? Do you enjoy attending? Are you nervous when the instructor asks you a question? To a great extent, the answers to these questions are contingent on your culture. The physical arrangement of classrooms, the social relationship between students and teachers, and the perceptual profiles of the students and teachers vary significantly from culture to culture.

Like communication, culture is difficult to define. Australian anthropologist Roger Keesing argues that

> culture does not have some true and sacred and eternal meaning we are trying to discover, but that like other symbols, it means whatever we use it to mean; and that as with other analytical concepts, human users must carve out—and try to partly agree on—a class of natural phenomena it can most strategically label.[24]

Just about everyone has a definition of culture. To be sure, over forty years ago two well-known anthropologists, Alfred Kroeber and Clyde Kluckhohn, found and examined three hundred definitions of culture, none of which were the same.[25]

Perhaps too often people think of culture only in terms of the fine arts, geography, or history. Small towns or rural communities are often accused of having no culture. Yet culture exists everywhere. There is as much culture in Gallup City, New Mexico (population 52), as there is in New York City (population 7,322,564). The two cultures are simply different. Simply put, culture is people.[26]

Although there may not be a universally accepted definition of culture, there are a number of properties of culture which, most people agree, describe its essence. In this textbook, *culture* is defined as *an accumulated pattern of values, beliefs, and behaviors shared by an identifiable group of people with a common history and a verbal and nonverbal symbol system.*

CULTURE AS AN ACCUMULATED PATTERN OF VALUES, BELIEFS, AND BEHAVIORS

Cultures can be defined by their value and belief systems and by the actions of their members. People who exist in the same culture generally share similar values and beliefs (see Table 1-2). In the United States, individuality is highly valued. An individual's self-interest takes precedence over group interests. Americans believe

TABLE 1-2 Values Across Cultures	
Saudi Arabia	**Maori (New Zealand)**
Islam	Land
Hospitality	Kinship
Cleanliness	Education
India	**Yemen**
Family Lineage	Islam
Supernatural Guidance	Self-Respect & Honor
Sexual Inequality	Family

that people are unique. Moreover, Americans value personal independence. Conversely, in Japan, a collectivistic and homogeneous culture, a sense of groupness and group harmony is valued. Most Japanese see themselves as members of a group first, as individuals second. Where Americans value independence, Japanese value interdependence. Norwegians value conformity. Norwegian children are taught to put the needs of society above their own. Cultural aspects of conformity are embodied in what Norwegians call *Janteloven*, which denotes the fear of individuality, of standing out in a crowd. Although the Norwegian literacy rate is among the highest in the world, Norwegian schools do not have accelerated programs for gifted and talented students. Norwegians believe that to divide students on the basis of intellectual ability would disrupt the social cohesion.[27]

The values of a particular culture lead to a set of expectations and rules prescribing how people should behave in that culture. Although many Americans prefer to think of themselves as unique individuals, most Americans behave in similar ways. Most work forty hours a week, receive some form of payment for their work, and pay some of their earnings in taxes. Most spend their money on homes and cars. Almost every home in the United States has a television. Observe the students around you in your classes. Although you may think that you are very different from your peers, you are really quite similar to them. Most of them follow a daily behavioral pattern very similar to your own, attending classes, taking examinations, going to lunch, studying, partying, writing papers, and so forth.

CULTURE AS AN IDENTIFIABLE GROUP OF PEOPLE WITH A COMMON HISTORY

Because the members of a particular culture share similar values, beliefs and behaviors, they are identifiable as a distinct group. In addition to their shared values, beliefs, and behaviors, the members of a particular culture share a common history. Any culture's past inextricably binds it to the present and guides its future. At the core of any culture are traditions that are passed on to future generations. In many cultures, history is a major component of the formal and informal education systems. To learn a culture's history is to learn that culture's values. One way children in the United States develop their sense of independence is by learning about the Declaration of Independence, one of this country's most sacred documents. Elementary school children in Iran learn of the historical significance of the political and religious revolution that took place in their culture in the 1970s and 1980s. Russian children are taught about the arts in Russian history, including famous Russian composers such as Tchaikovsky, Rachmaninoff, and Stravinsky. The arts of the past help Russians remember their culture as they face the disrupting social and political crises of the present. Such historical lessons are the glue that binds people to one another.[28]

CULTURE AS A VERBAL AND NONVERBAL SYMBOL SYSTEM

One of the most important elements of any culture is its communication system. The verbal and nonverbal symbols with which the members of a culture communicate are culture bound. To see the difference between the verbal codes of any two cultures is easy. The dominant verbal code in the United States is English whereas the dominant verbal code in Mexico is Spanish. Two cultures that share the same verbal code may have dramatically different verbal styles, however. Most white Americans use a very direct, instrumental, personal style in speaking English. Many Native Americans use an indirect, impersonal style in speaking English and may prefer the use of silence instead of words.[29]

Nonverbal code systems vary significantly across cultures also. Nonverbal com-

Gestures vary considerably across cultures. A common gesture in one culture may be very offensive in another. *(© James Neuliep)*

munication includes the use of body language, gestures, facial expressions, the voice, smell, personal and geographical space, time, and artifacts. Body language can communicate a great deal about one's culture. When adults interact with young children in the United States, it is not uncommon for the adult to pat the head of the child. This nonverbal gesture is often seen as a form of endearment and is culturally acceptable. In Thailand, however, where the head is considered the seat of the soul, such a gesture is unacceptable. Belching during or after a meal is viewed by most Americans as rude and impolite, perhaps even disgusting. But in parts of Korea and the Middle East, belching after a meal might be interpreted as a compliment to the cook.[30]

People also communicate nonverbally through smell. Americans, in particular, seem obsessed with the smell of the human body and home environment. Think of all of the products you used this morning before you left for class that were designed to mask the natural scent of your body, including soap, toothpaste, mouthwash, deodorant, cologne, or perfume. Persons from other cultures often complain that Americans tend to smell antiseptic.

MICROCULTURAL GROUPS

Within most cultures there are groups of people, or *microcultures,* that coexist within the mainstream society. Microcultures exist within the broader rules and guidelines of the dominant cultural milieu but are distinct in some way, perhaps racially, linguistically, or through their sexual orientation, age, or even occupation. In some ways, everyone is a member of some microcultural group. Often microcultures may have histories that differ from that of the dominant cultural group. In many cases, microcultural groups are subordinate in some way, perhaps politically or economically.

In the United States, Native American Indian tribes can be considered microcultures. In addition to the formal education provided by the larger culture, Navajo children informally learn their microculture's history by hearing the traditions of their people.[31] The Amish of Lancaster County, Pennsylvania, can also be considered a microcultural group. Although the Amish are subject to most of the same laws as any other group of citizens, they have unique values and communication systems that differentiate them from mainstream American life. Amish children are exempt from compulsory attendance in public schools after eighth grade. Although almost all Amish speak English, when they interact among themselves they speak German. During church services, a form of High German is used. Hence, most Amish of Lancaster County speak three languages.[32]

A Contextual Model of Intercultural Communication

Intercultural communication occurs whenever a minimum of two persons from different cultures or microcultures come together and exchange verbal and nonverbal symbols. A central theme throughout this book is that intercultural

FIGURE 1-3   A Contextual Model of Intercultural Communication

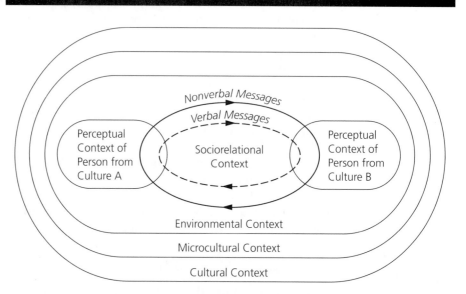

communication is contextual. A contextual model of intercultural communication is shown in Figure 1-3.

According to the model, intercultural communication occurs within a variety of contexts, including (1) cultural, (2) microcultural, (3) environmental, (4) perceptual, and (5) sociorelational contexts. A context is a complex combination of a variety of factors, including the setting, situation, circumstances, background, and overall framework within which communication occurs. The largest, outer circle of the model in Figure 1-3 represents the *cultural context*. This is the largest circle because the dominant culture permeates every aspect of the communicative exchange, even the physical geography. All communicative exchanges between persons occur within some culture. Cultural context is the focus of Chapter 2.

The next-largest circle in the model is the *microcultural context*. As mentioned earlier, within most cultures, separate groups of people coexist. These groups, called microcultures, are in some way different from the larger cultural milieu. Sometimes the difference is ethnicity, race, or language. Often microcultures are treated differently by the members of the larger culture. The microcultural context is the focus of Chapter 3.

The next-largest circle in the model is the *environmental context*. This circle represents the physical, geographical location of the interaction. While culture prescribes the overall rules for communication, the physical location indicates when and where the specific rules apply. For example, in the United States there are rules about yelling. Depending on the physical location, yelling can be prohibited or encouraged. In church, yelling is generally prohibited, whereas at a football game, yelling is the preferred method of communicating. The physical environment includes the physical geography, architecture, landscape design, and even the climate of a particular culture. All of these environmental factors play a key role in how people communicate. The environmental context is the focus of Chapter 4.

The two circles in the model on either side of the sociorelational context represent the *perceptual contexts* of the individuals interacting. The perceptual context refers to the individual characteristics of the interactants, including their cognitions, attitudes, dispositions, and motivations. How an individual perceives the environment and gathers, stores, and retrieves information is uniquely human but also culturally influenced. How an individual develops attitudes about others, including stereotypes, varies from culture to culture. The perceptual context of the individual is the focus of Chapter 5.

The circle intersecting the perceptual contexts in the model is the *sociorelational context*—that is, the relationship between the interactants. Whenever two people come together and interact, they establish a relationship. Within this relationship each person assumes a role. Right now, you are assuming the role of student. The person teaching your communication class is assuming the role of teacher. Roles prescribe how people should behave. Most of the people with whom you interact are related to you through your role as student. The reason you interact with so many professors is because you are a student. What you interact about—that is, the topic of your interaction—is also defined by your role as student. You and your professors interact about courses. How you interact with your professor—that is, the style of talk (for example, polite language)—is also prescribed by your role as student. The language and style of your talk with your professor is probably very different from the language and style of talk you use when you go back to your dorm room and interact with your friends. Probably the last ten people with whom you interacted were directly related to you through your role as student. When you go back to your hometown during semester break and step into the role of son or daughter, or brother or sister, you are assuming a different role, and your interaction changes accordingly. Your interaction varies as a function of the role you assume.

Roles vary from culture to culture. Although in just about every culture there are student/teacher role relationships, how those roles are defined varies significantly. What it means to be a student in the United States is very different from what it means to be a student in Japan. In Japan, students go to school six days a week. Japanese teachers are highly respected and play a very influential role in the Japanese student's life. What it means to be a mother or father also varies considerably from one culture to another. In the Masai culture of Kenya, a woman is defined by her fertility. To be defined as a mother in Masai culture, a woman must endure circumcision (clitoridectomy), an arranged marriage, and wife beating.[33] One's roles prescribe the types of verbal and nonverbal symbols that are exchanged. The sociorelational context and role relationships are the focus of Chapter 6.

In the model in Figure 1-3, the sociorelational context is graphically represented by two circles labeled "nonverbal messages" and "verbal messages." The nonverbal circle is larger of the two and is represented by a continuous line. The verbal circle is smaller and is represented as a series of dashes. The nonverbal-message circle is larger than the verbal-message circle because the majority of our communicative behavior is nonverbal. Whether we are using words or not, we are communicating nonverbally though eye contact, bodily stance, and space. In addition, our nonverbal behavior is ongoing—we cannot not behave. The verbal message circle is portrayed as a series of dashes to represent the *digital* quality of verbal communication.[34] By digital, we mean that, unlike our nonverbal communication, our verbal communication is made up of words that have recognizable and discrete beginning and ending points. A word is like a digit. We can start and stop talking with words. Our nonverbal behavior goes on continuously, however. Verbal communication codes are the focus of Chapter 7; nonverbal language is the focus of Chapter 8.

The general theme of this textbook, as represented in the model in Figure 1-3, is that intercultural communication is defined by the interdependence of these various contexts. The perceptual contexts combine to create the sociorelational context, which is defined by the verbal and nonverbal messages sent. The sociorelational context is influenced by the environmental context and is defined by the microcultural and cultural contexts. These contexts combine in a complex interaction to create the phenomenon of intercultural communication.

INTERCULTURAL COMMUNICATION AND UNCERTAINTY

When we interact with someone from a different culture, we are faced with a lot of uncertainty. We may not know anything about the person's culture, values, habits, behavior, dress, and so on. We may not know what to say or do in such circumstances. This uncertainty about the other person may make us feel nervous and anxious. Communication theorist Charles Berger contends that the task of interacting with someone from a different culture who may look, act, and communicate differently presents the intercultural communicator with some very complex predictive and explanatory problems. To some extent, to effectively interact with someone from a different culture, we must be able to predict how our interaction partner is likely to behave and, on the basis of those predictions, select our appropriate verbal and nonverbal messages.[35]

Berger theorizes that whenever we come together and interact with a stranger, our primary concern is to reduce uncertainty, especially when the other person is someone we will meet again or who provides rewards for us or behaves in some deviant way. Often when we are faced with high levels of uncertainty, we experience anxiety. In high-uncertainty situations, our primary goal is to reduce uncertainty and to increase the predictability about the other. This can be accomplished via specific verbal and nonverbal communication strategies such as question asking and appropriate nonverbal expressiveness.[36]

Some types of communication situations may be more or less anxiety producing than others. For example, Buss argues that situations that are novel, unfamiliar, and/or dissimilar lead to increased anxiety. Those situations containing new, atypical, and/or conspicuously different stimuli are likely to increase our sense of anxiety. By these criteria, initial interaction with someone or interacting with someone from a different culture may easily produce heightened anxiety.[37]

Intercultural communication experts William Gudykunst and Young Kim argue that when we interact with people from different cultures, we tend to view them as strangers. Strangers are unknown people who are members of different groups. Anyone entering a relatively unknown or unfamiliar environment falls into the category of stranger. Interaction with people from different cultures tends to involve the highest degree of "strangerness" and the lowest degree of familiarity. Thus, there is greater uncertainty in initial interaction with strangers than with people with whom we are familiar. According to Gudykunst and Kim, actual or anticipated interaction with members of different groups (for example, cultures or ethnic groups different from our own) leads to anxiety.[38]

If we are too anxious about interacting with strangers, we tend to avoid them. Neuliep and McCroskey state that this type of communication anxiety can be labeled intercultural communication apprehension—that is, the fear or anxiety associated with either real or anticipated interaction with people from different groups, especially different cultural or ethnic groups.[39]

INTERCULTURAL COMMUNICATION APPREHENSION

Successfully interacting with someone from a different culture requires a degree of communication competence. According to Brian Spitzberg, most models of communication competence include a cognitive, an affective, and a behavioral component. The cognitive component refers to how much one knows about communication. The affective component includes one's motivation to approach or avoid communication. The behavioral component refers to the skills one has to interact competently. An interculturally competent communicator is *motivated* to communicate, *knowledgeable* about how to communicate, and *skilled* in communicating. In addition, an interculturally competent communicator is *sensitive* to the expectations of the context in which communication occurs. Competent communicators interact effectively by adapting messages appropriately to the context. Competent communicators understand the rules, norms, and expectations of the relationship and do not significantly violate them. Communicators are effective to the degree that their goals are accomplished successfully.[40]

According to Neuliep and McCroskey, a person's affective orientation toward intercultural communication involves the individual's degree of motivation to approach or avoid a given intercultural context or person. Given that intercultural communication may be more anxiety producing than other forms of communication, the number of people suffering from intercultural communication apprehension (ICA) may be considerable. Identifying such individuals may be the first step toward more effective and successful intercultural communication.[41]

In Self-Assessment Box 1-2 is an instrument called the Personal Report of Intercultural Communication Apprehension (PRICA). This scale was developed by communication researchers Neuliep and McCroskey. The PRICA is very similar to the Personal Report of Communication Apprehension (PRCA) that you completed

---

Self-Assessment 1-2

Personal Report of Intercultural Communication Apprehension

The following self-report scale was designed by Neuliep and McCroskey to measure your intercultural communication apprehension. This instrument is composed of 14 statements concerning your feelings about communication with people from other cultures. Please indicate in the space provided the degree to which each statement applies to you by marking whether you (1) strongly agree, (2) agree, (3) are undecided, (4) disagree, or (5) strongly disagree with each statement. There are no right or wrong answers, and many of the statements are designed to be similar to other statements. Do not be concerned about this. Work quickly and record your first impressions. Respond to these statements as honestly as possible or else your score will not be valid.

1. _____ Generally, I am comfortable interacting with a group of people from different cultures.

2. _____ I am tense and nervous while interacting in group discussions with people from different cultures.

3. _____ I like to get involved in group discussions with others who are from different cultures.

4. _____ Engaging in a group discussion with people from different cultures makes me tense and nervous.

5. _____ I am calm and relaxed when interacting with a group of people who are from different cultures.

6. _____ While participating in a conversation with a person from a different culture, I feel very nervous.

7. _____ I have no fear of speaking up in a conversation with a person from a different culture.

8. _____ Ordinarily I am very tense and nervous in conversations with a person from a different culture.

9. _____ Ordinarily I am very calm and relaxed in conversations with a person from a different culture.

—Continued

10. _____ While conversing with a person from a different culture, I feel very relaxed.

11. _____ I'm afraid to speak up in conversations with a person from a different culture.

12. _____ I face the prospect of interacting with people from different cultures with confidence.

13. _____ My thoughts become confused and jumbled when interacting with people from different cultures.

14. _____ Communicating with people from different cultures makes me feel uncomfortable.

To score the instrument, reverse your original response for items 2, 4, 6, 8, 11, 13, and 14 (1 = 5, 2 = 4, 3 = 3, 4 = 2, and 5 = 1). For example, if your original score for item 2 was 1, change it to a 5. If your original score for item 4 was a 2, change it to a 4, and so forth. After reversing the score for these 14 items, sum all items. Scores cannot be higher than 70 or lower than 14. Higher scores (50–70) indicate high intercultural communication apprehension. Low scores (14–28) indicate low intercultural communication apprehension. To the degree to which you answered the items honestly, your score is a fairly reliable and valid assessment of your motivation to approach or avoid intercultural communication.

SOURCE: J. W. Neuliep and J. C. McCroskey, "The Development of Intercultural and Interethnic Communication Apprehension Scales," *Communication Research Reports,* 14 (1997), 145–156.

earlier in this chapter. The difference between these two scales is that the PRICA assesses your degree of apprehension about communicating with someone from a culture different from yours. After completing each scale you can compare your scores.

Spitzberg argues that people who are nervous and tense about interacting with people from different cultures are less likely to approach intercultural communication situations and probably are not confident about encountering new people from different cultures.[42]

Another key component of intercultural competence is knowledge. Communication knowledge refers to the ability to perceive situational variables that influence one's communicative choices and to select behaviors adaptive to those situational variables. Communication knowledge also involves understanding the consequences of enacting behaviors. Knowledgeable communicators have a relatively large repertoire of behavioral strategies for communicating. They are able to perceive how others are responding to their behaviors and refine and adapt their behaviors accordingly. To be interculturally competent, communicators need knowledge of other cultures. This textbook will help provide a foundation from which to build your communication knowledge about people from other cultures.

Intercultural communication competence also involves skill—that is, the ability to enact the desired and appropriate behavioral options. Because any given behavior might be judged competent in one culture and incompetent in another, skillful communicators are sensitive to the context in which communication occurs. They choose from their behavioral repertoires the kinds of verbal and nonverbal actions most appropriate for the culture and situation. Empathy, respect, interest in the particular culture, flexibility, and tolerance play key roles in intercultural sensitivity. Skillful intercultural communicators must be willing to modify their behavior as an indication of respect for people of other cultures.[43]

Fundamental Assumptions About Intercultural Communication

A central premise of this book is that intercultural communication is a complex combination of the cultural, microcultural, environmental, perceptual, and sociorelational contexts between two people who are encoding and decoding verbal and nonverbal messages. Because of the complexity of this process, a fundamental assumption about intercultural communication is that during intercultural communication, the message sent *usually is not* the message received.

> Assumption 1: During intercultural communication, the message sent usually is *not* the message received.

Whenever people from different cultures come together and exchange messages, they bring with them a whole host of thoughts, values, emotions, and behaviors that were planted and cultivated by culture. As we have said, intercultural communication is a symbolic activity where the thoughts and ideas of one person are encoded into a verbal and/or nonverbal message format and then transmitted through some channel to another person, who must decode it, interpret it, and respond to it. This process of encoding, decoding, and interpreting is filled with cultural noise. Noted intercultural communication scholar William Gudykunst has noted that during intercultural communication, culture acts as a filter through which all messages, both verbal and nonverbal, must pass. To this extent, all intercultural exchanges are necessarily, to a greater or lesser extent, charged with ethnocentrism. Hence, during intercultural communication, the message sent is not the message received.[44]

Ethnocentrism refers to the idea that one's own culture is the center of everything, and all other groups (or cultures) are scaled and rated with reference to it. Sociologist W. Sumner argued that ethnocentrism nourishes a group's pride and vanity while looking on outsiders, or outgroups, with contempt.[45] Although culture may mediate the extent to which we experience it, ethnocentrism is thought to be universal. One of the effects of ethnocentrism is that it clouds our perception of others. We have a tendency to judge others, and their communication, according to the standards set by our own culture. Neuliep and McCroskey have argued that the concept of ethnocentrism is essentially descriptive; not necessarily pejorative. Ethnocentrism may serve a very valuable function when one's in-group is under attack or threatened. Moreover, ethnocentrism forms the basis for patriotism, group loyalty, and the willingness to sacrifice for one's own group. To be sure, however, ethnocentrism can be problematic. In not looking past their own culture, people see little importance in understanding other cultures. At high levels, ethnocentrism is an obstacle to effective intercultural communication.[46]

Neuliep and McCroskey have developed the GENE scale, which is designed to measure ethnocentrism. The GENE scale and the directions for completing it follow.

Self-Assessment 1-3

The GENE scale is composed of 22 statements concerning your feelings about your culture and other cultures. In the space provided please indicate the degree to which each statement applies to you by marking whether you (5) Strongly agree, (4) Agree, (3) Are Undecided, (2) Disagree, or (1) Strongly Disagree with the statement. There are no right or wrong answers and some of the statements are similar to others. Remember, everyone experiences some degree of ethnocentrism. Fortunately, as we will see in Chapter 5, ethnocentrism can be managed and reduced. Be honest! Work quickly and record your first response.

1. _____ Most other cultures are backward compared to my culture.

2. _____ My culture should be the role model for other cultures.

3. _____ People from others cultures act strange when they come to my culture.

4. _____ Lifestyles in other cultures are just as valid as those in my culture.

5. _____ Other cultures should try to be more like my culture.

6. _____ I'm not interested in the values and customs of other cultures.

7. _____ People in my culture could learn a lot from people in other cultures.

8. _____ Most people from other cultures just don't know what's good for them.

9. _____ I respect the values and customs of other cultures.

10. _____ Other cultures are smart to look up to our culture.

—Continued

11. _____ Most people would be happier if they lived like people in my culture.

12. _____ I have many friends from different cultures.

13. _____ People in my culture have just about the best lifestyles anywhere.

14. _____ Lifestyles in other cultures are not as valid as those in my culture.

15. _____ I am very interested in the values and customs of other cultures.

16. _____ I apply my values when judging people who are different.

17. _____ I see people who are similar to me as virtuous.

18. _____ I do not cooperate with people who are different.

19. _____ Most people in my culture just don't know what is good for them.

20. _____ I do not trust people who are different.

21. _____ I dislike interacting with people from different cultures.

22. _____ I have little respect for the values and customs of other cultures.

To determine your ethnocentrism score complete the following four steps.

Step One: Add your responses to scale items 4, 7, and 9.
Step Two: Add your responses to scale items 1, 2, 5, 8, 10, 11, 13, 14, 18, 20, 21, and 22.
Step Three: Subtract the sum from Step One from 18 (i.e., 18 minus Step One Sum)
Step Four: Add results from Step Two and Step Three. This is your generalized ethnocentrism score. Higher scores indicate higher ethnocentrism. Scores above 55 are considered high ethnocentrism.

Assumption 2: Intercultural communication is primarily a nonverbal act between people.

Some foreign-language teachers might have us believe that competency in a foreign language is tantamount to effective and successful intercultural communication in the culture that speaks that language. To be sure, proficiency in a foreign language expedites the intercultural communication experience. But intercultural communication is primarily and fundamentally a nonverbal process. Some researchers have suggested that as much as 90 percent of all communication is nonverbal. Cultural values, the expression of intimacy, power, and status among communicators is typically accomplished nonverbally through paralinguistic cues, proxemics, haptics, oculesics, and olfactics. In Korea, for example, one's hierarchical position is displayed via vocal tone and pitch. When a student takes receipt of an important piece of paper, such as a graded exam from a respected professor, the student grasps it with both hands (not just one), giving a slight nod of the head and making only indirect eye contact—all nonverbal signs of deference.

The well-known anthropologist Edward Hall has argued that people from different cultures live in different sensory worlds. Hall claims that people from different cultures engage in a selective screening of sensory information that ultimately leads to different perceptions of experience.[47] Regarding olfactics (smell), most cultures establish norms for acceptable and unacceptable scents associated with the human body. When people fail to fit into the realm of olfactic cultural acceptability, their odor signals others that something is wrong with their physical, emotional, or mental health. In the United States we are obsessed with masking certain smells, especially those of the human body. In Western and Westernized cultures, body odor is regarded as unpleasant and distasteful, and great efforts are expended on its removal. Many Muslims believe that cleanliness of the body and purity of the soul are related. Muslim women are told to purify themselves after menstruation. As we will see in Chapter 8, our nonverbal messages complement, augment, accent, substitute for, and repeat our verbal messages.

Assumption 3: Intercultural communication necessarily involves a clash of communicator styles.

In the United States, talk is a highly valued commodity. People are routinely evaluated by their speech. Yet silence—that is, knowing when not to speak—is a fundamental prerequistite for linguistic and cultural competence.[48] The use and interpretation of silence varies dramatically across cultures. In many collectivistic cultures, like Japan and Korea, silence can carry more meaning than words, especially in the maintenance of intimate relationships. In fact, the Japanese and some Native American tribes in the United States believe that the expression of relational intimacy is best accomplished nonverbally. They believe that having to put one's thoughts and emotions into words somehow cheapens and discounts them.

In the United States we value and employ a very direct and personal style of verbal communication. Personal pronouns are an essential ingredient to the composition of just about any utterance. Our attitude appears to be "Get to the point"; "Don't beat around the bush"; "Tell it like it is"; "Speak your mind." Many cultures, however, prefer an indirect and impersonal communication style. In these cultures, there is no need to articulate every message. True understanding is implicit, coming not from words but from actions in an environment where speakers provide only hints or insinuations. The Chinese say, "One should use the eyes and ears, not the mouth," and "Disaster emanates from careless talk." The Chinese consider the wisest and most trustworthy person the one who talks the least but who listens, watches, and restricts his or her verbal communications.[49]

Chapter Summary

Recent technological, political, and sociological advancements have created a global village only dreamed about twenty years ago. However, while the dream of a global village holds great promise, the reality is that diverse people have diverse opinions, values, and beliefs that clash and too often result in violence. Only though intercultural communication can such conflict be managed and reduced.

The terms *communication* and *culture* are difficult to define. Communication involves the simultaneous encoding and decoding of verbal and nonverbal messages with someone else within some context. Culture, in part, can be defined as an accumulated pattern of values, beliefs, and behaviors shared by an identifiable group of people with a common history and a verbal and nonverbal symbol system. Intercultural communication is essentially contextual. The cultural, microcultural, and environmental contexts surround the communicators, whose sociorelational context is defined by the exchange of verbal and nonverbal messages that are encoded and decoded within each interactant's perceptual context.

The final part of this chapter has allowed you to discover something about yourself—your communication apprehension, your intercultural communication apprehension, and your ethnocentrism. Competent intercultural communicators are willing to approach intercultural situations and are sensitive to the differences in them.

GLOSSARY OF TERMS

Communication: The simultaneous encoding, decoding, and interpretation of verbal and nonverbal messages between people.

Communication apprehension: The fear or anxiety associated with either real or anticipated communication with another person or group of persons.

Context: The cultural, physical, social, and psychological environment.

Culture: An accumulated pattern of values, beliefs, and behaviors shared by an identifiable group of people with a common history and a verbal and nonverbal symbol system.

Dynamic: Active, forceful.

Environmental context: The physical, geographical location of communication.

Ethnocentrism: Tendency to place one's own group (cultural, ethnic, or religious) in a position of centrality and worth, and to create negative attitudes and behaviors toward other groups.

GENE: Self-report instrument disigned to measure generalized ethnocentrism.

Intentionality: During communication, the voluntary and conscious encoding and decoding of messages.

Interactive: A process between two people.

Intercultural communication: Two persons from different cultures or microcultures exchanging verbal and nonverbal messages.

Intercultural communication apprehension (ICA): The fear or anxiety associated with either real or anticipated communication with a person from another culture or coculture.

Microculture: An identifiable group of people coexisting within some dominant cultural context.

Perceptual context: The attitudes, emotions, and motivations of the persons engaged in communication and how they affect information processing.

Personal Report of Communication Apprehension (PRCA): Self-report instrument designed to measure communication apprehension.

Process: Anything ongoing, ever-changing, and continuous.

Sociorelational context: The role relationship between the interactants (for example, brother/sister).

Symbol: An arbitrarily selected and learned stimulus representing something else.

Transactional: Pertaining to the simultaneous encoding and decoding process during communication.

Uncertainty: The amount of unpredictability during communication.

REFERENCES

1. A. M. Schlesinger, *The Disuniting of America: Reflections of a Multicultural Society* (New York: Norton, 1993), p. 10.
2. Ibid.
3. J. Pomfret, "Resolving Crisis Was a Matter of Interpretation," *Washington Post* (April 12, 2001). Quotes from letter, page A1.: D. Rupple, "Equitable Resolution: Each Side Gained, Lost in US–China Plane Crisis" (abcnews.go.com...yNews/chinaplanecrisis 010411.html).
4. Ibid.
5. J. T. England, "Building Community for the 21st Century," *ERIC Digest,* ED347489 (1992) (www.ed.gov/databases/ERIC_Digests/ed347489.html).
6. M. S. Peck, *The Different Drum: Community Making and Peace* (New York: Touchstone, 1987).
7. United States Department of Commerce, "Big Emerging Markets" (1998) (www.ita.doc.gov/bems/index.html).
8. "The Numbers Game," *Time,* 142 (1993), 14.
9. U.S. Department of Commerce, U.S. Census Bureau, "Profiles of General Demographic Characteristics: 2000 Census of Population and Housing" (Washington, D.C.: United States Government Printing Office, 2001); M. Therrien and R. R. Ramirez, "The Hispanic Population in the United States: Population Characteristics" (Washington, D.C.: U.S. Government Printing Office, 2001); B. Guzman, "The Hispanic Population: Census 2000 Brief" (Washington, D.C.: U.S. Government Printing Office, 2001); E. M. Grieco and R. C. Cassidy, "Overview of Race and Hispanic Origin: Census 2000 Brief" (Washington, D.C.: U.S. Government Printing Office, 2001); "Population Estimates and Projections: The Changing American Pie, 1999 and 2025," Ameristat: A Population Reference Bureau and Social Science Data Analysis Network (www.ameristat.org/estproj/pie.htm).
10. Ibid.
11. J. McKinnon and K. Humes, "The Black Population in the United States: Population Characteristics" (Washington, D.C.: U.S. Government Printing Office, 2000); B. Guzman, "The Hispanic Population: Census 2000 Brief" (Washington, D.C.: U.S. Government Printing Office, 2001); "Population Estimates and Projections," Ameristat (www.ameristat.org/estproj/pie.htm).
12. *The American Tally* (Milpitas, Calif.: Toucan Valley Publications, 1993).
13. A. M. Schlesinger, *The Disuniting of America: Reflections of a Multicultural Society,* p. 15.
14. C. U. Larson, *Persuasion: Reception and Responsibility,* 6th ed. (Belmont, Calif.: Wadsworth, 1998), p. 5.
15. C. Safran, "Troubles That Pull Couples Apart: A Redbook Report," *Redbook,* 83 (1979), 138–141.
16. F. E. X. Dance, "The 'Concept' of Communication," *Journal of Communication,* 20 (1970), 201–210.
17. F. E. X. Dance and C. E. Larson, *The Function of*

Human Communication: A Theoretical Approach (New York: Holt, Rinehart & Winston, 1976).

18. B. A. Fisher, *Perspectives on Human Communication* (New York: Macmillan, 1978).

19. D. K. Berlo, *The Process of Communication* (New York: Holt, Rinehart & Winston, 1960), p. 24.

20. M. T. Motley, "On Whether One Can(not) Not Communicate: An Examination Via Traditional Communication Postulates," *Western Journal of Speech Communication,* 54 (1990), 1–20.

21. Ibid.

22. P. Watzlawick, J. Beavin, and D. Jackson, *Pragmatics of Human Communication: Patterns, Pathologies, and Paradoxes* (New York: Norton, 1967).

23. J. C. McCroskey, *An Introduction to Rhetorical Communication,* 8th ed. (Boston: Allyn and Bacon, 2001).

24. R. Keesing, "Theories of Culture," in *Annual Review of Anthropology,* ed. B. J. Siegel (Palo Alto, Calif.: Annual Reviews, 1974), p. 73.

25. A. I. Kroeber and C. Kluckhohn, eds., *Culture: A Critical Review of Concepts and Definitions* (New York: Random House, 1954); H. N. Seelye, *Teaching Culture: Strategies for Intercultural Communication* (Lincolnwood, Ill.: National Textbook Company, 1993).

26. *The American Tally* (Milpitas, Calif.: Toucan Valley Publications, 1993).

27. D. Yurkovich, K. Pliscott, and R. Halverson, "The Norwegian Culture" (unpublished student manuscript, St. Norbert College, De Pere, Wisc., 1996); A. R. Gayle and K. P. Knutson, "Understanding Cultural Differences: Jenteloven and Social Conformity in Norway," *Et Cetera,* 50 (1993), 449.

28. G. Westfahl, R. Koltz, and A. Manders, "Ethnic Russian Culture and Society" (unpublished student manuscript, St. Norbert College, De Pere, Wisc., 1996); A. Resnick, *The Commonwealth of Independent States* (United States: Childrens Press, 1993).

29. K. Basso, "To Give Up on Words: Silence in Western Apache Culture," in *Cultural Communication and Intercultural Contact,* ed. D. Car-

baugh (Hillsdale, N.J.: Erlbaum, 1990), pp. 303–320.

30. R. Axtell, *Gestures: Do's and Taboos of Body Language Around the World* (New York: Wiley, 1991).

31. J. McNeley, *Holy Wind in Navaho Philosophy* (Tucson: University of Arizona Press, 1981).

32. S. Moellendorf, H. Warsh, and K. Yoshimaru, "The Amish Culture: A Closer Look at the People of Lancaster County" (unpublished student manuscript, St. Norbert College, De Pere, Wisc., 1996).

33. K. Vandehey, C. Buerger, and K. Krueger, *Traditional Aspects and Struggles of the Masai Culture* (unpublished student manuscript, St. Norbert College, De Pere, Wisc., 1996); E. Angeloni, ed., *Mystique of the Masai* (Guilford, Conn.: Dushkin, 1995).

34. P. Watzlawick, J. Beavin, and D. Jackson, *Pragmatics of Human Communication.*

35. C. R. Berger, "Communicating Under Uncertainty," in *Readings on Communicating with Strangers,* ed. W. B. Gudykunst and Y. Y. Kim (New York: McGraw-Hill, 1992), pp. 5–15.

36. C. R. Berger and R. Calabrese, "Some Explorations in Initial Interaction and Beyond," *Human Communication Research,* 1 (1975), 99–112.

37. A. H. Buss, *Self-Consciousness and Social Anxiety* (San Francisco: W. H. Freeman, 1980).

38. W. B. Gudykunst and Y. Y. Kim, *Communicating with Strangers: An Approach to Intercultural Communication* (New York: McGraw-Hill, 1997).

39. J. W. Neuliep and J. C. McCroskey, "The Development of Intercultural and Interethnic Communication Apprehension Scales," *Communication Research Reports,* 14 (1997), 145–156.

40. B. H. Spitzberg, "A Model of Intercultural Communication Competence," in *Intercultural Communication: A Reader,* 8th ed., ed. L. A. Samovar and R. E. Porter (Belmont, Calif.: Wadsworth, 1997), pp. 379–391.

41. Neuliep and McCroskey, "The Development of

Intercultural and Interethnic Communication Apprehension Scales."

42. Spitzberg, "A Model of Intercultural Communication Competence," pp. 347–359.

43. D. P. Bhawuk and R. Brislin, "The Measurement of Intercultural Sensitivity Using the Concepts of Individualism and Collectivism," *International Journal of Intercultural Relations,* 16 (1992), 413–436.

44. W. Gudykunst, "Cultural Variability in Communication: An Introduction, "*Communication Research,* 24 (1997), 327–348.

45. W. G. Sumner, *Folkways* (Boston: Ginn, 1906).

46. J. W. Neuliep and J. C. McCroskey, "The Development of a U.S. and Generalized Ethnocen-

trism Scale," *Communication Research Reports,* 14 (1997), 385–398.

47. E. T. Hall, *The Silent Language* (New York: Doubleday, 1959).

48. C. Braithwaite, "Communicative Silence: A Cross-Cultural Study of Basso's Hypothesis," in *Cultural Communication and Intercultural Contact,* ed. D. Carbaugh (Hillsdale, N.J. Erlbaum, 1990), 321–328.

49. W. B. Gudykunst and S. Ting-Toomey, "Verbal Communication Styles," in *Culture and Interpersonal Communication,* ed. W.B. Gudykunst and S. Ting-Toomey (Newbury Park, Calif.: Sage, 1988), pp. 427–441.

The Cultural Context

CHAPTER OBJECTIVES

After reading this chapter, you should be able to:

- Compare and contrast individualism and collectivism.
- Identify some cultures that are individualistic and some that are collectivistic.
- Compare and contrast high- and low-context cultures.
- Identify some cultures that are high-context and some that are low-context.
- Compare value orientations among cultures.
- Compare and contrast high- and low-power-distance cultures.
- Identify some cultures that are high-power-distance and some that are low-power-distance.
- Compare and contrast high- and low-uncertainty-avoidant cultures.
- Identify some cultures that are high-uncertainty-avoidant and some that are low-uncertainty-avoidant.
- Assess your degree of individualism/collectivism, high/low-context, power distance, and uncertainty avoidance.

Cultural Context

The cultural context in which human communication occurs is perhaps the most defining influence on human interaction. Culture provides the overall framework in which humans learn to organize their thoughts, emotions, and behaviors in relation to their environment. Although people are born into a culture, culture is not innate. Culture is learned. Culture teaches one how to *think,* conditions one how to *feel,* and instructs one how to *act,* especially how to *interact* with others—in other words, communicate. In many respects, the terms *communication* and *culture* can be used interchangeably. The influence of culture on human interaction is paradoxical. As we conduct our daily lives, most of us are unaware of our culture. Yet culture influences our every thought, feeling, and action. As the internationally recognized anthropologist Edward Hall asserts in the quote at the beginning of this chapter, culture hides more than it reveals, particularly from its own members.

Australian anthropologist Roger Keesing argues that culture provides people with an implicit theory about how to behave and how to interpret the behavior of others. People from different cultures learn different implicit theories. These theories are learned through socialization. Through socialization individuals learn the dominant values of their particular culture and their self-identities.[2]

Over the past few decades, anthropologists, psychologists, and sociologists have isolated several dimensions of cultural variability that can be used to differentiate cultures. These dimensions are representative of the different implicit cultural theories. This chapter will focus on five dimensions of cultural variability: (1) *individualism/collectivism,* (2) *high/low context,* (3) *value orientations,* (4) *power distance,* and (5) *uncertainty avoidance.* Each of these dimensions affects how people communicate.

The five dimensions of cultural variability will be presented along cultural continua. The cultural continua allow for the representation of the dimensions as continuous and varying in magnitude by degree. No culture is purely and absolutely individualistic or collectivistic, for example. Rather, a culture may be more individualistic or more collectivistic than some other culture. Moreover, these cultural dimensions of variability are not opposites—in some cultures, they may coexist. In addition, many cultures are in a state of great transition. Collectivistic cultures might gravitate toward individualism while individualistic cultures adopt collectivistic values. For example, Japan is considered a collectivistic, group-oriented, society. Since the 1950s, Japan has been strongly influenced by Western culture. Many Japanese scholars have observed that the younger generation of Japanese, while still considered collectivistic, are more individualistic than their parents and even more so than their grandparents. Likewise, although the United States is considered one of the most individualistic cultures on the planet, many American businesses and corporations employ collectivistic management models in the workplace, focusing on teamwork and cooperation. While reading through this chapter, remember that cultures are not static; they are dynamic, continuously developing and evolving.

Individualism/Collectivism

Perhaps the single most studied dimension of cultural variability used to compare and contrast cultures and microcultures is individualism/collectivism. Along the cultural continuum shown in Figure 2-1, individualism is on the left end, and collectivism is on the right end.

Cultures falling toward the left side of the continuum are individualistic, whereas those falling toward the right side are collectivistic. Cultures falling at the midpoint may possess both individualistic and collectivistic characteristics. Gayle and Knutson write that Norwegians, for example, possess both individualistic and collectivistic tendencies. Norwegians are taught to put the needs of society above their own and to embrace a classless society. Simultaneously, however, Norwegians value personal independence. Although Norwegians conform to social norms, the individual Norwegian rebuffs traditional rules and standards. Norwegians strive for independence, yet do not depend on others to recognize their individual achievements. Norwegians believe that they must recognize their own good qualities to gain self-esteem.[3]

Perhaps Norway is unusual in the degree to which its people carry collectivistic and individualistic tendencies simultaneously, but regardless of culture, most persons carry to some degree both individualistic and collectivistic tendencies. The difference is that in some cultures, individualistic tendencies tend to dominate, whereas in others, collectivistic tendencies dominate.[4]

Harry Triandis, a psychologist at the University of Illinois, is well known for his work on individualism and collectivism. Triandis writes that in individualistic cultures, emphasis is placed on an individual's goals over group goals. In individualistic cultures, social behavior is guided by personal goals, perhaps at the expense of other types of goals. Individualistic cultures stress values that benefit the individual person. The self is promoted because each person is viewed as uniquely endowed and possessing distinctive talent and potential. Individuals are encouraged to pursue and develop their abilities and aptitudes. In many individualistic cultures, people are taught to be creative, self-reliant, competitive, and assertive.[5]

Triandis argues that an important ingredient of individualistic cultures is that the individual is emotionally disconnected from in-groups, such as the family. Because the individual has been taught to be independent, social control depends more on personal guilt than on shame or other social norms of conformity. Ironically, members of individualist cultures tend to belong to many groups, but their affiliation with them is short-lived. Many of the groups to which an individualist

FIGURE 2-1   The Individualism/Collectivism Continuum

Individualism   Collectivism

belongs are designed to enhance self-worth—for example, self-help, therapy, or occupational groups.[6]

Triandis traces the origins of individualism to ancient Greece, where literature (for example, the *Iliad* and the *Odyssey*) celebrated the accomplishments of individuals. Triandis notes that modern, industrial-urban, fast-changing cultures tend to be individualistic. In many cases, individualistic cultures are often highly complex and affluent. Complex cultures have heterogeneous populations and economies based on occupational specialization, in which individuals do different jobs. Cultural complexity also occurs in cultures in which people are separated from one another, either geographically or through migration patterns; for example, many individualistic cultures have a history of colonization.[7]

Affluence also correlates with individualism. Financial independence means that one may be less dependent on others to satisfy needs. As cultures become more affluent, they tend to become more individualistic. Some scholars even link climate to individualism and collectivism. Cultures in cooler climates tend to be individualistic, whereas cultures in warmer climates tend to be collectivistic. Colder climates are likely to foster and support individual initiative and innovative solutions to problems. Warmer climates render individual achievements less necessary. Many English-speaking Western cultures are considered individualistic (for example, the United States and Canada). Many Western European cultures are also individualistic (for example, Germany, Switzerland, and England).[8]

In contrast, according to Triandis, in collectivistic cultures, group goals have precedence over individual goals. Collectivistic cultures stress values that serve the in-group by subordinating personal goals for the sake of preserving the in-group. Collectivistic societies are characterized by extended primary groups—such as the family, neighborhood, or occupational group—in which members have diffuse mutual obligations and expectations based on their status or rank. In collectivistic cultures, people are not seen as isolated individuals. People see themselves as *interdependent* with others, with shared responsibility and collective accountability. A person is seen not as an individual, but as a member of a group.[9]

Triandis points out that although collectivistic cultures stress the importance of the group over the individual, their members tend to belong to fewer groups than persons in individualistic cultures. Unlike the individualist, the collectivist is emotionally connected to the in-group. A collectivist's values and beliefs are consistent with and reflect those of the in-group. Moreover, a collectivist's association with his or her in-groups may last a lifetime. In many collectivistic cultures, the primary value is harmony with others. Triandis observes that because group harmony is so highly valued, obedience to, and compliance with, in-group pressures is routine. One's behavior is role based, and deviations from the prescribed role are discouraged and often negatively sanctioned. A person's behavior is guided more by shame than by personal guilt. A collectivist who stands out from the group disrupts the harmony and may be punished. Most collectivistic cultures value social reciprocity, obligation, dependence, and obedience. But by far, the primary value stressed by many collectivistic cultures is harmony.[10]

Triandis believes that collectivism is based on the tenet that collaboration and cooperation ultimately lead to survival. Both collaboration and cooperation require obedience and harmony, which is typically managed and coordinated by someone in charge, such as an authority. Authority, or one's rank in the group, is a salient feature of many collectivistic cultures. Collectivists tend see each other in terms of hierarchically ranked roles, not as individuals. Collectivism can be found in parts of Europe, such as southern Italy and rural Greece. Much of Africa, Asia, and Latin America is considered collectivistic.[11]

Individualism and *collectivism* are terms that describe whole cultures. But cultures are not pure. As Triandis notes, members of collectivist cultures may practice individualistic tendencies, and members of individualist cultures may value collectivist ideals. Joe Feldhausen notes, for example, that Denmark has both collectivistic and individualistic tendencies. In Denmark, individual freedom is nurtured through a devotion to established traditions and customs. Regarding income and social rank, Danes are staunchly egalitarian. At the same time, however, Danes consider themselves free to be nonconformist and to stand out from the group. In this way, Danes may be at the theoretical midpoint of the individualistic/collectivistic cultural continuum. To account for this phenomenon, Triandis and other cross-cultural researchers distinguish between individualism and collectivism at the cultural level and idiocentrism and allocentrism at the individual psychological level. In other words, some cross-cultural researchers believe that individualism/collectivism cannot be measured at the cultural level. We should not label entire cultures as individualistic or collectivistic, because persons within those cultures may vary considerably. We can, however, measure an individual's degree of individualism/collectivism. When an individual carries individualistic

A person's individualistic or collectivistic tendencies will affect communication. Many Asian cultures are collectivistic while U.S. culture is considered individualistic.
(© James Neuliep)

Intercultural Conversation

An Intercultural Conversation: Individualist and Collectivist Cultures

In the following exchange, Mr. Patterson, an American manager working in Korea, is meeting with his supervisor, Mr. Wyman, who is also American. The United States is considered an individualistic culture, whereas Korea is considered collectivistic. In this scenario, Mr. Patterson reports to Mr. Wyman about some changes he has made within several of his sales teams. Later, Park Young Sam, their Korean counterpart, enters into the dialogue.

Mr. Patterson: Good morning, Mr. Wyman. Thanks for meeting with me this morning. As you know, our division has been doing very well this quarter. In fact, our numbers are up across the board.

Mr. Wyman: Yes, I've seen your quarterly reports. Nice job!

Mr. Patterson: Thanks. In order to recognize their hard work, I've made some changes in our sales teams. I've created team leaders in each group. In our product group, I promoted Lee Young-sam. In the marketing group, I promoted Chun Tae-woo, and in the technology group, I promoted Choi Mino. All of them have been real leaders. I think this idea will really motivate them. In fact, I met with the groups individually and announced the promotions.

Mr. Wyman: Good job, Patterson. I can see you're really on top of things. Good work.

Two Months Later

Mr. Patterson, Mr. Wyman, and Park Young Sam, a Korean manager, are discussing the poor performance of Mr. Patterson's sales teams.

Mr. Wyman: Well, just look at these dismal results. The numbers for this quarter are way down from last quarter. What's happened?

Mr. Patterson: I don't know. Ever since I introduced the team leader concept, the groups' productivity has really plummeted. I thought it was a great idea. I guess I chose the wrong people to lead the teams. I'll assign new leaders tomorrow.

Park Young Sam: Well . . . you may select new leaders if you desire, but the men you chose were all very capable. However, by elevating them you made them stand out and disrupted the harmony of each group. In Korea, we all work hard for the group . . . not for just one person.

Mr. Patterson: I guess I should have just left things as they were.

Following their individualistic orientations, Mr. Patterson and Mr. Wyman were perfectly comfortable with the idea of creating team leaders within the individual sales groups. However, as Park Young Sam mentions, by so doing, the harmony of the groups was upset, which, in turn, led to poor performance. In the United States, workers are often motivated by the opportunity for promotion and advancement as this serves the individualistic drive for individual achievement. In collectivistic cultures, however, workers may be motivated by being a part of a cohesive and productive team.

SOURCE: This dialogue is adapted from a scene in L. Copeland, producer, *Managing the Overseas Assignment* [videorecording] (San Francisco: Copeland Griggs Productions, 1983).

tendencies, we call him or her *idiocentric*. When an individual carries collectivistic tendencies, we call that person *allocentric*. Idiocentrism and allocentrism are the individual equivalents of cultural individualism and collectivism.[12]

William Gudykunst and his colleagues contend that another way to conceptualize individualism/collectivism at the individual level is to focus on self-construals—that is, how the individual thinks of the self. How individuals conceive of the self is one of the major determinants of their behavior. People use different construals of the self, including the independent and the interdependent self. The independent self predominates in individualistic cultures, and the interdependent self predominates in collectivistic cultures.[13]

CONSEQUENCES OF INDIVIDUALISM/COLLECTIVISM

A given culture's orientation toward individualism or collectivism has important behavioral consequences for that culture's members. Among collectivists, social behavior is guided by the group. Along with group membership come prescribed duties and obligations. Among individualists, social behavior is guided by one's personal attitudes, motivations, and other internal processes. Whereas individualists are taught to compete, the collectivist learns to cooperate. To be sure, individualistic cultures value and reward successful competition. The United States, for example, is replete with contests and ceremonies that recognize individual accomplishment. People are publicly rewarded for being the most beautiful, thinnest, strongest, fastest, tallest, smartest, youngest, oldest, funniest, or the "best" at something. Collectivistic cultures, on the other hand, stress harmony and cooperation. Collectivists strive for the approval of the in-group, which is attained not by standing out but by conforming to the group's norm. From the collectivist's perspective, an individual that stands out from the group disrupts harmony. In the United States "the squeaky wheel gets the grease," but in Japan "the tallest nail gets hammered down."[14]

Markus and Kitayama write that in individualistic cultures, how people see themselves privately is how they present themselves publicly. One's intrapersonal concept (for example, "I am scholarly," "I am trustworthy," "I am principled") is seen in the individualist's public behavior. The collectivist, however, may have an inconsistent public and private self. Collectivists are likely to behave publicly according to the in-group's norm regardless of their personal attitudes. Collectivists' self-esteem may depend on whether they can fit in and be a part of a relevant ongoing relationship with other group members. Collectivists see themselves as interdependent with others.[15]

Triandis maintains that a culture's individualistic or collectivistic orientation will likely affect child-rearing practices. Individualistic parents encourage their children to be unique, express themselves, and be independent. The children of individualistic parents understand that they are to leave home once they reach a certain age or education level. In fact, it is thought of as odd or unusual if children past the age of twenty-one or so still live at home with their parents. Though rank order exists in the individualist's family, decisions are often made democratically. Collectivistic parents teach their children the importance of family lineage and ancestry. Typically the father dominates the collectivist's home, and family rank is often determined by sex and age.[16]

Collectivists are more conscious of in-group/out-group distinctions than are individualists. According to Gudykunst and his colleagues, individualists tend to initiate and maintain specific friendships based on desirable qualities of the other person. Collectivists form friendships that are determined by their hierarchical role in society. Collectivists perceive and rate their in-group friendships as more intimate than do individualists. On the other hand, individualists tend to apply the same value standards to all, whereas collectivists tend to apply different value standards to members of their in-groups and out-groups. For example, collectivists are likely to use the equality norm (that is, equal distribution of resources) with in-group members and the equity norm (that is, unequal distribution of resources) with out-group members.[17]

HOFSTEDE'S CULTURAL PREFERENCES

In the late 1960s and early 1970s, Dutch social psychologist Geert Hofstede surveyed over 100,000 employees of a large multinational business organization in forty countries to measure work-related values. In 1991 Hofstede reformulated his results and included the findings of more recent research by himself and others, as well as survey data from ten additional countries and two areas.[18] Several of the items on Hofstede's survey measured individualism. The countries and their ranks for individualism appear in Table 2.1. According to Hofstede's scoring procedure, higher scores indicate a preference for individualism. Scores closer to zero indicate a preference for collectivism.

Individualism and collectivism are multidimensional. No single attribute is sufficient to classify a person as individualistic or collectivistic. That one or another culture may be more or less individualistic or collectivistic does not mean that they cannot share similar values related to other things. As Schwartz notes, wisdom, broad-mindedness, and inner harmony serve both personal and in-group interests. Cultures that are considered collectivistic may have values that are collective but are not those of the in-group. For example, equality for all, social justice, preserving the natural environment, and world peace are values that serve the larger cultural milieu and society, not only the in-group.[19]

VERTICAL AND HORIZONTAL INDIVIDUALISM AND COLLECTIVISM

While it is clear that individualistic cultures differ from collectivist cultures, individualistic cultures can, and do, differ from other individualistic cultures. The same can be said of collectivistic cultures. Some individualistic cultures, for example, link self-reliance with competition, whereas other individualistic cultures do not. Some collectivistic cultures emphasize in-group harmony above all else, whereas other collectivistic cultures do so not at all. To account for some of these finer distinctions among individualistic and collectivistic cultures, Triandis and

TABLE 2-1 Countries and Individualism Ranks

Country	Individualism Score	Individualism Rank	Country	Individualism Score	Individualism Rank
United States	91	1	Turkey	37	28
Australia	90	2	Uruguay	36	29
Great Britain	89	3	Greece	35	30
Canada	80	4/5	Philippines	32	31
Netherlands	80	4/5	Mexico	30	32
New Zealand	79	6	East Africa	27	33/35
Italy	76	7	Yugoslavia	27	33/35
Belgium	75	8	Portugal	27	33/35
Denmark	74	9	Malaysia	26	36
Sweden	71	10/11	Hong Kong	25	37
France	71	10/11	Chile	23	38
Ireland	70	12	West Africa	20	39/41
Norway	69	13	Singapore	20	39/41
Switzerland	68	14	Thailand	20	39/41
Germany	67	15	Salvador	19	42
South Africa	65	16	South Korea	18	43
Finland	63	17	Taiwan	17	44
Austria	55	18	Peru	16	45
Israel	54	19	Costa Rica	15	46
Spain	51	20	Pakistan	14	47/48
India	48	21	Indonesia	14	47/48
Japan	46	22/23	Columbia	13	49
Argentina	46	22/23	Venezuela	12	50
Iran	41	24	Panama	11	51
Jamaica	39	25	Ecuador	8	52
Brazil	38	26/27	Guatemala	6	53
Arab Countries	38	26/27			

SOURCE: From *Cultures and Organizations: Software of the Mind*, © 1991 Geert Hofstede. Reproduced with the author's permission.

his colleagues differentiate between vertical and horizontal individualism and collectivism.[20]

According to Singelis, Triandis, Bhawuk, and Gelfand, horizontal individualism is a cultural orientation in which an autonomous self is valued, but the individual is more or less equal in status to others. The self is perceived as independent but nevertheless the same as others. Vertical individualism is a cultural orientation in which an autonomous self is also valued, but the self is seen as different from, and perhaps unequal to, others. Status and competition are an important aspect of this orientation. The United States and France are examples of cultures oriented toward vertical individualism, whereas Sweden and Austria are oriented toward horizontal individualism.[21]

Horizontal collectivism is a cultural orientation in which the individual sees the self as part of an in-group whose members are similar to each other. The self is interdependent and the same as the self of others. Equality is expected and practiced within this orientation. China is probably a good example of a culture oriented toward horizontal collectivism. Theoretical communism is an example of extreme horizontal collectivism. Vertical collectivism is a cultural orientation in which the individual sees the self as an integral part of the in-group whose members are different from each other, some having more status than others. The self is interdependent, and inequality within the group is valued. In this orientation, serving and sacrifice are important. Japan, India, and rural traditional Greece are examples of cultures oriented toward vertical collectivism.

There are advantages and disadvantages to being an individualist just as there are to being a collectivist. Neither approach is better than the other; they are simply different orientations. The goal is to recognize and understand the differences, thereby increasing your intercultural competence.

To be sure, the individualism/collectivism dimension of cultural variability has been used extensively in describing cultural differences—perhaps too much. Asian cultures, in particular, are often branded as collectivistic. Recently the individualism/collectivism dichotomy has been the subject of criticism. In her analysis of Chinese culture, Hui-Ching Chang argues that by cultures' being described as only collectivistic, which focuses on the structure of society, much of the creativity of individual Asian cultures, including very rich histories, has been ignored. Chang asserts:

> Although it is through the lens of the metaphor "collectivism" that we are allowed to focus on group membership and patterns of relationships in Asian cultures, at the same time, we lose sight of other aspects of delicate cultural reasoning that underlie manifested behavior patterns.[22]

The essence of Chang's argument is that we cannot rely on single metaphorical distinctions such as individualism/collectivism if we really want to accurately describe and ultimately understand other cultures.

Self-Assessment 2-1

Measuring Horizontal and Vertical Individualism/Collectivism

Below are 32 statements designed to assess your attitudes and beliefs about yourself. There are no right or wrong answers, and some of the statements are similar to others. In the blank to the left of each item, indicate the degree to which you agree or disagree with each statement. If you are unsure or think that an item does not apply to you, enter a 5 in the blank. Use the following key:

Strongly Disagree 1 2 3 4 5 6 7 8 9 Strongly Agree

1. _____ I often do "my own thing."

2. _____ One should live one's life independently of others.

3. _____ I like my privacy.

4. _____ I prefer to be direct and forthright in discussions with other people.

5. _____ I am a unique individual.

6. _____ What happens to me is my own doing.

7. _____ When I succeed, it is usually because of my abilities.

8. _____ I enjoy being unique and different from others in many ways.

9. _____ It annoys me when other people perform better than I do.

10. _____ Competition is the law of nature.

11. _____ When another person does better than I do, I get tense and aroused.

12. _____ Without competition it is not possible to have a good society.

13. _____ Winning is everything.

14. _____ It is important that I do my job better than others.

15. _____ I enjoy working in situations involving competition with others.

16. _____ Some people emphasize winning; I'm one of them.

17. _____ The well-being of my coworkers is important to me.

18. _____ If a coworker gets a prize, I feel proud.

19. _____ If a relative were in financial difficulty, I would help within my means.

20. _____ It is important to maintain harmony within my group.

—*Continued*

21. _____ I like sharing little things with my neighbors.

22. _____ I feel good when I cooperate with others.

23. _____ My happiness depends very much on the happiness of those around me.

24. _____ To me, pleasure is spending time with others.

25. _____ I would sacrifice an activity I enjoy very much if my family did not approve of it.

26. _____ I would do what pleased my family, even if I detested that activity.

27. _____ Before taking a major trip, I consult with most members of my family and many friends.

28. _____ I usually sacrifice my self-interest for the benefit of my group.

29. _____ Children should be taught to place duty before pleasure.

30. _____ I hate to disagree with others in my group.

31. _____ We should keep our aging parents with us at home.

32. _____ Children should feel honored if their parents receive a distinguished award.

SCORING:

1. Add your responses for items 1 through 8. This is your Horizontal Individualism Score.
2. Add your responses for items 9 through 16. This is your Vertical Individualism Score.
3. Add your responses for items 17 through 24. This is your Horizontal Collectivism Score.
4. Add your responses for items 25 through 32. This is your Vertical Collectivism Score.

ALTERNATIVE SCORING METHOD:

1. Add your responses for items 1 through 16. This is your Individualism Score.
2. Add your responses for items 17 through 32. This is your Collectivism Score.

SOURCE: T. M. Singelis, H. C. Triandis, D. P. S. Bhawuk, and M. J. Gelfand, *Cross-Cultural Research*, Vol. 29, 1995, pp. 240–274. Copyright © 1995 Sage Publications. Reprinted by permission of the publisher.

High-Context/Low-Context Communication

Human communication is dependent on the context in which it occurs. In addition to the verbal and nonverbal codes that are exchanged between interactants, the salient features of a communicative context include the cultural, physical, sociorelational, and perceptual environments. The cultural context includes, among myriad other variables, such features as individualism and collectivism. The physical environment includes the actual geographical location of the interaction (for example, an office, classroom, bedroom). The sociorelational environment encompasses the relationship between the interactants (for example, superior/subordinate, teacher/student, husband/wife). The perceptual environment consists of the attitudes, motivations, and cognitive dispositions of the interactants. Each of these environments provides a wealth of information to the interactants about how to communicate. The degree to which interactants focus on these contexts while communicating varies considerably from culture to culture. For example, some persons choose to focus more on the verbal codes than on the nonverbal elements, whereas others will actively monitor the nonverbal elements of the context. Edward Hall describes the former as low-context and the latter as high-context. Hall asserts:

> A high-context (HC) communication or message is one in which most of the information is either in the physical context or is internalized in the person, while very little is in the coded, explicit, transmitted part of the message. A low-context (LC) communication is just the opposite; i.e., the mass of information is vested in the explicit code.[23]

Like individualism and collectivism, high/low-context is best conceptualized along the cultural continuum (see Figure 2.2). No culture exists exclusively on one end of the continuum.

CHARACTERISTICS OF HIGH-CONTEXT AND LOW-CONTEXT CULTURES

Hall argues that environmental, sociorelational, and perceptual contexts have an immense impact on communication. High-context cultures generally have restricted code systems. Users of a restricted code system rely more on the contextual elements of the communication setting for information than on the actual language code. Within a high-context transaction, the interactant will look to the physical, sociorelational, and perceptual environment for information. Of partic-

FIGURE 2-2   The Low-Context/High-Context Continuum

Low Context   High Context

ular importance is the social relationship between the interactants, especially their status. As Hall notes:

> Twins who have grown up together can and do communicate more economically (HC) than two lawyers in a courtroom during a trial (LC), a mathematician programming a computer, two politicians drafting legislation, two administrators writing a regulation, or a child trying to explain to his mother why he got into a fight.[24]

Because interactants in a high-context culture know and understand each other and their appropriate roles, words are not necessary to convey meaning. One acts according to one's role. Words and sentences may be collapsed and shortened. In this sense, restricted codes are not unlike local dialects, vernacular, or even jargon used by a well-defined group. Users of restricted codes interpret messages according to their accumulation of shared experiences and expectations.

Hall contends that persons communicating in high contexts understand that information from the physical, sociorelational, and perceptual environment already exists and need not be codified verbally. Therefore, high-context communication is fast, proficient, and gratifying. The burden of understanding in high-context communication rests with each interactant. The rules for communication are implicit, and communicators are expected to know and understand unspoken communication. High-context communication involves using and interpreting messages that are not explicit, minimizing the content of verbal messages, and being sensitive to the social roles of others. Though there are exceptions, many high-context cultures are collectivistic, including China, Japan, North and South Korea, Vietnam, and many Arab and African cultures.[25]

According to Hall, in a low-context transaction, the verbal code is the primary source of information. Low-context cultures generally rely on elaborated codes. Unlike users of restricted codes, users of elaborated codes rely extensively on the verbal code system for creating and interpreting meaning. Information to be shared with others is coded in the verbal message. Although persons in low-context transactions recognize the nonverbal environment, they tend to focus more on the verbal context. Moreover, the rules and expectations are explicitly explained. Users of elaborated codes are dependent upon words to convey meaning and may become uncomfortable with silence. In low-context transactions, the communicants feel a need to speak. People using low-context communication are expected to communicate in ways that are consistent with their feelings. Hence low-context communication typically involves transmitting direct, explicit messages. Though there are exceptions, many low-context cultures are individualistic, including Switzerland, Germany, Scandinavia, the United States, France, and the United Kingdom.[26]

COMMUNICATION CONSEQUENCES OF HIGH-CONTEXT AND LOW-CONTEXT CULTURAL ORIENTATIONS

Members of high-context and low-context cultures communicate differently, especially in regard to the use of silence. Charles Braithwaite argues that one of the

Self-Assessment 2-2

Assessing High-Context and Low-Context Communication

Below are 32 statements regarding how you feel about communicating in different ways. In the blank to the left of each item, indicate the degree to which you agree or disagree with each statement. If you are unsure or think that an item does not apply to you, enter a 5 in the blank. Use the following key:

Strongly Disagree 1 2 3 4 5 6 7 8 9 Strongly Agree

1. _____ I catch on to what others mean, even when they do not say it directly.

2. _____ I show respect to superiors, even if I dislike them.

3. _____ I use my feelings to determine whether to trust another person.

4. _____ I find silence awkward in conversation.

5. _____ I communicate in an indirect fashion.

6. _____ I use many colorful words when I talk.

7. _____ In argument, I insist on very precise definitions.

8. _____ I avoid clear-cut expressions of feelings when I communicate with others.

9. _____ I am good at figuring out what others think of me.

10. _____ My verbal and nonverbal speech tends to be very dramatic.

11. _____ I listen attentively, even when others are talking in an uninteresting manner.

12. _____ I maintain harmony in my communication with others.

13. _____ Feelings are a valuable source of information.

14. _____ When pressed for an opinion, I respond with an ambiguous statement/position.

15. _____ I try to adjust myself to the feelings of the person with whom I am communicating.

16. _____ I actively use a lot of facial expression when I talk.

17. _____ My feelings tell me how to act in a given situation.

18. _____ I am able to distinguish between a sincere invitation and one intended as a gesture of politeness.

—Continued

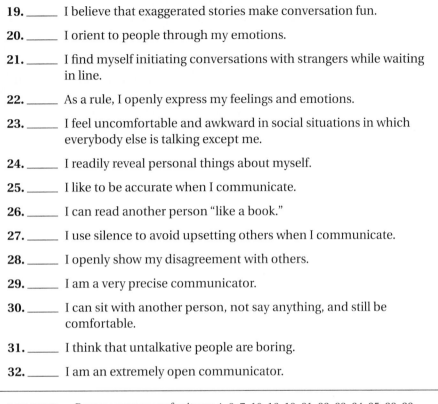

19. _____ I believe that exaggerated stories make conversation fun.

20. _____ I orient to people through my emotions.

21. _____ I find myself initiating conversations with strangers while waiting in line.

22. _____ As a rule, I openly express my feelings and emotions.

23. _____ I feel uncomfortable and awkward in social situations in which everybody else is talking except me.

24. _____ I readily reveal personal things about myself.

25. _____ I like to be accurate when I communicate.

26. _____ I can read another person "like a book."

27. _____ I use silence to avoid upsetting others when I communicate.

28. _____ I openly show my disagreement with others.

29. _____ I am a very precise communicator.

30. _____ I can sit with another person, not say anything, and still be comfortable.

31. _____ I think that untalkative people are boring.

32. _____ I am an extremely open communicator.

SCORING: Reverse your score for items 4, 6, 7, 10, 16, 19, 21, 22, 23, 24, 25, 28, 29, 31, 32. If your original score was 1, reverse it to a 9; if your original score was a 2, reverse it to an 8, and so forth. After reversing the score for those 15 items, simply sum the 32 items. Lower scores indicate low-context communication. Higher scores indicate high-context communication.

SOURCE: From W. B. Gudykunst, Y. Matsumoto, S. Ting-Toomey, et al., "The Influence of Cultural Individualism-Collectivism, Self Construals, and Individual Values on Communication Styles Across Cultures," *Human Communication Research*, Vol. 22 1996, pp. 510–543.

fundamental components of cultural and linguistic competence is knowing how and when to use silence as a communicative tactic.[27] During a high-context communicative exchange, the interactants generally are content with silence since they do not rely on verbal communication as their main source of information. Silence, in fact, communicates mutual understanding. In communicative exchanges between persons of differing status, the person with lower status may recognize the higher status of the other through silence. Lawrence Weider and Steven Pratt contend that many Native American tribes use silence as a way of recognizing "Indianness." A "real" Indian recognizes another real Indian with silence rather than speech. A recognizable Indian knows that neither he nor the other has an obligation to speak and that silence on the part of all conversants is permissible.[28] In her book on the contemporary Japanese woman, Sumiko Iwao writes that most Japanese feel that expressing especially personal or intimate details is best done nonverbally and/or intuitively—that is, without words. Iwao writes:

> There is an unspoken belief among the Japanese in general that putting deep feelings into words somehow lowers or spoils their value and that understanding attained without words is more precious than that attained through precise articulation.[29]

Of course, Japan is considered a high-context culture. In contrast, silence in most low-context transactions is uncomfortable. Persons who do not talk are often perceived negatively. When someone is quiet in a low-context transaction, others may suspect that something is amiss. Silence somehow communicates a problem. Low-context communicators are expected to be direct and to say what they think.

Persons in low-context cultures typically separate the issue of communication from the person with whom they are interacting. A manager might say, "Don't take it personally," as he or she reprimands an employee. High-context cultures, on the other hand, tend to see communication as intrinsic to the person. If an issue is attacked, so is the person. High-context communicators prefer indirectness typified by extreme politeness and discretion.

At this point in the chapter, you have been given the opportunity to assess your own level of individualism/collectivism and the degree to which your communication style is high- or low-context. Whatever the outcome on these surveys, one style is not better than the other; they are simply different. The goal is for you to have a better understanding of yourself and of people with different cultural backgrounds. Individualism/collectivism and high/low-context are two dominant ways that cultures differ. But perhaps what guides cultural behavior more than anything else are the values held by large collectives.

Value Orientations

In his seminal book on values, psychologist Milton Rokeach argues that

> the value concept, more than any other, should occupy a central position across all social sciences . . . it is an intervening variable that shows promise of being able to unify the apparently diverse interests of all sciences concerned with human behavior.[30]

Intercultural Conversation

An Intercultural Conversation: High-Context and Low-Context Cultures

In the following exchange, Mr. Hutchinson is the head of Information Technology within his organization. Mr. Wong is the lead computer programmer. Mr. Wong was born and raised in Malaysia, a high-context culture. The two are discussing when Mr. Wong will put a computer program into production. Note that Mr. Hutchinson's speech is direct and to the point, whereas Mr. Wong's speech is indirect and subtle. Mr. Hutchinson also uses four times as many words as Mr. Wong.

Mr. Hutchinson: The program looks good and passed the test run with only minor errors. When do you think you can put it into production? I don't see any production schedule here. The changes need to go into the system by the end of the month. Is that possible? When do you want to go with this?

Mr. Wong: Maybe I should review the requirements.

Mr. Hutchinson: The errors were minor. Quality Control needs to know when it will go into production. Let's set the production date now. Just tell me when you'll fix the errors. I'll tell QC.

Mr. Wong: Perhaps I can e-mail you an estimate. I'll talk to the team.

Mr. Hutchinson: Couldn't you just tell me when you'll have them fixed? Here, it's no big deal. (*Hands Mr. Wong the program*) Don't they seem like easy fixes?

Mr. Wong: (*Looks at the program but says nothing—as if not hearing Mr. Hutchinson's suggestion*)

Mr. Hutchinson: Mr. Wong? Just give me a date.

Mr. Wong: Yes. Whenever you prefer is fine. (*Hands the program back to Mr. Hutchinson*)

Mr. Hutchinson: I don't need this. (*Hands it back to Mr. Wong*) Well, it's got to go in by the first of next month. OK?

Mr. Wong: Yes, that is fine.

In the above dialogue, Mr. Hutchinson misses the hint that Mr. Wong is unable to set a production date. When Mr. Wong indicates that setting a date is difficult and will require some expertise, he is indirectly telling Mr. Hutchinson that he is not in a position to make the decision on his own and would prefer to discuss it with the team. Mr. Wong further signals his discomfort by telling Mr. Hutchinson that he could e-mail him the date. Mr. Hutchinson ignores Mr. Wong's status in the organization and further complicates the issue by handing Mr. Wong the program. Trying to avoid any disagreement, Mr. Wong simply asks Mr. Hutchinson to set the date for production and agrees to whatever he says.

SOURCE: Adapted from C. Storti, *Cross-Cultural Dialogues: Seventy-four Brief Encounters with Cultural Differences.* (Yarmouth, Maine: Intercultural Press, 1994).

Values affect intercultural communication. When people from different cultures come together to interact, their messages are guided by, and reflect, their fundamental value orientations. People who strongly value individuality will likely interact differently than people who strongly value collectivism. An understanding of cultural value systems can help to identify similarities and differences between people from different cultures, from which intercultural communication can proceed.

Like culture, values are learned; they are not innate or universal. Rokeach argues that values guide us in the selection and justification of social behavior. Values prescribe what is preferred or prohibited. Values are the evaluative component of an individual's attitudes and beliefs. Values guide how we think about things in terms of what is right/wrong and correct/incorrect. Values trigger positive or negative emotions. Values also guide our actions.[31] Israeli psychologist Shalom Schwartz asserts that values are concepts or beliefs that pertain to outcomes and behaviors, guide the selection and evaluation of behaviors, and are rank ordered according to their relative importance to the individual.[32]

HSU'S POSTULATES OF BASIC AMERICAN VALUES

Although any individual probably has a unique set of values, there are also sets of values that are representative of a particular culture. Francis Hsu, an anthropologist who has lived much of his life in China and the United States, has outlined what he thinks are the nine basic values of Americans. His list (see the Recap box on p. 55) was generated from his personal experiences, American literature and prose, social science research, and studies of criminal behavior in the United States.

Most of the values listed by Hsu reflect America's individualistic tendencies. In addition, they echo our emphasis on equality (discussed later under power distance), and our determination to push toward the future.

THE CHINESE VALUE SURVEY

In interesting contrast to the values of the United States, an individualistic low-context culture, are those of China, a collectivistic high-context culture. In 1987, the Chinese Culture Connection (CCC)—an international network of social scientists under the direction of Michael Bond, a professor in the Department of Psychology at Chinese University of Hong Kong—approached a number of Chinese social scientists and asked each of them to prepare a list of ten fundamental Chinese values. Although their procedure resulted in considerable overlap, they were able to eliminate redundancy by creating a master list of forty dominant Chinese values, as seen in the box on p. 56.

The CCC then analyzed this master list, noting the interrelations and underlying dimensions among many of the forty values. They then reduced the list to four

Hsu's Postulates of Basic American Values

1. An individual's most important concern is self-interest; self-expression, self-improvement, self-gratification, and independence. This takes precedence over all group interests.

2. The privacy of the individual is the individual's inalienable right. Intrusion into it by others is permitted only by invitation.

3. Because the government exists for the benefit of the individual and not vice-versa, all forms of authority, including government, are suspect. Patriotism is good.

4. An individual's success in life depends upon acceptance among his or her peers.

5. An individual should believe in or acknowledge God and should belong to an organized church or other religious institution. Religion is good. Any religion is better than no religion.

6. Men and women are equal.

7. All human beings are equal.

8. Progress is good and inevitable. An individual must improve himself/herself (minimize efforts and maximize returns); the government must be more efficient to tackle new problems; institutions such as churches must modernize to make themselves more attractive.

9. Being American is synonymous with being progressive, and America is the utmost symbol of progress.

SOURCE: H. N. Seelye, *Teaching Culture: Strategies for Intercultural Communication,* 3rd ed. (Lincolnwood, Ill.: National, 1993), pp. 128–129.

basic factors: integration, Confucian work dynamic, human-heartedness, and moral discipline (see Table 2-2).

The CCC then asked one hundred people in each of twenty-two different cultures to rate the importance of the forty values on a 9-point scale, where 9 meant "of supreme importance" and 1 meant "of no importance at all." With sophisticated statistical analysis it was possible to locate each of the twenty-two cultural groups on the four value factors (see Table 2-3). The numbers in Table 2-3 represent "factor scores." The higher the score, the more salient this value in that particular culture.

Fundamental Chinese Values

1. Filial piety (obedience to parents, respect for parents, honoring of ancestors)
2. Industry (working hard)
3. Tolerance of others
4. Harmony with others
5. Humbleness
6. Loyalty to superiors
7. Observation of rites and social rituals
8. Reciprocation of greetings, favors, and gifts
9. Kindness
10. Knowledge (education)
11. Solidarity with others
12. Moderation, following the middle way
13. Self-culturation
14. Ordering relationships by status and observing this order
15. Sense of righteousness
16. Benevolent authority
17. Noncompetitiveness
18. Personal steadiness and stability
19. Resistance to corruption
20. Patriotism
21. Sincerity
22. Keeping oneself disinterested and pure
23. Thrift
24. Persistence
25. Patience
26. Repayment of both the good or evil that another person has caused you
27. A sense of cultural superiority
28. Adaptability
29. Prudence (carefulness)
30. Trustworthiness
31. Having a sense of shame
32. Courtesy
33. Contentedness with one's position in life
34. Being conservative
35. Protecting your "face"
36. A close, intimate friend
37. Chastity in women
38. Having few desires
39. Respect for tradition
40. Wealth

SOURCE: From "Chinese Values and the Search for Culture-Free Dimensions of Culture" The Chinese Culture Connection, *Journal of Cross-Cultural Psychology,* Vol. 19, No. 2, pp. 143–164, 1987. Copyright © 1987 Western Washington University. Reprinted by permission of Sage Publications.

SCHWARTZ'S UNIVERSAL VALUES

Israeli Psychologist Shalom Schwartz and his colleagues have studied values across cultures with the goal of creating a comprehensive classification scheme of shared human values. Although some disagree with his position, Schwartz argues that there is a universal structure to values recognized by all cultures. Schwartz's work focuses on the structure of values, not on the universality of their relative importance. Schwartz argues that values represent goals and/or motivations. He contends that values represent, in the form of goals, three universal requirements for human existence to which all cultures must be responsive: (1) *the biological needs of individuals,* (2) *the need for social coordination,* and (3) *the survival and welfare needs of groups.* From these three universal human requirements Schwartz derived eleven distinct motivational types of values that lead to the formation of specific values and their priorities (see Recap box on p. 60).

TABLE 2-2

Integration	Confucian Work Dynamic	Human-Heartedness	Moral Discipline
Tolerance	Ordering relationships	Kindness	Moderation
Harmony	Thrift	Patience	Keeping disinterested
Solidarity	Persistence	Courtesy	Having few desires
Filial piety	Sense of shame	Righteousness	Adaptability
Trustworthiness	Reciprocation	Patriotism	Prudence
Contentedness	Personal steadiness		
Conservativeness	Protecting "face"		
Intimacy with friends	Respect for tradition		
Chastity in women			
Noncompetitiveness			

SOURCE: From "Chinese Values and the Search for Culture-Free Dimensions of Culture" The Chinese Culture Connection, *Journal of Cross-Cultural Psychology,* Vol. 19, No. 2, pp. 143–164, 1987. Copyright © 1987 Western Washington University. Reprinted by permission of Sage Publications.

TABLE 2-3 Factor Scores Across Culture for Chinese Values

Integration		Confucian Work Dynamic	
W. Germany	1.34	Hong Kong	.91
Netherlands	1.06	Taiwan	.74
Japan	.81	Japan	.59
New Zealand	.78	S. Korea	.49
Australia	.75	Brazil	.30
England	.75	India	.21
Brazil	.65	Thailand	.11
Sweden	.60	Singapore	−.04
Canada	.60	Netherlands	−.13
United States	.44	Bangladesh	−.20
Philippines	.42	Sweden	−.34
Poland	.39	Poland	−.36
S. Korea	.26	Australia	−.38
Singapore	.21	W. Germany	−.38
Zimbabwe	.13	New Zealand	−.39

—Continued

TABLE 2-3   Factor Scores Across Culture for Chinese Values (*continued*)

Integration		Confucian Work Dynamic	
Hong Kong	.10	United States	−.42
Thailand	−.02	England	−.50
Nigeria	−.13	Zimbabwe	−.50
Taiwan	−.19	Canada	−.53
Pakistan	−.65	Philippines	−.61
India	−.72	Nigeria	−.67
Bangladesh	−1.07	Pakistan	−1.00

Human-Heartedness		Moral Discipline	
Japan	1.42	Philippines	1.04
Philippines	1.10	S. Korea	.68
Canada	1.09	Poland	.54
Hong Kong	1.08	Pakistan	.33
England	1.01	Japan	.14
United States	1.00	W. Germany	.07
Zimbabwe	.96	India	−.02
New Zealand	.95	Taiwan	−.07
Australia	.87	Thailand	−.08
Singapore	.80	Hong Kong	−.17
Nigeria	.79	Nigeria	−.21
Brazil	.75	Singapore	−.32
Taiwan	.58	Netherlands	−.34
W. Germany	.50	Bangladesh	−.40
Thailand	.49	Australia	−.50
Sweden	.49	Brazil	−.66
Poland	.48	Canada	−.66
S. Korea	.45	England	−.66
Pakistan	.39	New Zealand	−.67
Bangladesh	.39	United States	−.71
India	.27	Zimbabwe	−.74
Netherlands	−1.09	Sweden	−.77

SOURCE: From "Chinese Values and the Search for Culture-Free Dimensions of Culture" The Chinese Culture Connection, *Journal of Cross-Cultural Psychology,* Vol. 19, No. 2, pp. 143–164, 1987. Copyright © 1987 Western Washington University. Reprinted by permission of Sage Publications.

KLUCKHOHN AND STRODTBECK'S VALUE ORIENTATIONS

In the early 1960s, Florence Kluckhohn and Fred Strodtbeck of Harvard University developed the concept of value orientations. They argued that in every culture there are universal problems and conditions that must be addressed. For example, every culture must deal with the natural environment. All cultures must feed themselves. All cultures must face the issues of child rearing, and so forth. For a given culture, however, there are only a limited number of solutions to these problems. These possible solutions are motivated by the values of the culture. Initially, Kluckhohn and Strodtbeck created five sets of value orientations.[33] Several years later, communication researchers John Condon and Fathi Yousef extended the set to a total of twenty-five value orientations. Condon and Yousef organized the value orientations around six dominant themes: (1) *self,* (2) *family,* (3) *society,* (4) *human nature,* (5) *nature,* and (6) *the supernatural* (see Table 2-4).[34]

The Condon and Yousef set of value orientations provides a structure and vocabulary that can be used to compare cultures. Although there are exceptions, many of the values on the left of the continuum in Table 2-4 are representative of individualistic low-context cultures, whereas those on the right are representative of collectivistic high-context cultures.

The Self.   In all cultures, people develop their self-identity. How that identity is fostered is influenced by the culture's values. For example, people in individualistic societies such as the United States tend to view their accomplishments and failures very personally. Conformity is viewed negatively. Hsu notes that in China, however, conformity and cooperation are highly valued. In the United States, a person is seen as a unique individual and strives for independence from others. When individuals succeed or win, they receive a great deal of attention and adulation, as in the case of winning an Olympic gold medal or an Academy Award. The individual is "put on a pedestal." Likewise, when individuals lose, they are often left to suffer alone. No one wants to be seen with a loser. Whether on top or on the bottom, the individual experiences intense emotions. Hsu contends that strong emotions are unavoidable since they are concentrated in one individual. The Chinese, however, are interdependent with others, and responsibility and accountability are shared and divided among the group members. If the group wins, everyone in the group wins—there is no "most valuable player." The intense emotions experienced in winning or failing are tempered and moderated because they are shared.[35]

The second variation on the self continuum is age. Western, individualistic, low-context cultures tend to value youth. Conversely, old age is valued in many cultures, such as Nigeria, where it is associated with wisdom. According to Harris and Moran, in Nigeria the elderly are respected because they have much experience and can pass on family history and tradition. Harris and Moran suggest that when conducting business with Nigerians, a firm would be wise to send an older person to meet with prospective business persons, as this will show respect for Nigeria's emphasis on age.[36]

Schwartz's Motivational Types of Values

1. *Self-Direction*: The defining goal of this value type is independent thought and action. (freedom, creativity, independence, choosing own goals, curiosity, self-respect)

2. *Stimulation:* The goal is derived from the need for variety and stimulation in order to maintain an optimal level of activation. Some of these needs are biological, whereas others are learned/cultural. (an exciting life, a varied life, daring)

3. *Hedonism:* The need and motivation for pleasure. (pleasure, enjoying life)

4. *Achievement:* The need and value of personal success and prestige. (ambition, influence, capability, success, intelligence, self-respect)

5. *Power:* Attainment of social status. (social power, wealth, authority, preserving public image, social recognition)

6. *Security:* Need for safety, harmony, and the stability of society and relationships. (national security, reciprocation of favors, family security, sense of belonging, social order, health, cleanliness)

7. *Conformity:* Restraint of actions, inclinations, and impulses. (obedience, self-discipline, politeness, honoring of parents and elders)

8. *Tradition:* The value of religious rites, beliefs, and norms of behavior that over time are valued and passed on by a collective. (respect for children, devotion, acceptance of one's portion in life, humility, moderation)

9. *Spirituality:* The goal of inner harmony through the transcendence of everyday life. (a spiritual life, meaning in life, inner harmony, detachment)

10. *Benevolence:* The need and motivation for positive interaction and affiliation. (helpfulness, responsibility, forgiveness, honesty, loyalty, mature love, true friendship)

11. *Universalism:* The value of understanding, appreciation, tolerance, and protection of the welfare of all people and of nature. (equality, unity with nature, wisdom, a world of beauty, social justice, broad-mindedness, protecting the environment, a world at peace)

SOURCE: Adapted from S. H. Schwartz, "Universals in the Content and Structure of Values: Theoretical Advances and Empirical Tests in Twenty Countries," in *Advances in Experimental Social Psychology,* vol. 25, ed. M. P. Zanna (San Diego, Calif.: Academic Press, 1992), pp. 6–7.

TABLE 2-4 Condon-Yousef's Value Orientations			
	Individualistic *Low-Context* Cultures		Collectivistic *High-Context* Cultures
SELF			
1. Individualism	Individualism	Individuality	Interdependence
2. Age	Youth	Middle years	Old age
3. Sex	Equality of sexes	Female superiority	Male superiority
4. Activity	Doing	Being-in-becoming	Being
THE FAMILY			
1. Relational Orientations	Individualistic	Collateral	Lineal
2. Authority	Democratic	Authority centered	Authoritarian
3. Positional Role Behavior	Open	General	Specific/prescribed
4. Mobility	High mobility	Phasic mobility	Low mobility/stasis
SOCIETY			
1. Social Reciprocity/	Independent	Symmetrical/ obligatory	Complementary/ obligatory
2. Group Membership	Many/brief membership	Balanced	Few/prolonged membership
3. Intermediaries	Few	Specialist only	Essential
4. Formality	Informal	Selective formality	Pervasive formality
5. Property	Private	Utilitarian	Communal
HUMAN NATURE			
1. Rationality	Rational	Intuitive	Irrational
2. Good/Evil	Good	Mixture	Evil
3. Happiness/ Pleasure	Happiness as goal	Inextricable bond of happiness and sadness	Life is mostly sad
4. Mutability	Change, growth, learning	Some change	Unchanging

—Continued

TABLE 2-4   Condon-Yousef's Value Orientations (*continued*)

	Individualistic *Low-Context* Cultures		Collectivistic *High-Context* Cultures
NATURE			
1. Relationship Between Humans and Nature	Humans dominate nature	Harmonious	Nature dominates humans
2. Ways of knowing Nature	Abstract	Circle of induction and deduction	Specific/direct
3. Structure of Nature	Mechanistic	Spiritual	Organic
4. Concept of Time	Future	Present	Past
SUPERNATURAL			
1. Relationship Between Humans and Supernatural	Humans as God	Pantheism	Humans controlled by supernatural
2. Meaning of Life	Physical/material goals	Intellectual goals	Spiritual goals
3. Providence	Good is unlimited	Balance of good and misfortune	Good in life is limited
4. Knowledge of Cosmic Order	Order is comprehensible	Faith and reason	Mysterious and unknowable

SOURCE: From *An Introduction to Intercultural Communication* by John C. Condon and Fathi Yousef, pp. 60–62. Copyright © 1975 by Allyn & Bacon. Reprinted by permission.

The third variation on the self continuum is activity. Americans identify themselves in terms of their activities, usually professions and occupations. Condon and Yousef hold that many English surnames indicate "doers"—for example, Baker, Smith, and Carpenter. In the United States, people are often asked about what they "do" for a living. Non-Western cultures emphasize being, a form of self-actualization. Life is an organic whole; it is human to embrace life and to become one with the universe.[37]

Family.   Familial relationships differ across cultures. Harris and Moran write that in Nigeria, for example, the family is the core group of society. Nigerians value their family lineage through the male head of the household. A Nigerian is known by his or her family lineage and may have privileges and responsibility based on the family name. Furthermore, marriage is seen as a way of producing more children to contribute to this lineage. If one's spouse is sterile, it is grounds for divorce. Nigerians also practice polygamy. Often wives are acquired through the payment of a bride price to the bride's parents.[38]

Positional role behavior within families refers to how strictly roles are prescribed among family members. The Guatemalan Ladinos (people born through interracial relationships or with Spanish and Indian blood) define a man's and woman's role within the family quite differently. *Machismo* is a Spanish term similar to the word *sexist* in English. Mike Keberlein notes that machismo is not quite the same as sexism, however. According to Keberlein, machismo deals mainly with how male and female roles are performed in the home. Ladinos view the man as protector and provider and women as child rearers and homemakers. Children are taught early by the mother to recognize their responsibilities as men and women. A boy may be sent to work in the fields as early as five years old. A young girl might start household chores at the same age, when she is taught to care for younger children of the house and to cook. Young boys are expected never to cry or show signs of pain, whereas young girls are taught to show emotion whenever appropriate.[39]

Society.   According to Condon and Yousef, social reciprocity refers to the mutual exchanges people make in their dealings with others. What is perceived as a relatively innocuous request in one country may be interpreted quite seriously in others. In the United States, a request for a favor (for example, "Can I borrow your car?") may imply no necessary reciprocity. In other cultures, one is required to return favors and obligations in kind. Equal exchanges are expected and obligated.[40]

The second value orientation, group membership, differs greatly among individualistic and collectivistic cultures. According to Condon and Yousef, members of individualistic cultures tend to join many groups throughout their lifetime, yet their affiliation with any particular group may be quite brief. The group is subordinate to the individual needs. In the United States, for example, people join political groups, social groups, hobby groups, occupational groups, self-help groups, fraternal groups, and so forth. In collectivistic cultures, people tend to belong to fewer groups (for example, family and occupational) but belong for a lifetime.[41]

An intermediary is a go-between or "middleman." Intermediaries are more common in collectivistic than in individualistic cultures. Many Chinese prefer to work through an intermediary. According to De Menthe, the concept of *mian-zi,* or "face," is a critical ingredient for Chinese. The Chinese believe that respect for others binds society together. *Mian-zi* is a sort of social status—how a person is ranked in relation to others. This is sometimes referred to as one's "face." A person's face is determined by such things as wealth and power. The more "face" a person has, the more he or she can "buy" with it. De Menthe writes that like a checking account, *mian-zi* can be overdrawn, and people are expected to balance their accounts. The

Chinese are very conscious of their "face" as well as the "face" of others. The higher in rank a person is, the more critical the concern with "face." In business dealings and in personal relationships, it is critical to the Chinese that they maintain "face" and avoid offending the "face" of others. Hence, it is difficult for the Chinese to be straightforward and open in their daily interactions with others. Intermediaries are therefore essential in both personal and business relationships.[42]

Human Nature.   The human nature orientation deals with how cultures perceive human character and temperament. In Western cultures like the United States, people are viewed as essentially rational. American children are taught to "use their heads" when making decisions. Americans frequently tell their friends to "stop being so emotional," as if being emotional implied some character flaw. Japanese children, on the other hand, are often taught to follow their intuition or to lead with their "hearts."

Condon and Yousef note that in the United States, happiness is viewed as a practical goal, even the primary goal—hence the popular song "Don't Worry, Be Happy." Moreover, the Declaration of Independence states that people "are endowed by their creator with certain unalienable rights, that among these are life, liberty, and the pursuit of happiness." Other societies and cultures view happiness and sadness as inseparable, as in the yin-yang philosophy of many Asian cultures. A Chinese proverb reads: "If a man's face does not show a little sadness, his thoughts are not too deep." Another one reads: "One should not miss the flavor of being sick, nor miss the experience of being destitute."[43]

Nature.   In the United States, high school students learn about the structure of nature in their biology, geography, and physics classes. Students learn about things they may never actually see, such as the structure of DNA. The models they see are not literal reproductions, but dramatic abstractions. Much of U.S. education is based on abstract concepts and constructs. Condon and Yousef maintain that in other cultures, perhaps those with little formal education, what a person knows about nature is learned through direct experience. Many Western cultures view nature as mechanistic, meaning that nature is structured like a machine or clock. The brain, for example, is explained in computer analogies. Models of DNA look like satellites. The organic orientation sees nature as an organic whole, interdependent with all other natural forces.[44]

The Supernatural.   Condon and Yousef assert that a culture's perspective on the cosmos reflects its philosophy about people's relationship with the supernatural and spiritual world. In many Western cultures, the supernatural is studied almost scientifically. Scientists study the structure of space and seek though scientific means to find the origins of the universe. We send out satellites equipped with printed messages and recordings in a (perhaps vain) attempt to communicate with extraterrestrials. Most Western cultures believe that the order of the cosmos is knowable. Conversely, other cultures see the cosmos with a great deal of fear and uncertainty. Condon and Yousef point to a farmer in Peru who relies on the phases of the moon and the cycles of the seasons to tell him when to plant or harvest his fields. The farmer thinks of the cosmos with a great deal of superstition and fear. To him, these mysteries are unexplainable.[45]

The value orientations presented above are not mutually exclusive or exhaustive. They are representative of the kinds of values held by cultures and the differences in those values. They also serve as a starting point for researchers to compare and contrast the myriad cultures that cohabit the planet.

Power Distance

According to Geert Hofstede, although many cultures declare and even legislate equality for their members, all cultures must deal with the issue of human inequality. A fundamental tenet expressed in the beginning of the Declaration of Independence is that "all men are created equal." In the United States, we treat others as equal, in both our personal and professional lives. Although some cultures, like the United States, affirm equality for their members, some form of inequality exists in virtually every culture. Inequality can occur in areas such as prestige, wealth, power, human rights, and technology. Issues of inequality fall within the rubric of what Hofstede calls "power distance." In his landmark survey research, Hofstede defined power distance as "the extent to which the less powerful members of institutions and organizations within a country expect and accept that power is distributed unequally."[46] Power distance can be seen in families, bureaucracies, and even friendships. For example, inequality of power within organizations is inevitable and is desirable in many instances for organizations to function effectively. Military organizations are defined by power distance.

Hofstede categorizes cultures as possessing either large or small power distance. Cultures with a smaller power distance emphasize that inequalities among people should be minimized and that there should be interdependence between less and more powerful people. In cultures with small power distance (for example, the United States, Canada, Austria), family members are generally treated as equal, and familial decisions are reached democratically. According to Hofstede, in low-power-distance schools, teachers expect a certain amount of initiative and interaction with students. The overall educational process is student oriented. In class, students are expected to ask questions and perhaps even challenge their teachers. In organizations, decentralization is popular, and subordinates engage in participative decision making. The organizational power hierarchy is mostly for convenience, and the persons who occupy powerful roles may change regularly. In fact, workers are expected to try to "climb the ladder of success" to more power and prestige. In this sense, persons in low-power-distance cultures may recognize "earned" power—that is, power that people deserve by virtue of their drive, hard work, and motivation. Moreover, low-power-distance cultures tend to resent people whose power is decreed by birth or wealth (that is, positional power).[47]

Hofstede maintains that in cultures with a larger power distance, inequalities

Power distance can be communicated in a variety of ways. In some cultures, to show deference to their husbands, women are required to walk several paces behind them in public. *(Jodi Cobb/National Geographic)*

among people are both expected and desired. Less powerful people should be dependent on more powerful people. In large-power-distance cultures (for example, the Philippines, Mexico, India), children are expected to be obedient. In many large-power-distance cultures, there is a strict hierarchy among family members; typically the father rules authoritatively, followed by the eldest son, then moving down the ladder by age and sex. In educational settings, teachers are treated as parents, with respect and honor, especially older teachers. Students who disobey may be punished severely. In the workplace, power is usually centralized, and workers and bosses are treated unequally. In many large-power-distance cultures, Hofstede observed, workers are generally uneducated and superiors are entitled to special privileges and status—in some cultures, by law.[48]

High-and-low-power-distance cultures may value different types of power. High-power-distance cultures tend to emphasize positional power. Positional power is based on formal authority (e.g., family rank). Persons with positional power have control over rewards, punishments, and information. Low-power-distance cultures recognize and respect earned power. Earned power is based on an individual's accomplishments, hard work, and effort.

HOFSTEDE'S POWER DISTANCE INDEX

Hofstede measured national differences in power distance with three survey items, as shown in Self-Assessment 2-3.

Scores on the power distance index for fifty countries and three regions were calculated, using 1 for the largest and 53 for the smallest power distance (see Table

Self-Assessment 2-3

The Power Distance Index

1. How frequently, in your experience, does the following problem occur? Employees being afraid to express disagreement with their managers.
   1. Very frequently
   2. Frequently
   3. Sometimes
   4. Seldom
   5. Very seldom

The descriptions below apply to four different types of managers. First, please read through these descriptions; then answer questions #2 and #3.

Manager 1
Usually makes his/her decisions promptly and communicates them to his/her subordinates clearly and firmly. Expects them to carry out the decisions loyally and without raising difficulties.

Manager 2
Usually makes his/her decisions promptly, but, before going ahead, tries to explain them fully to his/her subordinates. Gives them the reasons for the decisions and answers whatever questions they may have.

Manager 3
Usually consults with his/her subordinates before he/she reaches his/her decisions. Listens to their advice, considers it, and then announces his/her decision. He/she then expects all workers loyally to implement it whether or not it is in accordance with the advice they gave.

Manager 4
Usually calls a meeting of his/her subordinates when there is an important decision to be made. Puts the problem before the group and tries to obtain a consensus. If he/she obtains consensus, he/she accepts this as the decision. If consensus is impossible, he/she usually makes the decision him/herself.

2. For the above types of manager, please mark the *one* that you would prefer to work under.
   1. Manager 1
   2. Manager 2
   3. Manager 3
   4. Manager 4

3. And, to which *one* of the above four types of managers would you say your own manager *most closely corresponds?*

—Continued

The Power Distance Index (*continued*)

1. Manager 1
2. Manager 2
3. Manager 3
4. Manager 4
5. He/She does not correspond closely to any of them.

SOURCE: From G. Hofstede *Culture's Consequences: International Differences in Work-Related Values.* © 1980 Geert Hofstede. Used by permission of the author.

2-5). If we know the position of a culture on the power distance index relative to our own culture, we have a starting point from which to proceed in our understanding of that culture. In cultures with high rankings on the power distance index, subordinates are extremely submissive, whereas in cultures with low rankings on the power distance index, subordinates are confrontational. Hofstede concludes that power distance index scores tell us about dependence relationships in a given culture. In countries with a small power distance index (for example, Austria, Norway, the United States), there is limited dependence. Workers in these cultures prefer managers who consult with them in decision making; subordinates are generally comfortable approaching and interacting with their superiors. In

TABLE 2-5	Power Distance Index Ratings				
Country	Power Distance Score	Power Distance Rank	Country	Power Distance Score	Power Distance Rank
Malaysia	104	1	South Korea	60	27/28
Guatemala	95	2/3	Iran	58	29/30
Panama	95	2/3	Taiwan	58	29/30
Philippines	94	4	Spain	57	31
Mexico	81	5/6	Pakistan	55	32
Venezuela	81	5/6	Japan	54	33
Arab Countries	80	7	Italy	50	34
Ecuador	78	8/9	Argentina	49	35/36
Indonesia	78	8/9	South Africa	49	35/36

—Continued

TABLE 2-5	Power Distance Index Ratings (*continued*)				
Country	Power Distance Score	Power Distance Rank	Country	Power Distance Score	Power Distance Rank
India	77	10/11	Jamaica	45	37
West Africa	77	10/11	USA	40	38
Yugoslavia	76	12	Canada	39	39
Singapore	74	13	Netherlands	38	40
Brazil	69	14	Australia	36	41
France	68	15/16	Costa Rica	35	42/44
Hong Kong	68	15/16	Germany	35	42/44
Colombia	67	17	Great Britain	35	42/44
Salvador	66	18/19	Switzerland	34	45
Turkey	66	18/19	Finland	33	46
Belgium	65	20	Norway	31	47/48
East Africa	64	21/23	Sweden	31	47/48
Peru	64	21/23	Ireland	28	49
Thailand	64	21/23	New Zealand	22	50
Chile	63	24/25	Denmark	18	51
Portugal	63	24/25	Israel	13	52
Uruguay	61	26	Austria	11	53
Greece	60	27/28			

SOURCE: From *Cultures and Organizations: Software of the Mind*, © 1991. Reproduced with the author's permission.

cultures with a large power distance (for example, Malaysia, Mexico, India), there is considerable dependence of subordinates on superiors.

To some extent, a certain degree of power distance is essential if cultures are to survive. Legitimate power is a necessity of civilized life. Yet, on the other hand, independence from power, along with liberation and freedom of choice, are politically attractive alternatives. Perhaps the ideal situation is one in which individual families operate with internally driven large power distances while the larger cultural milieu restricts overbearing, omnipotent, and intimidating governments.

Intercultural Conversation

An Intercultural Conversation: Large- and Small-Power-Distance Cultures

Different power distance orientations manifest themselves in interaction. In the following dialogue, Jim Neuman is an American high school exchange student in Guatemala. Coming from a smaller-power-distance—oriented culture, Jim is accustomed to interacting with his teachers. Raising one's hand in a classroom in the United States is not only acceptable, but encouraged. In Guatemala, a larger-power-distance culture, the classroom is teacher centered. In Mr. Gutierrez's classroom, there is to be strict order, with Mr. Gutierrez initiating all of the communication. Teachers are to be treated with deference.

Mr. Gutierrez: This morning I will be discussing some points about Guatemala's geography. Guatemala is the northernmost country of Central America. *(Jim Neuman raises his hand)* To the north, it borders the countries of El Salvador and Honduras. To the west, its natural border is the Pacific Ocean. In the east is another natural border, the Atlantic Ocean, as well as the country of Belize.

Jim Neuman: (*Raising his hand and waving it slightly*) Mr. Gutierrez?

Mr. Gutierrez: Guatemala is called the "Land of the Eternal Spring." There are all of the same kinds of natural land forms as in Mexico, but they are *(Jim Neuman interrupts)*

Jim Neuman: Mr. Gutierrez, I have a question.

Mr. Gutierrez: Jim, stop interrupting, please.

Jim Neuman: May I ask a question?

Mr. Gutierrez: No! If you continue to disobey, I will punish you! Be quiet!

In the above dialogue, Jim does not understand Mr. Gutierrez's harsh reprimand. Coming from a low-power-distance culture, Jim recognizes that teachers have more power than students, but he does not see their power as absolute. Jim sees himself as an active participant in the class. After all, for most of his life Jim's teachers have encouraged him to speak up in class. Mr. Gutierrez, on the other hand, sees the classroom as his domain, one that he rules absolutely. By raising his hand, Jim demonstrates his insolence toward Mr. Gutierrez.

Uncertainty Avoidance

Gudykunst and Kim state that communicating with someone from an unknown culture can be uncomfortable because such situations are replete with uncertainty and unpredictability. When uncertainty is high, anxiety is usually high, and communication can be difficult and awkward. This may account for why some people avoid interacting with people from other cultures. By reducing uncertainty, however, anxiety can be reduced, which in turn facilitates effective and successful communication. Although uncertainty is probably a universal feature of initial intercultural communication, one's level of tolerance for uncertainty and ambiguity varies across cultures. In addition, argue Gudykunst and Kim, the communicative strategies for reducing uncertainty also vary across cultures. Persons in high-context cultures, for example, look to the environmental, sociorelational, and perceptual contexts for information to reduce uncertainty. People in low-context cultures tend to rely on verbal information-seeking strategies, usually by asking lots of questions.[49]

Hofstede asserts that although the extent to which an individual experiences uncertainty and the subsequent strategies for reducing it may be unique to that person, a general orientation toward uncertainty can be shared culturally. According to Hofstede, tolerance for uncertainty is learned through cultural socialization. Hofstede notes that a culture's technology, system of laws, and religion are markers for how that culture addresses and attempts to avoid or reduce uncertainty. Technology can help a culture manage natural uncertainty (for example, weather); systems of law are designed to prevent and account for behavioral uncertainties (for example, crime); and religion can help a culture cope with supernatural uncertainty (for example, death). A culture's technology, law, and religion are ingrained in the individual through socialization, education, and occupation. Hence, they lead to collective patterns of tolerance for ambiguity and uncertainty.[50]

Uncertainty avoidance is defined by Hofstede as the degree to which the members of a particular culture feel threatened by uncertain or unknown situations. Hofstede contends that this feeling is expressed through nervous stress and in a felt need for predictability and a need for written and unwritten rules. Hofstede categorizes cultures as possessing either weak or strong uncertainty avoidance orientations. In cultures with a weak uncertainty avoidance orientation, uncertainty is seen as a normal part of life, and each day is accepted as it comes. People are comfortable with ambiguity and are guided by a belief that what is different is curious. In school settings, students are comfortable with open-ended learning situations and enjoy classroom discussion. In the workplace, time is needed only as a guide, not as a master. Precision and punctuality are learned, because they do not come naturally. Workers are motivated by their achievements and personal esteem or belongingness. There is also a high tolerance for innovative ideas that may conflict with the norm.[51]

Hofstede explains that cultures with a strong uncertainty avoidance orientation sense that uncertainty in life is a continuous threat that must be fought. Life can be stressful, and a sense of urgency and high anxiety are typical. Hofstede maintains that strong-uncertainty-avoidant cultures are guided by the belief that what is different is dangerous. Uncertainty-avoiding cultures evade ambiguity in most situations and look for structure in their business organizations, home life, and relationships. At school, students are most comfortable in structured environments. The teachers are supposed to have all the right answers. On the job, time is money, and punctuality and precision are expected. There is generally a resistance to innovative ideas, and workers are motivated by job security.[52]

HOFSTEDE'S UNCERTAINTY AVOIDANCE INDEX

In his multinational survey, Hofstede assigned each country and region an uncertainty avoidance index based on respondents' answers to the three survey items shown in Self-Assessment 2-4.

Self-Assessment 2-4

The Uncertainty Avoidance Index

1. How often do you feel nervous or tense at work?
   1. I always feel this way
   2. Usually
   3. Sometimes
   4. Seldom
   5. I never feel this way

2. Company rules should not be broken—even when the employee thinks it is in the company's best interest.
   1. Strongly agree
   2. Agree
   3. Undecided
   4. Disagree
   5. Strongly disagree

3. How long do you think you'll continue working for IBM?
   1. Two years at the most
   2. From two to five years
   3. More than five years (but I probably will leave before I retire)
   4. Until I retire

SOURCE: G. Hofstede, From *Cultures, Consequences: Intercultural Work-Related Values.* © 1980 Geert Hofstede. Used by permission of the author.

The uncertainty avoidance index was calculated from the mean scores of questions 1 and 2 and the percentage score for question 3. Hofstede also multiplied each score by a fixed number so that the final index values would range from 0 for the country with the weakest uncertainty avoidance to around 100 for the country with the strongest. (The countries and their uncertainty avoidance indices are listed in Table 2-6).

Although the feelings associated with uncertainty are personal and subjective, they can be shared by whole cultures. Although anxiety creates the same physiological responses in humans, what triggers anxiety and one's level of tolerance for it are learned. A culture's orientation toward uncertainty can be found in its families, schools, and institutions. But uncertainty avoidance ultimately manifests itself in human interaction.

TABLE 2-6	Uncertainty Avoidance Scores and Ranks				
Country	Uncertainty Avoidance Score	Uncertainty Avoidance Rank	Country	Uncertainty Avoidance Score	Uncertainty Avoidance Rank
Greece	112	1	Ecuador	67	28
Portugal	104	2	Germany	65	29
Guatemala	101	3	Thailand	64	30
Uruguay	100	4	Iran	59	31/32
Belgium	94	5/6	Finland	59	31/32
Salvador	94	5/6	Switzerland	58	33
Japan	92	7	West Africa	54	34
Yugoslavia	88	8	Netherlands	53	35
Peru	87	9	East Africa	52	36
France	86	10/15	Australia	51	37
Chile	86	10/15	Norway	50	38
Spain	86	10/15	South Africa	49	39/40
Costa Rica	86	10/15	New Zealand	49	39/40
Panama	86	10/15	Indonesia	48	41/42
Argentina	86	10/15	Canada	48	41/42
Turkey	85	16/17	United States	46	43
South Korea	85	16/17	Philippines	44	44
Mexico	82	18	India	40	45
Israel	81	19	Malaysia	36	46
Colombia	80	20	Great Britain	35	47/48
Venezuela	76	21/22	Ireland	35	47/48
Brazil	76	21/22	Hong Kong	29	49/50
Italy	75	23	Sweden	29	49/50
Pakistan	70	24/25	Denmark	23	51
Austria	70	24/25	Jamaica	13	52
Taiwan	69	26	Singapore	8	53
Arab Countries	68	27			

SOURCE: From Cultures and Organizations: Software of the Mind, © Geert Hofstede. Reprinted by permission of the author.

Intercultural Conversation

An Intercultural Conversation: Weak and Strong Uncertainty Avoidance Cultures

There are any number of ways one's uncertainty avoidance orientation may manifest itself in interaction. In the dialogue presented below, Kelly and Keiko are interacting about a dinner invitation. Kelly, from the United States, possesses a relatively weak uncertainty avoidance index, while Keiko, a Japanese, comes from a culture with a relatively strong uncertainty avoidance index.

Keiko: Hey, Kelly, let's do something tonight.
Kelly: All right.
Keiko: Please come over to my house and I'll cook dinner for you.
Kelly: I have invited some friends over to my house for dinner tonight, but I don't know if they're coming.
Keiko: Well . . . as soon as you know if they're coming, let me know.
Kelly: I won't know until tonight.
Keiko: What time?
Kelly: I won't know until they call me. They'll probably call later this afternoon.

Keiko: How will you know whether or not to cook enough for everyone?
Kelly: Oh, I'll make up something on the spot. I like to cook. I'll whip up something fast.
Keiko: But . . . what if they don't come? Won't they call and let you know?
Kelly: No . . . if they don't come, I'll know that something else came up. I'll let you know as soon as I can.
Keiko: Maybe we should plan my dinner for some other night.

In the above dialogue, Keiko is confused by Kelly's easygoing attitude toward the evening's plans. Coming from a strong-uncertainty-avoidant culture, Keiko would prefer to plan ahead to avoid uncertainty and prepare her script for the evening. Kelly, on the other hand, is perfectly comfortable making plans based on how the evening progresses. Without a plan, how will Keiko know how to act?

Chapter Summary

In the contextual model of intercultural communication, culture is the largest context, surrounding all of the other contexts. This chapter has presented the paradox of culture. On the one hand, culture is amorphous; it is shapeless, vague, and nebulous. Most of us are not aware of its influence on our daily behaviors. On the other hand, culture is arguably the strongest influence on an individual's cognitive, affective, and behavioral choices. Over the past few decades, anthropologists, psychologists, and sociologists have isolated several dimensions of cultural variability by which cultures can be compared. This chapter has focused on five of these dimensions, including the extent to which we place individual goals over those of the group (individualism) or the degree to which we see ourselves as members of a group first, then as an individual (collectivism). Another dimension is high/low-context—the extent to which we gather information from the physical, social, and psychological context (high context) or the extent to which we gather information from the verbal code (low context). One of the most influential features of our lives is our value orientations. A culture's values guide its decisions as to what is right or wrong, decent or indecent, moral or immoral. Cultures also differ in the extent to which they accept and expect that power is distributed unequally (high power distance) or the extent to which they believe that people are inherently equal (low power distance). And finally, cultures differ in the extent to which people accept and tolerate uncertainty and unpredictability in their lives (weak uncertainty avoidance) or the extent to which uncertainty should be fought and conquered (strong uncertainty avoidance). These dimensions provide a starting point for our future examination of intercultural communication.

GLOSSARY OF TERMS

Collectivism: Cultural orientation in which the group is the primary unit of culture. Group goals take precedence over individual goals.

High context: Cultural orientation in which meanings are gleaned from the physical, social, and psychological contexts.

Horizontal collectivism: Cultural orientation in which the self is seen as a member of an in-group whose members are similar to each other.

Horizontal individualism: Cultural orientation in which an autonomous self is valued, but the self is more or less equal with others.

Individualism: Cultural orientation in which the individual is unique and individual goals are emphasized over group goals.

Low context: Cultural orientation in which meanings are encoded in the verbal code.

Power distance: The extent to which members of a culture expect and accept that power is unequally distributed.

Uncertainty avoidance: The degree to which members of a particular culture feel threatened by unpredictable, uncertain, or unknown situations.

Values: Criteria for selecting and justifying behavior. Values have a cognitive, affective, and behavioral component.

Vertical collectivism: Cultural orientation in which the individual sees the self as an integral part of the in-group whose members are different from each other (for example, in status).

Vertical individualism: Cultural orientation in which an autonomous self is valued, but the self is seen as different from, and perhaps unequal to, others.

REFERENCES

1. E. T. Hall, *The Silent Language* (Greenwich, Conn.: Fawcett, 1959), 39.
2. R. M. Keesing, "Theories of Culture," in *Annual Review of Anthropology,* ed. B. J. Siegel (Palo Alto, Calif.: Annual Reviews, 1974), pp. 73–97.
3. D. Yurkovich, K. Pliscott, and R. Halverson, "The Norwegian Culture" (unpublished student manuscript, St. Norbert College, De Pere, Wisc., 1996); A. R. Gayle and K. P. Knutson, "Understanding Cultural Differences: Janteloven and Social Conformity in Norway," *Et Cetera,* 49 (1993), 449.
4. H. C. Triandis, "Cross-Cultural Studies of Individualism and Collectivism," in *Nebraska Symposium on Motivation: 1989,* ed. J. J. Berman (Lincoln: University of Nebraska Press, 1990), pp. 41–133; H. C. Triandis, "Collectivism and Individualism as Cultural Syndromes," *Cross Cultural Research,* 27 (1993), 155–180; H. C. Triandis, *Individualism and Collectivism* (Boulder: Westview, 1995).
5. Triandis, *Individualism and Collectivism.*
6. Ibid.

7. Ibid.

8. Triandis, *Individualism and Collectivism*; F. L. K. Hsu, *Americans and Chinese: Passage to Differences*, 3rd ed. (Honolulu: University of Hawaii Press; 1981); S. H. Schwartz, "Individualism-Collectivism: Critique and Proposed Refinement," *Journal of Cross Cultural Psychology*, 21 (1990), 139–157; M. Lustig and J. Koester, *Intercultural Competence: Interpersonal Communication Across Cultures* (New York: HarperCollins, 1996).

9. Triandis, *Individualism and Collectivism*; Hsu, *Americans and Chinese: Passage to Differences*.

10. Triandis, "Cross-Cultural Studies of Individualism and Collectivism."

11. Triandis, "Cross-Cultural Studies of Individualism and Collectivism"; Triandis, *Individualism and Collectivism*; Schwartz, "Individualism-Collectivism: Critique and Proposed Refinement."

12. J. Feldhausen, "Collectivism and Individualism in Denmark" (unpublished student manuscript, St. Norbert College, De Pere, Wisc., 1998); Triandis, *Individualism and Collectivism*.

13. W. B. Gudykunst, Y. Matsumoto, S. Ting-Toomey, et al., "Measuring Self Construals Across Cultures" (paper presented at the meeting of the International Communicating Association, Sydney, Australia, 1994).

14. Triandis, *Individualism and Collectivism*; Hsu, *Americans and Chinese: Passage to Differences*.

15. H. Markus and S. Kitayama, "Culture and Self: Implications for Cognition, Emotion, and Motivation," *Psychological Review*, 98 (1991), 224–253.

16. Triandis, *Individualism and Collectivism*.

17. W. B. Gudykunst, Y. Matsumoto, S. Ting-Toomey, et al., "The Influence of Cultural Individualism-Collectivism, Self Construals, and Individual Values on Communication Styles Across Cultures," *Human Communication Research*, 22 (1996), 510–543; Gudykunst, Matsumoto, Ting-Toomey, et al., "Measuring Self Construals Across Cultures."

18. G. Hofstede, *Cultures and Organizations: Software of the Mind* (London: McGraw-Hill, 1991).

19. S. H. Schwartz, "Individualism-Collectivism: Critique and Proposed Refinement," 139–157.

20. T. M. Singelis, H. C. Triandis, D. P. S. Bhawuk, and M. J. Gelfand, "Horizontal and Vertical Dimensions of Individualism and Collectivism: A Theoretical and Measurement Refinement," *Cross Cultural Research*, 29 (1995), 240–275.

21. H. C. Triandis, "Cross Cultural Studies of Individualism and Collectivism," in *Nebraska Symposium on Motivation, 1989*, ed. J. J. Berman (Lincoln: University of Nebraska Press, 1990), pp. 41–133; Singelis, Triandis, Bhawuk, and Gelfand, "Horizontal and Vertical Dimensions of Individualism and Collectivism: A Theoretical and Measurement Refinement."

22. C. Hui-Ching, "'Collectivism' or 'Competitive Bidding': An Alternative Picture of Chinese Communication" (paper presented at the annual convention of the Speech Communication Association, San Diego, Calif.: 1996), p. 10.

23. E. T. Hall, *Beyond Culture* (Garden City, N.Y.: Anchor/Doubleday, 1976), p. 79.

24. Ibid. (Quote on page 79).

25. Ibid.

26. Ibid.

27. C. A. Braithwaite, "Communicative Silence: A Cross-Cultural Study of Basso's Hypothesis," in *Cultural Communication and Intercultural Contact*, ed. D. Carbaugh (Hillsdale, N.J.: Erlbaum, 1990), pp. 321–328.

28. D. L. Weider and S. Pratt, "On Being a Recognizable Indian Among Indians," in *Cultural Communication and Intercultural Contact*, pp. 45–64.

29. S. Iwao, *The Japanese Woman: Traditional Image and Changing Reality* (Cambridge: Harvard University Press, 1993), p. 98.

30. M. Rokeach, *The Nature of Human Values* (New York: Free Press, 1973), p. 3.

31. Ibid.

32. S. H. Schwartz, "Universals in the Content and Structure of Values: Theoretical Advances and Empirical Tests in Twenty Countries," in *Advances in Experimental Social Psychology*, vol.

25 (San Diego, Calif.: Academic Press, 1992), pp. 1–66.

33. F. Kluckhohn and F. Strodtbeck, *Variations in Value Orientations* (Evanston, Ill.: Row, Peterson, 1961); J. C. Condon and F. Yousef, *An Approach to Intercultural Communication* (Indianapolis: Bobbs-Merrill, 1975).

34. Condon and Yousef, *An Approach to Intercultural Communication;* Hsu, *Americans and Chinese: Passage to Differences.*

35. Hsu, *Americans and Chinese: Passage to Differences;* Hsu, *Americans and Chinese: Reflections on Two Cultures and Their People.*

36. P. R. Harris and R. T. Moran, *Managing Cultural Differences,* 4th ed. (Houston: Gulf, 1996).

37. Condon and Yousef, *An Approach to Intercultural Communication.*

38. Harris and Moran, *Managing Cultural Differences.*

39. M. Keberlein, "A Cultural Profile of the Guatemalan Ladinos" (unpublished student manuscript, St. Norbert College, DePere, Wisc., 1993).

40. Condon and Yousef, *An Approach to Intercultural Communication.*

41. Ibid.

42. B. Amraen, "China: A Populous Nation" (unpublished student manuscript, St. Norbert College, De Pere, Wisc., 1994); B. De Menthe, *Chinese Etiquette and Ethics in Business* (Lincolnwood, Ill.: NTC Publishing Group, 1992).

43. Condon and Yousef, *An Approach to Intercultural Communication.*

44. Ibid.

45. Ibid.

46. Hofstede, *Cultures and Organizations: Software of the Mind;* Hofstede, *Culture's Consequences: International Differences in Work-Related Values* (Beverly Hills, Calif.: Sage, 1980).

47. Ibid.

48. Ibid.

49. W. B. Gudykunst and Y. Y. Kim, *Communicating with Strangers: An Approach to Intercultural Communication* (New York: McGraw-Hill, 1997).

50. Hofstede, *Cultures and Organizations: Software of the Mind.*

51. Ibid.

52. Ibid.

CHAPTER THREE

The Microcultural Context

For those of us who live in/ between, being required, on the one hand, to cast off our cultural selves in order to don the worldview and ethos of an alien culture, on the other hand to cast off the influences of the alien culture as a means of puri- fication and identification is more than a personal dilemma; it is always and most of all a condition of living in/ between.

—Richard Morris[1]

CHAPTER OBJECTIVES

After reading this chapter, you should be able to:

- Define and explain the idea of a microculture.
- List and illustrate the five criteria for membership in a microculture.
- Recount the fundamental assumptions of the Muted Group Theory.
- Provide examples of the various microcultures in the United States.
- Identify and discuss two cultural values of the Hispanic microculture.
- Identify and discuss at least three aspects of African American communication.
- Identify and discuss at least three aspects of Amish communication.
- Identify and discuss at least three aspects of Hmong communication.

Within most cultures are groups of people who differ in some custom, habit, or practice from the general societal culture. These groups are sometimes called minorities, subcultures, or cocultures. In this textbook, the term *microculture* is used to refer to those identifiable groups of people who share a set of values, beliefs, and behaviors and who possess a common history and verbal and nonverbal symbol system that is similar to the dominant culture but which varies in some way, perhaps subtly. Most microcultural groups are groups of individuals who have much in common with the larger macroculture yet are bonded together by similar experiences, traits, values, or in some cases, histories. Hence the term *microculture* includes different types of groups that could be classified by age, class, geographic region, sexual preference, ethnicity, race, size, or even occupation. Perhaps most Americans are members of some kind of microcultural group.

Microcultures can be different from the larger culture in a variety of ways, often because of race or ethnicity. In the United States, for example, approximately 75 percent of the population is classified as white or Caucasian.[2] In this context, African Americans, Hispanics, and Hmong might be considered microcultural groups. Microcultures can also differ from the larger culture on account of language or religion. In the United States, Protestants outnumber all other religious groups. Other religious groups, then, such as the Amish or the Jews, might be considered microcultures. Specifically, Protestants make up approximately 55 percent of the population, Catholics about 28 percent, Jews approximately 2 percent. In the United States, there are approximately 600,000 Muslims (persons of Islamic faith). Indeed, Islam is one of the fastest growing religions in the country.[3] Finally, persons might be classified as members of microcultures because of their behavioral practices. Persons who use drugs are often said to belong to a "counter" or "drug" culture, not because of their race, ethnicity, or religion, but because they use drugs. Often such microcultures develop their own language for communicating outside the dominant or majority culture's context or value system.

Though not always, microcultural groups generally have less power than the majority, or "macro," culture. The majority group's power may be legal, political, economic, or even religious. The group with the most power is the dominant, or majority, group, and the less powerful groups have been known as "minority groups." Sociologist Richard Schaefer argues that the term *minority group* is a misnomer, however, in that it does not refer to the relative size of a group. According to Schaefer, a minority group is defined as "a subordinate group whose members have significantly less power and control over their own lives than members of the dominant or majority group."[4] Although defined as a minority, such groups may actually be larger (in population) than the majority group. For example, until just recently, whites, who were greatly outnumbered by blacks, ruled in South Africa under the political system of apartheid. In many countries colonized by Europeans, the indigenous people outnumbered the dominant Europeans. Moreover, in contemporary American society, the term *minority group* has taken on a negative connotation.

Often the term *subculture* is used to refer to microcultural groups. Like *minority groups,* the term *subculture* carries negative connotations. By definition, *sub-* means "beneath," "below," or "inferior." The perspective of this book is that no cultural group is beneath or below any other cultural group. To be sure, some cultures are subordinate to other groups (i.e., they have less power), but such groups should not be considered inferior. Hence, for the reasons cited above, we have chosen the term *microcultural group* as a more appropriate label for these groups.

Microcultural Group Status

In many cultures, including the United States, microcultural group status is determined by one's membership in sexual, racial, ethnic, or religious groups. Schaefer notes that social scientists generally recognize five characteristics that distinguish microcultural groups from the dominant culture: (1) *physical and cultural traits;* (2) *involuntary membership;* (3) *endogamy;* (4) *awareness of subordinate status;* (5) *unequal treatment by the dominant group.*

The first characteristic is that members possess some physical or cultural trait that distinguishes them from others. Two obvious distinguishing physical properties are skin color and sex. In the United States, for example, blacks and women are considered minorities (even though women constitute about 51 percent of the population). White males are considered the most powerful political and economic group in the United States. Blacks are also considered a minority in Brazil, which depended on slave trading much more than the United States. In fact, Brazil imported eight times the number of slaves brought to the United States.[5]

Other distinguishing physical or cultural traits are language or distinctive dress habits. The Rastafarians are a microcultural group in Jamaica. According to Penasa, Peters, and Smits, the "Rastas" are a relatively small group of about fourteen thousand persons. Rastas are recognizable by their dreadlocks and unique dress habits. Rastafarians also speak in a patois—an unofficial and informal language with a lyrical enunciation scheme. The Rastafarian patois has been traced back to slavery, when slaves were forced to learn the language of their masters (that is, English). Although it is mostly English, the Rastafarian patois takes words and phrases from African and other languages, including Spanish, French, and Portuguese. For example, the word *that* becomes *dat,* and *the* becomes *de. Me* is used for *I, me,* and *my.* Thus the phrase "I am Jamaican" becomes "Me Jamaican."[6] Regardless of culture, the dominant group decides, perhaps arbitrarily, what characteristics give a group its minority status. Such traits vary considerably across cultures.

The second distinguishing characteristic of microcultural groups is that membership is not voluntary. People are generally born into their microculture. People cannot choose to be of a certain race, ethnicity, or gender. Although people can choose their religion, most people are born into a religion and find it very difficult to leave. In tracing the history of the violence in Northern Ireland, Richard Schaefer notes that its roots are based in religion. According to Schaefer, in the twelfth century the English invaded Ireland but never completely conquered it. Schaefer maintains that the northernmost part of the island fell to the English in the seventeenth century and was soon populated by Protestant settlers from Scotland and England. Ireland was united with Great Britain in 1801 to form the United Kingdom. But the Irish never completely accepted British rule or London as their government. The Anglo-Irish war of 1919–1921 led to a treaty establishing an independent sovereign nation to the south, creating what is now the Republic of Ireland, which is 90 percent Catholic. The United Kingdom retained its control over the northern counties of Ulster, which is today's Northern Ireland, whose population is two-thirds Protestant and one-third Catholic. The Catholics in Northern Ireland, a minority in both numbers and power, complain of inadequate housing and education, low income, and high unemployment. They often blame the Protestant majority for their problems. Armed conflict has been the result.[7]

The third property that distinguishes a microcultural group from the macroculture is that microcultural group members generally practice endogamy (that is, marrying within the in-group). In many cultures, the dominant group staunchly discourages or even prohibits exogamy (marrying out of one's own group). Ethnologist Suzan Ilcan of the University of Windsor writes that majority groups believe that endogamy strengthens familial ties, preserves family property through inheritance, and upholds cultural and group traditions. Ilcan's work has focused on marital practices in Turkey, where endogamous marriages are viewed as a family or community affair. According to Ilcan, in the village of Sakli in the northwestern region of Turkey, spousal selection and all aspects of marriage are controlled by certain members of the family. Couples have little to do with the arrangements. Moreover, any meaningful romance between unmarried persons is not valued. Love and mutual attraction are expected to come after marriage and even then are not considered a necessity. In Sakli, people are considered suitable marriage partners on the basis of the compatibility of their families. Familial reputation and comparable economic and social class are the crucial elements for a marriage.[8] In cultures like Japan, Pakistan, China, India, and Laos, among others, endogamous marriages are often arranged.

The fourth characteristic that distinguishes a microcultural group from the dominant group is that microcultural group members are aware of their subordinate status. Because they know that they are less powerful within a particular culture, some microcultural groups are very cohesive. In the United States, for example, blacks have gained significant political and economic strength and are arguably the most powerful microcultural group in the country.

Finally, and perhaps the most disturbing aspect of microcultural group membership, is that such groups often experience unequal treatment from the dominant group in the form of segregation and discrimination. Catholics in Northern Ireland, blacks in the United States, mulattos in Brazil, and Muslims in Bosnia are all vivid examples of how membership in a minority group or microculture can affect one's life negatively.[9]

Muted Microcultural Groups

The experiences and perceptions of subordinate microcultural groups are often different from those of the dominant cultural group. For example, microcultural groups often are not as free or as capable as the dominant cultural group to communicate. Historically in the United States, for example, women and blacks could not vote or join the armed services. Only recently have black South Africans been granted the right to vote in their country. Hence, they had no legal voice or representation. In many cultures, the subordinate microcultural groups do not contribute to the construction of the language of the dominant group. In this sense, the language of a particular culture does not benefit its members equally. Yet the language of the dominant group may not provide the words and symbols representative of the microcultural group's perceptions and experiences. Thus, because such groups are forced to communicate (for example, to speak or write) within the dominant mode of expression, they become "muted." In essence, the language of the dominant cultural group contributes to the microcultural group's subordination. This idea is known as "The Muted Group Theory."[10]

The manifestations of the Muted Group Theory are that the speech and the writing of microcultural groups are not valued by the dominant cultural group. Moreover, microcultural groups experience difficulty expressing themselves fluently within the dominant mode of expression, and "micro/macro" interaction is difficult. Because the microcultural groups must communicate within the dominant mode, they must achieve some level of competence to survive. However, the dominant cultural group experiences more difficulty in understanding the communication of microcultural groups because they are not required to learn their code. Indeed, often the communication style of the microcultural group is considered substandard and/or inferior by the dominant group and is rejected as a legitimate form of communication.

Shirley Weber contends that microcultural groups may respond to the dominant mode of expression in two ways. Some will refuse to live by the standards set forth by the dominant group and will try to change the dominant mode of expression. In the United States, for example, the replacement of *chairman* with simply *chair,* or *mailman* with *mail carrier,* is demonstrative of this phenomenon. Another way subordinate groups respond is by using their own "private" language. They create symbols that are not understood or used by the dominant group. They use their own language in order to express their unique experiences. Weber argues that sometimes the language of the subordinate group serves as a political statement that the microcultural group has not relinquished or abandoned its political or social identity. The group's ability to sustain a living language indicates that they have control over a certain aspect of their lives and are determined to preserve their culture. As Weber notes, one's language is a model of his or her culture's adjustment to the world.[11]

Many social scientists consider the hip-hop/rap music generation a microcultural group that has been muted by mainstream culture. Christopher Tyson argues that hip-hop/rap has been the defining African American cultural movement in the United States over the past twenty-five years. As most college students know, rap is a very fast, rhythmical, accentuated singing and speaking style. Historically, the roots of rap are in African American popular music. Tyson contends that hip-hop culture and rap music are byproducts of the African American cultural heritage of jazz and blues. Unlike jazz or the blues, however, rap music reflects the growing flux of nonconformity among young African Americans (and now, other microcultural groups) in mainstream culture and the backlash against middle-class values.[12] Aino Konkka asserts that one of the most recognized styles of rap music is called *gangsta rap*. This style was invented on the West Coast, where inner-city gangs are prominent. Gangsta rap lyrics often tell the story of the desperate situation faced by many inner-city youths who feel rejected by and alienated from the dominant culture. Because the lyrics of gangsta rap are often profane, dealing with drugs and violence—especially violence against women and law enforcement—gangsta rap music has received a great deal of criticism from mainstream cultural critics. But as Konkka argues, it is the language that young African Americans understand. According to Konkka, "Using language that children can relate to, added with humor and catchy rhythms, helps getting the message through."[13] Well-known gangsta rappers include Snoop Doggy Dogg, Dr. Dre, Public Enemy, and Ice Cube.

Consistent with the tenets of the Muted Group Theory, rappers have created and developed a unique vocabulary that they use in their music and in communicating with each other. Although rappers speak English, the vocabulary and its meaning differ considerably from mainstream culture. Some examples of rap vocabulary are on the next page.

Another example is the Amish. Many Amish groups in the United States are trilingual. They speak Low German at home, High German at church, and English at school or with outsiders. High German is more formal, whereas Low German is a more relaxed oral dialect spoken at home. Koslow notes that in Canada, the people of Quebec define themselves as culturally unique from the rest of Canada because they speak French. In Quebec, the language debate is so great and emotional that many Quebecers are pushing for sovereignty. Quebecois (those who speak French) use French as a model and insist on keeping French in the home and on the street signs throughout the province.[14]

Microcultures in the United States

Many microcultures exist in the United States. The formation of microcultural groups is often the result of immigration, annexation, or colonization.[15] This chapter explores four United States microcultures, with particular attention to their communication and how it differs from the dominant macroculture. The first microcultural group to be examined is the Hispanic/Latino group. Hispanics/Latinos represent the largest microcultural group in the United States. The second group is

Intercultural Communication in Practice

Rap Vocabulary	Meaning
All that	In possession of all good qualities.
Ay yo trip	Phrase to seek attention, similar to "Check this out."
Bang	To fight or kill.
Be geese	To leave: "Yo, we be geese."
Bitch	Label generally for females, but not necessarily derogatory and not necessarily limited to women, as in "All yo niggas be bitches."
Bone	To have sexual intercourse: "Your aim is to bone."
Cave boy	White person.
Chill	To relax.
Homeboy	Close friend.
'Hood	The neighborhood, usually a poor community.
Nigga	Originally considered racist and profane, now used by rappers to express pride; "my friend," as in "my nigga."
Peckerwood	Derogatory term for a white person.
Roll up	To arrive on the scene.
Shank	A custom-made knife used in prisons.
Tag	The act of writing graffiti, as in "tagging up."
Tight	Feeling really good at the moment.

SOURCE: Excerpt from *The Rap Dictionary* by Patrick Atoon. www.rapdict.org. Reprinted by permission.

the African Americans, whose ancestors were brought to the United States as slaves. This group was selected because it is perhaps the most powerful microcultural group in the United States. African Americans have made great strides in social, legal, economic, and political power in the last century. The third group is the Amish, who originally immigrated to the United States from Europe to escape religious persecution. The Amish were chosen because, perhaps more than any other microcultural group, they have managed to maintain their cultural traditions in the face of immense pressure from the dominant culture to conform, and yet they have managed successfully to coexist within the dominant cultural milieu. The final group we will explore is the Laotian Hmong (pronounced *mung*), who began their immigration to the United States after the end of the Vietnam war in 1975. This group was chosen because they represent perhaps the newest microculture. They are also a relatively powerless group who lack social, political, and economic power.

Hispanics/Latinos

In the year 2000, for the first time in the history of the United States, Hispanics comprised the largest microcultural group in the country, surpassing African Americans. According to Census 2000 data, of the nearly 281 million people residing in the United States, just over 35 million, or approximately 13 percent, are Hispanic. You may recall from Chapter 1 that the United States government distinguishes between race and Hispanic origin, considering the two to be separate and distinct. Hence, Hispanics are not considered a racial group. Specifically, the government defines Hispanic or Latino as "a person of Cuban, Mexican, Puerto Rican, South or Central American, or other Spanish culture or origin regardless of race." According to Census 2000 data, nearly half of all Hispanics, about 17 million, reported their race as white. Six percent reported they were of two or more races, two percent reported their race as black or African American, while just over 1 percent indicated they were American Indian or Alaskan native. Forty-two percent of Hispanics indicated "some other race."[16]

Due mostly to immigration and high fertility rates, the Hispanic population in the United States increased by nearly 60 percent from 1990 to 2000, compared with an increase of approximately 13 percent by the rest of the population. Of the various groups represented under the Hispanic label, the Mexican population represents nearly 60 percent; Puerto Ricans comprise just under 10 percent; Cubans represent 3.5 percent. The remaining Hispanics of "some other origin" include Central Americans (5 percent), South Americans (4 percent), and Dominicans (2 percent). The remaining approximately 16 percent are labeled "all other Hispanics."[17]

Like other microcultural groups, Hispanics are concentrated in certain geographical areas in the United States. In fact, half of all Hispanics live in just two states: California and Texas. Other states with concentrated Hispanic populations include Arizona, Florida, Illinois, New Jersey, and New York. On the other hand, there are very small Hispanic populations in many states, such as Alabama, Kentucky, Maine, Mississippi, New Hampshire, North Dakota, South Dakota, Vermont, and West Virginia.[18]

In addition to its overall population trends, the Hispanic population has unique demographics, compared with the rest of the United States. Generally, the Hispanic population is younger than the U.S. population. Approximately 26 percent of the U.S. population is under the age of 18, compared with 35 percent of the Hispanic population. Nearly 31 percent of Hispanic households, in which a Hispanic is considered the "householder," consist of five or more people, while only 11 percent of households have been this large in the U.S. population. In terms of education, 27 percent of the Hispanic population have less than a ninth-grade education. Only 46 percent have a high school diploma and only 10 percent have a college degree. Economically, Hispanics are more likely than the general U.S. population to be unemployed. In 2000, almost 7 percent of Hispanics were unemployed, compared with 3.4 percent of non-Hispanic whites. In addition, when working, Hispanics tend to work in different jobs and earn less than non-Hispanic whites. Specifically, Hispanics are more likely to work in service occupations and much less likely to work in management or professional occupations. Among workers, just over 23 percent of Hispanics made $35,000 or more, compared with nearly half of non-Hispanic whites earning that much. Furthermore, the percentage of Hispanics earning over $50,000 was about 10 percent, compared with 27 percent of non-Hispanic whites. Thus, in the year 2000, almost 23 percent of Hispanics lived in poverty compared with about 8 percent of non-Hispanic whites. Hispanic children represented about 16 percent of all children in the United States but constituted nearly 30 percent of all persons living in poverty.[19]

CULTURAL VALUES OF HISPANICS

Although very diverse, the Hispanic microculture is united by values, language, and religion. Consultants AnneMarie Pajewski and Luis Enriquez argue that in Hispanic society, family or group needs take precedence over individual needs. This collectivistic tendency conflicts with the dominant U.S. culture's emphasis on individualism. Hispanics seem collectivistic across a variety of contexts, including academics. According to Pajewski and Enriquez, in school settings Hispanic students tend to be cooperative, whereas white students tend to be competitive and individualistic. When Hispanic students work in groups, not everyone is expected to do his or her equal share. A group member who does not work is not sanctioned, but in an Anglo group, each is expected to do his or her share. Moreover, Pajewski and Enriquez report that some Hispanic students are baffled by the idea of "cheating" in U.S. schools. During examinations, Hispanic students sometimes allow other students to copy their work and do not consider this cheating. Instead, such behavior is viewed as cooperative.[20]

Perhaps nowhere is the Hispanic group orientation more prevalent than in the family, or *familia*. Vasquez argues that commitment to the family is a dominant cultural value among virtually all Hispanics. According to Vasquez and others, family loyalty—the belief that a child's behavior reflects on the family honor, that sibling relationships are hierarchically ordered, and that family needs are to be met before individual needs—are dominant values in most Hispanic communities. Indeed, Shaefer argues that among Hispanics, the family is the primary source of both social interaction and caregiving. Griggs and Dunn maintain that the influence of the Hispanic family can be observed in the behavior of Hispanic adolescents, who are more likely than Anglo adolescents to model and adopt their parents' religious and political beliefs, occupations, and overall lifestyle.[21]

In general, Hispanics are a very religious people, with as many as 90 percent of all Hispanics belonging to the Roman Catholic faith. Clutter and Nieto point out that the church is a strong influence of Hispanic family life. In addition, many Hispanic communities celebrate their patron saint's day with more attention and ceremony than individuals give their own personal birthdays. Pajewski and Enriquez have observed that although Hispanics are generally very religious, they tend to believe in supernatural powers beyond their religious teachings. Many Hispanics believe in witchcraft and the curadora, and the healing powers of women and certain herbs.[22]

SPANGLISH: A LANGUAGE OF HISPANIC AMERICANS

The communication style of most Hispanics is more formal than that of white American culture. Pajewski and Enriquez maintain that Hispanics are sensitive to rank and customarily make use of formal titles. They also report that Hispanics tend to demonstrate affection nonverbally through touching, hugging, pats on the back, and cheek kissing.[23] Verbally, many Hispanics employ Spanglish. Linguists (people who study language) have noted that when groups of people from different cultures, who speak different languages, come together and live in the same society, a hybrid language sometimes evolves. This new language will take some of the phonological features (i.e., sounds) and syntactic structures (i.e., grammar) from each group's language and blend them; the resulting hybrid language serves as a vehicle for communication between the groups. According to Ilan Stavans, professor of Spanish at Amherst College, Hispanics have taken English words and "Spanish-ized" them and have taken Spanish words and "English-ized" them. The result is what linguists call "Spanglish": a bastard jargon, according to Stavans, that is part Spanish and part English. Although Spanglish appears to be a fairly recent phenomena, Stavans argues that it has been around for over 150 years.[24]

Scholars and laypeople alike agree that Spanglish unites the Hispanic community. Jane Rifkin of the *Hispanic Times* magazine points out that Spanglish is a widely accepted communication tool used by Spanish-speaking immigrants and native-born Americans. Although some Americans reject Spanglish as intellectually unsophisticated, Rifkin believes that the hybrid language is an expression of friendship, acceptance, and approval. She refers to it as the new national slang and contends that Spanglish is

> . . . truly a form of communicating among people that has a warmth about it and an inviting expression meant to be non-threatening to people who come together in spite of language barriers.[25]

Stavans argues that there are many variations of Spanglish, depending on the nationality, age, and class of its users. He contends that the Spanglish spoken by Cuban-Americans is different from that spoken by Dominicans, which is different still from Ganga Spanglish used by urban Hispanic gangs.[26] Although there may be many variations of Spanglish in the United States, Bill Cruz and Bill Teck, editors of *Generation ñ*, a magazine targeted primarily at Cuban-American youths, argue that authentic Spanglish is heard when a speaker switches from English to Spanish, or from Spanish to English, within the same sentence. They argue that Spanglish is commonplace in the homes of Hispanics who, as children, were educated in American schools but spoke Spanish at home. In their defense of Spanglish as a le-

Intercultural Communication in Practice

Spanglish	English
No creo que voy on the trip with you.	"I don't think I'm going on the trip with you."
"I'm *lonchando;* I don't wanna talk now."	"I'm having lunch; I don't wanna talk now."
"I think the *bacunclíner* swallowed my earring!"	"I think the vacuum cleaner swallowed my earring!"
Tiempo is money.	"Time is money."
"Turn up the heat; *¡estoy frizando!*"	"Turn up the heat; I'm freezing!"
el autopar	local auto parts store
guarejaus	a warehouse
Pisa Ho	Pizza Hut restaurant
Macdonal	McDonald's fast food restaurant
Sebenileben	7-11 convenience store
Guendis	Wendy's fast-food restaurant

gitimate language, Cruz and Teck maintain that often there are no words in English (or Spanish) that accurately express the speaker's intent. In such cases, the blending of the two languages allows the speaker to capture the essence of one culture in the language of the other. Cruz and Teck have compiled what they call "The Official Spanglish Dictionary." Above are some examples of Spanglish, taken from their work.[27]

STEREOTYPES OF HISPANICS

In most cultures, microcultural groups are often stereotyped by the dominant cultural group. In the United States, the Hispanic microculture has been the target of several unfortunate stereotypes. Perhaps the most common and most hotly debated stereotype about Hispanics revolves around the construct of male gender identity called *machismo*. Machismo centers on the notion of Hispanic masculinity and male superiority and dominance in the traditional patriarchal Hispanic society. Stereotypic characteristics associated with machismo males include aggressiveness, violence, dominance and supremacy over women, infidelity, and emotional insensitivity.[28] Manuel Roman, a Puerto Rican psychiatrist, argues that the concept of machismo is power based. Roman states:

> Men are physically more powerful than women. And machismo is derived from the natural state of being bigger, more muscular. It has to do with dominance, autocracy, having power over others. A macho man is somebody who is expected to

be sexually knowledgeable and aggressive with women, and to be fearless in his interactions with other males.[29]

To be sure, scholars disagree about the uniqueness of machismo in Hispanic culture. Counseling psychologist J. Manuel Casas and his associates argue that machismo has never been a uniquely Hispanic phenomenon. Instead, they propose that many of the traits associated with machismo can be found in virtually every culture. They note, however, that differences may exist in how the equivalent of the machismo construct is defined across cultures.[30] In other words, there may be many cultures in which the male gender identity is associated with aggressiveness, male supremacy, infidelity, and so on. Although there has not been a substantial amount of research conducted on the machismo identity, at least one characteristic associated with machismo—that is, infidelity—is not unique to Hispanic males. University of Chicago sociologists Michael, Gagnon, Laumann, and Kolata, authors of the widely publicized "Sex in America" study, found that the infidelity rate among Hispanics in the United States is about the same as for the general U.S. population.[31]

United States media, especially advertisers, have been particularly culpable in the dissemination of Hispanic stereotypes. Octavio Nuiry points out that one of the earliest images of Hispanics, and particularly Mexicans, is that of the ruthless *bandito*. This image has been depicted in all sorts of media from movie westerns to the famous advertising campaign for Frito Corn Chips. In 1967, Frito-Lay Corporation launched an advertising campaign for its brand of corn chips. The ads featured a cartoon character called the "Frito Bandito" whose persona was replete with a heavy Spanish accent, long handlebar mustache, sombrero, and pair of six-shooters. In the ads, the *bandito* was described as "cunning, clever, and sly." Contemporary ads, such as those of Taco Bell, encourage taco lovers to "Run for the Border!" in an apparent reference to the immigration issue. Interestingly, in what advertisers call crossover commercials, a Miller Lite beer advertisement features boxing champion Carlos Palomino encouraging viewers to "Drink Miller Lite, but don't drink the water."[32]

The influences of the Hispanic microculture in the United States are growing. Now more than ever, Hispanics are noticed by the dominant culture. We see images of Hispanics in television and movies. Hispanic cuisine is more popular than ever. Although their unemployment rates are high and their incomes low, as a microcultural group Hispanics are increasing their political and economic power. Soon, their voices will not be muted.

African Americans

According to Richard Schaefer, the history of African Americans in the United States dates as far back as the history of Euro-Americans (persons of European descent). Blacks arrived in the New World with the first white explorers. Schaefer reports that in 1619 twenty Africans arrived in Jamestown as indentured servants. At that time, their children were born free people. By the 1660s, however, the British colonies had passed laws making Africans slaves for life.[33]

According to Schaefer, the proportion of blacks in the United States has varied over the centuries and actually declined until the 1940s primarily because white immigration (mostly from Europe) far outdistanced population growth by blacks. In 1790, Africans represented a little over 19 percent of the total population of the United States. That percentage declined to 9.7 percent in 1910. Today blacks, or African Americans, represent 13 percent of the population.[34] Blacks are the second largest microcultural group in the United States. By 2000, blacks and Hispanics comprised nearly 27 percent of the U.S. population. Unlike the rapid and disproportionate growth of the Hispanic population since 1990, the rate of black population growth remains relatively stable.

Schaefer claims that blacks made significant progress in the twentieth century, mostly because of the civil rights movement. Although there remain gaps between blacks and whites in such areas as income, education, employment, and housing, blacks have made significant progress in the past fifty years. For example, in 2000, nearly 30 percent of all black families had incomes of $50,000 or more. Politically, the number of black elected officials has increased 271 percent since 1972. Schaefer notes that an interesting phenomenon is developing. An ever-growing proportion of the black population consists of blacks who are foreign born. Since 1984, the percentage of blacks in the United States born outside the United States (mostly in the Caribbean) has almost doubled.[35]

BLACK ENGLISH, DIALECT, AND EBONICS

One of the primary ways in which members of cultural groups define themselves and establish in-group and out-group identities is through verbal and nonverbal language—that is, through conversation. As groups residing in the same geographical country, African Americans and Euro-Americans differ significantly in their use of language codes. Some linguists maintain that 80 to 90 percent of African Americans engage in what is frequently labeled "black language" or "black dialect." Geneva Smitherman argues that black language is "an Africanized form of English reflecting black America's linguistic-cultural African heritage."[36]

Recently there has been a veritable fervor over the use of Ebonics in California school districts. The name Ebonics (from the terms *ebony* and *phonics*) was first coined in 1973 to refer to a grammatically complex African American speech pattern. Ebonics, or black language, is the language of the descendants of slaves that combines English vocabulary with a Niger-Congo grammatical structure. Many linguists recognize black language as a Creole that developed as a result of contact between Africans and Europeans. A new language was formed that was influenced by both languages and took on a variety of forms, depending on whether there was French, Portuguese, or English influence. According to Weber, there is evidence that these languages were spoken on the west coast of Africa as early as the 1500s. Some linguists believe that Africans responded to the English language as do all other nonnative speakers—that is, from the phonological and grammatical constructs of their native language.

Historically, blacks have been a muted group in the United States. Slaves and their descendants were denied access to educational institutions for two hundred years. Hence, there was no bilingual educational system available for them to learn English. In fact, slaves that risked learning English and were caught speaking it were often put to death. Moreover, they were not allowed to speak their own native language and were often separated from their ethnic groups when sold as slaves. Over time, Africans were forced to use English without the benefit of formal education; the result was what we now call black language or Ebonics. In Ebonics, the verb *to be* is not conjugated ("I be laughing at you"). The language is spoken very rhythmically and flows like other African languages in a consonant-vowel-consonant pattern in which some syllables are held longer and accented more strongly than in standard English, as in *DEE-troit*.[37]

In addition to its phonological and syntactic elements, black language includes other communication dimensions that distinguish it from other languages and mark its speakers as members of a unique group. Communication professor Thomas Kochman argues that African American expression is characteristically "emotionally intense, dynamic, and demonstrative," whereas Euro-American expression is "more modest and emotionally restrained."[38]

In comparing African American and Euro-American modes of expression, Kochman asserts that when engaging an issue, Euro-Americans use a detached and unemotional form of "discussion," whereas African-Americans use an intense and involving form of "argument." Kochman maintains that Euro-Americans tend to understate their talents, whereas African Americans tend to boast about theirs. In essence, African American speech acts and events are more animated, lively, and forceful than Euro-American speech acts. According to Kochman, the animation and vitality of black communication is due to the emotional force and spiritual energy that blacks invest in their public presentations and the functional role that emotions play in realizing the goals of black interactions, activities, and events. For example, a common goal of many African American speech events is to energize the audience into an emotional and spiritual release. Such speech events require a strong speaker, a medium that facilitates the emotional and spiritual release, and active participation from the audience. One type of communication that captures the essence of such revitalization is a call-and-response pattern involving reciprocal speech acts between speaker and audience. In the typical call-and-response mode, a speaker begins by calling—that is, by making some point or assertion to which the audience responds. African studies professor Shirley Weber describes an instance of call and response while teaching:

> During the lecture, one of my more vocal black students began to respond to the message with some encouraging remarks like "all right," "make it plain," "that all right," and "teach." She was soon joined by a few more black students who gave similar comments. I noticed that this surprised and confused some of the white students. When questioned later about this, their response was that they were not used to having more than one person talk at a time, and they really could not talk and listen at the same time. They found the comments annoying and disruptive. As the lecturer, I found the comments refreshing and inspiring.[39]

African Americans engage in call-and-response modes in a variety of formalized settings, such as church meetings, and during informal everyday gatherings.

THE DOZENS

Weber outlines other modes of African American communication, including rappin', runnin' it down, and doin'/playin' the dozens. The original meaning of the term *rappin'* was a dialogue between a man and a woman in which the man generates creative and imaginative statements designed to win the affection of the woman. *Runnin' it down* is a speech event in which the speaker's goal is to describe some event or situation in such detail that there is complete agreement and comprehension between speaker and audience. *Doin'/playin' the dozens* is a verbal battle of insults between speakers who are judged for their originality and creativity by a small group of listeners. This is the highest form of verbal warfare and impromptu speaking. The term *dozens* was used during slavery to refer to a selling technique used by slave owners. If an individual slave had a disability, he or she was considered damaged goods and was sold with eleven other damaged slaves at a discount rate. The term *dozens,* then, refers to negative physical attributes.[40]

In the early 1970s, University of Pennsylvania linguist William Labov conducted extensive field research in the inner cities of some of the major cities in the United States. He was interested in the language of the inner city, used primarily by African Americans. Labov called the language black English vernacular (BEV). One form of BEV studied by Labov was playin' the dozens. The dozens is gamelike interaction played according to a set of rules in which two players compete, in the form of insulting each other, for the admiration of the audience. There is a minimum of two players, and anyone within speaking distance can be forced by social pressure to play. Dozens players become well known for their unique styles as well as the ability to change styles depending on where the game is played and who the other players are. As in any speech community, dozens players unconsciously know the rules of their communities and the communication strategies they employ. Although they may not be able to explain the rules, dozens players know when the rules are broken. Playin' the dozens is also known as soundin', signifyin', woofin', cuttin', and so on, depending on the location. The dozens is a highly rule-oriented speech event. According to Labov, there are three participants: antagonist A, antagonist B, and the audience. A sounds against B in the form of some insult, the audience responds, then B responds to A's sound. Sounding is almost always about someone's mother: her age, weight, ugliness, blackness, smell, the food she eats, the clothes she wears, her poverty, and her sexual activity. Other relatives are mentioned, but their importance is secondary to the mother's. An important point here is that ritual insults are not intended as factual statements; they are not meant to be denied. This is a cardinal rule. Everyone knows that these propositions are not true. Yet there are some instances in which weak sounds can be interpreted as personal insults; they are denied, and conflict may follow. For example, "I fucked your mother" is not obviously untrue and could be interpreted as a personal insult. But "I fucked your mother from tree to tree" is obviously un-

Many microcultural groups develop unique verbal and nonverbal rituals. *(Mark Richards/Photo Edit)*

true and is interpreted as a ritual insult. Playin' the dozens is a language game of ritual insults.[41]

Out-groups or strangers are generally not welcome to join in sounding. Extended ritual sounding is an in-group process representing in-group rules. Moreover, obscenity does not play as large a role as one might think. To be sure, many of the sounds are obscene, but only within the rule structure of the dominant white adult middle-class society. The significance of the sound would be meaningless without reference to middle-class norms. In this sense, the sounds violate the rules of the middle-class speech community. According to Labov, one rule for the dozens is to insult your opponent's mother in a variety of ways as in

I hate to talk about your mother, she's a good old soul
She got a ten-ton pussy and a rubber asshole.

The simplest of sounds is to compare the opponent's mother with something old, ugly, or bizarre as in "Your mother look like Flipper" . . . "like a Milk Dud" . . . "a rubber dick." More complicated comparisons are done with a quantifier, an adjective, and an embedded sentence as in:

Your mother so old she can stretch her head and lick out her ass.
Your mother so skinny she do the hula hoop in a Applejack.
Your mother so dirty, when she get the rag an' take a bath, the water went back down the drain.

Another important type of sounds is directed against the home life of the opponent and the poverty that exists there. For example:

> I went to your house to ask for a piece of cheese. The rat jumped up and say, "Heggies, please."
>
> When I came across your house, a rat gave me a jay-walkin' ticket.

Whether a sound is good or bad is determined by the amount of laughter it receives. But, as Labov notes, an even more forceful mode of approving sounds is for the audience members to repeat them. Negative reactions include the absence of laughter and the response of "That's phoney" or "phoney shit!" Black English vernacular is the vehicle of communication used by some of the most talented and effective speakers of the English language.[42]

THE ORIGINS OF BLACK LANGUAGE

The origins of many of these African American communicative modes can be traced to ancient African philosophies about the relationship between humans, the spoken word, and the fostering of community. According to African scholar Janheinz Jahn, the traditional African view of the world is one of extraordinary harmony. All being, all essence, in whatever form it is conceived, is subsumed under one of four categories: (1) *muntu,* human being; (2) *kintu,* thing; (3) *hantu,* place and time, and (4) *kuntu,* modality. Everything that exists must necessarily belong to one of these four categories and is conceived of not as some tangible substance but as a force that affects, and is affected by, the other forces. All of the forces are interrelated and work together to accomplish a common goal. For example, scholar belongs in the *muntu* category, pen to the *kintu* category, university to *hantu,* and knowledge to *kuntu.* Anything that exists has distinct characteristics that combine with and relate to characteristics in the other categories. For example, the most distinguishing characteristic of *muntu* is the possession of *nommo*— that is, the magic power of the word. Through *nommo,* humans establish their mastery over the other things. According to Jahn, *nommo* is

> the life force, is the fluid as such, a unity of spiritual-physical fluidity, giving life to everything, penetrating everything, causing everything. . . . And since man has the power over the word, it is he who directs the life force. Through the word he receives it, shares it with other beings, and so fulfills the meaning of life.[43]

Nothing exists without *nommo;* it is the force that fosters the sense of community between speaker and audience in which they become one as senders and receivers.

Shirley Weber argues that the philosophy of *nommo* has been carried into contemporary African American society, in which an audience listening and responding to a message is equally as important as the speaker. One of the foremost goals within any African American communicative context is to bring speaker and audience together as one—hence the call-and-response mode. In contemporary and traditional African American speech contexts, the speaker and audience share the platform.[44]

The above discussion suggests that there are distinct differences in the language use of African Americans and Euro-Americans and that the reason for such differences may lie in the purpose of language. African Americans, more so than Euro-Americans, tend to use language to establish and maintain a sense of community. The use of a language that expresses their unique history, bridges social and economic gaps, and helps build their future is a critical ingredient in African American communication and membership in their microcultural group.

The Amish

A microcultural group that continues to fascinate much of America is the Amish. John Andrew Hostetler is a former Amish member who left his community and is considered the country's leading expert on Amish custom. Hostetler, now professor emeritus of anthropology and sociology at Temple University, has written a great deal about the Amish. He describes them as

> a church, a community, a spiritual union, a conservative branch of Christianity, a religion, a community whose members practice simple and austere living, a familistic entrepreneuring system, and an adaptive human community.[45]

The Amish, sometimes called "The Plain People" or "Old Order Amish," are an Anabaptist religious group who emigrated from Europe to the United States in the early 1700s to escape religious persecution. Today, Amish groups have settled in about twenty-two states and Ontario, Canada. Their name is derived from one of their earliest leaders, Jacob Ammann, a young Alsatian bishop and farmer who held a strong Bible-centered faith and was staunchly conservative. To his followers, Ammann advocated nonresistance, adult baptism, disciplinary dress standards, and separatism from worldly fashion and influence. From 1730 through 1770, between fifty and one hundred Amish families arrived in the United States and initially settled in Pennsylvania. Since then, several groups of Amish have moved farther west to settle in Ohio, Indiana, Illinois, Iowa, and Wisconsin, among other areas. Today some ninety thousand Amish inhabit the United States, with over 80 percent living in Pennsylvania, Ohio, and Indiana.[46]

AN ISOLATED MICROCULTURE

Perhaps more than any other microcultural group in the United States, the Amish have been relatively successful at isolating themselves from the influences of the dominant culture. Living what they call nonresistant lives, they do not serve in the military. According to Rich Huber, who was raised a Mennonite in Lancaster County, Pennsylvania, the Amish follow the Bible as literally as possible, citing "Be ye not conformed to the world" (Romans 12:2) as their fundamental principle. On the basis of their interpretation of this biblical passage, the Amish believe that true followers of Christ are to be separate from the world. Hence, to evade worldliness and the corruption and sin associated with it, the Amish have drawn strict boundaries between themselves and the dominant cultural milieu.[47]

Although they are successful at avoiding contemporary American society, the Amish are considered American citizens and observe most U.S. laws. Hostetler notes that the Amish pay income, property, and sales taxes like everyone else. They do not pay Social Security tax, nor do they receive Social Security benefits or any other type of government aid (for example, food stamps or welfare). In addition, they avoid the courts in settling disputes, are forbidden to take oaths, do not serve on juries, and do not collect settlements through the courts.[48] Moreover, they take full responsibility for the education of their children and generally do not send them to public schools. In fact, in 1972 the Supreme Court heard the case of *Wisconsin v. Yoder,* wherein the court exempted the various Amish sects from compulsory school attendance laws beyond eighth grade. *Wisconsin v. Yoder* represented the first time conflicts over education between the Amish and the government had been argued before the Supreme Court. This is significant because most Amish follow a "turn the other cheek" mentality and do not defend themselves. MacKaye notes that often, when confronted, many Amish simply pack up their belongings and move somewhere else in order to be left alone.[49]

Today, most Amish children are taught in one-room schoolhouses by teachers with no more than an eighth-grade education. Amish children attend school until the eighth grade, after which they are educated at home and go to work on the family farms. The Amish consider their society a form of schooling. The Amish train their children vocationally. Almost exclusively, Amish boys become farmers, carpenters, or tradesmen, and girls become homemakers. The Amish have virtually no unemployment.[50]

Like other religiously oriented microcultural groups, the Amish believe that God is the absolute power in the universe. They believe that their life on earth is preparation for their afterlife in heaven. As a result, many of the values and behaviors of the Amish may be similar to those of mainstream America, but for very different reasons. By the time they die, the Amish want their earthly sins settled. Hence, every day is to be lived well so as to please God. The Amish do not believe that entrance to heaven is guaranteed, however.[51] As Hostetler notes, complete assurance of heaven is seen as obnoxious because it smacks of pride and boasting. Hence, humility, self-denial, and submissiveness are at the core of Amish values.[52]

Because the Amish very much want their group to remain much as it was in the seventeenth century, they are very slow to change. They choose to examine change very carefully before they accept it. If a new idea or change does not help them keep their lives simple and their families together, they will probably reject it. Hence, the Amish eschew most modern technologies such as electricity, automobiles, and other conveniences.[53] Also, on the basis of the biblical passage "Thou shalt not make unto thee any graven image, or any likeness of anything that . . . is in the earth" (Exodus 20:4), the Amish do not take photographs.[54]

Unlike mainstream American society, the Amish are a collectivistic community, what they call *Gemeinde,* which translates into "redemptive community." From this perspective, individuals depend on their community for their identity. The Amish believe that a person's self-worth is defined by his or her role in the community. Individual achievement, self-ambition, power, and worldly acquisitions are not valued. Sharing, community effort, and trading are the core values of most

Amish communities. The Amish believe that community service gains access to God and eternal life.[55] Because of their collectivistic orientation, each member of the group has a well-defined role. For example, gender roles among Amish men and women are very clearly prescribed. Patterns of dress and a strict division of labor separate men and women in Amish society. Exclusively, Amish women are homemakers and Amish men are farmers, with the exception of those men who join the ministry.[56]

VERBAL COMMUNICATION AMONG THE AMISH

Most Amish are trilingual—that is, they speak three languages. They speak a dialect of German, called High German, during church services. At home or during informal gatherings, they speak Low German, sometimes called Pennsylvania Dutch (the term derived from non-Amish mispronunciation of *Deutsche*). They learn and speak English at school and when interacting with non-Amish persons. Like all other microcultures, the Amish frequently use phrases and sayings that carry meaning to them.

In their study of Amish verbal phrases and colloquialisms, Moellendorf, Warsh, and Yoshimaru report that one traditional Amish saying in German is "Das alt Gebrauch ist besser," which translates to "The old way is the better way." According to Moellendorf and her colleagues, the Amish believe that past traditions and the old way of living are superior to the conveniences of modern life and its new technologies. Occasionally, outsiders look to the Amish as an idyllic community. They see the Amish lifestyle as free from the pressures of the modern world. To this the Amish have a saying, "It's not all pies and cakes," meaning that the life of the Amish may appear simple and serene, but in reality the life of an Amish person is hard, disciplined, and strenuous. Although it happens only infrequently, sometimes an individual will leave the Amish community and join a less demanding church, such as the Mennonites, or other community. To this the Amish say, "He got his hair cut," as a polite way of communicating that the individual was unable to meet the rigorous standards of the Amish. The saying also suggests that the person has lost his masculine tie (that is, his long hair) to the community. Another way of communicating a similar phenomenon is "He went English," which is said when an Amish member has left the community to become a part of mainstream American culture.[57]

To enforce church order and discipline, the Amish engage in a form of excommunication called "the ban" or "shunning." Shunning includes prohibiting attendance at church and, in its most extreme form, most types of involvement with members of the community. The ban is particularly difficult for other members of a family who may have a member shunned. In such cases they are expected to cut off all communication with that person.[58]

NONVERBAL COMMUNICATION AMONG THE AMISH

Moellendorf and her colleagues also studied the nonverbal communication of the Amish and found that the Amish have a very distinct nonverbal communication system. According to Moellendorf, one's role in an Amish community is nonverbally communicated by his or her physical appearance and dress. For example, the style of hats worn by Amish men communicates their age and marital status. A black hat with three or more inches of brim is given to Amish boys at about the age of two. The larger brim is to communicate the young boy's innocence. A bride-groom's hat has a crease around the top and a wide seam along the brim signaling his marriage. Amish fathers wear hats with flat crowns. An Amish woman's bonnet is her way to communicate her marital status. All Amish women wear bonnets over the back part of their hair. Young girls wear colored bonnets and begin to wear black bonnets at about the age of nine. Married Amish women wear white bonnets.[59]

In addition to their hats and bonnets, Amish hairstyles communicate status. Young girls wear braids that are fastened around their foreheads. At about the age of ten, their hair is arranged into a bun. Adult Amish women never cut their hair; they part it in the middle and wear a bun. Most Amish women do not shave their legs or trim their eyebrows as such behavior is seen as interfering with God's work. Amish men shave until marriage, at which time they grow beards, which are analogous to wedding rings. If a single man reaches the age of forty, he may grow a beard. In all cases, married or not, the beard is left untrimmed, and moustaches are not allowed because of their long association with the military.[60]

To communicate submissiveness and pride, group unity, and the desire to be separate from the rest of the contemporary world, the Amish wear only very plain clothing. To the Amish, dress is a statement of conformity to group values. A man's shirt is pocketless, and his trousers do not have hip pockets and are worn with suspenders so that they are not tight. For women, ribbons, bows, makeup, and jewelry

The dress habits of the Amish communicate conformity to group values. *(David S. Strickler/Picture Cube)*

are forbidden as they are seen as haughty and vain. The dresses of older Amish women close in front, and their skirts touch the tops of their shoes. Women are never allowed to wear pants and typically wear an apron over the dress. Generally, the colors of both men's and women's clothing are restricted to white, green, blue, or purple.[61]

Another nonverbal dimension to the Amish is the horse and buggy. Kraybill argues that the horse and buggy serve as the prime symbol of Amish life. To the Amish, the horse communicates tradition, time, and proof that the Amish have not succumbed to the conveniences of modern life. The buggy, which is typically gray, communicates *Gelassenheit,* which means a surrender to communal values and modesty. Moreover, since the buggies all look alike, they serve as a kind of equalizer among the Amish.[62]

Amidst incredible societal and technological change, the Amish have maintained their lifestyle for over two hundred years. Although they are generally a quiet and reserved microculture that prefers to be isolated from the dominant culture, some Amish have recently become the target for hate crimes. Ironically, their nonflamboyant appearance and subdued behavior, along with their horses and buggies and their refusal to adopt modern technologies, have rendered the Amish an easy target. In a recent incident in which a young man shot at an Amish buggy full of children and then raped a young Amish woman, the assailant was quoted as saying that he wanted the Amish to know that they do not own this world and that there are other people in the world.[63] Father J. Mahoney, a priest who has studied various religious groups, argues that the Amish have tried to freeze their culture in the late seventeenth century. Throughout the centuries, as the mainstream culture of the United States has progressed technologically, the Amish have tried to preserve their lifestyle, creating a disparity between them and the dominant culture. That disparity, and disagreements as to how far they should go in accommodating to the dominant culture, will remain the major challenge in the coming decades for the Amish.[64] As Hostetler notes:

> Over the past three centuries the Amish and other Anabaptist groups have been suspended between two opposing forces: the political forces that would eliminate ethnicity from the face of the earth and the human communities who regard ethnicity as a natural and necessary extension of the familial bonds that integrate human activities. Caught between these forces the "plain" people have sometimes prospered and sometimes suffered for their faith.[65]

The Hmong

Although most students in the United States learn about America's involvement in the Vietnam war, probably few ever learn of the "Secret War" fought on behalf of the United States during this time. The "Secret War" refers to the thousands of Hmong who were recruited by the United States military through the Central Intelligence Agency (CIA) to help fight the war against communism in Southeast

Asia. According to Daphne Winland, the Hmong belong to the Sino-Tibetan language family. Being culturally similar to the Chinese, the Hmong can be traced back to China, where they lived peacefully for hundreds of years. Approximately 150 years ago, Chinese rulers began a campaign of persecution to extinguish the Hmong language. The Hmong moved southward and westward out of China and organized communities in Burma, Thailand, North Vietnam, and the mountains of Laos. Winland points out that the Hmong—whose name means "free people" or "mountain people"—were singled out by the CIA during the Vietnam war because of their geographically strategic location in the mountains of Laos.[66]

In the 1960s, the CIA began secretly enlisting Hmong to prevent North Vietnamese troops from entering and moving supplies to South Vietnam through Laos. The Hmong set up navigational aids for American bombers and fought to protect them when they were attacked by the North Vietnamese. In addition, Hmong soldiers were highly skilled in the operations required to rescue American pilots shot down over Laos (the United States flew more tactical missions over Laos than they did over Vietnam).[67] The Hmong were fierce fighters, yet suffered devastating losses, estimated at over one hundred times greater (proportionately) than those of the United States. Although estimates vary, most experts agree that over 25,000 Hmong lost their lives fighting for the United States during the Vietnam war.[68] Because of intense political pressures at home, the United States had vowed not to escalate the war into Laos. Hence, the Hmong became known as "The Secret Army," and their participation in the war was called "The Secret War."[69]

In 1975, the United States withdrew its forces from Vietnam. Concurrently, a Communist-backed government, supported by the Vietnamese and Soviets, assumed power in Laos. One of the foremost goals of the new Laotian government was to annihilate the Hmong people because of their alliance with the United States. The Communists tortured, raped, and murdered thousands of Hmong. They napalmed their villages and slaughtered their cattle. There is evidence that the Communists used chemical and biological weapons in their attempt to wipe out the Hmong. With the United States having withdrawn from Vietnam, the Hmong were left without any allies in the midst of their enemies and a new war.[70] Over 200,000 Hmong fled to Thailand, where they were housed in prisonlike conditions in refugee camps. Many Hmong emigrated to the United States, Australia, and France. Approximately 100,000 or so made it to the United States. Today, approximately 150,000 Hmong reside in the United States, with large concentrations in California, Wisconsin, and Minnesota. Although they were hired and paid by the United States, Hmong soldiers have received little or no recognition for their efforts and do not receive veteran's benefits. In May 1997, the United States finally acknowledged Hmong veterans with a granite marker in Arlington National Cemetery that reads: "The U.S. Secret Army in the Kingdom of Laos, 1961–1973." In both Lao and Hmong languages, the marker also reads: "You will never be forgotten."

Duffy alleges that life in the United States has been very difficult for many Hmong. For the most part, Hmong immigrants have not been welcome. Unfortunately, many people inaccurately associate the Hmong with the "enemy" in the Vietnam war. To add to their arduous situation, many stereotypes preceded their immigration to the United States. News coverage of the Hmong often referred to them as a "preliterate," "primitive," and "hilltribe" group.[71] Moreover, writes Winland, during this time period just about anything associated with the Vietnam war was anathema. Hence, the Hmong entered the United States being doubted and mistrusted by many and facing the straightforward bigotry of others. The Hmong find themselves in a situation of relative dependency on United States culture while simultaneously facing a real sense of cultural isolation.[72]

Unlike the African Americans or the Amish, who have been in the United States for centuries, the Hmong are unique in that they are first-generation immigrants. Their values, customs, and modes of communication have collided head-on with mainstream American culture. For example, like many of their Asian cousins, the Hmong are a collectivistic culture. According to Katie Thao, a native Hmong who emigrated to the United States when she was a teenager, the most important group is the family clan. Hmong family clans are patrilineal. Hmong males are given two names, one in childhood and the other when they reach adulthood. When children are born, they are given their father's clan name. When women marry, they keep their father's clan name and do not adopt their husband's even though they become formal members of his clan. Conversely, Hmong women do not receive an adult name, but become known by their husband's clan name. There are between twenty and thirty clan names. The most common clan names in the United States are Cha, Hang, Her, Kong, Kue, Moua, Lee, Lo or Lor, Thao or Thor, Vang, Vue, Xiong, and Yang.[73]

ROLE RELATIONSHIPS AND MARRIAGE

According to sociologists Ray Hutchison and Miles McNall, many of the Hmong customs associated with clan membership that have been imported to the United States have to do with sex role relationships and marriage practices. For the most part, these practices clash with American customs. For example, in traditional Hmong culture, women maintain clearly subordinate roles. Their role is to bear children, maintain the household, and be subservient to their husbands. One way Hmong women demonstrate their subordinate status is by walking directly behind their husbands when in public. Moreover, they have little or nothing to say in the decision making or political affairs of their clans. Some husbands refuse to allow their wives to learn English, hence keeping them muted and powerless in American culture. For the most part, first-generation Hmong women are not allowed an education and are expected to marry early, between the ages of thirteen to eighteen, whereas men marry between the ages of eighteen and thirty. Although practices are gradually changing, many Hmong marriages in the United States are still arranged. Many communities report that a high percentage of Hmong girls drop out of high school to get married. Indeed, Hmong women have the youngest average age of marriage of all Southeast Asian refugee groups. Moreover, Hmong fertility rates in the United States are much higher than those of any other refugee or immigrant group.[74]

Katie Thao participated in an arranged marriage. She did not meet her husband-to-be until the day of her wedding. To many Americans an arranged marriage seems ridiculous and absurd. But Thao asserts that she was completely comfortable with the idea because she had confidence that her parents, especially her father, would negotiate a good husband for her. Thao contends that an arranged Hmong marriage is a matter of considerable maneuvering and bargaining. Typically each family selects an elderly male spokesman. These spokesmen, usually the fathers, then negotiate and bargain a bride price that is to be paid to the bride's parents. The philosophy behind "buying a wife" is to assure that she will be highly valued by her new family. In many cases, the parents of the bride hold a feast of roasted pig in their home in celebration of the wedding. After the wedding ceremony, the souls and good fortune of the bride and groom are symbolically wrapped in an umbrella that is carried in procession to the groom's home, where another feast is held. If the bride is entering the groom's home for the first time (which is usually the case since the bride and groom are strangers), a rooster is waved over the bride to symbolize her membership in the groom's clan. In most cases, a Hmong marriage is seen not as a bonding of two people but as a union of two family clans. In some cases, if a married Hmong woman's husband dies, she automatically becomes the wife of his younger brother.[75]

COMMUNICATION PATTERNS AMONG THE HMONG

Like most microcultural groups, the Hmong share some unique verbal and nonverbal communication patterns. The overwhelming majority of the first Hmong immigrants entering the United States did not speak English. Historically, because the Hmong emigrated so often, their written language was eventually lost. Not until the 1950s were orthographies of the written language developed. Well over half of the Hmong who immigrated to the United States could not read or write. The Hmong who emigrated to Laos were taught in Buddhist temples in the Lao language and the Lao alphabet. In Laos today, there are two major dialects of Hmong language: Hmoob Dawb, meaning "White Hmong," and Hmoob Ntsuab, meaning "Blue Hmong." Since the White Hmong are in the majority, Hmoob Dawb is spoken more frequently.[76]

According to Thao, the phrase "playing a flute into a water buffalo's ear" is used by the Hmong when someone is trying, without success, to explain something to another who simply does not understand. Often Hmong will refer to someone who does not understand a message as some kind of animal, often a water buffalo. The idea of a flute is significant because in traditional Hmong culture, the flute communicates emotions, such as sorrow, love, and even anger or depression. Another phrase, "The grinder doesn't taste salty," is used to refer to a person who is bankrupt. Salt is a very valuable ingredient to the Hmong, and when there is no salt, it is an indication that the family is out of money. The Hmong are animistic, meaning that they believe that everything has a spirit. According to Thao, the supernatural is a very real part of the Hmong's lives. Evil spirits are thought to exist in unpopulated areas; therefore, many Hmong are afraid to travel alone in uninhabited places. The phrase "The devil will not eat or chew anyone for it" is said when an act or crime is committed in which no one will be caught or found guilty. The

Hmong believe that evil spirits such as the devil are omnipresent and can hear and see everything. If the devil will not eat anyone, the act will go unpunished. "Go check the mousetrap" is said in reference to a meal that is shared by an entire clan or village. The phrase indicates that going to the meal is similar to a mouse's going to a trap in search of food and getting caught. The person going to the meal gets trapped in the company of the clan or family. Many Hmong sayings and colloquialisms are indirect expressions. The Hmong believe that if the truth is spoken directly, evil spirits or unwanted guests can overhear it. Thao says that a Hmong farmer might call out to his family, "Come sharpen your knives," rather than calling out, "It's time to eat," because the latter might attract the evil spirits or animals who will eat up the meal.[77]

One of the most significant forms of nonverbal communication for the Hmong is their *paj ntaub,* pronounced *pandoa. Paj ntaub,* meaning "flower cloth," are sophisticated stitched quilts embroidered with bright threads. They often feature picturesque geometric designs that occasionally feature animals or other creatures. Since Hmong immigration to the United States, *paj ntaub* have evolved into "story cloths," often depicting the history and life experiences of the Hmong culture. Evolving from the Thai refugee camps, story cloths were a way to teach written language to Hmong children and others. Now they are treated as works of art and a vehicle for the Hmong to document their history and retain their cultural identity. Created exclusively by Hmong women, the cloths carry much significance. The quality of the needlework communicates the skill and creativity of the women who make them and may bring them a higher bride price at the time of marriage bargaining.[78]

Other nonverbal gestures used in Hmong culture include twitching the eyes to communicate contempt to another. Twitching the eyes during a long stare is very offensive and may lead to a physical confrontation. Slapping oneself on the buttocks is a nonverbal way of saying "Kiss my ass" or "Lick my ass." Kneeling is done only by men when they want to express their thanks or to ask another for mercy and forgiveness. A woman's kneeling has little or no value because of her low rank and position in Hmong clans.[79]

Elliot Barkan writes that acculturation in the United States has been difficult for the Hmong. The first-generation Hmong, arriving in the United States in the mid-1970s, have tried hard to preserve their culture, while their children, exposed to the values and the communication system of the dominant culture, are caught in between two cultures. The older-generation Hmong try to preserve the traditional ways, while contemporary culture, including the educational system, encourages their assimilation. Acculturation for the elderly Hmong has been particularly difficult. The age and gender hierarchies that prescribed their superior status are gone. In Laos, women have few, if any rights. In the United States, of course, wives have equal rights. Language has played a key role as well. A Hmong child's quick acquisition of English almost reverses traditional family roles. Unlike the traditional ways, the parents are now dependent on the child's communication skills to get along. Many parents feel that the learning of such skills undermines their authority. Hence some parents develop a sense of loss and worthlessness and fall into a deep depression.[80]

Chapter Summary

Within most cultures are groups of people who differ in some significant way from the general societal culture. In this textbook, the term *microculture* is used to refer to those identifiable groups of people who share a set of values, beliefs, and behaviors and who possess a common history and verbal and nonverbal symbol system that is similar to the dominant culture but which varies in some way, perhaps subtly. Microcultures can be different from the larger culture in a variety of ways, most often because of race, ethnicity, language, or behavior. But one's age group or occupation might also render one a member of a microcultural group. Perhaps every member of a culture is also a member of a microcultural group.

This chapter has profiled Hispanics, African Americans, Amish, and Hmong as microcultural groups in the United States. Due mostly to immigration and high fertility rates, Hispanics are now the largest microcultural group in the country. Like many other microcultural groups, Hispanics experience lower incomes, higher poverty, and higher unemployment rates than the non-Hispanic whites. The U.S. government estimates that the Hispanic population will continue to grow through the first half of this twenty-first century. By then, Hispanic economic influence will be significant. As an economic, political, and socially powerful group, African Americans have maintained an important part of their history—that is, their language. African American history is expressed in the language games African Americans play and in their daily communication with others in the form of Ebonics. More than any other microcultural group, the Amish have preserved their traditional culture while peacefully coexisting within the rule structure of the dominant cultural milieu. Unlike any other microcultural group, the Amish have successfully isolated themselves from most of mainstream American culture. Finally, possibly the newest microcultural group in the United States is the Hmong. The Hmong are a group of people who fought alongside American troops in the Vietnam war, only to be abandoned when the war was lost. Having emigrated to the United States, the Hmong try desperately to adapt to American culture while simultaneously maintaining some aspects of their traditional culture. Like African Americans, the Hmong face a great deal of racism and resentment.

While each of the microcultural groups portrayed in this chapter is obviously different from the others, they share at least one major feature—that is, language. Each group, while adapting and accommodating to the dominant cultural surroundings, has successfully preserved a part of their original culture through communication. The verbal and nonverbal language of any cultural group maintains its heritage and allows its people to pass along its ancestry for future generations.

GLOSSARY OF TERMS

African Americans: A microcultural group whose ancestors were brought to the United States as slaves.

Amish: A microcultural religiously oriented group whose members practice simple and austere living.

Dozens: A verbal battle of insults between speakers who are judged for their originality and creativity by a small group of listeners. This is the highest form of verbal warfare and impromptu speaking in many African American communities.

Ebonics: From the terms *ebony* and *phonics,* a grammatically robust and rich African American speech pattern whose roots are in West Africa.

Hispanic: Defined by the U.S. government as a person of Cuban, Mexican, Puerto Rican, South or Central American, or other Spanish culture or origin regardless of race.

Hmong: A microcultural group belonging to the Sino-Tibetan language family who are culturally similar to the Chinese. The Hmong, whose name means "free people" or "mountain people," fought for the United States during the Vietnam war, and many have immigrated to the United States since the end of the war.

Microculture: An identifiable group of people who share a set of values, beliefs, and behaviors and who possess a common history and verbal and nonverbal symbol system that is similar to, but systematically varies from, the larger, often dominant cultural milieu.

Minority group: Subordinate group whose members have significantly less power and control over their own lives than members of the dominant or majority group.

Muted groups: Microcultural groups who are forced to express themselves (for example, to speak or write) within the dominant mode of expression.

Spanglish: Hybrid language combining the phonological features (i.e., sounds) and syntactic structures (grammar) of English and Spanish.

REFERENCES

1. R. Morris, "Living In/between," in *Our Voices: Essays in Culture, Ethnicity and Communication,* ed. A. Gonzales, M. Houston, and V. Chen (Los Angeles: Roxbury, 1997), p. 172.
2. United States Department of Commerce, "Profiles of General Demographic Characteristics: 2000 Census of Population and Housing," U.S. Census Bureau (Washington, D.C.: United States Government Printing Office, 2001).
3. United States Department of Commerce, "Statistical Abstract of the United States: 2000," U.S. Census Bureau (Washington D.C.: United States Government Printing Office).
4. R. T. Schaefer, *Racial and Ethnic Groups,* 7th ed. (New York: Longman, 1998), p. 5.
5. This discussion of the defining characteristics of minority groups is based on the following sources: C. Wagley and M. Harris, *Minorities in the New World: Six Cases* (New York: Columbia University Press, 1958); B. Meyers, "Minority Group: An Ideological Formulation," *Social Problems,* 32 (1984), 1–15; Schaefer, *Racial and Ethnic Groups.*
6. A. Penasa, M. Peters, and S. Smits, "Jamaica: Out of Many, One People" (unpublished student manuscript, St. Norbert College, De Pere, Wisc., 1996); K. Lunatta, *Jamaica Handbook* (Chico, Calif.: Moon Publications, 1993).
7. Schaefer, *Racial and Ethnic Groups.*
8. S. M. Ilcan, "Marriage Regulation and the Rhetoric of Alliance in Northwestern Turkey," *Ethnology,* 33 (1994), 273–297.
9. Schaefer, *Racial and Ethnic Groups.*
10. The Muted Group Theory was first articulated by Shirley and Edwin Ardener. The sources used for this discussion include C. Kramarae, *Women and Men Speaking* (Rowley, Mass.: Newbury House, 1981); S. Ardener, ed., *Perceiving Women* (London: Malaby Press, 1975).
11. S. N. Weber, "The Need to Be: The Sociocultural Significance of Black Language," in *Intercultural Communication: A Reader,* 7th ed. (Belmont, Calif.: Wadsworth, 1994), pp. 221–226.
12. C. Tyson, "Exploring the Generation Gap and Its Implications on African American Consciousness," *Doula: The Journal of Rap Music and Hip Hop Culture* (2001) (www.urbanthinktank.org).
13. A. Konkka, "Power, Pride, and Politics in Rap Music," Department of Translation Studies, University of Tampere (www.uta.fi/FAST/US8/PAPS/ak-rap.html).
14. J. Koslow, "A World of Difference: An Introduc-

tion to the Culture of Quebec" (unpublished student manuscript, St. Norbert College, De Pere, Wisc., 1995).

15. Schaefer, *Racial and Ethnic Groups.*

16. E. M. Grieco and R. C. Cassidy, "Overview of Race and Hispanic Origin: Census 2000 Brief," U.S. Department of Commerce, U.S. Census Bureau (Washington, D.C.: United States Government Printing Office, 2001).

17. B. Guzman, "The Hispanic Population: Census 2000 Brief," U.S. Department of Commerce, U.S. Census Bureau (Washington, D.C.: United States Government Printing Office, 2001).

18. Ibid.

19. M. Therrien and R. R. Ramirez, "The Hispanic Population in the United States: Population Characteristics." U.S. Department of Commerce, U.S. Census Bureau (Washington, D.C.: United States Government Printing Office, 2001).

20. A. Pajewski and L. Enriquez, *Teaching from a Hispanic Perspective: A Handbook for Non-Hispanic Adult Educators* (Phoenix: The Arizona Adult Literacy and Technology Resource Center, Inc., 1996).

21. J. Vasquez, "Teaching to the Distinctive Traits of Minority Students," *The Clearing House,* 63 (1990), 299–304; Schaefer, *Racial and Ethnic Groups;* S. Griggs and R. Dunn "Hispanic-American Students and Learning Style," ERIC Clearinghouse on Elementary and Early Childhood Education (Urbana, Ill.: 1996), ERIC Identifier 393607.

22. A. W. Clutter and R. D. Nieto "Understanding Hispanic Culture," Ohio State University Fact Sheet (Columbus: Ohio State University Extension, 2000); Pajewski and Enriquez, *Teaching from a Hispanic Perspective.*

23. Pajewski and Enriquez, *Teaching from a Hispanic Perspective.*

24. I. Stavans, "The Gravitas of Spanglish," *Chronicle of Higher Education,* 47 (October 13, 2000), B7–B10.

25. J. M. Rifkin, "No Problema—Spanglish Language Abounds," *Hispanic Times Magazine,* 11 (1990), 30–31.

26. Stavans, "The Gravitas of Spanglish."

27. B. Cruz and B. Teck, "The Official Spanglish Dictionary," *Hispanic,* 11 (1998), 34–36; these examples of Spanglish can be found in B. Cruz, B. Teck, and the Editors of Generation Ñ, *The Official Spanglish Dictionary: Un User's Guia to More Than 300 Words and Phrases That Aren't Exactly Espanol or Ingles* (New York: A Fireside Book, Simon and Schuster, 1998).

28. Y. Q. Mayo and R. P. Resnick, "The Impact of Machismo on Hispanic Women," *Journal of Women & Social Work,* 11 (1996), 257–278; J. M. Casas, B. R. Wagenheim, R. Banchero, and J. Mendoza-Romero, "Hispanic Masculinity: Myth or Psychological Schema Meriting Clinical Consideration," *Hispanic Journal of Behavioral Sciences,* 16 (1994), 315–332.

29. G. Anders, "Machismo: Dead or Alive?" *Hispanic,* 6 (1993), 14–18.

30. Casas et al., "Hispanic Masculinity."

31. E. T. Michael, J. H. Gagnon, E. O. Laumann, and G. Kolata, *Sex in America: A Definitive Survey* (New York: Warner Books, 1995).

32. O. E. Nuiry, "Ban the Bandito!" *Hispanic,* 9 (1996), 26–31.

33. Schaefer, *Racial and Ethnic Groups.*

34. Ibid.

35. Ibid.

36. G. Smitherman, *Talkin' and Testifyin'* (Boston: Houghton Mifflin, 1972), p. 2.

37. This discussion of black language and Ebonics is based on the following sources: S. N. Weber, "The Need to Be: The Sociocultural Significance of Black Language," in *Intercultural Communication: A Reader,* 7th ed., ed. L. A. Samovar and R. E. Porter (Belmont, Calif.: Wadsworth, 1994); J. Leland, N. Joseph, and S. Rhodes, "Hooked on Ebonics," *Newsweek,* 129 (1977), 78–79; "A Case for Ebonics: An Interview with Noma Le Moine," *Curriculum Review,* 36 (1979), 5–6; C. A. Blackshire-Belay, "The Location of Ebonics Within the Framework of the Africological Paradigm," *Journal of Black Studies,* 27 (1996), 5–24.

38. T. Kochman, "Cultural Pluralism: Black and

White Styles," in *Cultural Communication and Intercultural Context*, ed. D. Carbaugh (Hillsdale, N.J.: Erlbaum, 1990), pp. 219–224.

39. Weber, "The Need to Be: The Sociocultural Significance of Black Language," p. 222.

40. Ibid.

41. This discussion of "the dozens" is based entirely on W. Labov, *Language of the Inner City: Studies of the Black English Vernacular* (Philadelphia: University of Pennsylvania Press, 1976).

42. All of the examples presented here are from Labov, *Language of the Inner City: Studies of the Black English Vernacular.*

43. J. Jahn, *Muntu* (New York: Grove Press, 1961), p. 124.

44. Weber, "The Need to Be: The Sociocultural Significance of Black Language."

45. J. A. Hostetler, *Amish Society* (Baltimore: Johns Hopkins University Press, 1993), p. 4.

46. Pennsylvania Dutch Country Welcome Center, "The Amish, the Mennonites, and 'The Plain People'" (1998) (www.800padutch.com/amish. html); D. Schlabach, "An Amishman's Personal Expression" (www.amish-heartland.com/amish/ stories/anamishman.htm). (Spectrum Publications, 1998).

47. R. Huber, "Be Ye Not Conformed to This World" (1997) (www.columbia.edu/cu/sipa/PUBS/ SLANT/SPRING97/huber.html).

48. Hostetler, *Amish Society;* S. Pearce, S. Suminski, and K. Tschudy, "The Amish: Simple Values in a Complex World (unpublished manuscript, St. Norbert College, De Pere, Wisc., 1996).

49. W. R. MacKaye, "High Court Hears Amish School Case," *Washington Post* (Dec. 9, 1971).

50. "Origins of the Old Order Amish" (1998) (holycrosslivonia.org/amish/origin.htm).

51. S. A., "Influences of World View on Individual Life and Culture" (www.missouri.edu/~rsocjoel/ rs150/papers/sall.html).

52. Hostetler, *Amish Society.*

53. Pennsylvania Dutch Country Welcome Center, "The Amish, the Mennonites, and 'The Plain People.'"

54. Huber, "Be Ye Not Conformed to This World."

55. S. A., "Influences of World View on Individual Life and Culture."

56. P. D., "Gender, Work, and Worldview: Reflections on Amish and American Society" (www. missouri.edu/~rsocjoel/rs150/papers/pdun. html).

57. S. Moellendorf, H. Warsh, and K. Yoshimaru, *The Amish Culture: A Closer Look at the People of Lancaster County* (unpublished student manuscript, St. Norbert College, De Pere, Wisc., 1997); Hostetler, *Amish Society;* D. B. Kraybill, *The Riddle of Amish Culture* (Baltimore: Johns Hopkins University Press, 1989).

58. Ontario Consultants on Religious Tolerance, "The Amish" (1998) (www.religioustolerance. org/amish.htm); J. Mahoney, *European Free-Church Family* (1998) (www.jmahoney.com/ european.htm).

59. Moellendorf, Warsh, and Yoshimaru, *The Amish Culture: A Closer Look at the People of Lancaster County;* B. B. Buch, "The Nonverbal Cues of Amish Dress" (unpublished manuscript, St. Norbert College, De Pere, Wisc., 1997); Hostetler, *Amish Society;* Kraybill, *The Riddle of Amish Culture.*

60. Moellendorf, Warsh, and Yoshimaru, *The Amish Culture: A Closer Look at the People of Lancaster County;* Buch, "The Nonverbal Cues of Amish Dress"; Hostetler, *Amish Society;* Kraybill, *The Riddle of Amish Culture.*

61. Ibid.

62. Ibid.

63. P. D., "Amish and Mainstream Culture Clash" (1998) (www.missouri.edu/~rsocjoel/rs150/ papers/pd4.html).

64. Mahoney, "European Free-Church Family."

65. J. A. Hostetler, "An Amish Beginning," *American Scholar,* 61 (1992), 562.

66. D. N. Winland, "The Role of Religious Affiliation in Refugee Resettlement: The Case of the Hmong," *Canadian Ethnic Studies,* 24 (1992), 96–120.

67. J. L. Tyson, "Congress and State Department Ignore Persecution of Hmong," *Human Events,* 50 (1994), 12–14.

68. "Honoring the Secret Warriors," *US News and World Report,* 122 (May 25, 1997), 13.

69. J. Duffy, "Who Are the Hmong?: Legends of Literacy, History of Struggle" (1996) (www.adone.com/ttj/news/050296/ent3.htm).

70. K. Thao, "The Hmong Culture" (unpublished student manuscript, St. Norbert College, De Pere, Wisc., 1995).

71. Duffy, "Who Are the Hmong? Legends of Literacy, History of Struggle."

72. Winland, "The Role of Religious Affiliation in Refugee Resettlement: The Case of the Hmong."

73. Thao, "The Hmong Culture."

74. R. Hutchison and M. McNall, "Early Marriage in a Hmong Cohort," *Journal of Marriage and the Family,* 56 (1994), 579–591.

75. Thao, "The Hmong Culture."

76. Ibid.

77. Ibid.

78. C. Guensburg, "The Fabric of Their Lives," *Milwaukee Journal Sentinel* (June 16, 1996); J. H. Lee, "Hmong Quilts—*Paj Ntaub*—Reflect Hmong History" (1998) (www.stolaf.edu/people/cdr/hmong/culture/pandau2.html).

79. Thao, "The Hmong Culture."

80. E. R. Barkan, "Out of Carnage and into the Crucible: Southeast Asian Refugees' Journey from Old Worlds to a New One," *Journal of American Ethnic History,* 14 (1995), 53–58.

The Environmental Context

Environment is heir to psyche.

—Howard F. Stein[1]

CHAPTER OBJECTIVES

After reading this chapter, you should be able to:

- Compare and contrast high- and low-load environments.
- Discuss the relationship between culture and the natural environment.
- Identify and describe fixed, semifixed, and informal built environments.
- Compare and contrast housing patterns of the Japanese, Navajo, and Marakwet cultures.
- Assess your orientation toward privacy.
- Assess your monochronic/polychronic time orientation.

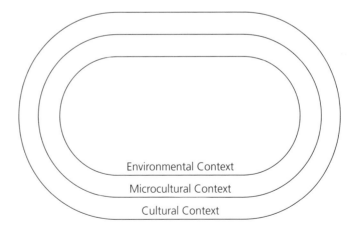

Environmental Context

Microcultural Context

Cultural Context

All human communication occurs within a physical and perceptual environment. These environments have a pervasive influence on the nature of communication. Consider the following two scenarios:[2]

Scenario 1: It is early evening, and you are alone in your dorm room. You're sitting on your bed reading a chapter in your intercultural communication textbook. You have some quiet music in the background that helps you concentrate. The room is quiet, as is the rest of the dormitory. Most of your friends are studying in their rooms as well.

Scenario 2: You are walking through the international terminal of a major airport. The terminal is very crowded, with people rushing to and from the various ticket counters. Announcements are coming in over the airport intercom system. The airport is very noisy, with people conversing, yelling, and laughing. You can hear the various jets landing and taking off as you rush to your gate. The lights are bright.

How would you compare these two environments? How might your verbal and nonverbal communication differ in each scenario? Would you feel and react the same in scenario 1 as in scenario 2?

This chapter explores the environmental context of intercultural communication. In the contextual model of intercultural communication presented in Chapter 1 (see Figure 1-2), the environmental context is the third largest circle surrounding the interactants. Recall that in the model, the cultural and microcultural contexts encircle the environmental context. How humans perceive the physical environment is very much affected by their culture and microculture. Furthermore, like the influence of the cultural and microcultural contexts, the influence of the physical environment is generally outside our conscious awareness.

How we see the physical world around us is very much influenced by our individual psychological perceptions, which, in turn, are shaped by culture. People from all cultures project their mental perceptions onto the physical environment and act as if what is projected is the true quality of the physical world. In other words, even the physical environment is subject to cultural interpretation. As Stein notes, far from being a passive component of culture, the environment is an active ingredient of the human experience.[3] In addition, the physical environment has a considerable impact on our communication. As we move from one physical location to another, our verbal and nonverbal messages adapt accordingly. The types of messages we send and receive in the classroom differ significantly from those we exchange in our dorm room or when we are out shopping in the mall. As the environment changes, our messages change as well.

This chapter discusses several aspects of the environment: the information load of an environment, the relationship between cultures and their natural environment, the *built* dimension of the physical environment, cross-cultural comparisons of housing, dimensions of privacy, and monochronic and polychronic time orientations. Each of these environmental dimensions affects how we communicate with others. And each varies considerably across cultures.

Environments and Information Load

Albert Mehrabian is well known for his work in environmental psychology. According to Mehrabian, there are a number of ways to compare one environment with another. One way is to calculate the *information rate*—that is, the amount of information contained or perceived in the environment per some unit of time. According to Mehrabian, the more information available to process, the greater the information rate. An environment having a high information rate has a *high load*, whereas one with a low information rate has a *low load*. Mehrabian and his colleagues developed a list of descriptive adjectives to describe the load of any given environment (see Table 4-1).

An environment that can be described by several of the adjectives in the left column of Table 4-1 has a high load, whereas an environment that can be described

TABLE 4-1 **High-Load Versus Low-Load Descriptors**	
Environment Type	
High-load	*Low-load*
Uncertain	Certain
Varied	Redundant
Complex	Simple
Novel	Familiar
Large-scale	Small-scale
Contrasting	Similar
Dense	Sparse
Intermittent	Continuous
Surprising	Usual
Heterogeneous	Homogeneous
Crowded	Uncrowded
Asymmetrical	Symmetrical
Immediate	Distant
Moving	Still
Rare	Common
Random	Patterned
Improbable	Probable

SOURCE: "High-Load Versus Low-Load Descriptors" from *Public Places and Private Spaces: The Psychology of Work, Plan, and Living Environment* by Albert Mehrabian. Copyright © 1976 by Basic Books, Inc. Reprinted by permission of Basic Books, a member of Perseus Books, L.L.C.

with adjectives from the right column has a low load. Some environments might contain a blend of terms from both columns. In regard to the scenarios presented at the beginning of the chapter, many of the right-column terms apply to scenario 1, such as *simple, small-scale, sparse, uncrowded, homogeneous, symmetrical, still, patterned,* and *probable.* In contrast, scenario 2 could be described with several of the left-column terms, such as *varied, complex, large-scale, contrasting, dense, surprising, heterogeneous, crowded, asymmetrical, moving, random,* and *improbable.* Using these criteria, we can say that scenario 1 has a low information load and that scenario 2 has a high information load.[4]

Mehrabian argues that to some extent, information load is equivalent to the level of uncertainty in a particular environment. The higher the information load, the higher the uncertainty, especially in novel and complex environments. The more familiar we are with a situation, the less uncertainty we experience. Of all the environmental factors, people are perhaps the greatest source of uncertainty. This is especially true of strangers, including people from different cultures. Hence, a crowded room of strangers contains high levels of uncertainty and a heavy information load, and the probability is high that when we are interacting with people from a different culture (especially in their environment), the information load will be high.[5]

Mehrabian contends that the information load of a particular environment can affect people's emotional responses in three dimensions: (1) *arousal/nonarousal,* (2) *pleasure/displeasure,* and (3) *dominance/ submissiveness.*[6] The arousal dimension refers to a person's level of stimulation and excitability. Pleasure refers to the degree of happiness and satisfaction. Dominance refers to feelings of control or command of the situation. These emotional responses cause people to approach or avoid an environment. Generally, lower-load environments produce less negative arousal and are more pleasant and more controllable. We are therefore likely to approach these kinds of environments. Conversely, heavily loaded environments produce anxiety (negative arousal) and are unpleasant and less controllable. We are more likely to avoid such environments.[7] Consider scenario 1 and scenario 2 from the beginning of this chapter. If you had the chance to choose one of the two scenarios, which would you choose? Of the two, which produces the most positive arousal and is more pleasant and more controllable? Likewise, how do you feel about approaching or avoiding communication situations with people from different cultures? Because such situations may be highly loaded, you may prefer to avoid them.

Culture and the Natural Environment

Jon T. Lang, a professor of urban design at the University of Pennsylvania, has written extensively about the relationship between people, culture, and their environment. Lang explains that the natural, or *terrestrial,* environment includes the physical geography of the earth, its climate, and its natural processes. The terrestrial environment for every person is the planet Earth.[8] Environmental psychologist Richard Knopf maintains that the natural environment is valued differently by different people. A culture's relationship with nature is culture bound. According to Knopf, culture influences how much people value nature and the symbols they use to communicate about it. Aivilik Eskimos, notes Knopf, have more than a dozen different terms to describe the winds and different snow conditions. People perceive and create symbols of their environment according to their cultural experiences with it. Knopf argues that it is not the natural environment per se that generates affect, but rather the verbal and nonverbal symbols that we use to communicate about nature. Moreover, how a culture values and treats the natural environment can change quickly, especially if that culture experiences shifts in religion or dramatic advances in science and technology.[9] The twentieth century in the United States, for example, witnessed immense changes in how we treat the natural environment. Because of scientific and technological progress we now see the environment as something we control and dominate.

Although all cultures exist within specific terrestrial contexts, some aspects of the terrestrial environment exist in every culture, whereas others do not. Gravity, for example, exists everywhere on earth. However, oceans, lakes, streams, mountain ranges, deserts, valleys, trees, and forms of vegetation vary considerably across cultures. Indonesia is composed of more than thirteen thousand islands covering over 700,000 square miles. The vegetation of Indonesia is very diverse, with over forty thousand species of flowering plants, including five thousand species of orchids.[10] The country of Laos, in Southeast Asia, has a monsoonal climate in which heavy rainfall sometimes averages ninety inches a year.[11] In contrast, in some areas of South Yemen, in the southwest corner of the Arabian Peninsula, only four inches of rain fall in a given year. Some northern and eastern sections of the country can go without rain for years.[12] Russia is the largest country in the world (geographically), with a land mass of over 6.5 million square miles and dramatic climatic extremes. Northern Siberia is covered with permafrost; snowdrifts can reach as high as sixty feet, and little vegetation is found.[13] Norway's land mass is just over 100,000 square miles, just slightly larger than Arizona, and only 3 percent of the land is usable as farmland.[14] As the physical environment of a culture varies, so will the vocabulary of the culture. Cultures with different environments create verbal and nonverbal symbols that enable them to adapt to and communicate about their environment.

Lang asserts that the natural environment of any culture influences life in that culture. Physical and climatic aspects of the environment can restrict the kinds of activities that occur.[15] In many cultures, the pace of daily activities reflects the natural climate of the area. In some southern European countries (for example, Spain, southern Italy), during the warm-weather season, many shop owners close their stores from about midday until late afternoon to avoid working in the hottest part of the day, when the temperatures can rise above 100 degrees Fahrenheit. Most of the stores in these countries are not air conditioned. Often visitors from other countries, particularly the United States, interpret this custom as laziness. In reality, the store owners are simply adjusting to the conditions of their natural climate.

WORLD VIEWS OF THE NATURAL ENVIRONMENT

Harvard University sociologist Florence Kluckhohn says that cultures can be described as having one of three orientations toward nature: (1) seeing *people as subjugated to nature*; (2) seeing *people as an inherent part of nature*; or (3) seeing *people as dominant over nature.*[16] A culture's orientation toward nature affects how people within that culture communicate about nature and organize their daily activities. Knowing and understanding a particular culture's orientation toward nature is a step in becoming a competent intercultural communicator.

Irwin Altman and Martin Chemers argue that in cultures in which nature is viewed as supreme, people believe they are at the mercy of an omnipotent nature. According to Altman and Chemers, in such cultures, nature is perceived as a dominant and unmanageable power. In biblical times, and even more recently, the natural environment and nature were viewed as threatening and dangerous. Altman and Chemers note that Western fairy tales are replete with references to such environmental features as "dark forests," where danger is lurking at every corner.[17] In her research on East India, Rebecca Jo Bishop found that many East Indians believe that the elements of the natural environment dictate the health and well-being of the people. Indeed, astrologers play an important role in India as the people believe that nothing in nature is accidental and that the universe and all living components have a fundamental order, over which they have no control.[18]

Kluckhohn claims that many cultures attempt a balancing act with nature and try to live in harmony with it. Indeed, argue Altman and Chemers, in these types of cultures, the natural environment is seen as orderly and cyclical. The days and seasons recur regularly, and natural events repeat themselves in consistent patterns. People and environment are viewed as one, changing together in what Altman and Chemers describe as a timeless mutual relationship.[19] Reick and Ogura hold that in many Eastern societies, nature is perceived as an ally that people draw on for spiritual support. The people of the island nation of Sri Lanka, which lies twenty miles off the southern coast of India, attempt a balancing act with nature. According to Reick and Ogura, their belief has its roots in Buddhism, which professes equality among all living things.[20] The Japanese are well known for their attempt to harmonize their relationship with nature, which can be seen in Japanese art forms such as gardening, flower arrangements, and haiku poetry. Altman and Chemers assert that the pygmies of Zaire, Africa, view themselves as an intrinsic part of the rain forest in which they dwell. To them, the forest is their mother and father, with whom they communicate on a personal basis.[21]

Kluckhohn's third orientation is seen in many Western societies, in which people believe that nature is something to be controlled, domesticated, and subjugated.[22] According to Altman and Chemers, some scholars attribute this view to Judeo-Christian doctrine, in which God is seen as the creator of the universe, who put humans on the earth to do his will. People are not just part of the environment, like trees, plants, or animals, but are of divine origin. Such philosophies have led to a separation between humans and the environment. When the scientific revolution developed, nature was seen as mechanistic, further separating people from nature. Through technology, buildings, and modern agricultural methods, humans were able to dominate their natural setting to their liking. In the United States, people separate themselves from nature and believe they have the power, and even the right, to dominate nature in just about any way they can. Many of our proudest achievements (for example, the moon landing, dams, indoor sports facilities) are based on conquering or exploiting nature. As in other countries in which European settlement has occurred, the environment is seen as an entity to be conquered. Much of Australia's economic activity is based on the extraction of natural resources such as timber, minerals, natural gas, and oil.[23]

CULTURE AND NATURAL DISASTERS

A culture's relationship with nature can be seen in how it deals with natural disasters. Whether drought, tornadoes, hurricanes, floods, or earthquakes, natural disasters occur in all cultures. How people manage such disasters is shaped by their culture and its view of nature. Moreover, many times when natural disasters strike, people from all over the world come together to help. Understanding the stricken culture's relationship with nature can facilitate communication between those directly affected and those offering aid and comfort. Ironically, natural disasters provide an opportunity for intercultural communication.

One model of human responses to natural disasters, reviewed by Sorenson and White, segregates cultures into three types: (1) *folk or preindustrial,* (2) *transitional,* and (3) *industrial.* Preindustrialized cultures, such as Nigeria, Malawi, and rural China, are characterized by primarily rural agrarian land use, have low income and literacy levels, underdeveloped communication systems, and simple technology. In these cultures, land use is primarily farming in small plots of land. Housing is typically adobe or mud. Many preindustrialized cultures believe in a harmonious relationship with nature. According to Sorenson and White, these societies have a low level of resource use, low material wealth, and less exposure to hazard risk; hence they are the least vulnerable to catastrophic natural events. They display resonance with the environment and have great resilience to most natural hazards. Although most people in most cultures believe that natural disasters are random occurrences, individuals in preindustrial cultures are more likely to perceive environmental hazards as cyclical or clustered than do people in industrialized societies.[24]

According to Sorenson and White, transitional societies like Sri Lanka, rural Turkey, and Brazil are characterized by rural-to-urban migration. These cultures may be investing in industry, may be seeing shifts from labor to capital-intensive land use, and may have low to moderate income, basic-level literacy rates, developing communication systems, and some trade. Land use may be semimechanized, and housing is unreinforced concrete and frame. Many transitional societies view nature as dominant. They have more wealth and more people living in high-risk areas than preindustrialized societies. Sorenson and White claim that because of their marginal economic status, which restricts their ability to prevent and recover from loss, these cultures are quite vulnerable to hazards, and their adaptability to disaster is low. Like preindustrialized cultures, people in transitional societies are more likely to perceive natural disasters as cyclical than are people in industrialized cultures.[25]

Industrial societies like Great Britain, urban Japan, and Australia are characterized by primarily urban land use. According to Sorenson and White, these cultures are capital-intensive and heavily mechanized and have high income and literacy levels, highly developed communication systems, and high trade. Land use is urban, suburban, residential, and industrial. Agriculture is highly mechanized, with large corporate farming operations. Contemporary architecture and housing in many industrialized societies is earthquake-resistant. These types of cultures believe that they are dominant over nature in a master/slave relationship. Although these societies have increased their exposure to natural disasters through intensive land use, their advanced technologies and greater wealth reduce the overall risk. Resilience is low, but different from that of transitional societies because vulnerability to disaster is decreased.[26]

The Built Environment

Jon Lang explains that the built environment of any culture consists mainly of adaptations to the terrestrial environment, including architecture, housing, lighting, and landscaping. The built environment artificially changes natural patterns

The built environment facilitates and restricts human behavior patterns.
(Emilio A. Mercado/ Picture Cube)

of behavior, heat, light, sound, odors, and human communication. Hence, the built environment affects the interaction between people and the natural environment. Moreover, many of these changes are specifically designed to facilitate or restrict human interaction. The built environment is not random; it is an intentionally designed pattern of spatial relationships between objects and objects, objects and people, and people and people. The built environment organizes and manages human communication between people and varies considerably across cultures.[27]

Lang notes that while sometimes designed for purely aesthetic reasons, the built environment is typically structured for specific activities. Classrooms, for example, are designed for a specific kind of communication. The size of the room, the positioning of the blackboards, and so forth, are all fashioned to facilitate interaction between teacher and student. Culture affects how the built environment is designed. Amos Rapoport argues that the interior of any given built environment influences and directs the way activities are carried out, how the family is structured, how gender roles are played, attitudes toward privacy, and the overall process of social interaction. Moreover, says Rapoport, how the built environment is planned and constructed reflects the values, motivations, and resources of the culture in which it exists. The overall economic, political, and legal system of a particular culture affects how that culture designs its built environment, including homes, schools, government, and private business buildings. As the built environments of cultures differ, so do communication patterns.[28]

Lang argues that the degree of ease or difficulty afforded by the built environment when moving from one place to another is a major predictor of human communication patterns. People are more likely to communicate with each other in those environments in which access to others is facilitated by the built environment than in environments in which access is restricted.[29] Anthropologist Edward Hall has identified three fundamental types of layout patterns in built environments: (1) *fixed-feature space*, (2) *semifixed-feature space*, and (3) *informal space*. Fixed-feature space is defined by immovable or permanent fixtures, such as walls, floors, and windows. Semifixed space includes that which is movable (usually within fixed-feature space), such as furniture and seating. Informal space is perceptual and varies according to the movement of the interactants. Informal space lasts only as long as the interactants communicate; it is not stated space and is usually outside the awareness of the people interacting.[30]

The variability of fixed, semifixed, or informal space influences human communication. Some environments must be restructured for certain kinds of activities, whereas others need not be adjusted at all. According to Lang, these kinds of environments are called adaptable or flexible. For example, in an adaptable fixed-feature space such as a gymnasium, many kinds of activities—sporting events, gym classes, commencement ceremonies, dances, plays, speeches, and so forth—can occur without any changes to the fixed features. In a flexible semifixed-feature space, changes are made to accommodate certain kinds of activities. Some schools and office buildings, for example, have portable walls. Informal (or dynamic) space between people is controlled, regulated, and managed by the nature of the relationship between the interactants.[31]

In addition to classifying fixed, semifixed, and informal space, Hall also developed a four-level classification of social distances. Hall argues that the physical environment guides behavior and the way that people define the space between themselves and others. Hall's classification scheme was modeled after that of ethologists (people who study animal behavior) who observed the various distances that animals maintain in their environments. Hall maintains that spatial distance between people is a vehicle for communication, much like that of sight, sound, smell, and touch. As distance decreases, people can see, hear, touch, and smell others differently than when distance increases. As the distance between interactants increases, the available visual, auditory, olfactic, thermal, and kinesthetic information decreases. As distance increases, the privacy of the person increases, but the privacy of the interaction decreases.[32]

Hall's four levels of social distance are (1) *intimate*, (2) *personal*, (3) *social-consultative*, and (4) *public*. Intimate distance is reserved for close, intimate contact, including touching. In this distance there is much visual, auditory, and olfactic sensation. In the United States, intimate distance is 9 to 18 inches and is usually reserved for highly personal relationships. The second type, personal distance, is 1.5 to 4 feet. This is sometimes called "arm's length" distance because a comfortable distance between interactants is literally about one human arm's length. Social-consultative distance is the spacing people practice at casual gatherings and in working situations. In the United States, this distance is 4 to 12 feet. In social distance, there is a more formal atmosphere. Public distance is used for talking across a room and for public speaking situations. In the United States, this distance extends from 12 feet and beyond. There is little olfactic sensation in this distance.[33]

To be sure, intimate, personal, social, and public distances vary by culture, and Hall's classification may not be universal. Hall argues that other factors, such as the relationship between interactants or external environmental factors, may influence distances between people. In addition, the built environment plays a key role in how space is used. Smaller, more confined spaces, insists Hall, increase interaction distances, whereas larger environments motivate people to adopt smaller distances. Lustig and Koester note, for example, that people in so-called high-contact cultures (Arabs, Latin Americans, southern Europeans) tend to use closer interaction distances than people in low-contact-oriented cultures. People in the United States, for example, prefer greater distances between themselves and others than do persons living in many Latin American cultures. People from colder climates have a tendency to use large physical distances when they communicate. Conversely, people from warmer climates tend to use small physical distances. Northern European cultures (for example, England, Germany, Scandinavia) are said to have larger personal space "bubbles" than southern European (for example, Greece, Italy, Spain).[34] In some Middle Eastern cultures, people stand close enough to smell each other's breath. Aiello has reviewed several studies and has found that Indonesians used less space than Australians and were more likely to initiate conversations with strangers. Other studies comparing Americans with other cultures have found no differences—that is, they share common spatial be-havior patterns. American, Australian, British, and South African young adults placed figures representing mental patients at approximately the same distances. In a similar study, American, British, Scottish, Swedish, and Pakistani subjects all rated different seating distances similarly for intimacy level. Another study found that when bilingual Japanese subjects spoke in their native tongue, they sat farther from a same-gender, same-nationality confederate than either Americans or bilin-gual Venezuelans. But when all subjects spoke English, the three groups approxi-mated the American seating pattern.[35]

Cross-Cultural Comparisons of Housing

The use of space is an integral part of every human being's communication. Deci-sions about where and when to perform our daily activities are based on spatial patterns that are learned culturally. We become so accustomed to our spatial defi-nitions and boundaries that many of us experience anxiety when forced to inter-act in novel or unusual environments. Many people complain that they do not sleep well when outside their regular home environments. How we organize space within the built environment says much about our culture, its values, and its way of life. Perhaps more than any other aspect of the built environment, *the home* presents a particularly rich source of information about a culture's perception and use of space.

JAPANESE HOUSING

In the past 150 years much has been written in the West about Japanese architec-ture, especially the Japanese home. Since World War II, great changes have oc-curred in Japanese housing. Many of the traditional Japanese homes, in which most of the daily activities occurred in one room, have been replaced by Western-style homes and highrises in which space is defined by walls.[36]

Houses of various types and styles can be found side by side in contemporary Japan. According to Kiyosi Sieke and Charles Terry, a fair number of homes still ex-ist that reflect traditional Japanese architecture dating back to the eighteenth cen-tury. Other homes reveal clear European influences. Many others, perhaps the majority, have almost completely adopted a Western look. Sieke and Terry believe that the design of contemporary Japanese homes has been influenced by the breakdown of the traditional family system in Japan. Many young people are leav-ing the traditional multigeneration family home situation and moving to apart-ments or small houses of their own. In homes in which two or three generations still live together, the main part of the house is intended for the second-generation husband and wife. A special section of the house may be designated for the family elders, and another section especially for the children. In many homes like this, the elders' section is organized and decorated in traditional Japanese style, the children's section will be completely Western, and the husband and wife's part a combination of the two styles. This type of home was unheard of before the war.[37]

Although many contemporary Japanese houses reflect a Westernized design, the Japanese attitude about life has not changed. Charles Terry, past editor of *The Japan Architect,* asserts that an essential point about Japanese houses and Japanese culture is the gap between the public and private Japanese person. According to Terry, the impression that a Japanese presents to society may be very different from what the person actually thinks or feels. In public settings, Japanese act according to clearly prescribed social rules. In private, Japanese think and act as they please. This philosophy is reflected in the contemporary Japanese home and its Western influence. According to Terry, most Japanese who build Western-style homes do so because it is fashionable and expected of them. Terry alleges that most Japanese probably prefer the traditional, however.[38] Likewise, Japanese author and scholar of traditional Japanese urban architecture Atsushi Ueda argues that the contemporary Japanese house is caught between tradition and modernism.[39]

Tetsuro Yoshida, one of Japan's leading contemporary architects, writes that because of the belief in harmony with nature, traditional Japanese homes fit unobtrusively into the landscape, not appearing human-made. The traditional Japanese house is a detached house with a garden. Yoshida states that among traditional Japanese, there is an intimate relationship between the house and garden.[40]

Since ancient times, the Japanese garden has been considered more as a work of art than as a simple plot of land where flowers and vegetables are cultivated. In Japan, the garden is treated as a painting or sculpture to be appreciated from some distance. Yoshida describes the traditional Japanese garden as a quiet monochrome compared to the colorful European or American garden.[41] However, writes Ueda, one seldom encounters anything resembling a proper Japanese garden in contemporary Japanese homes. Instead, one of the most visible features of the modern Japanese home is a car or a garage.[42]

In traditional Japanese homes, writes Ueda, rooms are separated by *shoji* or *fusuma*—opaque sliding screens. *Shoji* panels are very lightweight—usually made of cedar lattice with translucent paper stretched over it—and are easily slid open or closed with one finger. The purpose of, and major advantage to, *shoji* is that they can easily be removed to convert an entire floor of a house into a single open room. The traditional Japanese house is fundamentally a one-room home partitioned by *shoji.* Because of the versatility of *shoji,* the plan of a house is flexible, with the divisions of the rooms easily changed. According to Ueda, this is the major characteristic of space allocation in the Japanese home.[43]

Ueda alleges that regardless of how Westernized they may have become, the Japanese have not abandoned the custom of taking off their shoes when entering a house and sitting on the floor. The Japanese *yuka* floor developed as a result of this custom. The *yuka* is actually a raised floor that was developed to maintain sanitary conditions. Even contemporary homes have a raised floor.

According to Ueda, the size of a room in a Japanese home is measured by its number of *tatami* mats. The *tatami* mat is a modular floor mat made from straw and is used to cover the floor for sitting and sleeping. The principle room in a traditional Japanese home is the reception room, also called the sitting room. The average size of the room is eight to ten mats. The room usually faces the garden and incorporates an alcove, called the *tokonoma*. According to Ueda, the *tokonoma* is a recess arranged with staggered shelves, artistic ornaments, hanging scrolls, and perhaps a flower arrangement. The *tokonoma* is the most sacred place in the home, holding a sort of spiritual or moral place. The space immediately in front of the *tokonoma* is the most honored place in a traditional Japanese home.[44]

Two rooms not much discussed, but of primary importance in the Japanese home, are the kitchen and bathroom. The kitchen, even in modern Japanese homes, belongs to the wife. The kitchen is her place, not to be disturbed by other household members, and not to be entered or even observed by guests. The kitchen is a private place. In both traditional and contemporary Japanese homes, the bath is of utmost importance and is thought of as a time of recuperation and solitude. The bathroom, which is in a separate room from the toilet, consists of two separate places, one for bathing and the other for soaking. Initially, the Japanese will wash themselves with soap under a shower that is next to the bathtub. Following the shower, the Japanese will crouch in the tub, which is designed for sitting, not lying. The water is warmed and sometimes scented with flowers or lemons. The purpose is to relax and soothe the body. The water is kept for several days and used by all family members.

Japanese architect and author Atsushi Ueda maintains that the traditional Japanese house is a thing of the past. However, the contemporary Japanese house, he writes, is caught between tradition and modernism and is "nervously confessing its own insecurity."[45] Though dramatic changes have occurred in Japan in the last fifty years, much of the psychology driving the design of the traditional Japanese house lives in contemporary Japanese people.

AMERICAN NAVAJO HOUSING

Susan Kent, an ethnoarchaeologist, has studied extensively the use of space in Native American Navajo housing. In her pioneering work, Kent compared the use of space across three American cocultural groups, including Native American Navajos, Spanish-Americans, and Euro-Americans. Of particular interest is her work with Navajos. According to Kent's studies, many of the Navajos live in remote parts of reservations and have very limited contact with white Americans. Traditional Navajo families speak mostly Navajo and live in aboriginal dwellings called hogans. Hogans typically consist of three large converging support posts that interlock at the top with smaller support posts. The hogan is covered with earth. In addition to the hogan, the Navajo camp may consist of a wooden ramada (open porch), a wood-chip storage area, a horse corral, and small fields of corn. The hogan is occupied in the winter, and the ramada is used in the summer. The hogan is used for storage during the summer months. Water is hauled in from tribal wells. There is no outhouse. Some camps will have a sweathouse.[46]

In her research, Kent discovered that the space inside the hogan (see Figure 4-1) was used differently by the occupants according to their gender. The men

FIGURE 4-1   Navajo Hogan and Ramada

SOURCE: Based on graphics in S. Kent, *Analyzing Activity Areas: An Ethnoarchaeological Study of the Use of Space* (Albuquerque: University of New Mexico Press, 1984), p. 72.

stayed almost exclusively in one half of the hogan, and the women and children used the other half. Food preparation always took place in the half occupied by the women and children, but food was consumed in the half occupied by men.[47]

Kent writes that, in contrast to the gender-defined spaces inside the hogan, outdoors and in the ramada both genders of all ages performed activities at the same locale. Not only did both genders use the same activity area outside the hogan, but different types of activities were performed at the same place, including stripping hides, weaving, butchering, and washing. An individual's mood and season seemed to be the only factors affecting the activity areas of the Navajo camp.[48]

Kent observed that the use of space within the ramada differed significantly from that within the hogan. The men were active in all parts of the ramada. The women and children also used most of the ramada without restriction. Chairs and beds were used by each family member, regardless of age or gender. Kent also observed that the Navajos seemed to place little emphasis on the differences between the genders, and did not prescribe a traditional division of labor seen in many "Euro-American" homes. Moreover, asserts Kent, the Navajos had only a few gender-specific activities or gender-specific artifacts, and very few single-functional activity areas or artifacts. In fact, the only gender-specific activity areas used by the Navajos were in the hogan. Kent speculates that the reason for this is that the hogan is perceived as a sacred dwelling. According to Kent, the hogan is mentioned in important myths and prayers, and specific ceremonies must be conducted only in a hogan. Kent suggests that the circular hogan symbolizes the circular cosmos, whereas the rectangular ramada and the outdoors do not. The round, sacred hogan is divided into the same male and female areas as the round, sacred cosmos.[49]

HOUSING OF THE MARAKWET OF KENYA

The Marakwet people are a part of the Kalenjin tribe of western Kenya. In 1986, Henrietta Moore published an extensive anthropological study of the Marakwet people, focusing specifically on their use of space. The following discussion of the Marakwet is based on Moore's analysis.[50]

According to Moore, Marakwet country is one of the most secluded parts of Kenya. The Marakwet are divided into a number of villages called *kor*. The village is comprised of family compounds consisting of a family house, a "store" (storage structure), and a goat house. The Marakwet people are emotionally attached to the land and see themselves and the land they occupy as inseparable.[51]

Marakwet houses and their associated structures (stores and goat houses) are the only form of built environment in the Marakwet village. There is no physically constructed space outside of the family compound. According to Moore:

> The nature of village organisation is an interlocking set of social units which are also territorial units. At every moment, the life of the villages focuses down onto the household, and that of the household expands out to meet the world of the village: a world where social relations are also spatial relations.[52]

The Marakwet insist that a house must never face out over the valley. In addition, the houses within a particular compound must always face each other. The majority of Marakwet houses are subcircular, with a single entrance and a window (see Figure 4-2). They are constructed of wattle, a fabrication of poles interwoven with branches or reeds, and daub, a covering of some type, usually earth. The roofs are thatched. In the dry season, the houses are virtually indistinguishable from the natural terrain.

In her study, Moore observed that each house is divided into three areas: a sleeping area, a cooking area, and an area beneath the roof store. The bed is typically placed behind the door and is considered the most private place in the house. The fireplace/cooking place is just behind and to the side of the center post. The

FIGURE 4-2   The Interior of a Traditional Marakwet House in the Sibou Village

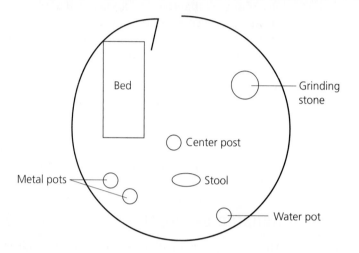

SOURCE: Based on H. L. Moore, *Space, Text, and Gender: An Anthropological Study of the Marakwet of Kenya,* *2/e.* © 1996 The Guilford Press. Used by permission.

area beneath the roof store is on the opposite side from the bed. Most family compounds within villages contain at least one house and a store or goat house. Like the houses, the stores are made of wattle and daub and are always elevated on stone stilts with a thatched roof. Stores must always be placed to the back of the family compound. Every Marakwet man starts with one house. After he marries, he may build a second house. Ideally, the second house would be for his wife.[53]

From her observations, Moore concluded that the internal organization of the Marakwet houses is based on the social relationships between family members—that is, men and women are segregated by space and activity. In Marakwet society, women are subordinate to men. Men spend the majority of their time away from the house, whereas women spend the majority of their time within the family house and compound. Men use the house primarily for sleeping and storage, whereas women use the house for cooking, childbearing, child rearing, entertaining, and family maintenance. Men spend most of their time tending to the herds or attending meetings with the other men in the village. Moore notes that because the women spend most of their time in the house, they exert considerable control over its possessions. Fellow villagers must ask for and receive permission to enter a house or to remove something from it. Although Marakwet women are subordinate to Marakwet men, they wield a great deal of power within the boundaries of the household.[54]

Moore explains that of particular importance to the Marakwet is the organization and disposal of refuse, which she argues also reflects a clear male/female dichotomy. The majority of refuse for the Marakwet is either ash, animal dung, or chaff (seed coverings). These three types of refuse hold symbolic meaning and have distinct disposal locations. Ash is the result of cooking and burning—that is, women's work. Hence ash is associated with womanliness and female fertility. Ash is always thrown behind the house. Chaff is placed in front of the compound, and dung is placed near the animal compound. Women are buried near the chaff because women's work is to dig and remove chaff. Men are buried near the animal dung because their work is to herd the cattle. Goat dung is symbolic of male fertility. The Marakwet are adamant about not mixing the three types of refuse because of their relationship to burial locations and their symbolic meaning.[55]

Privacy

Most social scientists agree that human beings, regardless of culture, are a social species with an innate propensity to affiliate and communicate with other human beings. At the same time, however, human beings cannot tolerate extended physical contact with other humans and need privacy.[56] According to Alan Westin, these same competing needs are found in the animal kingdom. Westin maintains that virtually all animals seek periods of time when they desire the company of other animals and other times when they seek individual seclusion.[57]

Although the need for privacy is innate and universal, the degree to which an individual human feels the need for seclusion varies considerably across cultures. For example, Americans value privacy so much that they have made it law. Junior high school students learn that Amendment 4 to the Constitution of the United States (part of the Bill of Rights) guarantees all citizens the right to be secure in their persons, houses, papers, and effects against unreasonable search and seizure. Americans literally believe that they have a *right to privacy.* Anthropologists contend that individuals in virtually all cultures engage in a continuous process of seeking privacy at some times and companionship at others. In this sense, privacy is culture bound and is considered a learned response to particular social situations. Irwin Altman argues that privacy is a "boundary control" process in which people sometimes make themselves accessible to others and sometimes close themselves off from others. The behavioral and environmental strategies that people use to accomplish this process are defined by culture.[58]

Westin maintains that privacy is a necessary condition for acceptable social behavior. In some circumstances, privacy is literally required in order to not violate cultural norms. Most cultures specify (sometimes legally) that certain behaviors must be enacted in private. Such rules and norms vary from culture to culture.[59]

Jon Lang states that privacy is closely linked to the built environment because it can be designed or maneuvered in a number of ways to promote, encourage, or restrict communication with others.[60] In his seminal work on privacy, Alan Westin identified four types of privacy: (1) *solitude,* being free from observation by others; (2) *intimacy,* being with another person but free from the outside world; (3) *anonymity,* being unknown, even in a crowd; and (4) *reserve,* using psychological barriers

The desire for and access to privacy varies across cultures.
(© James Neuliep)

to control unwanted intrusion.[61] These different forms of privacy serve different purposes, including personal autonomy, release of emotions, self-evaluation, and communication. Westin argues that the type and degree of privacy desired depends on the type of behavior in which one engages, the culture, and the individual personality traits of the individual. The location of sexual intercourse, for example, may vary from culture to culture. In cultures like the United States, where the nuclear family resides in a walled house that provides for privacy, sexual intercourse is likely to occur within the household. In cultures in which the extended family lives together in a communal dwelling without clear spatial divisions, sexual intercourse probably occurs outside the built environment.[62]

Extending on Westin's four categories of privacy, Darhl Pedersen identified six types of privacy: (1) *reserve,* an unwillingness to be with others, especially strangers; (2) *isolation,* a desire to be alone and away from others; (3) *solitude,* being alone and free from observation by others; (4) *intimacy with family,* being alone with members of one's own family; (5) *intimacy with friends,* being alone with friends; and (6) *anonymity,* the desire to go unnoticed in a crowd. With the exception of isolation and solitude, these types of privacy are independent—that is, one type of privacy does not necessarily go with another. To measure the types of privacy preferred by individuals, Pedersen developed a privacy questionnaire (see box on facing page), which has also been used in cross-cultural comparisons. A privacy profile may be expected to be unique for a particular person or culture.[63]

PERCEPTIONS OF PRIVACY IN THE UNITED STATES

Although the United States literally legislates privacy, perceptions of privacy differ throughout the country and among microcultural groups. Moreover, attitudes about privacy have changed dramatically in the past decade or so. Clay Calvert, a

Self-Assessment 4-1

Pedersen's Dimensions of Privacy Questionnaire

To complete the questionnaire, indicate how often you engage in the activity or state represented in each statement by marking whether it (1) never, (2) rarely, (3) occasionally, (4) sometimes, (5) often, or (6) usually applies. Scoring procedures are outlined following the scale.

1. _____ I sometimes need to be alone and away from anyone.

2. _____ I would be reluctant to engage in a prolonged conversation with someone I had just met.

3. _____ I like to go on vacation with just my family.

4. _____ I like my friends to sympathize with me and to cheer me up when I am depressed.

5. _____ I have to be encouraged to put on a stunt at a party even when others are doing the same sort of thing.

6. _____ I want my thoughts and ideas to be known by others.

7. _____ I'd like to work on a farm all by myself for a summer.

8. _____ I like to be the center of attention in my group.

9. _____ I like living in an apartment house because it prevents you from being alone.

10. _____ I do not like to be disturbed when I am at home engaged in a family activity.

11. _____ It would be fun to be alone on a high mountain peak, surveying the scene below.

12. _____ I like to be alone at home, where it is peaceful and quiet.

13. _____ I like to be at home with nobody else around.

14. _____ I have a special person that I can confide in.

15. _____ I like to attend meetings if I do not know others.

16. _____ At parties I am more likely to sit by myself than to join the crowd.

17. _____ I would like to have a mountain cabin where my family and I could be alone together.

18. _____ I like my friends to fuss over me when I am sick.

19. _____ I like other people to notice me when I am in public.

—Continued

20. _____ It pleases me when my accomplishments obtain recognition from my friends.

21. _____ I reserve displays of physical affection for a select few friends and family.

22. _____ I'd be happy living all alone in a cabin in the woods.

23. _____ Sometimes I like to be alone where I cannot be observed by anyone.

24. _____ I tell my problems only to my family.

25. _____ My personal relations with people are cool and distant.

26. _____ I think I'd like the kind of work a forest ranger does.

27. _____ I prefer doing things with only my family.

28. _____ I like to meet new people.

29. _____ Whenever possible, I avoid being in a crowd.

30. _____ I like being in a room by myself.

SCORING: Reverse your score for items 6, 8, 9, 15, 19, and 28, then follow the directions below.

Add your responses to items 1, 12, 13, 23, and 30. This represents your Solitude score.
Add your responses to items 4, 14, 18, 19, and 20. This represents your Intimacy with Friends score.
Add your responses to items 2, 16, 25, 28, and 29. This represents your Reserve score.
Add your responses to items 7, 9, 11, 22, and 26. This represents your Isolation score.
Add your responses to items 3, 10, 17, 24, and 27. This represents your Intimacy with Family score.
Add your responses to items 5, 6, 8, 15, and 21. This represents your Anonymity score.

Scores of 20 or higher on these subscales indicate a greater preference for the specific type of privacy.

SOURCE: "Privacy Instrument" reproduced with permission of author and publisher from D. M. Pedersen, "Dimensions of Privacy," _Perceptual and Motor Skills_, 48 (1979), 1291–1297. © Perceptual and Motor Skills 1979.

professor who holds degrees in communication and law, argues that Americans live in a "voyeur nation." A voyeur is one who seeks sexual stimulation by visual means or who is a prying observer of sordid or scandalous material. Calvert maintains that voyeurism has become a central theme of American entertainment and culture. He argues that the American public has access to information, not originally intended for public consumption, made available over television and the Internet, in what he calls "mediated voyeurism."

Calvert categorizes four types of mediated voyeurism. The first type is *video vérité voyeurism;* that is, unrehearsed and unscripted moments of actual events filmed by a video camera. The Rodney King beating and television program *Cops* are included as examples of video vérité voyeurism. The second type is *reconstruction voyeurism,* where some actual event is dramatized for the benefit of the viewer. The television show *America's Most Wanted* is an example of reconstructed voyeurism. The third type is called *tell-all/show-all voyeurism* and is typical of television shows such as *Jerry Springer.* Finally, the fourth type is *sexual voyeurism,* characterized by explicit Internet sites where hidden cameras are put into bathrooms, bedrooms, up women's skirts, and so on. Calvert maintains that the American voyeur mentality has serious implications for an individual's constitutional right to privacy, and he is not particularly optimistic about the future of privacy rights in the United States.[64]

Sociologist Sherry Turkle argues there is a tension in American culture between the individual's desire for and right to privacy and the invasion of personal privacy brought on by the computer age.[65] Because so much personal information about people is stored electronically, it is relatively easy to access, including virtually all of one's financial and medical data. According to Carole Lan, a paid Internet searcher:

> In a few hours, sitting at my computer, beginning with no more than your name and address, I can find out what you do for a living, the names and ages of your spouses and children, what kind of car you drive, the value of your house and how much in taxes you pay on it.[66]

Different groups of people throughout the United States have different concerns about privacy. Many college students, for example, are concerned about what type of information, and how much, their college or university can disclose about them. The 1974 Family Educational Rights and Privacy Act, also known as the Buckley Amendment, forbids colleges to disclose academic records without student approval. In October 1998, Congress amended the act in order to allow colleges and universities to inform parents any time a student under the age of twenty-one violates drug or alcohol laws. The privacy act still prohibits colleges and universities from releasing students' grades, but many colleges and universities are routinely calling parents and informing them about drug and alcohol policy violations. Moreover, colleges are not required to alert students when they have notified their parents. The new laws also allow colleges to disclose information regarding any violent crimes committed by students, and the 1998 amendment now permits a college to release a student's grades to a court.[67]

African Americans seem to have different views on privacy than do whites. For example, Gandy reports that educated African Americans extend broad privacy rights to individuals and, unlike whites, do not view information-gathering techniques used by businesses as invasions of privacy. In addition, when African Americans are concerned about privacy, it is because they sense that a loss of control over personal information renders them more susceptible to discrimination, especially in terms of employment, insurance, and credit. According to Gandy, African Americans are most concerned about privacy issues as they relate to relationships between individuals and the government, but no more so than other groups (e.g., whites).[68]

CROSS-CULTURAL VARIATIONS ON PRIVACY

Pedersen's privacy questionnaire is useful in determining the privacy preferences of a variety of cultural groups. Knowing a culture's preferences about privacy can help you determine when and where communication can and should take place. For example, if you know when and how a culture desires privacy, you would know when to restrict communication with persons from that culture. Invasions of privacy are negatively perceived across cultures and will be interpreted as a sign of incompetent communication.

Pedersen and Frances found that within the United States, men tended to score higher on isolation, whereas women scored higher on intimacy with family and intimacy with friends. People from the mountain states region preferred isolation, anonymity, and solitude more than people from the western states, where a preference for solitude ranked significantly higher. Persons from the Southeast showed a preference for isolation and a high preference for anonymity.[69]

Rustemli and Kokdemir administered Petersen's privacy questionnaire to Turkish students. The overall preferences of the Turkish subjects for solitude, isolation, anonymity, and intimacy were virtually the same as Pedersen and Frances's results with Americans. Preferences for reserve and intimacy with family differed across cultures, however. In contrast to American subjects, Turkish subjects demonstrated a lower preference for reserve and for intimacy with family members. The Turkish subjects preferred intimacy with friends over intimacy with family. This preference may be due to family structure in Turkish culture, in which the family is an intact group with intense concern for children. In the typical Turkish family, the children develop a very intimate and dependent, but restricted, relationship with their parents but have limited intimate communication with them. Issues of personal identity and intimacy are directed toward peers rather than toward parents.[70]

In referring to a paper delivered by Clifford Geertz, Westin describes the living arrangements of the people living in Java. According to Westin, the Javanese live in small bamboo-walled houses that have no interior walls or doors. Except for the bathroom, there are no private areas. Westin claims that because the Javanese have no physical privacy, they have developed a kind of psychological privacy in their everyday behaviors and communication. They speak softly, conceal their feelings, are emotionally restrained, and are indirect in their verbal and nonverbal communication.[71]

Irwin Altman has reviewed the privacy behaviors of several groups, including the Mehinacu Indians, a tribal culture in central Brazil. According to Altman, the Mehinacu live in communal villages, and there is virtually no privacy in their houses. To find privacy, the Mehinacu leave the village for extended periods of time, even years. Newly born children and their parents are isolated from the village in their homes for several weeks or months. Young boys are required to stay within the home behind a wooden partition and have virtually no communication with anyone. Food and bathing materials are brought to them. Altman states that during their seclusion, the boys are taught to speak quietly, are not allowed to play, and must abstain from emotional displays. Young women also go through a similar seclusion after their initial menstruation. Other forms of seclusion occur after the death of a spouse. Altman notes that the typical Mehinacu Indian may spend as much as seven to eight years of his or her life in isolation from others.[72]

While the Javanese and Mehinacu cultures may be characterized by having minimal privacy, the Balinese and Tuareg cultures desire maximum privacy. According to Altman, the Balinese live in houses surrounded by high walls and narrow doorways. The Tuareg, a Muslim culture in North Africa, wear clothes that cover the entire body except for the eyes, including a flowing outer garment that reaches from the shoulder to the ankle. A veil and headdress that cover the forehead and the bridge over the nose are worn continuously throughout life. Altman suggests that the veil is not unlike a door that allows some to enter and keeps others out.[73]

Hesselink, Mullen, and Rouse have studied privacy in Moroccan culture. They claim that Moroccans value privacy as a way of protecting themselves from the external environment and keep private the things they value most. The outside surfaces of Moroccan homes, for example, are very plain so as to expose little information about the people who live there. Hesselink notes that the walls of the homes are so tall that the only way to see into a home is to walk from the rooftop of one house to another. Moroccan women are also considered private and are hidden when males who are not a part of the immediate family enter a Moroccan home.[74]

The built environment is only one way a culture defines its communication with others. The way in which a particular culture achieves privacy involves a complex formula of environmental, verbal, nonverbal, and cultural factors. Focusing on only one of these dimensions provides a distorted view of the privacy regulation system of any culture.

Time

In addition to its physical and spatial components, the built environment also contains a perceptual/temporal feature. Human communication occurs in a physical space and in *perceptual time*. Edward Hall is well known for his discussion of time across cultures. Hall asserts:

> Time talks. It speaks more plainly than words. The message it conveys comes through loud and clear. Because it is manipulated less consciously, it is subject to less distortion than the spoken language. It can shout truth where words lie.[75]

Like other components of the environment, the perception and use of time is cultural. Unlike other elements of the built environment, time is not physical or tangible; it is a *psychological* component of the environment. Regarding time, Hall categorizes cultures as either (1) *monochronic* or (2) *polychronic*. Monochronic- and polychronic-oriented cultures organize time and space differently. According to Hall, monochronic (M-time) orientations emphasize schedules, the compartmentalization and segmentation of measurable units of time. Conversely, polychronic (P-time) orientations see time as much less tangible and stress multiple activities, with little emphasis on scheduling. P-time cultures stress involvement of people and the completion of tasks as opposed to a strict adherence to schedules. Hall maintains that the two orientations are incompatible.[76]

In M-time cultures, such as the United States, time is thought of as almost physical, like something you can touch and hold in your hand. Time is treated like money. We talk of saving, spending, wasting, and losing time. Hall argues that for M-time people, time is linear and compartmentalized into discrete units (minutes, hours, days). The schedule is paramount in monochronic cultures. In M-time cultures, scheduling dictates just about every activity of every day. In some ways, scheduling is like a computer program, specifying what actions will be performed while prohibiting others. Moreover, asserts Hall, scheduling allows only a limited number of activities to be performed in one place at one time. In M-time cultures, people are concerned with doing only one activity at a time. How often have we said aloud, "I can only do one thing at a time!"[77]

Hall explains that by its very nature, scheduling segments people from one another and dictates how people conduct their relationships. Because time is viewed as so valuable, people with the most power and prestige are given the most time (and space) and are allowed more flexibility and less accountability with their time. Physicians, for example, are routinely late for appointments without sanction. Late or "no show" patients, on the other hand, may pay heavily for their inconsideration of the physician's time.

Hall maintains that although an M-time orientation is learned and completely arbitrary, it becomes so ingrained in people that they have no other way of thinking about their world. At an early age, children are taught the importance of time, scheduling, and promptness. Moreover, they are often punished if they fail to adhere to cultural standards regarding time. A child learns when to eat, nap, and play. In schools, subjects are taught at certain times of the day for a specific duration. Through compartmentalizing and segmenting time, a person's day is completely planned and scheduled, including sleep, work, leisure, and even sex. Hall notes that tardiness and missed appointments are a source of extreme anxiety for many M-timers. He points out that perhaps the most important consequence of M-time is that it *denies the natural context and progression of human communication.* Rather than completing an assignment or finishing a conversation, scheduling forces people into an artificial pattern and sequence of behavior. Many M-time cultures are low-context, including those of the United States, Germany, Scandinavia, Canada, France, and most of northern Europe.[78]

On the other hand, Hall argues that in P-time cultures, schedules are not important and are frequently broken. Polychronic people can do many things at once, and relationships take priority over schedules. P-timers are often distractible and tolerant of interruptions. In P-time cultures, time is not thought of as tangible, and a person may be engaged in several activities in the same space and with several people simultaneously. P-time people are more interested in completing the task at hand than in leaving it because of some predetermined schedule. Hall contends that people in P-time cultures are not slaves to schedules and are frequently late for appointments or may not show up at all. The guiding principle behind polychronic cultures is that the natural context, *in the present,* guides behavior. Many P-time cultures are high-context, including those of southern Europe, Latin America, and many African and Middle Eastern countries.[79]

CONSEQUENCES OF MONOCHRONIC AND POLYCHRONIC ORIENTATIONS

Monochronic people have a particularly difficult time adjusting to polychronic time–oriented cultures. To an M-timer, people in P-time cultures may appear disorganized or even lazy. Harris and Moran warn American businesspersons traveling to Arab countries that they may find themselves waiting for days or even weeks to meet with their Middle Eastern affiliates. *"Bukra insha Allah,"* meaning "Tomorrow, if God wills," is a favorite traditional Arab expression. Unlike M-timers, Arabs believe that time is controlled by Allah. Hence, when trying to schedule an appointment, the Arab may respond, *"Insha Allah,"* or "If Allah wills," and he means this quite literally. To the Arab, a person who tries to influence the future via scheduling is either insane or irreligious.[80]

M-time and P-time cultures organize their space much in the same way as they do their time. Hence, the M-timer has a specific space set aside for specific activities, and generally these are the only activities allowed in that space. In M-time office buildings, for example, people have their own private offices to conduct their business. In contrast, in P-time cultures, where multiple activities occur simultaneously, multiple activities are conducted in the same place. Keberlein describes the inside of the municipal building in a small Guatemala town that has no interior walls to cordon people off from each other. Instead, the building is one large room in which all of the town's municipal needs are handled. There may be one desk surrounded by many people vying for the attention of the local mayor, who seems to be interacting with two or three people simultaneously. No lines are formed, and people compete for the mayor's attention. The mayor probably is a very important and informed person in this town.[81] Hall has observed that in many P-time cultures there is a defined centralization of bureaucratic control. This is because the leaders interact with many people, and the people are informed because they interact with each other. Polychronic people tend to be well informed of each other's business. Hall argues that their involvement with each other is the essence of their existence. Consequently, P-time bureaucracies can be slow and difficult to penetrate unless one knows an "insider."[82]

A similar contrast can be seen in the homes of M-time and P-time cultures. In most M-time cultures, the home is carefully planned and organized. It is compartmentalized with individual rooms, each with its specific purpose (for example, kitchen, dining room, bedroom, laundry room, bathroom). In many P-time cultures, on the other hand, homes may be defined by one large living area. In traditional Japanese homes, for example, the main living area is a single room where the entire family eats, sleeps, and interacts as a group.

Some cultures possess elements of both M-time and P-time. Vandehey, Buerger, and Krueger explain that the Masai, a nomadic culture of Kenya, do not compartmentalize time into seconds, minutes, and hours but instead have specific periods of the day that are scheduled around the rising and setting sun and the feeding of their cattle. The typical Masai day begins just prior to sunrise, when the cattle go to the river to drink. This period is called "the red blood period" because of the color of the sunrise. The afternoon consists of a period of time when the "shadows lower themselves." The evening begins when "the cattle return from the river."[83]

According to Vandehey and her colleagues, the Masai have a unique way of classifying people by age. Rather than using a calendar of years like most cultures, the Masai belong to age sets. One's age set determines his or her privileges and responsibilities. Similarly, the duration of Masai seasons and months is determined by rainfall. A particular month lasts as long as the rains continue, and a new month does not begin until the rains have ceased.[84]

Intercultural Conversation

An Intercultural Conversation: Monochronic and Polychronic Cultures

Mr. Paul Bersik is the international sales representative for his computer equipment company. His most recent trip takes him to Saudi Arabia, where he is scheduled to meet with his Saudi counterpart, Abdul Arami. In the following scenario, Mr. Bersik comes face to face with P-time.

Mr. Bersik and his training team arrived in Saudi Arabia three days ago for a scheduled appointment with Mr. Arami. However, Mr. Arami has not yet met with Mr. Bersik or his team. Finally, a call to Mr. Bersik's hotel room indicates that Mr. Arami is prepared to meet with him. When Mr. Bersik arrives at the location, he is asked to wait outside Mr. Arami's office. As he waits, he notices many people entering and leaving Mr. Arami's office at a very quick pace. The hallways of this building are a hustle and bustle of activity, with people shuffling in and out of many rooms. Finally, after several hours, Mr. Bersik is called in to meet Mr. Arami.

Mr. Bersik: Ah, Mr. Arami, it's so good to finally see you. Gosh, I've been waiting for days. Did you forget our appointment?

Mr. Arami: Hello, Mr. Bersik. Please sit down. Everything is fine?

Mr. Bersik: Actually no . . . *(Phone rings)* . . . the problem is . . .

Mr. Arami: Excuse me . . . *(Takes the phone call and speaks in Arabic. After several minutes he concludes the phone conversation)* Yes, now . . . everything is fine?

Mr. Bersik: Well, actually, I've got a small problem. You see, the computer equipment you ordered . . . *(A staff person enters the room and hands Mr. Arami something to sign)*

Mr. Arami: Oh, excuse me . . . *(Signs the document)* Yes, now, everything is fine?

Mr. Bersik: As I was saying . . . all of the computer equipment you ordered is just sitting on a ship at the dock. I need your help in getting it unloaded. I mean, it's been there for two weeks!

Mr. Arami: Hmmm. I see . . . This is no problem.

Mr. Bersik: Well, if it sits in the heat much longer, it could be damaged. Could I get you to sign a work order to have it unloaded by Friday?

—Continued

Mr. Arami: There is no need for that. The job will get done, *insha Allah.*

Mr. Bersik: Well, could we set up some kind of deadline? You see, I have a staff of people here waiting to train your people on the equipment. I need to let them know when it will be ready. How about this Friday? Could we do it then? My people are here now, and they're waiting to begin training.

Mr. Arami: There is no great rush. We have lived for many generations without this equipment. We can wait a few more weeks, if necessary. This is not a problem. (*Two men enter the room and begin a conversation with Mr. Arami*)

There is little chance that Mr. Arami will sign any kind of work order for Mr. Bersik. Within the context of the Saudi culture, Mr. Bersik's behavior is inappropriate. His emphasis on deadlines is perceived by Mr. Arami as either insane or irreligious. Mr. Bersik is also distressed by the constant interruptions. To Mr. Arami, Mr. Bersik is in too much of a hurry. When Mr. Arami says to Mr. Bersik that the job will get done *"insha Allah,"* he means it quite literally. Unless God decrees it, a plan or schedule is useless. In the future, Mr. Bersik must learn that the Saudis' perception of time is much different from his own. Mr. Bersik is monochronic, whereas Mr. Arami operates from a polychronic time orientation. When he does business in Saudi Arabia, Mr. Bersik must understand the temporal feature of the culture.

SOURCE: The model for the dialogue is adapted from L. Copeland, producer, *Managing the Overseas Assignment* [videorecording] (San Francisco: Copeland Griggs, 1983).

Self-Assessment 4-2

Assessing Time Orientation

The following scale is designed to measure one's monochronic and/or polychronic time orientation. In the blank before each item, indicate the degree to which you (1) strongly agree, (2) agree, (3) are neutral, (4) disagree, or (5) disagree with the statement. There are no right or wrong answers, and many of the statements are similar by design. Work quickly and record your first impression.

1. _____ I usually feel frustrated after I choose to do a number of tasks when I could have chosen to do one at a time.

2. _____ When I talk with my friends in a group setting, I feel comfortable trying to hold two or three conversations at a time.

3. _____ When I work on a project around the house, it doesn't bother me to stop in the middle of one job to pick up another job that needs to be done.

—Continued

4. _____ I like to finish one task before going on to another task.

5. _____ At church it wouldn't bother me to meet at the same time with several different people who all had different church matters to discuss.

6. _____ I tend to concentrate on one job before moving on to another task.

7. _____ The easiest way for me to function is to organize my daily activities with a schedule.

8. _____ If I were a teacher and had several students wishing to talk with me about assigned homework, I would meet with the whole group rather than with one student at a time.

9. _____ I like doing several tasks at one time.

10. _____ I am frustrated when I have to start on a task without first finishing a previous one.

11. _____ In trying to solve problems, I find it stimulating to think about several different problems at the same time.

12. _____ I am mildly irritated when someone in a meeting wants to bring up a personal topic that is unrelated to the purpose of the meeting.

13. _____ In school, I prefer studying one subject to completion before going on to the next subject.

14. _____ I'm hesitant to focus my attention on only one thing because I may miss something equally important.

15. _____ I usually need to pay attention to only one task at a time to finish it.

SCORING: For items 2, 3, 5, 8, 9, 11, reverse your response: (5=1), (4=2), (3=3), (2=4), (5=1). For example, if your response to item #2 was 5, reverse it to 1. If your response to item #3 was 4, reverse it to a 2. Once you have reversed your responses to those 6 items, sum the entire 15 items. Scores of approximately 30 and below indicate a monochronic orientation. Scores of approximately 42 and above indicate a polychronic orientation.

SOURCE: This scale was developed by Charles A. Phipps and appears in C. H. Dodd, *Dynamics of Intercultural Communication,* 5th ed. (New York: McGraw-Hill, 1998), p. 265. Used by permission of Carley Dodd.

Chapter Summary

The relationship between humans and their environment is complex. By its very nature the environment, natural or built, is loaded with information. How that information is perceived and processed is strongly influenced by culture and can dramatically affect communication. In this chapter we saw that cultures vary considerably in how they view the natural environment. Some see the environment as a dominating force that cannot be harnessed. Other cultures perfer a balancing act between the environment and their needs and try to coexist with nature peacefully. Still others see nature as a slave and try to control and rule it. Whether dominated by it, living in harmony with it, or treating it as a slave, humans are in constant interaction with their environment.

As the contextual model of intercultural communication shows, all human communication exists within some kind of environment. Most human communication occurs within a built environment that is specifically designed either to restrict or to facilitate human interaction. How a culture designs its built environment says much about how it approaches communication, especially through its housing. Understanding how cultures manage their built and home environments leads one to a better understanding of cultures and to more competent intercultural communication.

This chapter has also discussed issues of privacy. People of all cultures have an innate inclination to affiliate and communicate with other human beings. At the same time, however, people cannot tolerate extended physical contact with others; they develop a need for privacy. The degree to which one senses privacy is learned and varies from culture to culture.

Finally, this chapter has described two orientations toward the perceptual environmental variable of time: monochronic and polychronic. Monochronic orientations emphasize schedules, the compartmentalization and segmentation of measurable units of time, and promptness. Polychronic orientations see time as much less tangible and stress simultaneous multiple activities, with little emphasis on scheduling. P-time cultures stress involvement of people and the completion of tasks as opposed to a strict adherence to artificial schedules. The natural, built, and perceptual aspects of the environment are pervasive influences on how people communicate with each other. Moreover, our perceptions of the environment are largely molded by our culture.

GLOSSARY OF TERMS

Built environment: Adaptations to the terrestrial environment, including architecture, housing, lighting, and landscaping.

Fixed-feature space: Space bounded by immovable or permanent fixtures, such as walls.

High-load: Situation with a high information rate.

Informal space: Space defined by the movement of the interactants.

Information rate: The amount of information contained or perceived in the physical environment per some unit of time.

Low-load: Situation with a low information rate.

Monochronic time orientation: Cultural temporal orientation that stresses the compartmentalization and segmenting of measurable units of time.

Polychronic time orientation: Cultural temporal orientation that stresses the involvement of people and the completion of tasks, as opposed to strict adherence to schedules. Time is not seen as measurable.

Privacy: The degree to which an individual can control the visual, auditory, and olfactory interaction with others.

Semifixed-feature space: Space bounded by movable objects, such as furniture.

Terrestrial environment: The physical geography of the earth.

REFERENCES

1. H. F. Stein, *Developmental Time, Cultural Space* (Norman: University of Oklahoma Press, 1987), p. 15.
2. The idea of comparing two scenarios is adapted from A. Mehrabian, *Public Places and Private Spaces: The Psychology of Work, Play, and Living Arrangements* (New York: Basic Books, 1976).
3. Stein, *Developmental Time, Cultural Space.*
4. Mehrabian, *Public Places and Private Spaces.*
5. Ibid.
6. Ibid.
7. Ibid.
8. J. Lang, *Creating Architectural Theory: The Role of the Behavioral Sciences in Environmental Design* (New York: Van Nostrand Reinhold, 1987).
9. R. C. Knopf, "Human Behavior, Cognitions, and Affect in the Natural Environment," in *Handbook of Environmental Psychology,* vol. 1, ed. D. Stokols and I. Altman (New York: Wiley, 1987), pp. 783–826.
10. A. K. Wibisono and W. Schultz, "Cultural Examination of Indonesia" (unpublished student manuscript, St. Norbert College, De Pere, Wisc., 1996); J. E. Safra, "Indonesia," *The New Encyclopaedia Britannica,* vol. 6 (Chicago: Encyclopaedia Britannica, 1997), pp. 298–299.
11. K. Thao, "The Hmong Culture" (unpublished student manuscript, St. Norbert College, De Pere, Wisc., 1995); D. Yang, *Hmong at the Turning Point* (Minneapolis: Worldbridge Associates, 1993).
12. S. Bichler, R. Jaeger, and B. Schiefelbein, "Life and Culture in South Yemen" (unpublished student manuscript, St. Norbert College, De Pere, Wisc., 1996); R. F. Nyrop, ed., *The Yemens: Country Studies* (Washington, D.C.: United States Government Printing Office, 1986).
13. G. Westfahl, R. Koltz, and A. Manders, "Ethnic Russian Culture and Society" (unpublished student manuscript, St. Norbert College, De Pere, Wisc., 1996); M. W. Shoemaker, *Russia, Eurasian States, and Eastern Europe: 1996* (Harpers Ferry, W. Va.: Stryler-Post, 1996).
14. D. Yurkovich, K. Pliscott, and R. Halverson, "The Norwegian Culture" (unpublished student manuscript, St. Norbert College, De Pere, Wisc., 1996); Central Intelligence Agency, *The World Fact Book* (Washington, D.C.: United States Government Printing Office, 1995).
15. Lang, *Creating Architectural Theory.*
16. F. R. Kluckhohn, "Dominant and Variant Value Orientations," in *Personality in Nature, Culture and Society,* ed. C. Kluckhohn, H. A. Murray, and D. M. Schneider (New York: Knopf, 1953), pp. 342–357.
17. I. Altman and N. M. Chemers, "Cultural Aspects of the Environment-Behavior Relationship," in *Handbook of Cross-Cultural Psychology,* vol. 5, ed. H. C. Triandis and R. W. Brislin (Boston: Allyn and Bacon, 1980), pp. 335–394.
18. R. J. Bishop, "Cultural Profile, Examination of Value Orientations and Sociocultural Influences, and Verbal and Nonverbal Language Aspects of the East Indian Culture" (unpublished

manuscript, St. Norbert College, De Pere, Wisc., 1995); R. Srinivasan, *India* (New York: Marshall Cavendish, 1951); P. R. Harris and R. T. Moran, *Managing Cultural Differences,* 4th ed. (Houston: Gulf Publishing, 1996).

19. Kluckhohn, "Dominant and Variant Value of Orientations."

20. S. Rieck and M. Ogura, "Sri Lanka: The Pearl of the Indian Ocean" (unpublished student manuscript, St. Norbert College, De Pere, Wisc., 1996); G. A. Borden, W. A. Conaway, and T. Morrison, *Kiss, Bow, or Shake Hands* (Holbrook, Mass.: Bob Adams, Inc., 1993).

21. Altman and Chemers, "Cultural Aspects of the Environment-Behavior Relationship."

22. Kluckhohn, "Dominant and Variant Value Orientations."

23. Altman and Chemers, "Cultural Aspects of the Environment-Behavior Relationship"; R. Thorne and R. Hall, "Environmental Psychology in Australia," in *Handbook of Environmental Psychology,* vol. 2, ed. D. Stokols and I. Altman (New York: Wiley, 1987), pp. 1137–1154.

24. J. H. Sorenson and G. F. White, "Natural Disasters: A Cross-Cultural Perspective," in *Human Behavior and Environment: Advances in Theory and Research,* ed. I. Altman, A. Rapoport, and J. F. Wohlwill, vol. 4, *Environment and Culture* (New York: Plenum, 1980), pp. 279–318.

25. Ibid.

26. Ibid.

27. J. Lang, *Creating Architectural Theory;* A. Rapoport, "Cross-Cultural Aspects of Environmental Design," in *Human Behavior and Environment: Advances in Theory and Research,* pp. 7–46

28. A. Rapoport, *House Form and Culture* (Englewood Cliffs, N.J.: Prentice-Hall, 1969).

29. Lang, *Creating Architectural Theory.*

30. E. T. Hall, *The Hidden Dimension* (New York: Doubleday, 1966).

31. Lang, *Creating Architectural Theory.*

32. Hall, *The Hidden Dimension;* I. Altman and A. M. Vinsel, "Personal Space: An Analysis of E. T. Hall's Proxemics Framework," in *Human Behavior and Environment: Advances in Theory and Research,* vol. 2, ed. I. Altman and J. F. Wohlwill (New York: Plenum, 1977), pp. 181–260.

33. Hall, *The Hidden Dimension.*

34. M. W. Lustig and J. Koester, *Intercultural Competence: Interpersonal Communication Across Cultures,* 2nd ed. (New York: HarperCollins, 1996).

35. For an excellent summary of research related to personal space across cultures see J. Aiello, "Human Spatial Behavior," in *Handbook of Environmental Psychology,* vol. 1, ed. D. Stokols and I. Altman (New York: Wiley, 1987), pp. 389–504.

36. G. Hagino, M. Mochizuki, and T. Yamamoto, "Environmental Psychology in Japan," in *Handbook of Environmental Psychology,* vol. 2, ed. D. Stokols and I. Altman (New York: Wiley, 1987), pp. 1155–1170.

37. K. Sieke and C. S. Terry, *Contemporary Japanese Houses* (Tokyo: Kodansha, 1970).

38. Ibid., pp. 11–12.

39. A. Ueda, *The Inner Harmony of the Japanese House* (Tokyo: Kodansha, 1990).

40. T. Yoshida, *The Japanese House and Garden* (London: Pall Mall Press, 1969).

41. Ibid.

42. Ueda, *The Inner Harmony of the Japanese House.*

43. Ibid.

44. Ueda, *The Inner Harmony of the Japanese House;* Yoshida, *The Japanese House and Garden.*

45. Ueda, *The Inner Harmony of the Japanese House,* p. 9.

46. S. Kent, *Analyzing Activity Areas: An Ethnoarchaeological Study of the Use of Space* (Albuquerque: University of New Mexico Press, 1984).

47. Ibid.

48. Ibid.

49. Ibid.

50. H. L. Moore, *Space, Text and Gender: An Anthropological Study of the Marakwet of Kenya* (Cambridge: Cambridge University Press, 1986).

51. Ibid.

52. Ibid, p. 45.

53. Ibid.

54. Ibid.

55. Ibid.

56. J. K. Burgoon, "A Communication Model of Personal Space Violations: Explication and an Initial Test," *Human Communication Research,* 4, no. 2 (1978), 124.

57. A. F. Westin, *Privacy and Freedom* (New York: Atheneum, 1967).

58. I. Altman, "Privacy Regulation: Culturally Universal or Culturally Specific?" *Journal of Social Issues,* 83, no. 3 (1977), 66–84.

59. Westin, *Privacy and Freedom.*

60. Lang, *Creating Architectural Theory.*

61. Westin, *Privacy and Freedom.*

62. Ibid.

63. D. M. Pedersen, "Dimensions of Privacy," *Perceptual and Motor Skills,* 48 (1979), 1291–1297.

64. C. Calvert, *Voyeur Nation: Media, Privacy, and Peering in Modern Culture* (Boulder, Colo.: Westview Press, 2000); C. S. Stepp, "Playing at Peeping Tom," *Ameican Journalism Review,* 23 (2001), 58.

65. J. Quittner and W. Dowell, "Invasion of Privacy," *Time,* 150, (1997), 28–36.

66. Ibid.

67. S. Burd, "Colleges Allowed to Tell Parents About Alcohol Use," *Chronicle of Higher Education,* 46 (2000), A31; L. Reisberg, "2 Years After Colleges Started Calling Home, Administrators Say Alcohol Policy Works," *Chronicle of Higher Education,* 47 (2001), A34.

68. O. H. Gandy Jr., "African-Americans and Privacy: Understanding the Black Perspective in the Emerging Policy Debate," *Journal of Black Studies,* 42 (1993), 178–196.

69. D. M. Pedersen and S. Frances, "Regional Differences in Privacy Preferences," *Psychological Reports,* 66 (1990), 731–736.

70. A. Rustemli and D. Kokdemir, "Privacy Dimensions and Preferences Among Turkish Students," *Journal of Social Psychology,* 133, no. 6 (1993), 807–814.

71. Westin, *Privacy and Freedom.*

72. Altman, "Privacy Regulation: Culturally Universal or Culturally Specific?" 66–84; J. M. Roberts and T. A. Gregor, "Privacy: A Cultural View," in *Privacy,* ed. J. R. Pennock and J. W. Chapman (New York: Atherton Press, 1971).

73. Altman, "Privacy Regulation," 66–84.

74. R. C. Hesselink, R. T. Mullen, and J. M. Rouse, "Moroccan Culture: An In-Depth Study" (unpublished manuscript, St. Norbert College, De Pere, Wisc., 1996); P. Bowles, *Morocco* (New York: Harry N. Abrams, 1996); P. Seward, *Cultures of the World: Morocco* (New York: Marshall Cavendish, 1995); "Overview of Islamic Architecture" (http://venture.cob.ohio-state.edu:1111/khalid/pages/archtcre/overview.htm).

75. E. T. Hall, *The Silent Language* (Greenwich, Conn.: Fawcett, 1959), p. 15.

76. E. T. Hall, *The Dance of Life* (New York: Doubleday); Hall, *The Silent Language.*

77. Ibid.

78. Ibid.

79. Ibid.

80. Harris and Moran, *Managing Cultural Differences.*

81. M. C. G. Keberlein, "A Cultural Profile of the Guatemalan Ladinos" (unpublished manuscript, St. Norbert College, De Pere, Wisc., 1993).

82. Hall, *The Silent Language.*

83. K. Vandehey, C. Buerger, and K. Krueger, "Traditional Aspects and Struggles of the Masai Culture" (unpublished manuscript, St. Norbert College, De Pere, Wisc., 1996); A. C. Hollis, *The Masai: Their Language and Folklore,* rev. ed. (New York: Clarendon Press, 1965).

84. Ibid.

The Perceptual Context

It seems to me that we have sound reasons for thus considering theoretical knowledge as more objective than immediate experience.

—Michael Polyani[1]

CHAPTER OBJECTIVES

After reading this chapter, you should be able to:

- List and discuss the three stages of human information processing.
- Discuss cross-cultural differences in perception.
- Define and discuss short- and long-term memory.
- Discuss cross-cultural differences in memory and recall.
- Define and discuss at least four types of mental categories.
- Define and discuss racial and ethnic stereotypes.
- Identify and discuss at least two reasons why people stereotype.
- Define and discuss ethnocentrism.
- Define and discuss the nature of racism.

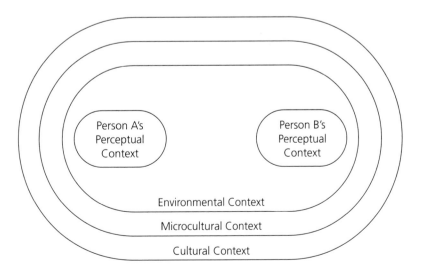

C onsider the following interaction between Jim, an American college student, and Olga, a Ukrainian exchange student studying at the same college in the United States.

Jim: You know, Olga, I've been thinking about America's involvement in the war in Afghanistan. I see reports of people starving and dying and it's just so depressing. I hope this is over soon.

Olga: Yes, I know, it's a terrible thing. My country has experienced a lot of starvation and war.

Jim: Really?

Olga: Oh yes. My country has been fought over and suppressed for centuries. We gained our independence from Russia for a short time between 1917 and 1920, but that was followed by ruthless Soviet rule that was responsible for two famines in which over 8 million people died. Can you relate to that, Jim? And then World War II, where the German and Soviet armies killed some 7 million of my people. So in the twentieth century alone, over 15 million people died, some say for no good reason.

Jim: I had no idea. I can't imagine how that makes you feel.

Olga: Right, I understand. Our history give my people a whole different perspective on life and how we see and live our lives. It's almost impossible to not carry a little sadness in our hearts.

Jim: My generation has never experienced anything like that. This is brand new to us. It's very confusing.

Whenever two people come together and interact, like Jim and Olga, they process great quantities of information. In addition to the cultural, microcultural, and environmental contexts influencing their interaction, Jim and Olga both bring with them their unique perceptual experiences. The perception context refers to how people take in, store, and recall information. In this brief conversation, Jim and Olga encode, decode, and interpret a vast amount of information about themselves, their cultures' histories, current events, their surroundings, and each other. Because they come from different cultures, they see the world differently. Their interpretation of world events differs dramatically. Intercultural communication is a process of connecting perceptual contexts.

The higher mental processes required for human communication include the gathering, storing, and retrieval of information. Although human information processing is a universal phenomenon, it is influenced by culture. This chapter discusses the higher mental activities of the individual that constitute the perceptual context of intercultural communication. In addition to the cultural, microcultural, and environmental contexts, the perceptual context affects how people interact. Every time we enter into a communicative exchange with someone, we bring with us a perceptual frame of reference through which all of our messages are filtered. The cultural, microcultural, environmental, and perceptual contexts are interdependent influences that combine in a complex formula that ultimately defines our interaction with others.

From an information-processing perspective, the human mind is seen as a complex information-processing system that takes in, stores, and retrieves information. The first part of this chapter introduces the idea of culture and cognition and outlines a model of human information processing. The second part of the chapter explains a common form of information processing called categorization. The third part of the chapter focuses on two attitudinal dimensions of information processing: stereotyping and ethnocentrism. The overall purpose of the chapter is to explain how the human mind processes information during communication, especially intercultural communication.

Culture and Cognition

People from different cultures think about different things. The Aleutian Eskimos of western Alaska and the Marakwet tribe of western Kenya think about different things because of the extreme differences in their natural environments. Moreover, people from different cultures think differently about their life experiences. The life experiences of a Guatemalan Ladino are markedly different from those of a Ukrainian. Few people question that the content of thought for people in different cultures varies. What is open to speculation, however, is whether higher mental processes, such as perception and remembering, differ across cultures. How much do the cultural, microcultural, and environmental contexts affect how the human brain processes information?

A Model of Human Information Processing

Roy Lachman and his colleagues maintain that when it comes to processing information, the human mind is analogous to a computer. Information is entered, stored, and retrieved in a sequence of stages in which each stage performs a specific operation on the information.[2] According to Lachman, Lachman, and Butterfield, during stage 1, the *input* stage, information is taken in via the senses, attended to, and then interpreted. In stage 2, the *storage* stage, information is held in short-term and long-term memory. During stage 3, the *retrieval* stage, information is recalled. For people to communicate with each other in any culture, they are required to take in, store, and recall information. Although these stages are probably universal, culture influences the specific strategies and styles of processing information in each stage.

STAGE 1: INPUT

The first stage of information processing is the input stage, in which information is taken in and interpreted (see Figure 5-1). This is the stage in which raw

FIGURE 5-1   The Input Stage of Information Processing

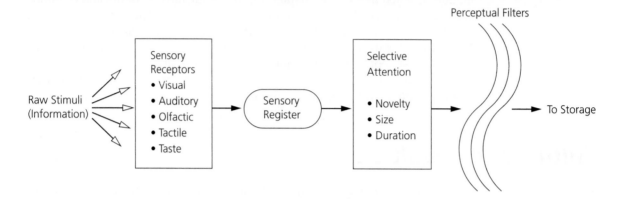

information is taken in through the senses and interpreted by the brain. The essential cognitive process during this stage is *perception*. Margaret Matlin defines perception as the mental interpretation of external stimuli via sensation.[3]

According to Matlin, at any given point in time, especially during human communication, human beings are bombarded with external stimuli (see Figure 5-2). Humans take in visual stimuli with their eyes, auditory stimuli with their ears, olfactic stimuli with their nose, taste stimuli with their mouth, and tactile stimuli through the skin. Although humans tend to favor visual and auditory sensation, olfactic, tac-

FIGURE 5-2   Sources of Sensory Stimuli

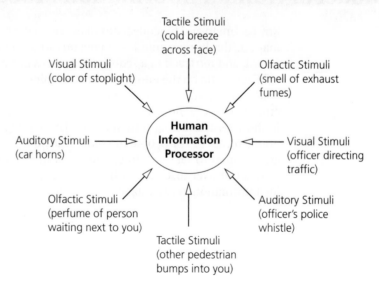

tile, and taste sensations are very informative. Although most stimuli come from external sources, information can come from within the human processor as well. During intercultural communication, many of the stimuli come from the cultural, microcultural, and environmental contexts. Matlin maintains that at the point of sensation, the external stimuli are raw and unprocessed. At the very moment the stimuli are sensed, they are transferred to a *sensory register*, which holds the unprocessed stimuli for a very short period of time until they can be further processed and interpreted. Matlin points out that information in the sensory register is a nearly literal record of its sensory image. The entry of information into the sensory register is passive and is lost very quickly.[4] Visual sensory memory (called *iconic memory*) can be demonstrated by taking a flashlight into a dark room. Holding the flashlight firmly and pointing it at a wall, make a circular motion with the flashlight in such a way as to produce a "circle" of light on the wall. You can actually see the complete circle even though the light is at only one physical location on the wall at any time. Tactile sensory memory can easily be demonstrated by clapping your hands loudly. You can still feel the clap after the completion of the act.[5]

The sensory register holds stimuli long enough for an individual to decide which stimuli to process further and which to ignore. This is the *attention phase of perception*, in which the human processor becomes conscious of the incoming stimuli. During the attention phase, the individual selects which information to process further. Because the person is bombarded with so many stimuli, only certain kinds will be attended to, whereas others will be ignored. According to Jim McCroskey and Virginia Richmond, novel or unusual stimuli generally attract attention. Hence, interacting with someone from a different culture may heighten one's attention. If you have ever walked through the international terminal of a major airport, you may have found yourself staring at people you considered "different" or "unusual." If the cultural or environmental context is unusual or new, an individual may feel information overload. Although there may not be any more stimuli in one context than in another, the novelty of one context may lead one to think there are more stimuli. This may account for why entering into a new culture may be overwhelming to some. McCroskey and Richmond point out that the size of the stimuli also affects attention; generally the larger the stimulus, the more likely one is to attend to it. Finally, the duration of the stimulus will also affect one's attention. Stimuli that fade quickly may not be attended to, and stimuli that last for excessively long periods of time may eventually be ignored.[6]

Immediately after information passes through the sensory register and is attended to, it passes through *perceptual filters*. Perceptual filters alter and change how humans interpret incoming information. According to Blaine Goss, people filter information physiologically, sociologically, and psychologically.[7] *Physiological filters* are the natural or genetic differences in how one sees, hears, smells, tastes, or feels. For example, eyesight varies considerably from person to person. Many people are required to wear eyeglasses to accommodate for poor visual sensation. When light waves are sensed by the eye, they are transmitted via the optical nerve to the brain. The brain then interprets the stimuli. The eyes of a nearsighted person sense visual stimuli (for example, light waves) differently than do the eyes of a farsighted person. Hence the brain of the nearsighted person interprets the stimuli differently than does the brain of a farsighted person. People everywhere have natural physiological differences in their ability to see, hear, taste, touch, and smell incoming stimuli.

Sociological filters represent demographic data and one's membership in groups, such as one's culture, microculture, or hometown. The groups to which people belong influence how they perceive incoming stimuli. For example, in the National Football League, a fierce rivalry exists between the Chicago Bears and the Green Bay Packers. People from Chicago and Green Bay view their respective football teams differently. In the last seconds of a game played a few years ago, the quarterback for the Green Bay Packers, Don Maijkowski, threw a touchdown pass that would have won the game for the Packers. A penalty was called on the play, indicating that Maijkowski had stepped over the line of scrimmage—a violation of the rules that nullified the winning touchdown. Upon further review, the penalty was reversed, the touchdown was counted, and Green Bay won the game. Chicago fans were outraged because they were convinced Maijkowski had crossed the scrimmage line. Packer fans were joyous because they could see that he had not crossed the line. Even to this day, Chicago fans watching replays of that play are certain Maijkowski crossed the line, whereas Green Bay fans, watching the very same replay, are equally convinced he did not. Both sets of fans perceiving the very same play have very different perceptions.

The third set of filters outlined by Goss are the *psychological filters,* which include the attitudes, beliefs, and dispositions of the individual. A person's likes, dislikes, and beliefs about what is right or wrong filter the perception of incoming stimuli. If someone has a negative attitude about a professor, he or she may perceive that class as especially boring or uninformative. If people believe that abortion is immoral, they may perceive an abortion rights speaker as unattractive. At the point of passing through the perceptual filters, the information is no longer considered raw and unprocessed. Although all of us are bombarded with the same visual, auditory, tactile, olfactic, and taste stimuli, our sensations and perceptions of these stimuli will differ considerably, especially if we come from different cultures.

Cross-Cultural Differences in Sensation and Perception.   Data from some studies suggest that people differ across cultures in their ability to gather incoming information. John Berry and his associates outline four explanations for cross-cultural differences in the perception of sensory stimuli: (1) *conditions of the physical environment,* (2) *indirect environmental conditions,* (3) *genetic differences,* and (4) *cultural differences in how people interact with their environment.*[8]

Conditions in the physical environment may affect one's ability to gather incoming information. In the early 1970s, Reuning and Wortley conducted a cross-cultural study on auditory acuity. In comparing Kalahari Bushmen, Danish, and American subjects, they found less hearing loss in the Kalahari sample than in the Danish or American samples, particularly among older subjects. Reuning and Wortley attributed their findings to the low levels of ambient noise in the Kalahari desert region. They also cited other studies that found a slower loss of hearing in nonindustrialized societies. These findings may suggest that environmental noise, such as that heard in industrialized societies, may have a negative effect on people's hearing.[9]

In his study, Wyndham attributed an indirect environmental factor, specifically poor nutrition, as the reason that it took longer for the eyes of black South African miners to adapt to the dark conditions of the mines than it did for the eyes of white miners to adapt. Wyndham suggests that many of the black mine workers might suffer from forms of liver ailments, which in turn were associated with nutritional deficiencies in early childhood.[10]

Berry and his associates argue that genetic factors seem to account for red-green colorblindness, tasteblindness, and the "alcoholic flush" phenomenon. Many studies have demonstrated that the frequency of red-green colorblindness is much lower in non-Caucasian groups than among Caucasians. Approximately 30 percent of all Caucasians are tasteblind to certain substances that taste bitter to Africans and Native American Indians. The alcoholic flush, a reddening of the face after consuming only a few alcoholic drinks, is much more common in Asian populations than in Caucasians.[11]

According to Berry, one's experience and enculturation with the environment plays a role in sensory stimulation. People can be conditioned to prefer and select some stimuli over others. Children are taught to pay attention to certain kinds of stimuli. Africans, for example, tend to excel at auditory tasks, whereas Europeans tend to excel at visual tasks. Cultural groups are taught to favor some sensory receptors over others. These people are called sensotypes—that is, they favor the relative importance of one sensory modality over the others.[12]

An extensive body of cross-cultural research on perception has been accumulated by Marshall Segall and his colleagues, who studied the perception of optical illusions in almost two thousand subjects from fourteen non-Western cultures.[13] Segall believes that repeated experience with perceptual objects affects how those objects are perceived and argues that optical illusions occur because previously learned interpretations of visual cues are misapplied, owing to unusual or misleading characteristics of stimuli.

One hypothesis that explains vulnerability to illusions is called the *carpentered-world hypothesis*.[14] According to the carpentered-world hypothesis, people raised in an environment shaped by carpenters (for example, one with rectangular furniture, rectangular houses, and right angles) have a learned tendency to interpret nonrectangular figures as representations of rectangular figures seen in perspective. Segall described this hypothesis by applying it to the Sander parallelogram (see Figure 5-3).

FIGURE 5-3   The Sander Parallelogram

FIGURE 5-4   The Muller-Lyer Illusion

People living in carpentered societies tend to judge the leftmost diagonal line within the parallelogram as longer than the two lines on the right side. This illusion is a result of their tendency to perceive a parallelogram drawn on a flat surface as a representation of a rectangular surface extended in space. Here the viewer is actually judging distance covered by the left diagonal as greater than the distance covered by the right diagonal.

Subjects in Segall's study were also shown the Muller-Lyer illusion (see Figure 5-4). Again, Segall assumed that people from carpentered societies would perceive the figures as representations of three-dimensional objects extended in space. For example, these illusions can be found in the corners of rooms extending away from the observer. The figure on the right tends to be interpreted as farther away, and therefore the line is seen as longer. The figure on the left is found in corners of objects extending toward the observer, and therefore the line is seen as shorter.

In related research, Dawson, Young, and Choi compared the optical illusion susceptibility of Hong Kong Chinese, Americans, and Australian aboriginal Arunta desert dwellers. When shown the Muller-Lyer and the Sander parallelogram illusions, the American subjects were the most susceptible, followed by the Chinese and then the Arunta. These results lend support to Segall's carpentered-world hypothesis.[15]

Segall spent many years gathering data and found a strong tendency for illusion susceptibility across cultural groups. Although Segall's findings have not gone unchallenged, the general consensus among most cognitive psychologists is that learned experiences do, in fact, affect how people perceive their surroundings. Culturally learned experiences filter how we see, hear, smell, feel, and taste the world around us.[16]

STAGE 2: STORAGE

Lachman, Lachman, and Butterfield argue that once information has passed through the perceptual filters, it is processed into memory. Memory involves maintaining information over time.[17] Memory is required for virtually all human communication. Without the ability to store information over time, we could not communicate with others. Imagine not being able to remember your own name or recognize your family members. Without memory, you could not read this book, nor would you be able to construct a single spoken sentence. Many cultures regard memory as the most important component of human intelligence.

According to Lachman and his colleagues, cognitive psychologists recognize three kinds of memory: (1) *sensory memory,* or sensory register (discussed above);

FIGURE 5-5 **Stages of Mental Storage**

(2) *short-term memory;* and (3) *long-term memory* (see Figure 5-5). These three memory stores preserve information in different formats, for different time intervals, and in different ways.[18]

Sensory memory may only last a second or two, and the information is generally stored in its original form. Once the information has passed through the perceptual filters, it travels either directly to long-term memory or through short-term memory. According to Robert Logie, *short-term memory,* sometimes called working memory or active memory, refers to the cognitive storage area in which small amounts of information are held for relatively brief periods of time.[19] In some cases the information is committed to long-term memory, and in many other cases the information is simply lost. The amount of information stored in short-term memory is quite limited. Although psychologists disagree, many concur with George Miller's conclusion that short-term memory is limited to seven items, plus or minus two.[20]

Lachman, Lachman, and Butterfield suggest that short-term memory is relatively fragile. Information held in short-term memory is easily lost because of interference from other information entering the cognitive system or from other external distractions, such as noise. Although short-term memory is temporary, limited, and fragile, it is essential for human communication. Most communicative tasks, such as reading, writing, listening, and speaking, are entirely dependent on the ability to maintain information for short periods of time. The ability to finish a spoken sentence is contingent on remembering its first words.[21]

On the other hand, according to Robert Howard, *long-term memory* is a virtual warehouse of stored information. A major difference between short-term and long-term memory is the duration of storage. Unlike short-term memory, information in long-term memory may be held for a lifetime. People may be able to recall events that took place thirty or forty years ago. A second major difference between the two stores is their capacity. Whereas the short-term store may be limited to seven items, plus or minus two, the storage capacity in long-term memory is virtually unlimited. Another difference between the two memories is their method of forgetting. Information in short-term memory seems to be lost because of *decay*—that is, if the information is not used, it simply fades away. Although long-term memories also decay, long-term store seems most disrupted by *interference*—that is, other information gets in the way of stored information.[22]

Many cognitive psychologists distinguish between two types of long-term memory: *episodic long-term memory* and *semantic long-term memory*.[23] According to Endel Tulving, episodic long-term memory refers to that type of stored information pertaining to the unique experiences of the individual. Episodic memory is autobiographical. One's birthday, first-grade teacher, first date, and so forth, are different for each person and are representative of the type of information stored in episodic long-term memory. On the other hand, according to Tulving, semantic long-term memory preserves a person's general conceptual information, world knowledge, and language abilities. How to spell, ride a bike, and construct sentences would be information preserved in semantic long-term memory. Semantic long-term memory is not autobiographical. Although these two types of long-term memory appear to be different, they are also highly interconnected and probably operate in tandem.[24]

STAGE 3: RETRIEVAL

Once information has been stored, it is relatively useless unless it can be retrieved. The human information processor excels at retrieval. Information that has been stored for a lifetime yet rarely used can be recalled in an instant. At other times, however, recently stored information seems very difficult to recall. Most adults can easily recall the name of their first-grade teacher but can not remember what they had for dinner three nights ago. Moreover, the quality of human information retrieval is typically approximate rather than literal. People have global memories of conversations or events rather than verbatim transcriptions.

According to Lachman and his colleagues, forgetting is memory failure—the inability to recall or recognize stored information. Forgetting in sensory or short-term store is necessary in order to process new incoming information. Forgetting information in long-term storage may have serious consequences, especially on a multiple-choice or essay exam. Cognitive psychologists now treat long-term-memory forgetting as an asset rather than a liability because it is a useful way to prevent long-term memory from being cluttered up with information that is not being used. Forgetting often follows what is called a negatively accelerated curve. Most forgetting occurs rapidly, then levels off over time. Other researchers contend that information is never really forgotten; people just lose access to it.[25]

Matlin points out that there are several reasons why we might forget something: (1) *decay*, (2) *interference*, (3) *arousal*, (4) *repression*, and (5) *depth of processing*. Forgetting due to decay occurs when a memory is not rehearsed or used over time. Eventually the information diminishes or fades from memory. Interference occurs when other information intrudes on stored information. Sometimes forgetting occurs when old memories interfere with the storage of new information. At other times, forgetting occurs when new information disrupts previously stored "old" memories. Matlin devised a miniexperiment, shown in the accompanying box, that demonstrates the effect of interference.

Negative arousal, or anxiety, may be another source of forgetting. One study that supports this view was conducted by Goss, Neuliep, and O'Hair. In their study, two groups of students were shown the same videotaped conversation between a student and a teacher interacting about an alleged cheating incident. The student in the video was being accused of cheating by the teacher. One week later, individual students from one of the two groups were individually taken to a room where they were told they were about to testify before a university tribunal where the student in the videotape was on trial for cheating (there was no actual trial). Prior to entering the trial each student was given a multiple-choice recall test and asked to recall as much as possible about the videotape seen one week earlier. The other group of students was given the same recall test but was not informed of any trial. In a comparison of the recall tests, the students in the group who were told they would have to testify scored significantly lower than the other group. Goss, Neuliep, and O'Hair attributed the lower recall scores to increased negative arousal.[26]

According to Matlin, another source of forgetting may be repression. Repression occurs when people actively, but unconsciously, forget unpleasant material. Similarly, pleasant material may be more easily processed than unpleasant. Refer back to the interference experiment in the box. After your friend completes

---

The Effect of Interference on Recall

Present the following word list to a friend or roommate:

River	Card
Door	Test
Cat	Tree
Plate	Ball
Book	Road

Allow a few moments for your friend to read the list. After he or she finishes, ask him or her to either write down or recite orally a list of 10 vegetables. When he or she has finished the list, ask him or her to recall the words on the above list. See how many he or she recalls and with what degree of accuracy. Repeat the experiment with another friend, but this time delete the vegetable list exercise. Compare their results. Theoretically, the vegetable word list exercise should interfere with your friend's ability to store the word list in memory.

SOURCE: "The Effect of Interference on Recall" from M. Matlin, *Cognition*. Copyright © 1983 Holt, Rinehart Winston. Reprinted by permission of John Wiley & Sons, Inc.

the experiment, make note of the first few and the last few vegetables on the list. Chances are that those vegetables listed first are the ones your friend enjoys, whereas those listed toward the end are those your friend dislikes.[27]

Matlin suggests that the effort required to gather and store information may also affect its retrieval. Meaningful information that requires deeper cognitive processing to store may be easier to recall than information that requires minimal effort to encode. Likewise, the context in which the information is encoded may facilitate recall. Called encoding specificity, the contextual cues present during the gathering and storing of information may serve as cues for the memory of stored information.[28] For example, witnesses often will return to the scene of the crime to help themselves remember what happened.

Cross-Cultural Differences in Memory and Retrieval.   Several studies indicate that culture affects information retrieval. In addition to culture, two other variables strongly linked to recall are age and education. Age and recall are curvilinearly related (see Figure 5-6). Up to a point, one's age facilitates recall. However, when many people reach a certain age, their memory skills deteriorate. Education and recall are related in that educated persons seem to employ different kinds of memory strategies. Barbara Rogoff claims that to the extent that cultures have different educational systems and methods, their peoples may have different memory skills. Persons educated in industrialized cultures have been taught to remember disconnected bits of information, such as names and dates. These persons may be more likely than nonschooled individuals to use memory strategies that facilitate the organization of unrelated items. Moreover, Rogoff asserts that schooled individuals are more likely to classify similar objects together, whereas nonschooled persons classify objects according to their functional similarity. For example, in many memory tests, persons are presented with lists of unrelated pieces of information, not unlike the word list in the interference experiment box. This type of

FIGURE 5-6   Relationship Between Recall and Age

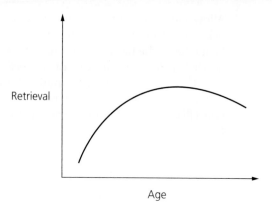

information may be remembered better if the person employs some sort of mnemonic (pronounced *ne-monic,* meaning a technique for improving memory) device, such as rehearsing or classifying. Nonschooled persons, including pre-school children, generally do not employ such mnemonic strategies and have difficulty with such tasks.[29]

With contextually organized information, however, fewer memory differences are observed between schooled and nonschooled persons. In one study reported by Rogoff, for example, Guatemalan Mayan and American nine-year-olds watched an experimenter place twenty miniature objects, such as cars, animals, furniture, people, and household items, in a panorama model of a town. The twenty items were then removed from the panorama and put into a pool of eighty other objects. The children were then asked to reconstruct the panorama, using as many of the original twenty items as they could remember. The Mayan children performed slightly better than the American children. The performance of the Mayan children may have been due to the fact that about one-third of the American children used rehearsal strategies typical for remembering unrelated bits of information, such as rehearsing the names of the objects. This type of strategy may be inappropriate for remembering spatially oriented, contextual information.[30] In related research, Yoshida, Fernandez, and Stigler explored Japanese and American students' recognition memory for statements made during a videotaped mathematics lesson. Japanese and American fourth- and sixth-graders watched either a Japanese or an English version of the same lesson and then were tested for recognition of teacher statements that were relevant or irrelevant to the content of the lesson. The Japanese and American students were equally successful at recognizing relevant statements, but American students remembered more irrelevant statements than the Japanese.[31]

Cole and Gay assert that a culture's language and literacy rate may affect recall. Some evidence indicates that nonliterate societies develop mnemonic skills different from those of literate societies. In nonliterate societies, there may be no written language to facilitate memory. Cole and Gay note that in nonliterate societies, people must store information in memory rather than on a piece of paper. Likewise, the histories of nonliterate societies must be stored in the memories of their people rather than on paper or in books.[32] In a study conducted by Ross and Millson, two groups of university students, one from Ghana and the other in New York, were read several stories aloud and then asked to recall them. Generally, the Ghana students had better recall of the stories than the American students.[33] Harris, Schoen, and Hensley, in a related study, examined the effects of culturally based knowledge on memory. College students from America and Mexico read three brief stories of everyday activities. There were two versions of the same story, each consistent with either an American or a Mexican cultural script. The students read each version. Researchers then administered memory tests, first immediately after the reading, then thirty minutes after the reading, and finally one week after the reading. After one week, both groups of students mistakenly recalled the stories from the other cultures as being more like their own culture than the stories in fact were.[34] Other memory research reviewed by Liu indicates that Chinese persons may have superior memory. For example, in word-pair-association memory tasks, Chinese college students usually attain perfect recall within two or three trials, whereas the recall of students from other cultures is typically below 70 percent.[35]

Until more is known, conclusions about the relationship between culture and memory should be made with some degree of caution. Although several studies indicate a connection between culture and memory, these studies may actually be revealing differences in other factors that affect recall, such as socialization or education. Because cultures differ in so many ways, it is difficult to pinpoint culture as the sole mechanism for memory ability.

Categorization and Mental Economy

Humans are besieged by so many stimuli simultaneously that they cannot possibly process all of them. In order to manage these enormous quantities of information, humans tend to engage in strategies of mental economy. One such strategy is called categorization. *Categorization* is classifying, sorting, or arranging information into identifiable compartments that share certain features or characteristics. Most cognitive psychologists argue that all people, regardless of culture, engage in categorization. Gordon Allport argues that humans cannot avoid categorization and that orderly living depends on it.[36] Gudykunst and Kim suggest that categories are useful because they help the information processor reduce uncertainty and increase the accuracy of predictions about others. Moreover, categories help us to make attributions about the behavior of others and to recall and recognize information. Understanding categorization is particularly important for intercultural communication because whenever we interact with someone from a different culture, we are faced with high levels of uncertainty and with unfamiliar stimuli to process.[37]

Cross-cultural researcher Richard Brislin argues that people categorize for a number of reasons, including reducing uncertainty and maintaining self-esteem. According to Brislin, the kinds of information upon which people form categories include, but are not limited to, (1) *conspicuous differences*, (2) *familiarity*, (3) *functional importance*, (4) *maximizing the relative advantage of the in-group*, (5) *projection and externalization*, (6) *belief similarity*, (7) *desirable and undesirable qualities*, and (8) *salient information*. The examples provided here are particularly relevant to intercultural communication. Keep in mind that these examples are not the actual categories themselves. Rather, they illustrate the kinds of information used to formulate categories.[38]

Conspicuous-difference categories are based on easily seen similarities or differences. According to Brislin, these types of categories are formed quickly during initial interaction with someone from a different culture. Conspicuous similarities or differences help us classify others as members of in-groups and out-groups. Conspicuous differences may stem from skin color, dress, language, or occupation.[39]

Sometimes we form categories on the basis of information that is familiar to us. Brislin points out that although people from different cultures may be conspicuously different from us, we may be quite familiar with them and their culture. Familiar stimuli are more efficiently processed than unfamiliar stimuli. The use of familiar categories facilitates accurate predictions about the behavior of others.[40]

Sometimes categories are formed that help us adjust and function. These functionally important categories may help us to meet needs and to achieve goals. For example, when needed, a person may categorize himself or herself as a member of a particular kind of group that receives special benefits or entitlements. At other times, the same person may not categorize himself or herself that way because it is not "functionally important." For example, students wishing to obtain a scholarship or loan may highlight their membership in an ethnic or racial group to obtain the assistance. Their group membership, in this circumstance, becomes functionally important.[41]

Most persons have a tendency to think of others in terms of in-group and out-group membership. In doing so, people also have a tendency to create categories that maximize the advantage of the in-group. An example provided by Brislin suggests that when members of the in-group constantly lose at sporting competitions, they may be categorized as "sportsmanlike." If in-group members share their resources, they may be categorized as "generous." Conversely, if the out-group loses at sporting events, they are categorized as "losers," and when they share their resources, they are categorized as "irresponsible."[42]

Projection refers to a shift of one's negative feelings onto someone or something else. In the case of categories, people may project in-group troubles to an out-group. For example, if a high percentage of the members of an in-group are unemployed, they may blame members of the out-group for taking all of "their" jobs. Brislin claims that externalization is related to projection in that people categorize members of the in-group as more like themselves than may actually be the case. For example, a student may complain to an advisor that "all students" hate to take the required math class.[43]

Perceived similarity may be the best predictor of positive affect toward others. People who perceive an out-group as similar to their in-group are likely to think positively about that out-group and to engage them in interaction. People can perceive themselves as similar to others in a variety of ways, such as physically, socially, morally, experientially, or economically. When people categorize others as similar, they reduce uncertainty about them, which, in turn, facilitates interaction.[44]

People have a tendency to label out-groups with undesirable qualities and to classify in-groups with desirable qualities. For example, out-group members may be categorized as bitter, arrogant, or strange, whereas in-group members are categorized as loyal, honest, and trustworthy. Brislin argues that people are socialized to believe in the superiority of the groups of which they are members.[45]

Salient information is that which is most noticeable, pronounced, or striking. When interacting with someone from another culture for the first time, there may be many salient features about that person that could lead to categorizing the entire culture. For example, when you enter into another culture, if the first person with whom you interact treats you disrespectfully, you may categorize the entire population as disrespectful.[46]

Brislin asserts that there are several consequences of categorization, some positive

People are often attracted to others they perceive as similar to themselves.
(© James Neuliep)

and others potentially negative. On the positive side, categorization helps to confirm thinking. Categorization reduces the amount of incoming information to a manageable size and increases the availability of incoming information. Categorization also reduces uncertainty and stress, especially in situations in which we are interacting for the first time with someone who belongs to a culture with which we are unfamiliar. Categorization also helps integrate incoming information and may help to link our own culture with others. On the potentially negative side, when we categorize others, we ignore individual elements of the person. We must be careful not to categorize too quickly or carelessly. We must be conscious that categorizing minimizes in-group differences and maximizes out-group differences.[47]

Stereotyping

By constructing categories, the human mind processes information more efficiently. Once created, categories are the basis of prejudgment, such as stereotyping. Considered a subset of categorization, stereotyping involves members of one group attributing characteristics to members of another group. These attributions typically carry a positive or negative evaluation. In this sense, stereotypes are categories with an attitude. Stereotypes typically refer to membership in social categories, such as sex, race, age, or profession, that are believed to be associated with certain traits and behaviors. In the United States, race and gender groups are often stereotyped. The meaning of the term *stereotype* has changed considerably since its introduction in 1824 by James Morier to describe a printing duplication process "in which the original is preserved and in which there is no opportunity for change or deviation in the reduplications."[48] A century later, Walter Lippman defined stereotypes as "pictures in our heads" and argued that stereotypes are not merely descriptions of others, but include an affective component that is driven by one's self-respect and value orientations.[49] In more recent times, the word *stereotype* has taken on negative connotations. In 1998, Richard Schaefer defined stereotypes as exaggerated images of the characteristics of a particular group held by prejudiced people who hold ill feelings toward that group.[50] Gudykunst and Kim define stereotypes as cognitive representations of another group that influence one's feelings about the group. They argue that stereotypes provide the content of social categories.[51]

Although we hesitate to admit it, we all stereotype. Stereotyping is a natural and universal information-processing strategy. Taylor and Porter maintain that stereotyping should be seen as a normal and essentially benign process that is a useful information-processing tool in diverse societies. The difficulty arises when stereotypes carry a negative connotation and are used to overgeneralize negative traits to an entire group of people when, in reality, few members of the group actually possess such traits.[52] Victoria Esses and Mark Zanna found that simply being in a "bad mood" may incline people to negatively stereotype. Several studies have demonstrated that when individuals are in a negative mood, they are especially likely to attribute stereotypes that they consider to be very unfavorable to certain ethnic groups.[53] In this way, stereotyping can lead to ethnocentrism.

RACIAL AND ETHNIC STEREOTYPES

Social scientists have long been interested in stereotypes and prejudice, two concepts that are often related. The systematic study of racial and ethnic stereotypes in the United States began in the 1930s with a study conducted by David Katz and Kenneth Braly. In their study, college students were presented with a list of eighty-four adjectives and were asked to indicate which traits were characteristic of ten ethnic groups, including Americans, blacks, Chinese, English, Germans, Italians, Irish, Japanese, Jews, and Turks. The results of their study showed that the college students consistently agreed on which traits described which group. The results were particularly consistent for blacks and Jews.[54]

In their original study, Katz and Braly found a high level of consistency in the adjectives respondents associated with the black stereotype. Moreover, the adjectives selected were generally negative. Several other researchers have since replicated Katz and Braly's stereotype checklist method, using the same eighty-four adjectives that were in the original study. Gilbert replicated it at Princeton in 1950, and Leonard Gordon replicated it at Arizona State University in 1969 and 1982. Recently, Patricia Devine and Andrew Elliot replicated that research at the University of Wisconsin. In their work, however, Devine and Elliot added nine new characteristics to the original eighty-four–item adjective checklist. The nine characteristics added included the terms *athletic, criminal, hostile, low in intelligence, poor, rhythmic, sexually perverse, uneducated,* and *violent.* The accompanying stereotype checklist is similar to the one used by Katz and Braly and includes the nine characteristics added by Devine and Elliot.

Self-Assessment 5-1

Stereotype Checklist

Below are several adjectives that may or may not describe groups of people. On a scale of 1 to 5, which of the following traits are representative of blacks?

1 = Not representative
2 = Rarely representative
3 = Sometimes representative
4 = Generally representative
5 = Very representative

_____ Superstitious
_____ Lazy
_____ Happy-go-lucky
_____ Ignorant
_____ Ostentatious (showy or conspicuous)
_____ Stupid
_____ Physically dirty
_____ Naive
_____ Sly
_____ Aggressive
_____ Loud
_____ Arrogant
_____ Unreliable
_____ Musical
_____ Intelligent
_____ Materialistic
_____ Sportsmanlike
_____ Pleasure-loving
_____ Sensitive
_____ Athletic
_____ Criminal
_____ Hostile
_____ Low in intelligence
_____ Poor
_____ Rhythmic
_____ Sexually perverse
_____ Uneducated
_____ Violent

On a scale of 1 to 5, which of the following traits are representative of Jews?

1 = Not representative
2 = Rarely representative
3 = Sometimes representative
4 = Generally representative
5 = Very representative

_____	Shrewd
_____	Mercenary (greedy)
_____	Grasping
_____	Sly
_____	Aggressive
_____	Ostentatious (showy or conspicuous)
_____	Extremely nationalistic
_____	Industrious
_____	Intelligent
_____	Ambitious
_____	Loyal to family
_____	Persistent
_____	Talkative
_____	Very religious
_____	Materialistic
_____	Sophisticated
_____	Alert

SOURCE: Adapted from D. Katz and K. W. Braly, "Racial Stereotypes of One Hundred College Students," *Journal of Abnormal Sociology and Psychology,* 28 (1933), 280–290. P. G. Devine and A. J. Elliot, "Are Racial Stereotypes Really Fading? The Princeton Trilogy Revisited," *Personality and Social Psychology Bulletin,* 21 (1995), 1139–1150.

After completing the Stereotype Checklist above, you can compare your results with those across seven decades. Remember that the 1932 percentages are from the original Katz and Braly study conducted at Princeton University. The 1950 data are also from Princeton, but reported by Gilbert. The 1969 and 1982 data were collected at Arizona State University by Gordon, and the 1995 data were collected at the University of Wisconsin by Devine and Elliot. In the Devine and Elliot study, which focused exclusively on black stereotypes, respondents were asked to indicate which traits made up the *cultural stereotype* of blacks, not necessarily ones that reflect the respondents' personal beliefs.

A close examination of Table 5-1 reveals both positive and negative trends regarding stereotypes of blacks and Jews in the United States. On a positive note,

TABLE 5-1 White College Student Stereotypes of Blacks and Jews Spanning 50 Years				
	Katz & Braly 1932 (%)	Gilbert 1950 (%)	Gordon 1969 (%)	Gordon 1982 (%)	Devine & Elliot 1995 (%)
Blacks *Negative Trait Selections*					
Superstitious	84	42	10	9	0
Lazy	75	32	18	18	45
Happy-go-lucky	39	17	5	1	3
Ignorant	38	24	8	9	14
Ostentatious	26	11	14	10	0
Stupid	22	10	2	1	11
Physically dirty	17	-	1	1	9
Naive	14	-	0	0	0
Sly	-	-	1	15	-
Aggressive	-	-	6	13	5
Loud	-	-	9	11	40
Arrogant	-	-	1	10	3
Unreliable	-	-	10	6	6
Athletic	-	-	-	-	74
Rhythmic	-	-	-	-	57
Low in intelligence	-	-	-	-	46
Poor	-	-	-	-	45
Criminal	-	-	-	-	35
Hostile	-	-	-	-	25
Other Trait Selections					
Musical	26	33	25	11	11
Intelligent	-	-	13	13	-
Materialistic	-	-	8	11	0
Sportsmanlike	-	-	6	9	-
Pleasure-loving	-	19	12	4	1
Sensitive	-	-	8	4	0
Very religious	24	17	-	-	11

	Katz & Braly 1932 (%)	Gilbert 1950 (%)	Gordon 1969 (%)	Gordon 1982 (%)	Devine & Elliot 1995 (%)
Jews *Negative Trait Selections*					
Shrewd	79	47	37	15	
Mercenary	49	28	8	2	
Grasping	34	17	1	1	
Sly	20	14	8	9	
Aggressive	12	-	10	6	
Ostentatious	-	-	9	3	
Extremely nationalistic	-	-	8	2	
Other Trait Selections					
Industrious	48	29	25	9	
Intelligent	29	37	33	21	
Ambitious	21	28	20	10	
Loyal to family	15	19	22	11	
Persistent	13	-	2	2	
Talkative	13	-	9	2	
Very religious	12	-	12	14	
Materialistic	-	-	19	11	
Sophisticated	-	-	5	9	
Alert	-	-	10	4	

SOURCES: Data from Katz and Braly, "Racial Stereotypes of One Hundred College Students"; G. Gilbert, "Stereotype Persistence and Change Among College Students," *Journal of Abnormal and Social Psychology,* 46 (1951), 245–254; L. Gordon, "The Fragmentation of Literary Stereotypes of Jews and Negroes Among College Students," *Pacific Sociological Review,* 16 (1973), 411–425; L. Gordon, "College Student Stereotypes of Blacks and Jews on Two Campuses: Four Studies Spanning 50 Years," *Sociology and Social Research,* 70 (1986), 200–201; P. G. Devine & A. J. Elliot, "Are Racial Stereotypes Really Fading? The Princeton Trilogy Revisited," *Personality and Social Psychology Bulletin,* 21 (1995), 1139–1150.

many of the more negative traits associated with blacks and Jews diminished from 1932 to 1982. For example, the percentage of respondents stereotyping blacks as lazy, ignorant, stupid, physically dirty, and naive dropped considerably. The percentage of respondents stereotyping Jews as shrewd and mercenary also dropped significantly. Unfortunately, the percentage of people characterizing blacks with some of the same negative traits actually rose from 1982 to 1995. Moreover, seven of the nine characteristics added by Devine and Elliot indicate that in contemporary American culture, some stereotypes remain deeply embedded. For example, 46 percent of respondents in the Devine and Elliot survey indicated that "low in intelligence" was characteristic of blacks. Thirty-five percent indicated that blacks were criminal, 25 percent that blacks were hostile, and 40 percent that blacks were loud. In addition, two stereotypical behaviors long associated with blacks—that is, that they are athletic and rhythmic—remain a staple of the black stereotype. Devine and Elliot argue that despite a shift in social norms discouraging the overt expression of prejudice and discrimination, stereotypical images of blacks remain salient (i.e., pronounced or conspicuous) in U.S. culture. Devine and Elliot conclude:

> Although efforts such as affirmative action and increased sensitivity to media portrayals of Blacks may ultimately have positive effects and facilitate the fading of cultural racial stereotypes, it is likely that such changes will take place over a protracted period of time.[55]

American Stereotypes.   Canadian psychologists Donald Taylor and Lana Porter examined some of the socially desirable aspects of stereotyping and allege that the negative connotation associated with stereotyping may be uniquely American. Taylor and Porter argue that historically the study of stereotypes in the United States has focused mainly on white stereotypes of African Americans, which have been particularly brutal and negative. Second, Taylor and Porter suggest that the essence of the political doctrine in the United States is modeled after the "melting pot" metaphor in which the peoples of all the different cultures immigrating to the United States get "stirred up in the great pot until cultural differences are boiled away and a single culture remains—American." Because stereotyping, by definition, recognizes and highlights differences between groups, it directly conflicts with the melting-pot image. Third, Taylor and Porter suggest that psychologists studying interpersonal attraction have long understood that perceived similarity is a major determinant in how much people are attracted to and will like others. The more we perceive people to be similar to us, the more likely we are to be attracted to and to like them. Hence, stereotypes that emphasize group differences essentially block the potential for intergroup friendships. Given these trends, Taylor and Porter assert that there are compelling reasons why Americans view stereotyping as a destructive social force. This, they argue, has led to an enormous investment in human and financial resources to rid people of their stereotypes.[56]

Taylor and Porter recognize that people in countries different from the United States are brought up in entirely different cultural contexts, in which it is perfectly acceptable to categorize people into groups. In Europe and Canada, for example, people presume that society is culturally diverse and are proud of their various group memberships. Taylor and Porter suggest that this philosophy contrasts sharply with the American melting-pot metaphor, which emphasizes cultural homogeneity. In other countries, the significance of cultural diversity is symbolized through metaphors very different from the melting pot, such as a mosaic or a montage.

Taylor and Porter claim that a fundamental feature of any pluralistic society is that ethnic attitudes exist between different groups, particularly in-groups and out-

Some studies indicate that because stereotypes are learned at such a young age, they become automatically activated in the presence of a member of the stereotyped group. *(© James Neuliep)*

groups. Ethnic attitudes and stereotypes are a part of all cultures; no one can avoid learning them.[57] In fact, research conducted by Trice and Rush indicates that stereotypes are well established in children's memories long before they acquire the intellectual ability to question or evaluate them. In their study of American four-year-olds, Trice and Rush found that boys were significantly more likely to aspire to male-stereotyped occupations (for example, police officer, truck driver, house builder) than female-stereotyped occupations (for example, teacher, nurse, secretary). Likewise, girls were significantly more like to aspire to female-stereotyped occupations than male-stereotyped occupations.[58]

Attitudes about ethnic groups may be relatively independent of ethnic group stereotypes, however. That is, although people may have knowledge of a stereotype, their personal beliefs may or may not be congruent with the stereotype. Some studies indicate that the degree of stereotyping of an ethnic group is unrelated to the evaluation of that group. Indeed, other studies demonstrate that stereotypes and personal beliefs are conceptually distinct cognitive structures. Psychologist Patricia Devine has shown that stereotyping is an *automatic* information-processing strategy, whereas prejudice is a *controlled* process.[59] According to Devine, automatic information processing is the unintentional and/or instinctive activation of thoughts that have been learned through repeated stimulation in memory. Automatic processes are largely unconscious and appear to be triggered by environmental stimuli (for example, a person from a different ethnic or cultural group). Devine notes that an important point about automatic processes is that they seem to be inescapable despite our conscious attempts to ignore them. Controlled processes, on the other hand, are intentional and require the conscious attention of the processor. Because they are intentional, controlled processes are useful in decision-making and problem-solving tasks.

Devine's model assumes that high- and low-prejudiced persons are equally knowledgeable of cultural stereotypes. Moreover, because stereotypes are learned at such an early age, they become automatically activated in the presence of a member of the stereotyped group. Devine contends that although just about everyone possesses knowledge of cultural stereotypes, not everyone believes or endorses them. Devine argues that the unintentional activation of the stereotype is equally strong and inescapable for the high- and low-prejudiced person. Devine's major thesis is that high- and low-prejudiced persons differ with respect to their personal beliefs about the stereotype. High-prejudiced persons have personal beliefs consistent with the stereotype, whereas low-prejudiced persons understand that the stereotype is inappropriate or inaccurate. Instead of believing in the stereotype, low-prejudiced persons create new thoughts or images (of the person or group) that require intentional activation. In her research, Devine found that high- and low-prejudiced individuals do not differ in their knowledge of stereotypes but diverge sharply in their sanction of the stereotype. For example, whereas most white Americans possess knowledge of the black stereotype, only a subset of these individuals actually endorses the stereotype and believes its validity. Such findings lend support to the idea that ethnic stereotyping simply may be a useful information-processing approach that is relatively innocuous.[60]

When stereotyping is viewed as a natural information-processing strategy, there are several explanations as to why it is so common and universal, none of which relate to prejudice. One explanation is called the *out-group homogeneity effect*. According to Judd and Park, the out-group homogeneity effect is the tendency for people to see members of an out-group as less diverse and more stereotypic than the members of that group see themselves. We have a tendency to see out-group members as highly similar (that is, homogeneous) yet view ourselves and our in-group members as unique and individual. For example, students may think that all professors are the same. Likewise, professors may think that all students are alike. Yet neither professors nor students see themselves as "just like" all the others. The out-group homogeneity effect is not necessarily the consequence of prejudice. Taylor and Porter contend that because in-groups and out-groups do not interact much, they may be unable to develop accurate representations of each other.[61]

A second plausible explanation for stereotyping is called the *illusory correlation principle*. According to Taylor and Porter, when two objects that are unfamiliar or unusual in some way are observed to be connected on one occasion, we have the tendency to believe that they are always connected. For example, if we observe an out-group member participating in some atypical incident or behavior, such as a felony, out-group members and felonies become associated in our minds. Then, the next time we see a member of the same out-group, we will stereotype the person as a felon. The correlation between the out-group members and felonies is illusory and/or unreal because the out-group is linked to felonies on account of only one or relatively few observed occurrences.[62]

Neither the out-group homogeneity effect nor the illusory correlation principle is necessarily wrong or socially "bad." They are naturally occurring information-processing strategies that are a part of everyone's normal cognitive repertoire. The problem is that they may lead to negative attitudes and subsequent prejudice.

Richard Schaefer offers two other reasons why stereotypes are so widely held. First, he argues that stereotypes may arise out of real conditions. For example, a disproportionate number of people from a particular racial or ethnic group may live in poverty, so members of other groups may stereotype all of them as poor or even lazy. A second explanation of stereotypes is their role in self-fulfilling prophecies. The dominant group in a particular culture may construct social or legal obstacles, making it hard for members of the stereotyped group to act differently from the stereotype. Hence, conformity to the stereotype, although forced, validates the stereotype in the minds of the dominant group. For example, members of a subordinate stereotyped group may have difficulty obtaining high-paying, prestigious employment because members of the dominant group refuse to hire them. Hence members of the subordinate group must accept low-paying, less prestigious jobs and thereby become stereotyped.[63]

Henri Taifel contends that another reason why people retain stereotypes is because they help us develop and maintain a positive self-esteem. Our membership in various groups constitutes a major aspect of our self-concept. Our social identities essentially are made up of our group memberships (for example, husband, professor, colleague, friend, counsel). Taifel asserts that our sense of self-esteem is nourished when we differentiate our in-groups from out-groups, usually by assigning traits (that is, stereotypes) that are favorable to the in-group and ones that are negative to the out-group. Typically, we differentiate our in-groups on the basis of power, ancestry, religion, language, culture, and race, as well as a host of other variables.[64]

According to Steele and Aronson, some members of stereotyped groups actually start to believe the stereotype. They call this phenomenon *stereotype threat*. Stereotype threat occurs when we sense that some aspect of our self (for example, our behavior, physical characteristics, or social condition) seems to match the stereotype, thus making it appear valid. Steele and Aronson believe that stereotype threat is experienced essentially as a self-evaluative threat. Culturally held stereotypes pose the most danger for stereotyped groups since large numbers of people may hold them, leading members of the group to sense that the stereotype is valid. When the stereotype is negative, the effects can be disastrous to the stereotyped group. In their research on stereotype threat, Steele and Aronson varied the stereotype vulnerability of blacks taking a difficult verbal test. In one condition, blacks were told that the test was a valid measure of intellectual ability. In a second condition, they were told that the test was simply a problem-solving activity that was not designed to measure ability. Their results showed that blacks performed worse than whites when the test was presented as a measure of their intellectual ability but improved dramatically, matching the performance of whites, when the test was presented as not reflective of ability. Steele and Aronson theorize that stereotype threat inhibits efficient information processing, as do other evaluative pressures. Stereotype-threatened persons alternate their attention between trying to accomplish the task at hand and trying to assess their self-significance, resulting in reduced speed and less accuracy.[65]

FIGURE 5-7   Expectations Affect Perception

Although evidence suggests that stereotyping may be independent of one's attitudes about others, some studies have demonstrated that stereotypes distort the social perception of others. Human perception is not necessarily accurate and honest. Perception is influenced by one's needs, wishes, and expectations. In many instances, people perceive what they expect to perceive, regardless of reality. Figure 5-7 illustrates how expectations affect perception.

Most read the words in the triangle as "Paris in the spring," failing to notice the duplication of the word *the*. By definition, stereotyping is categorizing people according to some easily identifiable characteristic and then attributing to them qualities or behaviors believed to be typical of members of that classification. In this sense, stereotyping leads to expectations that, in turn, affect our social perception of others. In what is now considered a classic experiment, Bruner and Goodman found that persons of lower socioeconomic status tended to accentuate the size of coins.[66] In related research, Duncan found that perceptions of an ambiguously aggressive act are strongly influenced by racial stereotypes. In Duncan's study, ninety-six white male college students coded the behaviors observed in what they thought was a live conversation on a television monitor. The conversation ended with an ambiguous shove. Half of the students were shown a black actor shoving another person, whereas the other half were shown the identical act performed by a white actor. Thirty-five of forty-eight observers coded the shove as violent behavior when it was performed by a black actor, yet only six of forty-eight observers coded the identical act as violent behavior when it was performed by a white actor. Duncan argued that because of stereotypes associating blacks with violence, the violent-behavior category is cognitively more accessible to observers viewing a black perpetrator than to those viewing a white one.[67] The results of Duncan's study were replicated by Sagar and Schofield, who studied black and white sixth-graders. The students were shown a variety of ambiguously aggressive acts performed by black and white actors. Both black and white students rated the behaviors of black actors as more mean and threatening than the identical behaviors performed by white actors. Sagar and Schofield argue that stereotypes create expectations and conclude that "in the existing social order, the stereotype is all too real. To activate it, the person engaging in an ambiguous behavior need only be black."[68]

Intercultural Conversation

An Intercultural Conversation: Stereotyping

Akira is an exchange student from Japan who is spending a semester at an American university. Jim is a student at the same university who was born and raised in Milwaukee. Jim and Akira meet for the first time.

Jim: Hi. (*Thinks to himself, "Man, he's so short, he's just like all the other Asians I've seen"*)

Akira: Hi, I'm Akira. (*Thinks to himself, "Wow, he's pretty tall"*)

Jim: I'm Jim. Are you a student here? (*Thinks to himself, "He's probably a math major"*)

Akira: Yes. (*Thinks to himself, "He probably thinks I'm Chinese"*)

Jim: Are you from Japan? (*Thinks to himself, "He probably wonders if I drive a Honda . . . I wonder if he realizes how many Americans are unemployed because of all the imported Japanese cars"*)

Akira: Yes, I am. (*Thinks to himself, "What will he ask me now . . . these Americans are so impolite"*)

Jim: Yeah? That's cool. How do you like it in the United States? Have you been here before? (*Thinks to himself, "He must love it here . . . it's got to be better than his country"*)

Akira: I like it here a lot. (*Thinks to himself, "I'd better not tell him that the food here is horrible . . . it might upset him"*)

In this brief exchange, both Jim and Akira engage in categorization and stereotyping. Initially Jim categorizes Akira based on conspicuous differences ("Man, he's short"), familiarity ("He's probably a math major"), and projection ("I wonder if he realizes how many Americans are unemployed because of all the imported Japanese cars"). Jim also stereotypes Akira as good in math. Akira categorizes and stereotypes Jim in much the same way.

Ethnocentrism

All along, this textbook has described intercultural communication as a symbolic activity where the thoughts and ideas of one person are encoded into a verbal and/or nonverbal message format, then transmitted through some channel to another person, who must decode it, interpret it, and respond to it. And at this point you understand that because your messages are filtered by your cultural upbringing, the messages you send are not necessarily the messages received by others, especially others from cultures different than your own. Because we are naturally biased by our culture, our intercultural exchanges are necessarily, to a greater or lesser extent, charged with ethnocentrism. Near the end of Chapter 1 is the General Ethnocentrism (GENE) scale, designed to assess your level of ethnocentrism. You may want to refer back to Chapter 1 for a moment and review your score on the GENE scale.

One of the central concepts in understanding out-group attitudes and intergroup relations is ethnocentrism. Nearly a century ago, sociologist W. G. Sumner defined ethnocentrism as "the technical name for this view of things in which one's own group is the center of everything, and all others are scaled and rated with reference to it."[69] Sumner argued that ethnocentrism nourished a group's pride and vanity while looking on outsiders, or out-groups, with contempt. According to Segall, ethnocentrism is now recognized as a universal phenomenon experienced in all cultures.[70] Many scholars maintain that ethnocentricity is a natural condition and that most peoples of the world do not like foreigners and openly display feelings of hostility and fear toward them.[71] Lustig and Koester contend that all cultures have an ethnocentric tendency. Cultures teach their members to use the categories of their own cultural experiences when they judge persons from other cultures, microcultures, races, or religions. They argue that it is natural for humans to prefer what is typically experienced, but that ethnocentrism is learned.[72] At the core of ethnocentrism, asserts Segall, is the tendency for any people to put their own group in a position of centrality and worth, while creating and reinforcing negative attitudes and behaviors toward out-groups.[73] As Dutch sociologist Geert Hofstede argues, ethnocentrism is to a people what egocentrism is to an individual.[74]

Donald Klopf notes that the etymology of the term *ethnocentrism* is from the Greek words *ethnos*, which refers to nation, and *kentron*, which refers to center. Literally, then, this terms refers to the view that one's country is the center of the universe.[75] Neuliep and McCroskey assert, however, that the term can also be applied to an ethnic or microcultural group within a country. Similar views can be held on the basis of religion (for example, "Judaism is the only true religion") or region of origin (for example, "Texans are the only real Americans"). Moreover, Neuliep and McCroskey contend that ethnocentrism is essentially descriptive, not necessarily pejorative. They argue that "ethnocentrism may serve a very valuable function when one's central group is under actual, or the threat of, attack. Ethnocentrism forms the basis for patriotism and the willingness to sacrifice for one's central group."[76] Ethnocentrism might also emerge in the business world. Varner and Beamer note that business organizations that succeed in their own culture often adopt an ethnocentric stance when they take their business to other cultures, believing that if they know how to make it work at home, they can make it work anywhere.[77]

The facets of ethnocentrism are exemplified by attitudes and behaviors toward in-groups versus attitudes and behaviors toward out-groups. Attributions made about the attitudes and behavior of the in-group and out-group are biased in favor of the in-group at the expense of the out-group.[78] According to Levine and Campbell, ethnocentric groups see themselves as virtuous and superior, see their own standards of value as universal and intrinsically true, and their customs as original and centrally human. On the contrary, out-groups are seen as contemptible, immoral, inferior, and weak. Behaviorally, ethnocentric groups foster cooperative relations and obedience with in-group members while maintaining a willingness to remain an in-group member. Simultaneously, ethnocentric groups compete with, and are not obedient to, out-group members and are unwilling to convert to their group. In many cases, out-groups are often blamed for in-group troubles and serve as bad examples in the training of in-group children.[79] Sharma, Shimp, and Shin argue that ethnocentrism functions by helping to secure the survival of the in-group by increasing its solidarity, conformity, cooperation, loyalty, and effectiveness.[80]

In 1950, a series of studies was published representing the first systematic social scientific treatment of ethnocentrism: *The Authoritarian Personality*, by Adorno, Frenkel-Brunswik, Levinson, and Sanford, dealt with the psychology of fascism, anti-Semitism, and what the authors called the "antidemocratic" personality. They argued that nationalism is a species of ethnocentrism, that ethnocentrism is an expression of authoritarianism, and that authoritarianism is a personality defect.[81] In *The Authoritarian Personality*, ethnocentrism is defined as "based on a pervasive and rigid ingroup-outgroup distinction; it involves stereotyped, negative imagery and hostile attitudes regarding outgroups, stereotyped positive imagery and submissive attitudes regarding ingroups, and a hierarchical, authoritarian view of group interaction in which ingroups are rightly dominant, outgroups subordinate."[82]

A central thesis of *The Authoritarian Personality* is that prejudices against minorities and ethnic groups constitute a generalized personality profile and that prejudices should not be studied in isolation. The theoretical explanation for an individual's prejudice toward Jews, for example, is that this particular prejudice is representative of an entire set of negative attitudes about ethnic, racial, or gender out-groups. This generalized attitude profile is called ethnocentrism. Although *The Authoritarian Personality* has been sharply criticized for a variety of reasons by a number of researchers, a general consensus has been reached that prejudices against minority and ethnic groups constitute a general attitudinal profile.[83]

Another line of research deals with a phenomenon called *ethnocentric attributional bias*. This effect was introduced by Taylor and Jaggi, who argue that in-group members have a tendency to make internal attributions for the positive behavior of other in-group members while making external attributions for their negative behavior. For example, if we observe a member of our in-group engaging in a positive behavior, such as assisting an elderly person across the street, we tend to attribute the cause of the behavior to some internal disposition of the individual, such as good values or strong conviction. On the other hand, if we observe a member of our in-group engaged in some negative behavior—for example, a fist fight—we may attribute the cause of the behavior to external factors (for example, the other guy started it, or the in-group person was acting in self-defense). The reverse is true for attributions of out-group members. That is, external attributions are made for the positive behavior of out-group members, whereas internal attributions are made for their negative behavior.[84]

The research of Peter Grant indicates that a threat to one's social identity fosters ethnocentrism. Grant's premise is that our group memberships are a fundamental part of our social identities and that we constantly make social comparisons between in-groups and out-groups. Most of the time, our comparisons are biased in favor of the in-group. Grant argues that virtually all groups maintain a positive social identity by differentiating themselves from out-groups. In some situations, out-groups may threaten the in-group in some way. In such cases, the in-group members tend to engage in a kind of collective ethnocentric action to counter the threat. Grant's studies show that when our in-group identity is threatened, we tend to respond ethnocentrically by differentiating the out-group from our in-group along stereotyped and attitudinal dimensions. The strength of group identification is significantly related to differentiation for these groups.[85] The more we differentiate, the more strength of group identification.

Another body of research has emerged focusing on *consumer ethnocentrism*. Shimp and Sharma use the phrase "consumer ethnocentrism" to represent the beliefs held by American consumers about the appropriateness and morality of purchasing foreign products. Consumer ethnocentrism may partially explain why consumers evaluate domestic products more favorably than they do foreign goods.[86]

ETHNOCENTRISM AND INTERCULTURAL COMMUNICATION

Ethnocentrism can be an obstacle to intercultural communication competence. Gudykunst and Kim assert that high levels of ethnocentrism are dysfunctional with respect to intercultural communication and expand upon Peng's concept of communicative distance and Lukens's concept of ethnocentric speech.[87] Peng alleges that ethnocentric attitudes are reflected in linguistic diversity and create communicative distance between interactants that manifests itself in the expressions, idioms, and words of the speakers.[88] Lukens claims that ethnocentric speech results in three types of communicative distance: indifference, avoidance, and disparagement.[89] The *distance of indifference* is communicated in speech patterns such as talking loudly and slowly to a nonnative speaker of the language, with exaggerated pronunciation and simplification. The communicative distance of indifference is also communicated in such expressions as "Jew them down," "top of the totem pole," and "the blind leading the blind." The *distance of avoidance* communicates that the speaker prefers to minimize or avoid contact with persons from other cultures through the use of in-group jargon or slang that members of other cultures or out-groups do not understand. The *distance of disparagement* is communicated to openly express contempt for persons of different cultures and is communicated through ethnophaulisms such as "nigger," "nip," "chink," and so forth.[90] Although ethnocentrism has potential positive as well as negative consequences, it is an orientation that is presumed to have important effects on an individual's communication behavior, particularly when the context of that communication involves people with diverse cultural, ethnic, religious, or regional backgrounds.

ETHNOCENTRISM AND RACISM

Although the terms *racism* and *ethnocentrism* are not synonymous, they are related. Ethnocentrism refers to the degree to which one sees his or her culture as superior and the standard by which other cultures should be judged. Racism refers to a belief that one racial group is superior to others and other racial groups are necessarily inferior. To be ethnocentric but not racist is possible. To be racist and not ethnocentric is probably unlikely. In other words, you may believe your culture is superior to other cultures, but not necessarily believe that your race is superior. However, if you believe that your race is superior, chances are very good that you also believe your culture is superior. There is a biological component at the core of racist ideology that does not exist in the concept of ethnocentrism. Racist ideology is a belief in the moral and intellectual superiority of one race over the others. This alleged superiority is biologically based. Because such superiority is biological rather than social, it cannot be conditioned by culture or education. However, racist ideology asserts that racial-biological superiority does, in fact, translate into cultural and/or social superiority. Hence, superior race produces superior culture. While racism refers to the hierarchical ranking of one race above the others, ethnocentrism refers to the strong preference of one's own culture over other cultures. As racism is rooted in biology, ethnocentrism is rooted in ethnicity and culture. Racial groups are biological. Ethnic groups can be based on blood, common history, nationality, religion, or even geographic region.[91]

In addition to their conceptual differences, racism and ethnocentrism have different origins. As mentioned previously, many scholars believe that ethnocentrism is a universal phenomenon that reflects a biologically rooted survival instinct experienced, to some degree, by all people in all cultures. Hence, it is thought that ethnocentrism is innately human—that is, we are born ethnocentric. Racism, on the other hand, is not universal, and is thought to be learned, which raises this question: Why would anyone teach others to be racist? One argument, espoused by scholars from across a wide variety of disciplines, is that racism is the byproduct of ignorance, fear, and hate. Although this argument is attractive, it fails to take into account the fact that many of the leading philosophers of Western civilization espoused undeniably racist views. David Hume wrote, "I am apt to suspect Negroes, and in general all the other species of men, to be naturally inferior to the whites." Immanuel Kant wrote that "the Negroes have received from nature no intelligence that rises above the foolish." George Hegel wrote, "The Negro race has perfect contempt for humanity."[92]

Although slavery is not unique to the United States, in American history racism is often associated with the forced immigration and enslavement of Africans. Because the U.S. Constitution was predicated on the tenet that all men are created equal, slavery presented a moral dilemma for the country. The enslavement and brutal treatment of Africans was a blatant violation of any sort of equality creed. But if whites could define blacks as biologically inferior, then they could justify slavery and do so with a clear conscience. Thus a flagrantly racist system of unequal treatment was established.[93]

Many political scientists offer a socioeconomic-political explanation of the causes of racism, an explanation frequently called the frustration-aggression hypothesis. During times of social, economic, or political stress (e.g., depressed economy, mass immigration) the dominant cultural group often will place blame on subordinate racial groups. Racism becomes a way of releasing the stress and frustration associated with difficult social, economic, or political times. In these situations, the dominant group often will act out its frustration against the subordinate racial group, via prejudice and discrimination.[94] Racism, stereotyping, prejudice, and discrimination are often linked. When a racial group is labeled inferior, stereotypes emerge, like those presented earlier in this chapter. Because racial stereotypes are often negative, people become prejudiced toward the racial group and discriminate against them. Prejudice is how people feel or think about a particular group, and discrimination is the behavioral outcome: that is, action against that group.

Chapter Summary

This chapter has described and explained the perceptual context of intercultural communication. Whenever two people come together and interact, they process immense amounts of information. Some communicative situations, especially intercultural communication contexts, have higher information rates than others and require the interactants to reduce more uncertainty than usual. Regardless of culture, human beings, for the most part, process information similarly. Although culture impacts the types of information we process, all humans take in, store, and recall information in much the same way. Culture's role in this process leads us to make different kinds of interpretations about the information we process. All persons categorize, stereotype, and to some extent are ethnocentric with the information they process.

GLOSSARY OF TERMS

Carpentered-world hypothesis: Learned tendency by those living in industrialized cultures to interpret nonrectangular figures as rectangles seen in perspective.

Categorization:: Classifying or sorting of perceived information into distinct groups.

Cognition: Higher mental processes, such as perception and memory.

Decay: Memory loss due to lack of use.

Discrimination: Acting or behaving in a negative way toward members of a distinct group (e.g., ethnic or racial) because of membership in the distinct group.

Encoding specificity: The degree to which the content in which an item is put into memory facilitates the recall of that item.

Episodic memory: A component of long-term memory in which private individual memories are stored.

Ethnocentric attributional bias: The tendency to make internal attributions for the positive behavior of the in-group and external attributions for its negative behavior.

Ethnocentrism: Tendency to place one's own group or ethnicity in a position of centrality and worth, and to create negative attitudes and behaviors toward other groups.

Iconic memory: Visual sensory memory; the brief visual impressions left after seeing an object or a person.

Illusory correlation principle: The tendency to believe that when two objects or persons are observed to be linked on one occasion, they are always linked (or correlated).

Interference: Obstruction of recall by old or new information.

Long-term memory: Cognitive storage area in which large amounts of information are held relatively permanently.

Memory: The storage of information in the human brain over time.

Out-group homogeneity effect: The tendency to see members of an out-group as highly similar while seeing the members of the in-group as unique and individual.

Perception: The mental interpretation of external stimuli via sensation.

Perceptual filters: Physical, social, and psychological processes that screen and bias incoming stimuli.

Prejudice: A preconceived judgment or opinion about a person or group of people based on their membership in a distinct group (often ethnic or racial). The preconceived opinion is usually, if not always, without merit.

Racism: An ideology promoting the superiority of one racial group over the others. The alleged superiority is ascribed to biological (i.e., racial) differences between groups.

Recall/retrieval: Calling to mind or recollecting stored information.

Semantic memory: A part of long-term memory in which general information such as how to read and write and the meanings of words are stored.

Sensation: Gathering of visual, auditory, olfactic, haptic, and taste stimuli/ information.

Sensory receptors: Eyes, ears, nose, mouth, and skin.

Sensory register: Storage center for raw sense data.

Short-term memory: Cognitive storage area in which small amounts of information are held for short periods of time, usually less than twenty seconds.

Stereotypes: A subset of categorizing that involves the attribution of characteristics of a group to an individual based on the individual's membership in that group. Stereotypes are categories with an attitude.

REFERENCES

1. M. Polyani, *Personal Knowledge: Towards a Post-Critical Philosophy* (Chicago: University of Chicago Press, 1958), p. 4.
2. R. Lachman, J. L. Lachman, and E. C. Butterfield, *Cognitive Psychology and Information Processing: An Introduction* (Hillsdale, N.J.: Erlbaum, 1979); N. A. Stillings, S. E. Weisler, C. H. Chase, et al., *Cognitive Science: An Introduction* (Cambridge: Massachusetts Institute of Technology Press, 1995).
3. M. Matlin, *Cognition* (New York: Holt, Rinehart, and Winston, 1983).
4. Ibid.
5. These demonstrations are from Matlin, *Cognition.*
6. J. C. McCroskey and V. P. Richmond, *Fundamentals of Human Communication: An Interpersonal Perspective* (Prospect Heights, Ill.: Waveland, 1996).
7. B. Goss, *The Psychology of Human Communication* (Prospect Heights, Ill.: Waveland, 1989).
8. J. W. Berry, Y. H. Poortinga, M. H. Segall, and P. R. Dasen, *Cross-Cultural Psychology: Research and Applications* (Cambridge: Cambridge University Press, 1992).
9. H. Reuning and W. Wortley, "Psychological Studies of the Bushmen," *Psychologia Africana* (Monograph Supplement 7), cited in Berry et al., *Cross-Cultural Psychology.*
10. C. H. Wyndham, "Ergonomic Problems in the Transition from Peasant to Industrial Life in South Africa," in *Ethnic Variables in Human Factor Engineering,* ed. A. Chapanis (Baltimore: Johns Hopkins University Press, 1975), pp. 115– 134); Berry et al., *Cross-Cultural Psychology.*
11. Berry et al., *Cross-Cultural Psychology.*
12. Ibid.
13. M. H. Segall, "A Cross-Cultural Research Contribution to Unraveling the Nativist-Empiricist Controversy," in *Psychology and Culture,* ed. W. J. Lonner and R. Malpass (Boston: Allyn and Bacon, 1994), pp. 135–138.
14. Ibid.; M. H. Segall, *Cross-Cultural Psychology: Human Behavior in Global Perspective* (Monterey, Calif.: Brooks/Cole, 1979).

15. S. L. M. Dawson, B. M. Young, and P. P. C. Choi, "Developmental Influences on Geometric Illusion Susceptibility Among Hong Kong Chinese Children," *Journal of Cross-Cultural Psychology,* 4 (1973), 49–74.

16. Segall, *Cross-Cultural Psychology.*

17. Lachman, Lachman, and Butterfield, *Cognitive Psychology and Information Processing.*

18. Ibid.

19. R. H. Logie, *Visual-Spatial Working Memory* (Hillsdale, N.J.: Erlbaum, 1995).

20. G. A. Miller, "The Magical Number Seven, Plus or Minus Two: Some Limits on Our Capacity for Processing Information," *Psychological Review,* 63 (1956), 81–97.

21. Lachman, Lachman, and Butterfield, *Cognitive Psychology and Information Processing.*

22. R. W. Howard, *Learning and Memory: Major Ideas, Principles, Issues and Applications* (Westport, Conn.: Praeger, 1995).

23. Howard, *Learning and Memory;* Stillings et al., *Cognitive Science.*

24. E. Tulving, "Episodic and Semantic Memory," in *Organization of Memory,* ed. E. Tulving and W. Donaldson (New York: Academic Press, 1972).

25. Lachman, Lachman, and Butterfield, *Cognitive Psychology and Information Processing;* Howard, *Learning and Memory.*

26. B. Goss, J. W. Neuliep, and D. O'Hair, "Reduced Conversational Recall as a Function of Negative Arousal: A Preliminary Analysis," *Communication Research Reports,* 2 (1985), 202–205.

27. Matlin, *Cognition.*

28. Ibid.

29. B. Rogoff, *Apprenticeship in Thinking: Cognitive Development in Social Context.* New York: Oxford University Press, 1990.

30. Ibid.

31. M. Yoshida, C. Fernandez, and J. W. Stigler, "Japanese and American Students' Differential Recognition Memory for Teachers' Statements During a Mathematics Lesson," *Journal of Educational Psychology,* 85 (1993), 610–617.

32. M. Cole and J. Gay, "Culture and Memory," *American Anthropologist,* 74 (1972), 1066–1084.

33. B. M. Ross and C. Millson, "Repeated Memory of Oral Prose in Ghana and New York," *International Journal of Psychology,* 5 (1970), 173–181.

34. R. J. Harris, L. M. Schoen, and D. I. Hensley, "A Cross-Cultural Study of Story Memory," *Journal of Cross-Cultural Psychology,* 23 (1992), 133–147.

35. I. Liu, "Chinese Cognition," in *The Psychology of the Chinese People,* ed. M. H. Bond (Hong Kong: Oxford University Press, 1986), pp. 73–105.

36. G. Allport, *The Nature of Prejudice* (New York: Doubleday, 1958).

37. W. B. Gudykunst and Y. Y. Kim, *Communicating with Strangers: An Approach to Intercultural Communication* (New York: McGraw-Hill, 1997).

38. R. Brislin, *Cross-Cultural Encounters* (Elmsford, N.Y.: Pergamon, 1981).

39. Ibid.

40. Ibid.

41. Ibid.

42. Ibid.

43. Ibid.

44. Ibid.

45. Ibid.

46. Ibid.

47. Ibid.

48. F. Rudmin, "The Pleasure of Serendipity in Historical Research: On Finding 'Stereotype' in Morier's (1824) Haiji Baba," *Cross-Cultural Psychology Bulletin,* 23 (1989), 8–11; D. M. Taylor and L. E. Porter, "A Multicultural View of Stereotyping," in *Psychology and Culture,* pp. 85–90.

49. W. Lippman, *Public Opinion* (New York: Macmillan, 1992).

50. R. Schaefer, *Racial and Ethnic Groups,* 7th ed. (New York: Longman, 1998).

51. Gudykunst and Kim, *Communicating with Strangers.*

52. Taylor and Porter, "A Multicultural View of Stereotyping"; Berry et al., *Cross-Cultural Psychology.*

53. V. M. Esses and M. P. Zanna, "Mood and the Expression of Ethnic Stereotypes," *Journal of Personality and Social Psychology,* 69 (1995), 1052–1068.

54. D. Katz and K. W. Braly, "Racial Stereotypes of One Hundred College Students," *Journal of Abnormal Sociology and Psychology,* 28 (1933), 280–290.

55. P. G. Devine and A. J. Elliot, "Are Racial Stereotypes Really Fading? The Princeton Trilogy Revisited," *Personality and Social Psychology Bulletin,* 21 (1995), 1139–1150; quote at p. 1149.

56. Taylor and Porter, "A Multicultural View of Stereotyping"; quote at p. 87.

57. Ibid.

58. A. D. Trice and K. Rush, "Sex-Stereotyping in Four-Year-Olds' Occupational Aspirations," *Perceptual and Motor Skills,* 81 (1995), 701–702.

59. P. G. Devine, "Stereotypes and Prejudice: Their Automatic and Controlled Components," *Journal of Personality and Social Psychology,* 56 (1989), 5–18.

60. Ibid.

61. C. M. Judd and B. Park, "Outgroup Homogeneity: Judgments of Variability at the Individual and Group Levels," *Journal of Personality and Social Psychology,* 54 (1988), 778–788; B. Park and C. M. Judd, "Measures and Models of Perceived Out-Group Variability," *Journal of Personality and Social Psychology,* 59 (1990), 173–191; Taylor and Porter, "A Multicultural View of Stereotyping."

62. Taylor and Porter, "A Multicultural View of Stereotyping."

63. Schaefer, *Racial and Ethnic Groups.*

64. H. Taifel, *Differentiating Between Social Groups: Studies in Intergroup Behavior* (London: Academic Press, 1978).

65. C. M. Steele and J. Aronson, "Stereotype Threat and the Intellectual Performance of African Americans," *Journal of Personality and Social Psychology,* 69 (1995), 797–811.

66. J. A. Bruner and C. C. Goodman, "Value and Need as Organizing Factors in Perception," *Journal of Abnormal Social Psychology,* 42 (1947), 33–44.

67. B. L. Duncan, "Differential Social Perception and Attribution of Intergroup Violence: Testing the Lower Limits of Stereotyping of Blacks," *Journal of Personality and Social Psychology,* 34 (1976), 590–598.

68. A. H. Sagar and J. W. Schofield, "Racial and Behavioral Cues in Black and White Children's Perceptions of Ambiguously Aggressive Acts," *Journal of Personality and Social Psychology,* 39 (1980), 590–598.

69. W. W. Sumner, *Folkways* (Boston: Ginn, 1906).

70. Segall, *Cross-Cultural Psychology.*

71. I. M. Lewis, *Social Anthropology in Perspective* (Cambridge: Cambridge University Press, 1985); R. Lynn, "The Sociobiology of Nationalism," *New Society,* (July 1976), 11–14; J. P. Rushton, "Genetic Similarity, Human Altruism, and Group Selection," *Behavioral and Brain Sciences,* 12 (1984), 503–559.

72. M. W. Lustig and J. Koester, *Intercultural Competence: Interpersonal Communication Across Cultures* (New York: HarperCollins, 1996).

73. Segall, *Cross-Cultural Psychology.*

74. G. Hofstede, *Cultures and Organizations: Software of the Mind* (London: McGraw-Hill, 1991).

75. D. W. Klopf, *Intercultural Encounters: The Fundamentals of Intercultural Communication* (Englewood, Colo.: Morton, 1995).

76. J. W. Neuliep and J. C. McCroskey, "The Development of a U.S. and Generalized Ethnocentrism Scale," *Communication Research Reports,* 14 (1997), 385–398.

77. I. Varner and L. Beamer, *Intercultural Communication in the Global Workplace* (Chicago: Irwin, 1995).

78. M. Hewstone and C. Ward, "Ethnocentrism and Causal Attribution in Southeast Asia," *Journal of Personality and Social Psychology,* 48 (1985), 614–623; M. Islam and M. Hewstone, "Intergroup Attributions and Affective Consequences in Majority and Minority Groups," *Journal of Personality and Social Psychology,* 64 (1993), 936–950; J. G. Weber, "The Nature of Ethnocentric Attribution Bias: Ingroup Protection or Enhancement?" *Journal of Experimental Social Psychology,* 30 (1994), 482–504.

79. R. A. Levine and D. T. Campbell, *Ethnocentrism: Theories of Conflict, Ethnic Attitudes, and*

Group Behavior (New York: John Wiley and Sons, 1972).

80. S. Sharma, T. A. Shimp, and J. Shin, "Consumer Ethnocentrism: A Test of Antecedents and Moderators," *Journal of the Academy of Marketing Science,* 23 (1995), 26–28.

81. T. W. Adorno, E. Frenkel-Brunswik, D. J. Levinson, and R. N. Sanford, eds., *The Authoritarian Personality* (New York: Harper & Brothers, 1950); H. D. Forbes, *Nationalism, Ethnocentrism, and Personality* (Chicago: University of Chicago Press, 1985).

82. D. J. Levinson, "Politico-Economic Ideology and Group Memberships in Relation to Ethnocentrism," in *The Authoritarian Personality,* p. 150.

83. M. M. Bierly, "Prejudice Toward Contemporary Out-Groups as a Generalized Attitude," *Journal of Applied Social Psychology,* 15 (1985), 255–260; G. Murphy and R. Likert, *Public Opinion and the Individual* (New York: Harper & Brothers, 1983); J. J. Ray and F. A. Lovejoy, "The Generality of Racial Prejudice," *Journal of Social Psychology,* 126 (1986), 563–564; G. Rubinstein, "Two Peoples in One Land: A Validation Study of Altmeyer's Right Wing Authoritarianism Scale in the Palestinian and Jewish Societies in Israel," *Journal of Cross-Cultural Psychology,* 27 (1996), 216–230.

84. D. M. Taylor and V. Jaggi, "Ethnocentrism and Causal Attribution in a South Indian Context," *Journal of Cross-Cultural Psychology,* 5 (1974), 162–171; J. G. Weber, "The Nature of Ethnocentric Attribution Bias: Ingroup Protection or Enhancement?" *Journal of Experimental Social Psychology,* 30 (1994), 482–504.

85. P. R. Grant, "Ethnocentrism Between Groups of Unequal Power in Response to Perceived Threat to Social Identity and Valued Resources," *Canadian Journal of Behavioral Science,* 24 (1992), 348–370; P. R. Grant, "Ethnocentrism in Response to a Threat to Social Identity," in

Replication Research in the Social Sciences, ed. J. W. Neuliep [special issue], *Journal of Social Behavior and Personality,* 8 (1993), 143–154; P. R. Grant and R. Brown, "From Ethnocentrism to Collective Protest: Responses to Relative Deprivation and Threats to Social Identity," *Social Psychology Quarterly,* 58 (1995), 195–211.

86. T. A. Shimp and S. Sharma, "Consumer Ethnocentrism: Construction and Validation of the CETSCALE," *Journal of Marketing Research,* 24 (1987), 280–289; R. G. Netemeyer, S. Durvasula, and D. R. Lichtenstein, "A Cross-National Assessment of the Reliability and Validity of the CETSCALE," *Journal of Marketing Research,* 28 (1991), 320–328.

87. Gudykunst and Kim, *Communicating with Strangers.*

88. F. Peng, "Communicative Distance," *Language Science,* 31 (1974), 32–28.

89. J. Lukens, "Ethnocentric Speech," *Ethnic Groups,* 2 (1978), 35–53.

90. Gudykunst and Kim, *Communicating with Strangers*; Peng, "Communicative Distance"; Lukens, "Ethnocentric Speech."

91. This discussion of racism is based on A. de Benoist, "What Is Racism?" *Telos,* 114 (1999) 11–49; and on D. D'Souza, *The End of Racism: Principles for a Multiracial Society* (New York: The Free Press, 1995).

92. D'Souza, *The End of Racism,* pp. 28–29.

93. This slavery argument is found in a variety of sources. The sources used here include "A Learned Behaviour," *Canada & the World Backgrounder,* 61 (1996), 4–10; M. T. Briggs, director and producer, *Ethnic Notions* [film] (1987; available from California Newsreel, Berkeley, Calif.)

94. C. T. Wolfe and S. J. Spencer, "Stereotypes and Prejudice," *American Behavioral Scientist,* 40 (1996), 177–187; S. Castle, "Explaining Racism in the New Germany," *Social Alternatives,* 12 (1993), 9–13.

The Sociorelational Context

CHAPTER OBJECTIVES

After reading this chapter, you should be able to:

- Compare and contrast membership and nonmembership groups.
- Compare and contrast voluntary and involuntary groups.
- Define and discuss the significance of reference groups.
- Define and discuss the concept of group roles.
- Compare and contrast formal and informal roles across cultures.
- Compare and contrast family roles across cultures.
- Compare and contrast sex roles across cultures.

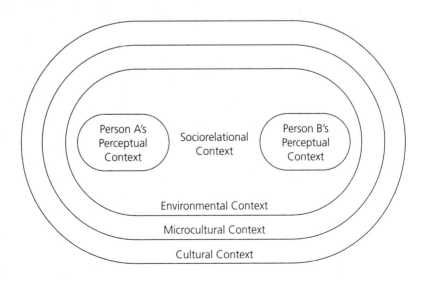

All human beings, regardless of culture, belong to groups. Although some cultures (such as the United States) promote individuality and independence, our survival depends on our interdependency and cooperation with other humans. This, of course, requires human communication. Historians believe that it was through social cooperation, social organization, the initiation of group hunting methods, a system of distributing work, and our ability to share knowledge that our human ancestors were empowered to survive when other related species, such as Neanderthals, became extinct.[2]

In many ways intercultural communication is a group phenomenon experienced by individuals. In other words, when people from different cultures come together to interact, they typically view each other not as unique individuals, but as members of a different cultural *group*. Think about your own communication experiences with strangers from different cultures. When you meet a stranger from a different culture, do you see that person as an individual or as a member of a cultural group that is different from your own? Even intraculturally—that is, within our own culture—when we meet strangers, we typically see them in terms of the groups to which they belong (sex, race, age, etc). In fact, there is no other way to describe a stranger than by the groups to which he or she belongs. The sociorelational context refers to how group memberships affect communication. Whenever people from different cultures come together to interact, their verbal and nonverbal messages are defined by, and filtered through, their group memberships. The social relationships they develop are significantly influenced by the groups to which they belong; hence the term *sociorelational context*.

Although all people belong to groups, the nature of group membership and group behavior, especially group communication, differs considerably across cultures. The number of social groups to which a person belongs, the length of association with those groups, whether group membership is determined by birth or eligibility, and the purpose of the groups varies from one culture to the next. Our membership in groups represents the sociorelational context of intercultural communication.

This chapter explores the idea of groupness and how social groups vary across cultures. The first part of the chapter focuses on definitional aspects of group memberships and categories of groups. The second part of the chapter discusses role relationships, social hierarchies, and stratification across cultures. The third part of the chapter looks at family groups, and the final part of the chapter examines gender groups.

Dimensions of Group Variability

All people in all cultures are affected by social groups. Those groups to which we belong and even those to which we do not belong have a dramatic effect on how we perceive the world around us, how we make decisions, and how we communicate with others. Three categories of groups that exist in all cultures include membership/nonmembership, in-groups/out-groups, and reference groups. These three types of groups are discussed below.

MEMBERSHIP AND NONMEMBERSHIP GROUPS

Much of what makes each of us human is our membership in social groups. Regardless of our culture, we all belong to groups. For individuals in any culture, there are those groups to which they belong—called membership groups—and those groups to which they do not belong—called nonmembership groups. There are two classes of membership groups: voluntary and involuntary. *Involuntary membership groups* are those groups to which people have no choice but to belong, such as age, race, sex, and biological family groups. Obviously, we can not choose our age, race, or sex. Although we may choose to interact or not to interact with our biological family group, we can not choose our biological father, mother, brother, or sister. *Voluntary membership groups* are those groups to which people consciously choose to belong through political affiliation, religion, occupation, and to some extent, economic status.[3] Whether group membership is voluntary or involuntary varies according to culture. In some cultures, like China, people may have no choice but to belong to a particular religion or political party. In fact, there may be strong sanctions for not belonging to a group. For example, Islam is the official religion of the Kingdom of Saudi Arabia. According to Saudi law, the public practice of any religion other than Islam is illegal. Hence, essentially 100 percent of the native population practices some form of Islam.[4] In contrast, the U.S. Constitution guarantees freedom of religion. There are over 130 organized religions in the United States, and a person can choose to belong to any one of them.

Nonmembership groups are those groups to which people do not belong. Like membership groups, nonmembership groups can be voluntary or involuntary. Some people may want to belong to a group but are ineligible to join because they do not possess the needed qualifications (for example, age, education). In other cases, people may be eligible for membership in a group but choose not to join. The distinction is important because people who are eligible to join a group but choose not to belong may be more likely than ineligible nonmembers to accept and embrace the norms and behaviors of the group. Nonmembers may also differ regarding their ability and motivation to become members: some nonmembers may aspire to membership, some may be indifferent, and others may be motivated to remain unaffiliated. For example, in India, people are born into social classes called castes. According to Bishop, there are dramatic social disparities between the different levels of the caste system. Usually members of the lower levels are exploited and treated very harshly. Hence, a native Indian is born into an involuntary membership group (his or her caste) and is ineligible for membership in any other caste group.[5]

IN-GROUPS AND OUT-GROUPS

In 1906, sociologist William Graham Sumner introduced the concepts of in-group and out-group when he wrote:

A differentiation arises between ourselves, the we-group, or in-group, and everybody else, or the others-group, out-groups. The insiders in a we-group are in a relation of peace, order, law, government and industry, to each other. Their relation to all outsiders, or others-groups, is one of war and plunder, except as agreements have modified it . . . the relation of comradeship and peace in the we-group and that of hostility and war towards the others-group are correlative to each other.[6]

According to Sumner's thesis, in-groups represent a special class of membership group characterized by a potent internal cohesiveness among its members and a sometimes intense hostility toward out-groups. To be sure, however, earnest loyalty to one's membership group does not necessarily mean hostility toward nonmembership groups or out-groups. Sumner's dichotomy of in-group/out-group animosity can be seen in cases of extreme nationalism. According to Merton, nationalists are members of a group, usually ethnic and/or religious, who believe that their group should dominate and rule a political entity, such as a state or nation. A nationalist state, then, is dominated by an ethnic or religious group. The symbols and laws of a nationalist state are reflective of the particular ethnic or religious group. Nationalist groups believe that political organizations within the state or nation should be ethnic or religious in character and may take extreme measures to see that they are so. Intense nationalism has been blamed for the atrocities in the war in the former Yugoslavia. In countries such as Bosnia, Serbia, Croatia, and Herzegovina, being a member of an out-group (for example, Muslim) has cost more than 200,000 lives. The term *ethnic cleansing,* used often to describe aspects of the conflict in Yugoslavia, refers to a process of systematically killing people on the basis of their ethnicity and/or religion. Although this is an extreme example of the in-group/out-group phenomenon, it vividly demonstrates how much group membership and nonmembership can affect our lives.[7]

Harry Triandis defines an *in-group* as a group whose norms, aspirations, and values shape the behavior of its members. An *out-group,* on the other hand, is a group whose attributes are dissimilar from those of the in-group, or who oppose the accomplishment of the in-group's goals. Triandis maintains that in order to be classified as an out-group, the group must be perceived as threatening in some way to the in-group, be relatively stable and impenetrable, and be dissimilar. An important point articulated by Triandis is that persons can be perceived as in-group members in one context and out-group members in another.[8] For example, a white American may view a black American as a member of an out-group within the boundaries of the United States but see the same person as an in-group member while visiting a foreign country. Furthermore, definitions of in-groups and out-groups differ widely across cultures. In Greece, for example, family and close friends are considered in-group members, whereas other Greeks are out-groups.

Brewer and Campbell assert that the tendency to distinguish between in-groups and out-groups is universal.[9] When we meet someone from a different culture for the first time, we immediately categorize the other as an in-group or out-group member. Attributions about in-group and out-group members are typ-

In order to be classified as an out-group, the group must be perceived as threatening to the in-group. *(Charles Gupton/Stock Boston)*

ically biased in favor of the in-group at the expense of the out-group. Some theorists argue that in-group biases function to promote, enhance, protect, and maintain the in-group's self-esteem. Others maintain that in-group biases function to preserve in-group solidarity and to justify the exploitation of out-groups. Taifel and Turner argue that the mere presence of an out-group is sufficient to provoke intergroup competition or discriminatory responses on the part of the in-group. Moreover, the magnitude of in-group and out-group dissimilarity tends to intensify in-group biases. That is, the more the groups appear different (for example, in sex, race, religion, or status), the greater the extent of in-group bias.[10]

Richard Schaefer points out that in-group bias can manifest itself in what he calls in-group virtues and out-group vices. Often the behaviors and practices of the in-group are perceived by the in-group as virtuous (in-group virtues), yet when the very same behaviors are practiced by the out-group, they are seen as unacceptable (out-group vices).[11] For example, Christians may view the fervor with which they practice their religion as commendable yet think of Islamic or Jewish fundamentalism as unprogressive and backward.[12] White students on some college campuses complain that formation of black student unions and black fraternities and sororities constitutes a kind of "self-segregation" of blacks. Blacks, however, may label their behavior as "self-affirmation."

REFERENCE GROUPS

Another type of group that affects our communication and our relationships with others is the reference group. A reference group is a group to which we may or may not belong but with which we identify in some important way. A reference group possesses some quality to which we aspire and hence serves as a "reference" for our decisions or behavior. From time to time we are faced with decisions about matters of which we know very little or need direction. We may not know how to feel about a particular political issue or which way to vote in an upcoming referendum. In these kinds of situations, we often look to others whose opinions we value and trust to help us make our decisions. For example, students often look to teachers for guidance. In this way, teachers are a reference group for students. Attorneys may be a reference group for law students. We use the group's position on an issue as a reference, standard, or barometer in developing our own attitudes. Reference groups can be membership or nonmembership and positive or negative. In deciding for which political candidate to cast your vote, you may look to your political party (a membership group) for guidance. A law student may view lawyers or judges as a reference group (a nonmembership group, since the student does not yet belong to the group). Usually, though not necessarily, voluntary membership in-groups serve as positive reference groups, whereas voluntary nonmembership out-groups are seen as negative reference groups.

Napier and Gershenfeld point out that reference groups serve two functions: (1) a *comparative function* and (2) a *normative function*.[13] We often use reference groups for comparison in making judgments and evaluations about ourselves. For example, when professors return examinations, students try very hard to see the grades of their peers in an effort to determine their own relative standing. If a student fails an examination but learns that most of the class failed, she or he does not feel as bad.

Individuals also use reference groups to establish the norms and standards to which they conform. For example, many students on college campuses dress according to how other students dress. Our reference groups influence our self-concept, self-esteem, and relationship with others. In most cultures, children look to their elders as a positive reference group. The Masai culture of southern Kenya is a gerontocracy—that is, social power is based on age. Wisdom, insight, and sound judgment are associated with age and are highly respected. Elders have moral and political authority, and the younger Masai look to them for advice and direction. Through their age-based level in the hierarchy, the elders are the central reference group of their culture.[14]

Role Relationships, Role Differentiation, and Social Stratification

By virtue of our membership in groups, we assume roles. Roles exist only in relationship with other roles. The definition of one's role is cultural, however. In other words, what it means to be a student (or a teacher) in one culture is different than what it means in another culture. Moreover, all roles in all cultures are ranked hierarchically; that is, some roles are more highly valued in some cultures than in others. The following is a discussion of role relationships, role differentiation, and social stratification.

ROLE RELATIONSHIPS

Whenever we join a group, voluntarily or involuntarily, we assume a role. A role is one's relative position in a group—that is, one's rank. Any group role exists in relation to some other role in that group. Roles do not exist in isolation; they are always related to some other role. You cannot be a son without a father. You cannot be a student without a teacher. Leaders cannot lead without followers.

With all roles, in all groups, certain behaviors are expected. A role, then, can be defined as one's relative position in a group along with its expected set of verbal and nonverbal behaviors. By virtue of our membership in groups, even family groups, we are expected to behave in certain ways, usually according to some set of standards or norms established by the group. In your role as student, for example, you are expected to attend class, write papers, and complete examinations. Within groups, roles are hierarchically organized, with some roles having more influence and prestige than others. In this sense, our role in a group represents our relative position or rank in the group.[15]

There are two types of roles in most cultures: formal and informal.[16] *Formal roles* have very well defined, and often contractual, behavioral expectations associated with them. The chief executive officer of a corporation, the president of a college or university, and the president of the United States have a clearly prescribed set of behaviors that they are expected to enact by virtue of their role. Most fraternities and sororities and academic organizations have constitutions or charters that very specifically spell out the roles of their officers and members. In many instances, the person assuming a formal role takes an oath declaring his or her allegiance to the group and promises to make a faithful effort to follow the expectations prescribed. Violations of such prescriptions are often subject to negative evaluation and even removal from the role. An important point about formal roles is that regardless of who assumes the role, the behavioral expectations remain the same. Formal roles and their prescriptions vary across cultures.

Informal roles are learned informally and are much less explicit than formal roles. Unlike formal roles, the behavioral expectations associated with informal roles must be mastered by experience and vary considerably from person to person and from group to group. Your roles as son or daughter, brother or sister, or even boyfriend or girlfriend are learned through experience. What it means to be a son or daughter in your family may be quite different from what it means to be a son or daughter in the family of your next-door neighbor. Informal roles and their prescriptions vary across and within cultures.

Roles and communication are integrally linked. Roles prescribe (1) *with whom,* (2) *about what,* and (3) *how* to communicate with others.[17] Because you are assuming the role of student, most of the people with whom you communicate include teachers, students, resident hall assistants, librarians, and so forth. If not for your role as college student, you probably would not have communicated with any of the people with whom you have already communicated today. In addition to prescribing with whom you communicate, your role prescribes the topic of your communication. With teachers, for example, much of your interaction is about class-related topics and assignments. Finally, your role defines how you communicate, or your style of communication. When you are interacting with your professors about class-related topics, you probably engage in a more formal communication pattern than when you interact with other students. You probably use less slang and perhaps speak more politely with professors than with fellow students.

Henri Taifel contends that our social identity is created by our total combination of roles. He argues that one's *social identity* is that part of the individual's self-concept derived from his or her membership in social groups, together with the value and significance attached to that membership.[18] Because the nature and prevalence of formal and informal roles vary so much across cultures, the roles we assume in our native culture may not be practiced or valued similarly in another culture. This would include the roles we assume in our cultural, national, ethnic, demographic, and various other in-groups.

Because roles and communication are so closely related, they must be considered cross-cultural—that is, roles vary significantly across cultures. For example, although there are probably teachers and students in every culture, what it means to be a teacher or student in the United States may differ remarkably from what it means in China or Japan. Gudykunst and Kim argue that there are at least four dimensions in which roles vary across cultures: (1) *personalness,* (2) *formality,* (3) *hierarchy,* and (4) *deviation from the ideal role enactment.*[19] According to Gudykunst and Kim, roles can vary from personal to impersonal. Some role relationships are quite close and perhaps intimate, whereas others are distant. The degree of formality between roles varies from formal to informal. Some of our role relationships are prim and proper, whereas others are casual and relaxed. The degree of hierarchy refers to how strictly roles are ranked in relation to one another. In some cultures there may be a very rigid hierarchical distinction between student and teacher, whereas in others the difference is quite loose and flexible. The degree of deviation allowed refers to how much a person is permitted to deviate from the prescribed role expectation without significant negative sanction.

The following comparison of student/teacher role relationships in the United States and Korea illustrates how Gudykunst and Kim's four dimensions can be applied. In Korea, there is an old adage, "One should not step even on the shadow of one's teacher." This expression, emphasizing the degree of respect accorded teachers, has been a guiding tenet in Korean education for years. Social order in Korea is based on Confucianism, whose central axiom is obedience to superiors. At just about any type of social gathering, who greets whom first, who sits where, who sits first, who speaks first, and so forth is of utmost importance. In Korea, special attention must be taken not to upset the social order, for to do so is interpreted as uncouth and lacking in social decorum. In Korea, the recognition of one's place in the social hierarchy is communicated by specialized vocabularies consisting of special terms and phrases for addressing one who is superior, equal, or of lower status.[20]

In the United States, most students respect their teachers but do not recognize

FIGURE 6-1   Comparison of Student/Teacher Roles in Korea and the United States

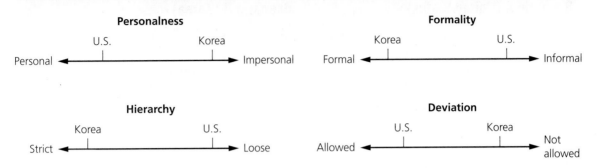

the strict adherence to formality and hierarchy to the degree that is seen in Korea. In Korea, the student/teacher role relationship is quite proper and formal, and the communication is scripted. Similarly, the difference in rank between Korean student and teacher is very strict and recognized. The student/teacher role relationship in the United States is more personal and probably allows for more deviation from the ideal role prescription. Students and teacher can interact informally and may even engage in activities outside the formal classroom.

Figure 6-1 illustrates where Korean and American student/teacher relationships fall along Gudykunst and Kim's four role dimensions. Generally, the student/teacher relationship in Korea is less personal, more formal, more hierarchical, and with less room for deviation from the ideal role enactment than in the United States.

ROLE DIFFERENTIATION AND SOCIAL STRATIFICATION

Whenever we assume a role in a group, that role represents our rank or relative position within the group. On a much larger scale, our roles are ranked by our culture as well. Some roles are at the top of the hierarchy, whereas others are at the bottom. In the United States, for example, physicians and attorneys are highly ranked occupational roles, whereas used-car salespeople are low-ranked roles. The rank ordering of roles within a culture is called *social stratification*. Social stratification varies across cultures. Not all roles are valued the same across cultures.

The complexity of role hierarchy varies from culture to culture, too. Some cultures make relatively few distinctions, whereas others make many. This is called *role differentiation*. For example, a relatively undifferentiated culture might distinguish among only a few types of roles, such as family, social, and occupational roles. A highly differentiated culture may make numerous role distinctions, such as corporate roles (owner, vice president, manager, worker, retiree); religious roles (pope, cardinal, bishop, priest, parishioner); educational roles (superintendent, principal, teacher, senior, junior, sophomore, freshman); and military roles (general, colonel, major, captain, lieutenant), among others. According to cross-cultural

Intercultural Conversation

Scenario A (United States)

Because roles prescribe with whom, about what, and how people communicate, differences in the four role dimensions manifest themselves in communication. In the following two conversations, scenario A is between a student and a teacher in the United States. Scenario B is between a student and a teacher in Korea. Note the differences in formality and personalness and the degree to which the students recognize the hierarchical difference between themselves and the teacher. In each case the student wishes to speak to the teacher about an assignment.

Jeff: (*Approaches Dr. Neuliep's office unannounced*) Hey, Dr. N., how's it goin'?

Dr. Neuliep: Hey, Jeff, what's up?

Jeff: (*Steps into the office*) I thought I would stop by an' see if I could talk to ya about my paper assignment.

Dr. Neuliep: Sure, c'mon in, have a seat. What are you thinking about?

Jeff: Well . . . I'm kinda havin' some trouble coming up with a topic. Do you have any ideas?

Dr. Neuliep: I suggest doing something that's very interesting to you—otherwise the assignment might bore you to death. Stay away from topics that have very little research associated with them. Also . . . you might try doing a search on the Internet. Sometimes you'll find topics that you might not ever have thought of yourself.

Jeff: Yeah . . . that's a good idea. If I find somethin' can I stop by and show it to you before I get started?

Dr. Neuliep: Sure; just stop by or leave a message on my voice mail.

Jeff: OK, yeah. OK, well . . . thanks a lot.

Dr. Neuliep: Sure.

Scenario B (Korea)

Mino: (*Approaches Dr. Choi's office and knocks on the door*) Good morning, Professor Choi.

Dr. Choi: Hello, Mino.

Mino: I am here for my appointment.

Dr. Choi: Yes.

Mino: May I come in?

Dr. Choi: Yes.

Mino: Thank you. (*Enters Dr. Choi's office*) I am here to approve my topic for the research paper assignment, as you requested.

Dr. Choi: Yes, what have you decided?

Mino: I would like to research the natural resources of Northern India, if that is acceptable.

Dr. Choi: Yes, that topic is fine.

Mino: Thank you. Thank you for seeing me this morning,

Dr. Choi: Yes, you are welcome. Good day.

The conversation between Jeff and Dr. Neuliep in scenario A is generally smooth and coordinated. The situation is informal enough that Jeff shows up unannounced, without an appointment. Jeff uses informal dialect ("havin'," "ya,") and refers to Dr. Neuliep as "Dr. N," demonstrating a degree of personalness. Dr. Neuliep invites Jeff to sit down, reducing the hierarchical distance between them. Generally, their conversation, though perfectly respectful, is informal. In scenario B, Mino has set up an appointment with Dr. Choi prior to the meeting, shows up at the appointed time, and asks permission to enter the office. The conversation is rather formal and impersonal. Mino does not engage in any slang or informal vocabulary, does not sit down, and keeps the conversation as short as possible. Unlike Jeff, Mino is prepared to state his choice of subject. To ask the professor for a suggestion, as Jeff does in scenario A, would be impertinent in Korean culture, where responsibility rests entirely on the student.

researcher John Berry and his colleagues, social stratification exists in a culture with a highly differentiated role hierarchy that is organized in a vertical status structure. Most cultures have some form of role hierarchy that distinguishes among high- and low-ranking roles. Berry maintains that cultural role differentiation and stratification appear to be related to ecological systems among cultures. For example, nomadic hunting-and-gathering cultures tend to have less role differentiation and stratification, whereas industrialized urban cultures are typically quite differentiated and stratified. Sedentary agricultural societies fall somewhere in the middle.[21]

Although it is impossible to generalize across every culture, many collectivistic, high-context, and high-power-distance cultures possess a relatively strict hierarchical role stratification compared with low-context, individualistic, low-power-distance cultures. Recall from Chapter 2 that individualistic, low-power-distance cultures believe that all people are created equal and have inalienable rights. Collectivistic cultures, on the other hand, see people not as individuals, but as members of groups. In these cultures, often one's level in the role stratification hierarchy is based on one's membership in sex, age, family, and occupational groups. In such cultures, one person is almost always more powerful than another. Mike Keberlein points out that the Guatemalan Ladino stratification is vertically shaped like a pyramid, with the wealthy on top and the poor on the bottom. Belonging to an upper class means owning a home and having land to work and rent. The upper class have their own social in-groups, such as the International Rotary Club, to which only they are accepted for membership. Lower-class Ladinos are left to work the land. They are also the ones who attend church most often. The upper class, however, establish the rules considered socially acceptable. Interestingly, according to Keberlein, the lower-class Ladinos practice the values of the culture more than any other social class.[22]

Perhaps the most notorious system of social stratification is the caste system of India. According to Duley, castes (or *jatis*) are endogamous groups in which membership is by birth. A Hindu is born into a caste and cannot leave it until the beginning of the next lifetime. The caste system prescribes a very strict and practiced code of conduct. A person's social status depends on the caste to which he or she belongs. Although made illegal fifty years ago, the caste system still operates in many parts of India today, especially rural areas. Although the system contains literally thousands of subcastes, there are four or five generally recognized levels. At the top are the Brahmins, priests or seers who possess spiritual power. Next are the Kshatriyas; that is, warriors and rulers. Third are the Vaishyas, or merchants. Fourth are the Sudras, who may be farmers. Outside the caste system are the untouchables, or as Gandhi termed them, the Dalit, meaning "children of God." Untouchables are workers who take on the lowest of jobs: they are the sweepers, butchers, potters, and so forth. Also outside the system are tribal groups (called *adivasis*) with unique ethnic, linguistic, and cultural histories.[23]

Because roles prescribe with whom, about what, and how to communicate with others, communication in cultures with a rigid social stratification system is very predictable. Verbal and nonverbal messages are prescribed according to a person's role and rank in the social hierarchy. Accepted forms of address, vocabulary, non-verbal behavior such as eye contact, and social manners are defined for practically every social situation. When two strangers interact for the first time, much uncertainty is reduced simply by recognizing role differences. The two people only need to know each other's roles in order to communicate appropriately. Though not exclusively, many of these cultures can be found in the East (for example, China, Japan, India, Korea).

Many individualistic, low-context, low-power-distance cultures profess equality and minimize role stratification. In the United States, for example, children are taught that they are equal to everyone else. In fact, in many of these cultures, equality is legislated. Although role differences are recognized and respected, these cultures believe that a person occupying a role is a unique individual. Therefore, knowing someone's role provides only minimal information about the person and does not reduce as much uncertainty as it would in a high-context, high-power-distance culture. Many of these cultures can be found in the West (for example, Australia, New Zealand), but there are certainly exceptions.

Understanding a culture's role differentiation and stratification is important for communication because special vocabularies exist for different roles. Donald Klopf notes that in Korea, the terms a husband will use to refer to his wife vary depending on with whom he is interacting. She is his *cho* when he is speaking to someone of higher rank, his *chip saram* when he is speaking to an equal, and his *ago omoni* when he is speaking to a person of lower rank or status.[24] Communication problems often result when persons from different cultures do not understand or recognize the role differences between the cultures. Many international exchange students find American teachers rather informal and personal compared with their teachers. Students from Eastern cultures find an American teacher's use of humor quite strange, since teachers in their cultures would never act in such a way.

Family Groups

All human beings, regardless of culture, belong to a family. One's biological family is the first and probably most significant socialization influence on a child. The structure of the family and the degree of influence a family has on its children differ notably across cultures. Biology determines membership in the nuclear family, which consists of the father, mother, and children. The extended family consists of the nuclear family plus other relatives, including grandparents, uncles, aunts, cousins, and in-laws. As a unit, the nuclear family is prevalent in most low-context, individualistic, low-power-distance cultures, such as the United States, Canada, England, Ireland, Germany, and France. Extended families are common in Central and South America, Africa, the Middle East, and Asia, although trends are changing even in these parts of the world. There are, clearly, exceptions to the above list, such as African American families in the United States, who have a cultural pat-

Intercultural Conversation

Role Hierarchies

In cultures such as the United States, Canada, and Australia people are accustomed to treating everyone else as equals, regardless of sex, age, occupation, and so on. This can lead to misunderstandings in intercultural interactions with people who, in their culture's role hierarchy, are accorded special privileges. In the following conversation, Mr. Mammen, a native of India now living in the United States, has taken his wife and family to a very nice restaurant. When he arrives at the restaurant, he expects to be seated even though he has not made dinner reservations. Because of his social standing, he assumes that he will be accommodated.

Mr. Mammen: (*Approaches the host*)
Host: Good evening, may I help you?
Mr. Mammen: Yes, my wife and family are here for dinner.
Host: Certainly, your name please?
Mr. Mammen: I am Mr. Mammen.
Host: I'm sorry, I don't see your name on our reservations listing.
Mr. Mammen: I don't have reservations, but I can make them now.
Host: I'm sorry, but this evening's dinner reservation list is completely full.

Mr. Mammen: No . . . I disagree. This restaurant is not full. I see empty tables.
Host: Yes, but these tables are reserved for those people who have reservations for this evening.
Mr. Mammen: I will make reservations right now.
Host: I'm sorry, but the evening is completely full.
Mr. Mammen: I can see that it is not full. I want to see the manager right now! I am here to have dinner!

Because of Mr. Mammen's cultural role position, in his native culture he probably would have been seated in the restaurant even though he did not have a reservation. In the United States, however, one's occupational role will not ensure any special favors outside that occupation. The host of this restaurant is simply following his culture's way of treating everyone—that is, equally. Such cultural differences can lead to conflict and misunderstanding.

SOURCE: Dialogue adapted from a scene in L. Copeland, producer, *Managing the Overseas Assignment* [videorecording] (San Francisco: Copeland Griggs, 1983).

tern of a very strong extended-family interaction and kinship network. In collectivistic cultures, families are generally cohesive and well integrated. Familial relations are caring and warm, but also hierarchical. The decision-making process typically is not democratic. The interests of the family group take precedence over those of individual family members. Familial role prescriptions are clearly defined not only within the family, but in the larger cultural context. In individualistic cultures, on the other hand, there is less emphasis on hierarchy and more emphasis on individual development. Family decisions may be more participative than in collectivistic cultures. Familial role prescriptions are open and may vary considerably across the cultural context.

In the Hmong culture of Laos, the most important sociocultural groups are the family and the clan, both of which are headed by men. According to Katie Thao, the Hmong clan system combines social, political, economic, and religious dimensions and is the primary guide for Hmong behavior. Within a clan, each person has certain obligations to others. When one shares with fellow clan members, the act is returned. Clan members of the same generation (but of different biological families) will call each other "brothers" and "sisters." Although the bond is not biological, it is so close that marriages between members of the same clan are seen as almost incestuous, leading to the Hmong practice of clan exogamy.[25]

In most cultures the family group is the most valued societal structure. Familial role prescriptions differ widely across cultures, however. For example, two important variables in understanding Korean family structure are family surname and Confucianism. According to Sungjong Paik, there are only about 250 family names in South and North Korea. In fact, over half the population use one of five family names, including Kim, Yi, Pak, Ch'oe, and Chong. One in five family names in Korea is Kim. Fifteen percent of Koreans use Yi, 9 percent use Pak, 5 percent use Ch'oe, and 4 percent use Chong. By comparison, in many other countries, like the United States, literally hundreds of thousands of family names are used.[26]

Many Koreans believe that because of their common family names, they are descended from a common ancestor. Hence, many Koreans belong to family-name organizations called *taejonghoe*. According to Paik, *taejonghoe* are rather formal organizations with head offices in Seoul and hundreds of branch offices throughout the country. *Taejonghoe* publish newsletters, award scholarships, and sponsor sporting events. Paik argues that *taejonghoe* exercise great influence on Korean social life. For example, one's social status is often determined by membership in a specific family-name lineage. Moreover, Paik asserts that many politicians try to use the family names to gain political influence.[27]

As in many other cultures, the family is the foundation of Korean society. Historically and in traditional Korean society, family roles and social interaction were governed by patriarchal Confucianism. Kyung-Sup Chang asserts that patriarchal Confucianism prescribes a social structure of *authoritarian collectivism*. According to Chang, traditional Korean patriarchal Confucianism imposes a rigid hierarchy and inequality between different age groups and between men and women. Males dominate females and elders dominate young. In traditional Confucian families, children are socialized to conform with traditional gender stereotypes and are segregated by sex. Following the father, the eldest son has the highest social status in the family.[28] Kim notes also that in traditional Korean families, certain rooms in the home are reserved for communication, men interacting only with men in the outer room (*sarangbang*) and women interacting only with women in the *anbang* (inner room).[29] Communication in Confucian familial relationships would require the use of a restricted code. In the United States, when speaking to a brother, sister, aunt, or uncle, English speakers use the generic terms *brother, sister, aunt,* or *uncle.* Linguistically, one's age or status is irrelevant. In Korean language (i.e., Hangul), the relationship term used to refer to a familial relative changes according to the sender's and receiver's familial rank, which is based on their age and sex.

Family life in Korea is changing. Levande, Herrick, and Sung maintain that while filial piety (loyalty and obedience to parents, elderly) remains a central value among Koreans, familial relationships between parents and children are changing from a sense of duty and obligation to intergenerational affection. Levande, Herrick, and Sung argue that Korean families are moving away from the authoritarian and patriarchal norms of the past to more egalitarian and reciprocal patterns of mutual support between generations. For example, younger Koreans, in pursuit of educational and occupational opportunities, are increasingly moving to urban areas. The effect has been a decrease in the number of multigenerational coresiding nuclear families. In 1975 over 90 percent of elderly Koreans lived with their children. That number decreased to 53 percent in 1996. Such trends are observed mostly in rural areas where elderly people constitute the majority of the population. In urban areas, such as Seoul, the capital of South Korea, 65 percent of persons age sixty or older lived with their children. The majority of these persons live with their married sons.[30] Kim argues that living apart does not necessarily translate into autonomy from parents. Korean sons are still responsible for the parents' well-being and are expected to provide emotional and material support for them. Kim maintains that in contemporary Korean society, nuclear families are faced with the social dilemma of having to appear both autonomous and interdependent, private and communal. Chun and MacDermid agree; they also assert that contemporary Korean families still value connectedness over separateness and that Korean children associate strict parental control with warmth rather than hostility.[31]

As in Korea, filial piety is the dominant force in Chinese families, where in the home the elders maintain complete control. Michael Bond has written extensively about the Chinese and maintains that Chinese women are beginning to make inroads toward equality. For example, half of the physicians in China are women. In the past, Chinese families had many children, but today family planning is required. Abortions are easy to obtain and sometimes forced. Although the Chinese government seems coercive, Chinese parents seem to be extremely lenient and even lax in their child-rearing attitudes toward obedience with infants and young children. This is in sharp contrast to the strict discipline they impose on older children (beginning at about four to six years of age). According to Bond, communication between parents and their children is based on obedience, morality, and the acceptance of social obligation. A child's adventurous or risky activities are discouraged. On the other hand, sex training and control of aggression are severe. The father is the harsher disciplinarian, and fathers seem more distant toward their children than do mothers. In terms of communication, some studies have demonstrated that Chinese babies are less vocal, less active, less likely to smile, and more apprehensive in social situations than Caucasian babies.[32]

According to Tehmina Basit, the family group represents the foundation of Islamic society. Basit argues that obedience and respect for parents are repeatedly stressed in Islamic teachings. Mohammed Haroun maintains that in Islam, the individual is not allowed to be just an individual who is free to do whatever he or she desires. Haroun alleges that any political or social system that makes the individual the basic unit of society does not take into account the natural bonds and needs of family. He maintains that the most *natural* unit of society is the family. According to Haroun, in Islam there are three factors that keep the family together, including kinship or blood ties, marital commitments, and faith. The traditional Muslim household is multigenerational, including grandparents, parents, married sons, their wives and children, unmarried sons and daughters, and sometimes an unmarried, widowed, or divorced uncle or aunt. Although Islamic teachings stipulate that men and women are equal, within the context of marriage the man is endowed with authority both over the woman and in the family setting. Pels maintains that the role of the eldest male is that of patriarch and therefore his authority is undisputed and paramount.[33]

Sex and Gender Groups

One group to which all human beings belong, regardless of culture, is their biological sex group. Biological differences between males and females are universally recognized. But, as in any group, to be a member of a sex group is to assume a role—in this case a sex role. And like any other role, one's sex role, or gender, is a set of expectations about how one should behave.

Often the terms *sex* and *gender* are used interchangeably, but as Sandra Bem notes, the terms are not synonymous. Bem recognizes that sex refers to the biological and anatomical classifications of males and females. Gender, on the other hand, is a social and symbolic creation that we learn through enculturation and socialization. Whereas sex is innate, gender is learned. In most cultures, there is a close association between sex and gender, however. That is, most cultures establish norms and expectations that they assign people on the basis of their biological sex. According to Bem, our *sex-role orientation* (that is, *gender*) is based on the extent to which we internalize our culture's sex-type expectations of desirable behavior for men and women. In most cases, there is a high correlation between biological sex and sex-role orientation. In other words, most people assume the gender roles that their culture prescribes. We are taught by our parents, teachers, and peers how to behave on the basis of our culture's standards. Boys are taught to be masculine (however the culture defines it), and girls are expected to act feminine (however the culture defines it). Thus, when cultures recognize some behaviors as masculine and others as feminine, they are saying that the majority of people taking on these roles should be male (for the former) and female (for the latter). *Gender,* then, can be defined as the behavioral, cultural, and psychological traits typically associated with one's sex. To be sure, as Bem notes, this is not to say that a certain sex cannot fulfill the other role, but rather that the characteristics of the person assuming the role are associated with that sex. Indeed, some people possess both feminine and masculine traits. These persons may be classified as androgynous, a term that combines *andro* ("male/masculine") and *gyne* ("woman").[34]

Nearly thirty years ago, Bem developed an instrument designed to measure an individual's sex-role orientation. The instrument, called the Bem Sex Role Inventory (BSRI), consists of a list of sixty personality traits, of which twenty are considered masculine; twenty feminine; and twenty neither masculine nor feminine, included as neutral traits.[35] Examples of masculine traits on the BSRI include the terms *assertive, dominant, forceful,* and *aggressive.* Examples of feminine traits on the BSRI include the terms *yielding, understanding, tender,* and *warm.* Neutral traits include the terms *helpful, moody, conscientious,* and *reliable.* In completing the BSRI, respondents are instructed to indicate on a seven-point scale (1 = Never, to 7 = Always) the extent to which each of the sixty traits describes them. On the basis of the respondents' self-ratings, they can be classified as androgynous (high masculine score and high feminine score), masculine (high masculine score and low feminine score), feminine (low masculine score and high feminine score), or undifferentiated (low masculine score and low feminine score).

The BSRI has been used in a number of cross-cultural studies. Typically researchers will have people of one culture complete the BSRI; then the researchers compare the results from people of a different culture. For example, Zhang, Norvilitis, and Jin compared BSRI scores between Americans and Chinese and found that the majority of BSRI scores for both masculine and feminine traits were lower among the Chinese sample. Zhang, Norvilitis, and Jin reasoned that according to American standards for gender roles, Chinese men are less male oriented than American men and Chinese women are less female oriented than American women. Another possible interpretation is that according to Confucian philosophy, moderation is highly valued: one is encouraged to take the "middle road." Such philosophy may have led the Chinese participants to respond differently than Americans when completing the BSRI—that is, they were less likely to use extreme ratings (*1*s or *7*s) in their responses.[36]

The BSRI also has been used to examine masculinity and femininity in Japan. In traditional Japanese society, sex roles were clearly differentiated between men and women. According to Sugihara and Katsurada, Japanese males were taught to be strong and maintain control and dominance over children and women. Japanese women were taught to be subservient to their husbands and, in their old age, to their male children. Sugihara and Katsurada also point out that the Japanese adopted the traditional division of labor in which the man provides for his family thorough his occupation, and the woman stays at home and does housework and childrearing.[37] In related work, Sugihara and Katsurada argue that contemporary Japanese society has changed over the years in terms of the number of Japanese women in higher education, the increasing number of Japanese women in the work force, women delaying marriage, high divorce rates, and low birthrates. In addition, the number of men involved in domestic activities and the number enrolling in women's studies is increasing. Sugihara and Katsurada maintain that along with these changes in Japanese society, gender-role expectations have changed accordingly. In two separate studies, Katsurada and Sugihara had Japanese college students complete the BSRI. In one of the studies, results showed that male students rated the feminine items significantly higher than did female students in terms of their desirability for men. No gender difference was found in the desirability items of feminine characteristics for women, however. In the other study, Sugihara and Katsurada found no significant differences between Japanese males and Japanese females on either the masculinity or femininity scales of the

BSRI. However, a comparison of the masculinity and femininity scores within male and female samples indicated that both male and female students scored higher on the femininity scale than on the masculinity scale of the BSRI.[38] In related work, Shimonaka, Nakazato, and Kawaai examined the BSRI scores among elderly Japanese men and women and found that, like the Japanese college students, both elderly men and elderly women scored higher on the femininity scale than on the masculinity scale.[39]

The value associated with masculinity seems to vary across cultures. Although he did not use the BSRI, in his seminal cross-cultural survey of over fifty countries, Dutch sociologist Geert Hofstede asked participants to rate the value of masculinity. According to Hofstede, masculinity stands for a society in which social gender roles are clearly distinct. In masculine cultures men are conditioned to be assertive, tough, and focused on material success. In these same cultures women are conditioned to be modest, tender, and concerned with the quality of life. Hofstede argues that feminine oriented cultures see sex roles as overlapping in some cases. The rankings of the cultures on Hofstede's masculinity index are presented in Table 6-1 below. The lower the score, the more masculinity is valued in the culture.[40]

TABLE 6-1 Masculinity Index Values for 50 Countries and 3 Regions		
Masculinity Rank	**Country**	**Masculinity Score**
1	Japan	95
2	Austria	79
3	Venezuela	73
4/5	Italy	70
4/5	Switzerland	70
6	Mexico	69
7/8	Ireland	68
7/8	Jamaica	68
9/10	Great Britain	66
9/10	Germany (FR)	66
11/12	Philippines	64
11/12	Colombia	64
13/14	South Africa	63
13/14	Equador	63
15	USA	62
16	Australia	61
17	New Zealand	58
18/19	Greece	57
18/19	Hong Kong	57

Masculinity Rank	Country	Masculinity Score
20/21	Argentina	56
20/21	India	56
22	Belgium	54
23	Arab Countries	53
24	Canada	52
25/26	Malaysia	50
25/26	Pakistan	50
27	Brazil	49
28	Singapore	48
29	Israel	47
30/31	Indonesia	46
30/31	West Africa	46
32/33	Turkey	45
32/33	Taiwan	45
34	Panama	44
35/36	Iran	43
35/36	France	43
37/38	Spain	42
37/38	Peru	42
39	East Africa	41
40	Salvador	40
41	South Korea	39
42	Uruguay	38
43	Guatemala	37
44	Thailand	34
45	Portugal	31
46	Chile	28
47	Finland	26
48/49	Yugoslavia	21
48/49	Costa Rica	21
50	Denmark	16
51	Netherlands	14
52	Norway	8
53	Sweden	5

SOURCE: "Masculinity Rankings" from G. Hofstede, *Cultures and Organization: Software of the Mind,* © 1991, p. 84. Reproduced with the author's permission.

The expectations and behaviors associated with masculinity and femininity can vary remarkably across cultures. In his study of the Sambian society of Papua New Guinea, anthropologist Gilbert Herdt found that adolescent boys are required to perform fellatio (oral sex) on older men as a part of the initiation into manhood. Their culture holds that a Sambian boy cannot mature physically or emotionally unless he ingests another man's semen over a period of several years. In Sambian culture, such behavior is considered masculine.[41]

When people deviate from their cultural sex-role expectations, they are often negatively sanctioned. Some researchers have argued that collectivistic cultures are more traditional than individualistic cultures and are more likely to punish persons who violate cultural sex-role expectations. Recall from Chapter 2 that collectivistic cultures stress interdependence, prescribe very clear role expectations, and value conforming to the needs of the group. Violating one's role prescription (including sex role) disrupts the harmony of the group. Individualistic cultures, on the other hand, value independence, self-expression, and the pursuit of individual goals over group goals. Promotion of an individual's uniqueness is common in individualistic cultures. Therefore, when an individual violates a cultural sex-role expectation, it is likely to be more tolerated in an individualistic culture than in a collectivistic culture.[42]

GENDER STEREOTYPES

In most cultures, men and women carry out different sex roles, yet there is remarkable consistency in how cultures view the roles of men and women. Since 1990, psychologists John Williams and Deborah Best have conducted a series of cross-cultural studies investigating gender stereotypes. Williams and Best asked university students in more than thirty countries to consider a list of three hundred adjectives and to indicate whether in their culture the adjectives are more frequently associated with men or women, or equally with both. The responses of the participants in each country were tallied to determine the frequency with which each adjective was associated with men and/or women. A surprising degree of cross-cultural agreement was found among one hundred of the three hundred adjectives (see Table 6-2). Some of the countries surveyed included Canada, Finland, England, Italy, Pakistan, Malaysia, Nigeria, Singapore, India, Japan, Netherlands, Venezuela, Germany, the United States, New Zealand, Peru, Australia, South Africa, and Brazil.

Williams and Best also scored each of the adjectives in terms of its affective meaning (that is, its favorability, strength, and activity). They found that the characteristics associated with men were generally stronger (for example, "tough") and more active (for example, "robust") than those associated with women, but that the adjectives were equally favorable for both men and women. Williams and Best also concluded that the male stereotypes were more favorable than the female stereotypes in certain countries, such as Japan, South Africa, and Nigeria, whereas the female stereotypes were more favorable in other countries, such as Italy, Peru, and Australia. They also found that gender stereotypes were more differentiated in Protestant countries than in Catholic countries.[43]

In a related study, Williams and Best surveyed five- and eight-year-old children

TABLE 6-2 The 100-Item Pancultural Adjective Checklist

Male-Associated Adjectives		Female-Associated Adjectives	
Active	Loud	Affected	Modest
Adventurous	Obnoxious	Affectionate	Nervous
Aggressive	Opinionated	Appreciative	Patient
Arrogant	Opportunistic	Cautious	Pleasant
Autocratic	Pleasure-seeking	Changeable	Prudish
Bossy	Precise	Charming	Self-pitying
Capable	Progressive	Complaining	Sensitive
Coarse	Quick	Complicated	Sentimental
Conceited	Rational	Confused	Sexy
Confident	Realistic	Curious	Shy
Courageous	Reckless	Dependent	Softhearted
Cruel	Resourceful	Dreamy	Sophisticated
Cynical	Rigid	Emotional	Submissive
Determined	Robust	Excitable	Suggestible
Disorderly	Serious	Fault-finding	Superstitious
Enterprising	Sharp-witted	Fearful	Talkative
Greedy	Show-off	Fickle	Timid
Hardheaded	Steady	Foolish	Touchy
Humorous	Stern	Forgiving	Unambitious
Indifferent	Stingy	Frivolous	Unintelligent
Individualistic	Stolid (detached)	Fussy	Unstable
Initiative	Tough	Gentle	Warm
Interests wide	Unfriendly	Imaginative	Weak
Inventive	Unscrupulous	Kind	Worrying
Lazy	Witty	Mild	Understanding

SOURCE: "Pan-Cultural Checklist" from J. L. Williams and D. L. Best, "Cross-Cultural Views of Women and Men," in Walter J. Lonner and Roy S. Malpass (eds.), *Psychology and Culture*, pp. 191–196. Copyright © 1994 by Allyn & Bacon. Reprinted by permission.

in twenty-five countries. In this study, the children were shown silhouettes of a man and a woman and were asked to select between the ones described in brief stories. The stories were written to reflect the more important features of the adult sex-stereotype characteristics. For example, children were asked to select "the person who gets into the most fights" or "the person who cries a lot." The results of the study indicate that the children in each culture showed at least a beginning knowledge of the adult stereotypes. The stories most frequently associated with the male figures were those involving strong, aggressive, and cruel characteristics, whereas the stories associated with women showed emotional, weak, and softhearted characteristics. Pakistani children seemed to show the most developed gender stereotypes, whereas Brazilian children showed the least. In each country, the eight-year-old children showed a significant increase in stereotype knowledge in comparison to the five-year-old children.[44]

Sex and Gender Roles Across Cultures

The variability of sex roles across cultures is dramatic. Yet many anthropologists and some feminist writers contend that whereas the customs and practices with which women's subordination is expressed differ from culture to culture, the secondary status of women across the globe is one of the few universal cross-cultural truisms. No book or chapter could possibly describe all of the sex-role differences between male and females across all cultures. The following sections discuss sex roles in three cultures, with special attention to women's roles.

MOROCCO

Leila Hessini has written about women's roles in Moroccan culture and points out that Moroccan society defines physical space according to male and female roles. Private space within the home is for family and is considered female space. Public space, on the other hand, is male space. Women are to fulfill their roles inside the female space—that is, the interior of the home. Men fulfill their roles in public spaces, which means almost anywhere outside the home. Men are free to sit in public spaces where women are not welcome. Thus, communication between husband and wife is likely to be restricted to the home. According to Hessini, the Moroccan Personal Status Code, called the Mudwanna, stipulates a wife's duties to her husband, including (1) fidelity, (2) obedience according to accepted custom, (3) breast-feeding of children, (4) management of the household, and (5) deference toward the husband's father, mother, and close relatives. Article 35 of the Mudwanna specifies the husband's duties to his wife, including (1) financial support, (2) equal treatment of all spouses (in the case of polygyny), (3) authorization for his wife to visit her parents within the limits of socially accepted norms, and (4) protecting the wife's total freedom to administer her possessions independent of the husband's control. Hessini notes, however, that a gap has grown between what the Mudwanna legally stipulates and how people actually behave.[45]

JAPAN

Sumiko Iwao has written a fascinating book portraying the role of women in contemporary Japan. Iwao notes that the "kimono clad, bamboo parasol-toting, bow-

Today, many Japanese women pursue professional careers. *(Ryan McVay/Getty Images)*

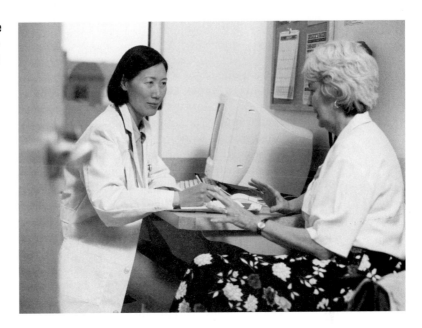

ing female walking three paces behind her husband" is still seen in some parts of Japan. But Iwao contends that the lives and attitudes of many younger contemporary Japanese women have undergone dramatic changes in the past twenty years. The postwar Japanese Constitution stipulates that all Japanese are equal under the law and outlaws discrimination on the basis of sex. To be sure, most private and political organizations that comprise the dominant Japanese culture are controlled by men. However, Japanese women enjoy more freedom today than perhaps ever before in their history. Iwao remarks that in terms of communication, today's Japanese women are much more outspoken and direct than their mothers. Sugihara and Katsurada report that the traditional gender division of labor inside and outside the home has diminished and that accordingly, traditional sex-role stereotypes have diminished. For example, contemporary stereotypic traits associated with Japanese males include intellectual and economic achievement, interpersonal skills, and emotional maturity. Japanese women appear to have become more masculine. Therefore communication between men and women approaches a more egalitarian perspective. But even modern Japanese women recognize their secondary status and have not completely discarded their traditional passivity. Moreover, when asked, many Japanese women acknowledge their fate as a subordinate group. The modern Japanese woman's happiness remains tied to her family, so much so that she will repress her personal feelings to an extent that many American women would find unendurable. Following their collectivistic histories, most Japanese women continue to sacrifice personal goals for the sake of the harmony of the family. Because they have fewer opportunities than men, maintaining interpersonal harmony is their utmost concern.[46]

INDIA

India is one of the few countries of the world where men outnumber women. According to Margot Duley, the Indian Constitution guarantees all citizens "equality of status." Unfortunately, writes Duley, legal equality remains elusive for most Indian women. The subordination of women in India is mainly economically based. Most women work in agricultural jobs. In fact, female farmers in northern India work nearly 3,500 hours per year, almost three times as many as men. Although laws favoring women's rights have been passed, they have not had much impact. For example, there are no uniform statutes governing marriage and inheritance laws. In most areas there is a very strong emphasis on chastity for women. Most young women marry by the age of seventeen. Even though the Dowry Prohibition Act was passed in 1961, the practice of dowry giving has actually spread in recent years because of the overwhelming pressure on girls to marry. After parents arrange the marriage of their children, the groom's parents expect and receive a dowry in the form of cash, jewelry, and other goods from the bride's parents. The amount of the dowry is often calculated according to the groom's potential financial prospects. Grooms in well-paying jobs demand larger dowries. Often the bride's parents cannot afford expensive dowries, and the in-laws continue to extort goods from the bride after the wedding. If their demands are not met, they often murder her. These so-called "dowry deaths" have increased dramatically in the past decade to nearly 6,000 a year (although many believe the number is much higher). Often the deaths are made to look like accidents. For example, brides are doused with kerosene and set on fire in or near the kitchen of their home.[47]

Because of the expenses associated with dowries, many Indian women engage in female infanticide and a relatively new phenomenon called female feticide. Female infanticide occurs when a mother kills her newborn female baby. Female feticide is basically the act of aborting a female fetus. Abortion is legal in India, but feticide is questionable legally. Essentially, women are seen as an economic liability.[48]

Because of the secondary status accorded to women, communication between men and women is often restricted. For example, Derne writes that an Indian's family honor is confirmed by a daughter's marriage into a family of appropriate status. To protect the marriage prospects for their daughters, fathers carefully monitor the daughter's interaction with unmarried men. In addition, in his interviews of Hindu men, Derne learned that most husbands actively restrict their wives' interaction outside the home. Hindu men expect their wives to be modest, shy, ashamed, and docile when they go outside the home. Moreover, much communication time between husband and wife focuses on when she can go outside and with whom. Apparently, protecting the family's honor is an important reason for restricting the woman's movement outside the home. Communication within the home is also restricted. Many Hindu men believe that wives are a threat to harmonious family life. They fear that their wives might gain control over them and tempt them away from familial obligations to brothers and parents. Thus, husband-and-wife interaction is controlled and limited. Derne notes that an Indian woman is generally taught to be passive and silent in the presence of her husband. As one of Derne's Hindu interviewees asserted, "The most important quality of an ideal wife is that she obey her husband. She should do whatever the husband says."[49]

Chapter Summary

Our lives are inextricably tied to our group memberships and the roles that we play. How we see ourselves and how our culture treats us are based on the total accumulation of roles we assume. Our roles represent our social standing in our culture. This chapter has focused on the sociorelational context of intercultural communication—that is, the group memberships we assume. All of us belong to any number of groups. Groups to which we belong are called membership groups. Some of these are voluntary, whereas others are involuntary. Often voluntary in-groups serve as reference groups. These are groups that help us make decisions about significant issues in our lives. The reference group serves as a standard by which we judge ourselves.

As group members, we assume roles that define with whom, about what, and how we communicate with others. Some of our roles are formal, whereas others are informal. Regardless, roles prescribe how we should communicate with others. Roles are a set of expectations that if violated, are subject to negative sanctions. Roles vary considerably across cultures, especially family and sex roles. In order for us to be competent communicators across cultures, we must understand the expectations of the roles we assume. We must also understand and appreciate that the roles we assume in our native culture may be quite different in other cultures.

GLOSSARY OF TERMS

Gender: The behavioral, cultural, and psychological traits associated with one's sex.

In-group: A membership group whose norms, goals, and values shape the behavior of the members. Extreme in-groups see the actions of an out-group as threatening to the in-group.

Involuntary membership group: A group to which a person belongs and has no choice but to belong, such as a person's sex, race, and age group.

Involuntary nonmembership group: A group to which a person does not belong because of ineligibility.

Membership group: A group to which a person belongs in which there is regular interaction among members who perceive themselves as members.

Nonmembership group: A group to which a person does not belong.

Out-group: A group whose attributes are dissimilar from those of an in-group and who oppose the realization of the in-group's goals.

Reference group: A group to which a person may or may not belong, but whose values and goals the person identifies with in some way.

Role: One's relative hierarchical position or rank in a group. A role is a prescribed set of behaviors that are expected in order to fulfill the role. Roles prescribe with whom, about what, and how to interact with others.

Role differentiation: The degree and complexity with which cultures distinguish among roles. Highly differentiated cultures distinguish among several roles—for example, corporate (owner, vice president, manager, worker, retiree), and religious (pope, cardinal, bishop, priest, parishioner) roles. Less differentiated cultures make fewer and more general distinctions among societal roles.

Sex: A classification of people based on biological genital differences.

Sex role: A prescribed set of behaviors assigned to different sexes.

Social identity: The total combination of one's group roles; the part of the individual's self-concept that is derived from the person's membership in groups.

Social stratification: A culture's organization of roles into a hierarchical vertical status structure.

Voluntary membership group: A membership group to which a person belongs out of choice, such as a political party or service organization.

REFERENCES

1. A. de Tocqueville, *Democracy in America,* vol. 2, trans. Henry Reeve (New York: Vintage Books, 1957), p. 114.
2. J. W. Johnson and F. P. Johnson, *Joining Together: Group Theory and Group Skills* (Boston: Allyn and Bacon, 1994).
3. This discussion of membership, nonmembership, voluntary, and involuntary groups can be found in a number of textbooks. The source used here is R. K. Merton, *Social Theory and Social Structure* (Glencoe, Ill.: The Free Press, 1959).
4. A. Wolter, "Saudi Arabia and Its Culture" (unpublished manuscript, St. Norbert College, De Pere, Wisc., 1994); "Saudi Arabia Culture and Religion" (www.arab.net/saudi/culture) (1997).
5. Merton, *Social Theory and Social Structure*; R. J. Bishop, "Cultural Profile, Examination of Value Orientations and Sociocultural Influences, and Verbal and Nonverbal Language Aspects of the East Indian Culture" (unpublished manuscript, St. Norbert College, De Pere, Wisc., 1995); W. B. Gudykunst and Y. Y. Kim, *Communicating with Strangers: An Approach to Intercultural Communication* (New York: McGraw-Hill, 1997).
6. W. G. Sumner, *Folkways* (Boston: Ginn, 1906), pp. 12–13.
7. Merton, *Social Theory and Social Structure.*
8. H. Triandis, "Cross-Cultural Studies in Individualism and Collectivism," in *Nebraska Symposium on Motivation, 1989,* ed. J. J. Berman (Lincoln: University of Nebraska Press, 1990), pp. 41–133.
9. M. B. Brewer and D. T. Campbell, *Ethnocentrism and Intergroup Attitudes* (New York: Wiley, 1976).
10. J. Weber, "The Nature of Ethnocentric Attribution Bias: Ingroup Projection or Enhancement?" *Journal of Experimental Social Psychology,* 30 (1994), 482–504; M. B. Brewer, "Ingroup Bias in the Minimal Intergroup Situation: A Cognitive Motivational Analysis," *Psychological Bulletin,* 86 (1979), 307–324; H. Taifel and J. Turner, "An Integrative Theory of Intergroup Conflict," in *The Social Psychology of Intergroup Conflict,* ed. W. Austin and S. Worchel (Monterey, Calif.: Brooks/Cole, 1979).
11. R. T. Schaefer, *Racial and Ethnic Groups,* 7th ed. (New York: Longman, 1998).
12. These examples of Christians and Jews are adapted from Schaefer, *Racial and Ethnic Groups.*
13. R. W. Napier and M. K. Gershenfeld, *Groups,*

Theory and Experience, 5th ed. (Boston: Houghton Mifflin, 1993).

14. T. Spear and R. Waller, eds., *Being Maasai* (London: James Currey, 1993); K. Vandehey, C. M. Buerger, and K. Krueger, "Traditional Aspects and Struggles of the Masai Culture" (unpublished manuscript, St. Norbert College, De Pere, Wisc., 1996).

15. The discussion of roles can be found in any number of group textbooks; the particular one used here was B. A. Fisher and D. G. Ellis, *Small Group Decision-Making,* 3rd ed. (New York: McGraw-Hill, 1990).

16. This discussion of formal and informal roles was based on J. K. Brilhart and G. J. Galanes, *Effective Group Discussion,* 9th ed. (Boston: McGraw-Hill, 1998).

17. R. B. Adler and N. Towne, *Looking Out, Looking In,* 8th ed. (Fort Worth: Harcourt Brace, 1996).

18. Gudykunst and Kim, *Communicating with Strangers*; H. Taifel, ed., *Differentiation Between Social Groups* (London: Academic Press, 1978), p. 63.

19. Gudykunst and Kim, *Communicating with Strangers.*

20. "Customs and Traditions in Korea" (www.emb. washington.dc.us/Korea/Scustoms.html) (1997).

21. J. W. Berry, Y. H. Poortinga, M. H. Segall, and P. R. Dasen, *Cross-Cultural Psychology: Research and Applications* (Cambridge: Cambridge University Press, 1992).

22. M. Keberlein, "A Cultural Profile of the Guatemalan Ladinos" (unpublished manuscript, St. Norbert College, De Pere, Wisc., 1993).

23. M. I. Duley, "Women in India," in *The Cross-Cultural Study of Women,* ed. M. I. Duley and M. I. Edwards (New York: The Feminist Press, 1986), pp. 127–236; Bishop, "Cultural Profile, Examination of Value Orientations and Sociocultural Influences, and Verbal and Nonverbal Language Aspects of the East Indian Culture."

24. D. Klopf, *Intercultural Encounters: The Fundamentals of Intercultural Communication,* 3rd ed. (Englewood, Colo.: Morton, 1995).

25. S. Chan, *Hmong Means Free* (Philadelphia: Temple University Press, 1984); K. Thao, "The Hmong Culture" (unpublished manuscript, St. Norbert College, De Pere, Wisc., 1995).

26. S. Paik, "The Formation of the United Lineage in Korea," *History of the Family,* 5 (2000), 75–90.

27. Ibid.

28. K. S. Chang, "Modernity Through the Family: Familial Foundations of Korean Society," *International Review of Sociology,* 7 (1997), 51–64.

29. M. Kim, "Transformation of Family Ideology in Upper-Middle-Class Families in Urban South Korea," *Ethnology,* 32 (1993), 69–86.

30. D. Levande, J. Herrick, and K. Sung, "Eldercare in the United States and South Korea," *Journal of Family Issues,* 21 (2000), 632–652.

31. Kim, "Transformation of Family Ideology in Upper-Middle-Class Families in Urban South Korea"; Y. Chun and S. M. MacDermid, "Perceptions of Family Differentiation, Individuation, and Self-Esteem Among Korean Adolescents," *Journal of Marriage and the Family,* 59 (1997), 451–463.

32. M. H. Bond, ed., *The Psychology of the Chinese People* (Hong Kong: Oxford University Press, 1986); B. Amraen, "China: A Populous Nation" (unpublished manuscript, St. Norbert College, De Pere, Wisc., 1994).

33. T. Basit, "'I Want More Freedom, but Not Too Much': British Muslim Girls and the Dynamism of Family Values," *Gender & Education,* 9 (1997), 425–440; M. Haroun, "Family Life in Islam," *The Lahore Ahmadijya Movement for the Propagation of Islam* (www.aaiil.org/text/articles/others/ familylifeinislam.shtml); T. Pels, "Muslim Families from Morocco in the Netherlands: Gender Dynamics and Fathers' Roles in a Context of Change," *Current Sociology,* 48 (2000), 75–94.

34. S. L. Bem, "The Measurement of Psychological Androgyny," *Journal of Consulting and Clinical Psychology,* 81 (1974), 506–520; J. Wood, "Gender, Communication, and Culture," in *Intercultural Communication: A Reader,* 9th ed. L. A. Samovar and R. E. Porter (Belmont, Calif.: Wadsworth, 2000), pp. 170–179.

35. Bem, "The Measurement of Psychological Androgyny."

36. J. Zhang, J. M. Norvilitis, and S. Jin, "Measuring Gender Orientation with the Bem Sex Role Inventory in Chinese Culture," *Sex Roles*, 44 (2001), 237–251.

37. E. Katsurada and Y. Sugihara, "Gender Differences in Gender-Role Perceptions Among Japanese College Students," *Sex Roles*, 41 (1999), 775–786; Y. Sugihara and E. Katsurada, "Masculinity and Femininity in Japanese Culture: A Pilot Study," *Sex Roles*, 40 (1999), 635–646.

38. Ibid.

39. J. Shimonaka, K. Nakazato, and C. Kawaai, "Rounenki Ni Okeru Seiyakuwari To Shinnritekitekiou" ["Sex Roles and Psychological Adjustment in Old Age"], *Shakai Ronenngaku*, 31 (1990), 3–11.

40. G. Hofstede, *Cultures and Organization: Software of the Mind* (New York: McGraw-Hill, 1991).

41. G. H. Herdt, ed., *Ritualized Homosexuality in Melanesia* (Berkeley and Los Angeles: University of California Press, 1984).

42. T. E. Lobel, S. Mashraki-Redhatzur, A. Mantzur, and S. Libby, "Gender Discrimination as a Function of Stereotypic and Counterstereotypic Behavior: A Cross-Cultural Study," *Sex Roles*, 43 (2000), 395–406.

43. J. E. Williams and D. L. Best, *Measuring Sex Stereotypes Across Cultures: A Multi-Nation Study* (Newbury Park: Calif.: Sage, 1990).

44. J. E. Williams and D. L. Best, "Cross-Cultural Views of Women and Men," in W. J. Lonner and R. Malpass, eds., *Psychology and Culture* (Boston: Allyn & Bacon, 1994), pp. 191–196.

45. L. Hessini, "Wearing the Hijab in Contemporary Morocco: Choice and Identity," in F. M. Gogek and S. Balaghi, eds., *Reconstructing Gender in the Middle East* (New York: Columbia University Press, 1994), pp. 40–56.

46. S. Iwao, *The Japanese Woman: Traditional Image and Changing Reality* (Cambridge.: Harvard University Press, 1993); Sugihara and Katsurada, "Masculinity and Femininity in Japanese Culture."

47. Duley, "Women in India"; "India: Dowry Deaths Still Increasing," *Women's International Network News*, 22 (1996), 67; P. Mandelbaum, "Dowry Deaths in India," *Commonweal*, 126 (1999), 18–21.

48. "India: Actions to Stop Feticide," *Women's International Network News*, 26, (2000), 47.

49. S. Derne, "Hindu Men Talk About Controlling Women: Cultural Ideas as a Tool of the Powerful," *Sociological Perspectives*, 37 (1994), 203–228.

The Verbal Code: Human Language

CHAPTER OBJECTIVES

After reading this chapter, you should be able to:

- Explain the relationship between language and culture.
- Explain the principles of linguistic relativity and linguistic determinism.
- Define the three levels of language.
- Explain the principles of universal grammar.
- List and define three universals of language.
- Compare and contrast elaborated and restricted codes.
- Compare and contrast cross-cultural communication styles.

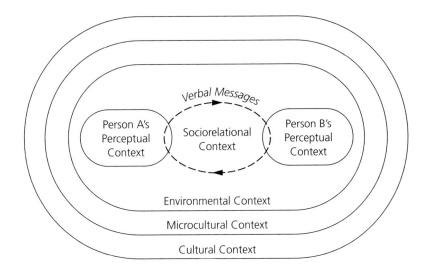

The capacity of the human brain to acquire language may be the distinguishing feature that separates humans from the rest of the living beings on the planet. Our ability to put thoughts into a code in order to communicate with someone else empowers us beyond imagination. Other living beings are larger, stronger, faster, and smaller, but no other living being has the capacity for language. Language has put humans on top of the evolutionary ladder. Because of their capacity for language, humans have become the most powerful living beings on earth. This chapter explores the idea of language and how it varies across cultures. The first part of the chapter outlines the relationship between language and culture by exploring the Sapir-Whorf hypothesis. The second part of the chapter outlines the fundamental structure of language, including the concept of a universal grammar that applies to all languages. The third part of the chapter looks at universals of language that are shared across cultures. The fourth part of the chapter focuses on how the use of language differs across cultures, including a look at elaborate and restricted codes and cross-cultural comparisons of language style.

The Relationship Between Language and Culture

Linguist and cultural anthropologist Zdenek Salzmann points out that historically, anthropologists and linguists have often grouped language, culture, and race together as though any one of them automatically implied the other two. Contemporary linguistic anthropologists generally agree, however, that culture, race, and language are historically distinct. In other words, a person's race does not determine what language he or she will speak. As we saw in Chapter 5, however, the language of a particular culture and the thought processes of its people are closely related.[2]

THE SAPIR-WHORF HYPOTHESIS

In 1928, anthropologist and linguist Edward Sapir published a paper in the journal *Language* that changed the face of the study of language and culture. Sapir's thesis was that the language of a particular culture directly influences how people think. Sapir wrote:

> . . . the network of cultural patterns of a civilization is indexed in the language which expresses that civilization. . . . Language is a guide to "social reality." . . . Human beings do not live in the objective world alone . . . but are very much at the mercy of the particular language which has become the medium of expression for their society.[3]

Sapir continued to argue that the ways in which people perceive the world around them, including their natural and social environments, is essentially dictated by their language. In fact, Sapir argued that the speakers of different languages see different worlds. Strongly influenced by Sapir was one of his students, Benjamin Whorf, who further developed this line of thought.[4] In 1940, Whorf wrote:

... the background linguistic system (in other words the grammar) of each language is not merely a reproducing instrument for voicing ideas but rather is itself the shaper of ideas.... We dissect nature along lines laid down by our native languages.[5]

Like Sapir, Whorf believed that people who speak different languages are directed to different types of observations; therefore, they are not equivalent as observers and must arrive at somewhat different views of the world.[6] Sapir and Whorf's ideas received a great deal of attention and have become well known as the Sapir-Whorf hypothesis. Salzmann contends that the Sapir-Whorf hypothesis delineates two principles: (1) the *principle of linguistic determinism,* which says that the way one thinks is determined by the language one speaks, and (2) *the principle of linguistic relativity,* which says that the differences among languages must therefore be reflected in the differences in the worldviews of their speakers. These principles raise some important issues for cross-cultural communication. If how we think is a reflection of the language we speak, then the speakers of two very different languages must think very differently. This could render effective and successful intercultural communication extremely difficult, if not insurmountable.

Salzmann and other contemporary linguists and anthropologists maintain that the Sapir-Whorf hypothesis may be a bit exaggerated. Today, most linguists believe that the vocabulary and grammar of a particular language parallel the nonverbal culture. In other words, the geographic, climatic, kinesic, spatial, and proxemic aspects of a culture are emphasized and accented in a culture's language. Salzmann notes, for example, that in Pintupi (one of the aboriginal languages of Australia), there are at least ten words designating various kinds of holes. *Mutara* is a special hole in a spear, *pulpa* refers to a rabbit burrow, *makarnpa* is the burrow of a monitor lizard, and *katarta* is the hole left by a monitor lizard after it has broken the surface after hibernation.

Moreover, linguists believe that the syntactic features of a language influence how speakers of that language categorize and mentally organize their worlds. For example, speakers of English use the personal pronoun *you* whether they are addressing one or several children, adults, old persons, subordinates, or individuals much superior to themselves in rank. Other languages operate differently. When addressing someone, speakers of Dutch, French, German, Italian, Russian, and Spanish must choose between the "familiar" personal pronoun and the "polite" personal pronoun and/or the corresponding verb forms. In English, the word *teacher* refers to a person who teaches, whether it is a man or a woman. In German, *Lehrer* is the masculine form of teacher, and *Leherin* is the feminine form. In this way, speakers of Dutch, French, German, and Italian may be more conscious of the status differences between themselves and another person because their language requires them to use words designating the power differential.[7]

Therefore, most linguists now believe that the users of a particular language may overlook or ignore objects or events that speakers of another language may emphasize. John B. Carroll modifies the Sapir-Whorf hypothesis by arguing that to the extent that languages differ, language users organize their experiences differently, according to the vocabularies and grammars provided by their respective languages. Carroll notes that these cognitions will affect behavior.[8]

The Structure of Human Language

All languages are a systematic set of sounds combined with a set of rules for the sole purpose of creating meaning and communicating.[9] Any human language is made up of a set of sounds. These sounds are represented symbolically in the language's alphabet. In English, for example, there are approximately forty sounds represented in an alphabet of twenty-six letters. The Korean script, called Hangul, consists of sixteen consonants, of which there are five basic forms, and ten vowels. According to Kenneth Katzner, the Hebrew alphabet of twenty-two letters (five of which have a different form when they appear at the end of a word) consists entirely of consonants. The language is written from right to left without vowels. Thus the word *kelev* ("dog") appears as the Hebrew equivalents of, from right to left, *k, l,* and *v.* If you are not familiar with Hebrew, it is impossible to know how to pronounce a word from the way it is written. During the eighth century, a system was developed for indicating vowels through the use of small dots and dashes placed above and below the consonants. These signs are still in use today, but they are confined to schoolbooks, prayerbooks, and textbooks for foreigners and are not to be seen in newspapers, magazines, or books for general use.[10]

The written form of Japanese consists of three major systems. A fourth system, called *romaji,* is a romanization using English letters. All four systems are used simultaneously in any given piece of writing. The first system, called *kanji,* consists of over five thousand characters borrowed from Chinese. The word *kanji* means "Chinese character." *Kanji* are the Chinese characters used in written Japanese. Each *kanji* character represents an idea or concept, rather than a simple sound. The meaning of the character changes when the combination of characters varies (see Figure 7-1). To be able to read a Japanese newspaper, you would need to know and understand at least two thousand basic characters. Moreover, you would have to learn the different readings or compounds of two or more *kanji.* There are over four thousand *kanji* compounds. The Japanese also have two phonetic systems, called *hiragana* and *katakana. Hiragana* consists of forty-six characters. These are phonetic sounds that make up the *kanji* and are used to change verb tenses. The *katakana* also consists of forty-six sounds. The *katakana* sounds coincide with the *hiragana,* but the characters are different. *Katakana* is used for all foreign words coming from outside Japan.[11]

SOUNDS AND SYMBOLS

The letters of a language's alphabet are symbols representing sounds. These small units of sound are called *phonemes.* In English, the letter *c* represents the sound *see,* or *ka;* the letter *a* represents the sound *ah;* and the letter *t* represents the sound

FIGURE 7·1   Kanji Examples

hito: human being, man, person

otona: adult (big + person)

tee. In combination, phonemes become words—that is, morphemes, the smallest meaning-unit of sound. When coarticulated, the sounds *ka, ah,* and *tee* create the word/morpheme *cat.*

There is no natural or inherent relationship between the sounds and their accompanying alphabet. That is, there is no intrinsic or immanent relationship between the symbol *c* and the *see* sound, the *a* and the *ah* sound, or the letter *t* and the *tee* sound. That *c* represents the *see* sound is completely random and arbitrary. Likewise, there is also no natural relationship between any word and its referent. In other words, there is no natural or necessary relationship between the word *cat* and that fuzzy little animal walking across the room. In Spanish, which uses a similar but different sound system, the fuzzy little animal walking across the floor is called *gato;* in Japan it is *neiko;* and in French it is *chat.* Each of the different languages uses a different set of sounds for the same referent.

Although the letters and the sound systems of any two languages may be different, the function of an alphabet is the same across languages—that is, to symbolize sound. A *symbol* is an arbitrarily selected and learned stimulus representing something else. The ability to represent sounds with symbols seems to be limited to humans. To be sure, animals can learn to associate sounds with behaviors, but they can do so only at a very rudimentary level. Jo Liska has developed a hierarchy of symbolic abstraction that allows us to see where humans and animals are distinct in terms of language and symbol use.[12] The hierarchy includes, from bottom to top, symptoms, ritual semblances, iconic semblances, proper symbols, conceptual symbols, and syntactic symbols. According to Liska, *symptoms* constitute the foundation for all animal communication. These are biologically "hard-wired" in the central nervous system, meaning they are a natural part of human and animal biology. The employment of symptoms is unconscious and is stimulated by events in the physiological conditions of the animal. Examples of symptoms include pupil dilation, blushing, piloerection, estrus, and vocalizations. A dog's growl at the sign of another dog is symptomatic. Liska maintains that these behaviors are fixed and immune to short-term environmental changes. Symptoms are automatic, involuntary, and primary. *Ritual semblances* are exaggerated symptoms that are relatively conscious, such as posed facial expressions, gestures of pantomime, begging, and signs of submission. Dogs and cats often exaggerate their begging routines in order to receive table scraps. *Iconic semblances* are related to ritual semblances in that these are signs that represent their referents, such as a map, a blueprint, or a photograph of a dog. Liska suggests that iconic semblances are probably restricted to humans. Early cave drawings by our ancestors can be considered iconic semblances. Next up Liska's ladder of symbolic abstraction are *proper symbols,* which label some aspect of reality. Proper symbols provide the means for naming others, objects, or events. The word *cat* is a proper symbol for the fuzzy little animal. Proper symbols are acquired through stimulus-response learning. Over time, we learn to associate the fuzzy little animal with the word *cat.* On the other hand, *conceptual symbols* create symbolic reality and refer to concepts that exist only in the minds of the users, such as "liberty," "democracy," and "freedom." Unlike proper symbols, conceptual symbols have no physical referent. The stimulus-response pattern for acquiring proper symbols cannot account for the acquisition of conceptual symbols since there is no external stimulus (such as a cat) with which to associate the symbol. Finally, at the top of the symbolic hierarchy are *syntactic symbols.* These symbols express grammatical relationships between other symbols, such as possession, function, and tense. Syntactic symbols are the means by which language is patterned, organized, and structured.[13]

According to Liska, many mammals and birds communicate using ritual semblances, and some species of primates seem to be able to acquire and use proper symbols. When well trained and monitored, apes seem to acquire language presented to them visually. Yet their natural communication repertoire appears to be based on symptoms and ritual semblances. Apes seem to have the capacity for language, but as humans use it, language has not yet emerged among wild-living apes. Liska contends that all animals "communicate," but we humans have made it our single most distinguishing characteristic. To be sure, argues Liska, other animal species may possess "advanced" communication systems. Apes engage in a whole host of symptomatic and semblamatic signs. Whales sing intricate songs that vary over time. Killer whales (orcas) use calls that seem to vary from group to group. Wolves use a complicated set of postures for coordination of the pack. But, unlike animals, we seem compelled to create and invent symbols. As Liska avows, humans seem to communicate because we *need to.*[14]

SYNTAX AND UNIVERSAL GRAMMAR

Along with a system of sounds, all languages have a set of rules for combining the sounds to create meaning. The set of rules, or grammar, is called syntax. Through syntax, sentences are generated. Through syntax, sound and meaning are connected. Noam Chomsky is perhaps the most recognized linguist in the world. For the past forty years, Chomsky has developed a fascinating theory about syntax.[15] Chomsky contends that although the five thousand or so languages that are spoken in the world today appear to be very different, they are, in fact, remarkably similar. Moreover, Chomsky asserts that the obvious differences between languages are actually quite trivial. Chomsky maintains that all languages spoken on the planet today are dialects of one common language: human language.[16]

Chomsky argues that all human languages share a *universal grammar* that is in-

Unlike animals, humans seem compelled to create and invent symbols. Humans need to communicate. *(© James Neuliep)*

nate in the human species and culturally invariant. Chomsky and other linguists claim that every normal child is genetically programmed for human language. Just as humans are programmed to walk upright, so are humans programmed with universal grammar. Chomsky says that language is as much a part of the human brain as the thumb is a part of the human hand. Linguist Lila Gleitman maintains that human language is not innate in the same way as bee-language or horse-language may be innate, or in the sense that human visual sensation is innate. Humans do not "learn" how to see. Humans, do, however, learn a specific language. The acquisition of a particular language (for example, English or Japanese) is influenced by the specific cultural environment in which a child is born.[17] In other words, no individual language is universal to human beings. Children learn their specific language by being exposed to it in their cultural environment. Children born and raised in China learn to speak Chinese, whereas children born and raised in Norway learn to speak Norwegian, not because of their race or ethnicity, but because of their cultural environment.

The commonalities among the different languages (for example, Chinese and Norwegian) are so striking that Chomsky and other linguists are convinced that the fundamental syntax for all languages is universal and that the particular languages of particular cultures are simply dialects of the universal grammar. For example, there are two fundamental syntactical structures to all human languages. The first is that all languages, the world over, rely on either word order or inflection to convey meaning. Most languages rely on both to a greater or lesser extent. English, for example, relies heavily on word order. The phrase "The man is in the car" means something very different from "The car is in the man." English also uses inflection to carry meaning. Inflections are changes to words to indicate grammatical relationships, such as number, case, gender, tense, and so forth. For example, to indicate the plural of something in English, we add the letter *s* to the end of nouns. A single fuzzy little animal is called a *cat*, and two fuzzy little animals are called *cats*. The language of the Warlpiri people of Australia relies almost exclusively on inflection rather than word order. Latin also relies heavily on inflection. The point is that word order and inflection are a part of all languages. As linguist Dan Slobin asserts:

> In a way [language] it's like the human face. A human face is very simple, two eyes, a nose, and a mouth. You can draw a simple sketch of it. But look at the incredible diversity. Each one of us has a uniquely different face. Yet each face is obviously a human face. Languages are the same. Each one is obviously a different language but they're clearly examples of the same kind of system.[18]

Gleitman forwards two additional arguments in favor of the universality of language.[19] The first is that language learning proceeds uniformly among children within and across cultures. Chinese children and Norwegian children learn language at the same time in their development. All normal children begin to use language at about the same time across cultures. Linguist Steven Pinker has observed that sometime around their first birthday, babies start to understand and use words. At about eighteen months, children's vocabulary across all cultures increases at a rate of one word every two hours and continues to grow through adolescence. At this time, two-word strings appear. These two-word combinations are highly similar across cultures. Children announce when objects appear, disappear, and move about. According to Pinker, by the age of three years, a child's vocabulary grows dramatically and he or she can produce fluent grammatical conversation. Such sentences, though quite short, illustrate the child's knowledge of, and competence in, the basic structure of language (appropriate word order, and so forth). For example, even though he or she has never had a lesson on English grammar, an English-speaking child might say, "I want cookie," but would never say, "Want I cookie." By the age of five or so, children in normal learning settings begin to use complex sentences.[20]

Gleitman argues that even when the learning environment changes, children learn language at essentially the same rate. Studies indicate that a child's language learning rate is basically unaffected by differences in the mother's speech. Furthermore, deaf or blind children learn language at the same time and rate as children with normal hearing and sight. Gleitman points out that the vocabulary and syntax of sign languages are essentially the same as those of spoken languages. At about the age of two, deaf children start to put gestures together into elementary two- and three-gesture sentences. By five years of age, they are constructing complex multigesture sentences. In addition, blind children have little trouble acquiring terms that describe visual experiences. Gleitman suggests that since blind children are unable to see, one might expect that phrases referring to sight (such as "Look at that!") would be absent from their speech. Yet such terms are some of the first to appear in blind children's vocabulary. In response to the command

Although very young, children are competent users of language.
(© James Neuliep)

"Look up," blind children raise their hands instead of their heads. When they are told that they can "look but not touch," blind children very slowly stretch out their hands and cautiously touch the object. When told, "Go ahead and look," they handle the object with enthusiasm.[21]

The second point supporting the universality-of-language argument is that children across cultures acquire many linguistic generalizations that experience alone could not have taught them. Children of all cultures say things that no one could have taught them. Chomsky argues that in advance of experience, children of all cultures are already equipped with an understanding of the basic structure of any human language. Like walking, or growing hair, language is encoded into the genetic makeup of normal functioning human beings. By the age of three, for example, there are any number of things children cannot do, such as tie their own shoes, perform mathematical computations, or spell most words. By age three, however, children can construct meaningful sentences in ways that no one has ever taught them.[22] Moreover, as Pinker notes, the sentences they create are grammatically correct. Indeed, asserts Pinker, children never make some mistakes. For example, a child might ask, "What did you eat your eggs with?" but the child would never say, "What did you eat your eggs and?" which seems to be a straightforward extension of the statement "I ate ham and eggs." The interesting point here is that no one has ever taught the child not to end sentences with the word *and*. Pinker and Chomsky argue that children never make such errors because to do so would violate some principle of universal grammar.

In another example provided by Pinker, a language learner who hears the sentences (a) and (b) below could quite sensibly extract a general rule that when applied to sentence (c) would yield sentence (d). But sentence (d) is something no one would say.

(a) We expect the bird to fly.
(b) We expect the bird will fly.
(c) The bird is expected to fly.
(d) The bird is expected will fly.[23]

The proposition that all languages share a universal grammar that is innate to humans is widely accepted among contemporary linguists. But these linguists also recognize that all human languages are somewhat different. For example, although virtually all languages rely on some form of word order to construct sentences, the word order may vary across languages. The word order for a sentence in most European languages is subject-verb-object, as in the sentence "I watch television." In Japanese, however, the order is subject-object-verb, as in the sentence "I television watch." In addition, Japanese, like other Asian languages, does not contain a grammatical equivalent to plurality as can be found in English.[24] The Swahili alphabet lacks the letters *c, q,* and *x* but contains a number of letters of its own. The letter *dh* is pronounced like the *th* of *this; gh* is pronounced like the German *ch.* Whereas English grammatical inflections occur at the end of a word, in Swahili everything is done at the beginning. *Kitabu* is the Swahili word for "book," but the word for *books* is *vitabu.* Many languages are read from left to right, like English. Most languages of the Middle East, including Arabic, Hebrew, and Persian, are read from right to left, however. Korean writing differs considerably from most other languages in that the letters of each syllable are grouped together into clusters, as if the English word "seldom" were written in the following way:

SD   SEL
EO   or   DOM
LM

The point here is that even though human languages across the globe have much in common, each is unique in some way.[25]

All human languages have a set of rules that are used to combine the language's sounds into meaningful units. Complex languages exist even in remote parts of the world where people have yet to be exposed to modern technology and media. Papua New Guinea, for example, is where some of the most isolated people on earth live, yet it is probably the most linguistically diverse country on earth. Among the population of 3 million people, there are over 750 spoken languages, about one-fifth of the total number of languages on earth. Some of the languages are spoken by less than one thousand people. In his longitudinal work with the Menya people of Papua New Guinea, Carl Whitehead has found that the Menya use a language that is as complex as any other. Whitehead argues that one of the most remarkable features of the Menya language is its verb system. Some Menya verbs can have as many as 2,000 to 3,000 different forms; English verbs can have up to 5 forms. Languages such as Menya are as highly rule-governed as any other language. In this sense there is no such thing as a primitive language.[26]

UNIVERSALS OF LANGUAGE

Another reason why so many linguists believe that all languages evolved from a universal grammar is because of their numerous commonalities. All languages have some way of labeling objects, places, or things (such as the English noun). All languages have a way of naming action (such as the English verb). All human languages have some way of stating the negative, a way to construct interrogatives, and a way of differentiating between singular and plural.[27]

According to Salzmann, the uniquely human way of communicating through speech shares several other universal features, regardless of culture, race, and particular vocabulary. (1) All human speech is transmitted via a vocal-auditory channel. Conversely, some sounds produced by animals are not vocal or are not received auditorily (for example, bees have no ears). An important advantage of the vocal-auditory channel for humans is that the rest of the body is left free to carry on other activities. (2) Speech sounds are emitted from their source of origin in all directions, making it possible to determine the location of the source. Functionally this phenomenon is important because it enables speakers to communicate without necessarily being face to face—for example, from around corners or in the dark. (3) Speech sounds are heard within a very limited range and only during production. Soon after, they are lost. In this sense, speech is transitory. (4) Speech is interchangeable. We are capable of repeating what others say. This is not true of many animal species. (5) Human speakers are equipped with complete intrapersonal feedback. As speakers, we can hear ourselves and are capable of monitoring our own messages. (6) Speech is specialized. Human speech has only a single function—that is, to communicate. (7) Speech can be displaced from time and space. We can talk about something that happened one thousand years ago, or project what we think will happen one thousand years from now. (8) What a person may say can be completely false. (9) Speech is reflexive. We use language to talk about language. (10) The speakers of any language can learn a second language or even several languages in addition to their native tongue.[28]

GENERATIVE GRAMMAR

One of the most remarkable features of any language's rule structure is that it allows the speakers to generate sentences that have never before been spoken. Chomsky refers to this aspect of language as its *generative grammar.* From a finite set of sounds and a finite set of rules, speakers of any language can create an infinite number of sentences, many of which have never before been uttered yet are easily comprehended by other speakers of the same language.[29]

Most of the sentences you have produced today have never before been spoken by anyone on the planet, and yet everyone understood them. Linguist George A. Miller contends that any sentence over twenty words in length has probably never before been spoken. According to Miller, suppose it is possible for someone to choose the next word that he or she is going to say from a list of 10 possible words.

Continuing on, assume that the second word someone is going to speak is also one of 10 possible words. At this point the total number of possible combinations of two-worded sentences is 10 times 10, or 100 possible two-word sentences (see Table 7-1). Now assume that the person is to select a third word out of a possible 10 words. The number of possible three-worded sentences is 10 to the third power, or 1,000 possible sentences.

Moving on to a fourth possible word out of a list of 10 possible words, the number of potential four-worded sentences is 10 to the fourth power, or 10,000 possi-

TABLE 7·1   Number of Possible Two· and Three-Word Sentences

First-Word Options	Second-Word Options	
Blue	dog	
Green	cat	
Yellow	bird	
Red	pig	
Black	cow	Number of possible two-word
Brown	horse	sentences is 10 × 10 = 100
Orange	chicken	
Gray	rat	
White	mouse	
Violet	fish	

First-Word Options	Second-Word Options	Third-Word Options	
Jan	ran	fast	
Jim	walked	slow	
Gary	jumped	quickly	
Karen	limped	rapidly	
Kevin	opened	leisurely	Number of possible
Donna	cried	gradually	three-word sentences
Jeff	laughed	briefly	is 10 × 10 × 10 =
Judy	rode	promptly	1,000
Henry	drove	swiftly	
Susan	flew	fashionably	

ble sentences. The number of possible messages increases very rapidly as the length of the message increases. Following this example, the number of possible 20-word sentences is 10 to the twentieth power, or 100,000,000,000,000,000,000 possible sentences. On the basis of this example, Miller asserts that the number of possible sentences in any language is essentially infinite.[30]

Elaborated and Restricted Codes

Although the world's five thousand or so languages have much in common, the style or fashion in which they are used by the people who speak them differs from culture to culture. In fact, speakers of the same language often use it differently. Some of these differences may be explained by Hall's concept of high- and low-context cultures. Persons in high-context cultures generally rely more on their nonverbal code than on their verbal code to communicate, whereas members of low-context cultures rely extensively on the verbal code during communication.

Basil Bernstein argues that the use of linguistic codes is closely related to the social structure of a particular culture. First, Bernstein differentiates between language and speech. He agrees that language is a system of sounds and syntax that allows speakers to represent their reality and generate an infinite number of sentences. In fact, he argues that all languages are equal in terms of their ability to represent reality. Speech, on the other hand, is at the mercy of the social circumstances in which it is employed. Bernstein maintains that while language symbolizes what is *possible* to do, speech symbolizes what is actually occurring. The social context of communication sets up the boundaries for the type of speech that is preferred, obligated, or prohibited. As the social context varies, the speakers of the language will generate different kinds of speech, even if they speak the same language. The social system delimits the speaker's options in terms of language use. The speech codes, then, are not defined in terms of vocabulary or syntax, but by the social structure of the culture.[31]

Broadly speaking, Bernstein identifies two types of linguistic/speech codes: elaborated and restricted codes. A *restricted code* is one in which the options (not necessarily the vocabulary) are limited as to what the speakers can say or do verbally. A restricted code is considered a status-oriented speech system. The code reinforces the social system by restricting or limiting its speakers to a limited number of linguistic options during communication. Restricted codes are most often seen in high-context cultures in which the status of the interactants dictates who says what to whom and how it is said. When interactants of a high-context collectivistic culture communicate, their words and phrases are strictly prescribed, leaving them little choice about what to say or how to say it. In this way, their code is "restricted" and is highly predictable. Bernstein points out that the Chinese, for example, operate with a restricted code, yet have one of the most complex languages on earth. Chinese need to learn several thousand characters in order to read and write, but they speak with a restricted code because the social system (highly status and group oriented) dictates what can be said to whom in a given social circumstance. Restricted codes also emerge in individualistic cultures as interactants develop close relationships. Restricted codes can be found in what Bernstein calls "closed" communities, such as prison camps and criminal subgroups, but can develop within any social structure in which the individuals share social identifications (for example, spouses or coworkers). In this way, restricted codes show up in both high- and low-context cultures, although they tend to be more salient across the entire culture in a high- rather than low-context culture.[32]

With an *elaborated code*, speakers can choose from among a variety of linguistic options to communicate. Bernstein argues that speakers using an elaborated code are able, via the social system, to put their thoughts, intents, and goals into an explicit verbal message. Bernstein argues that elaborated codes develop in circumstances in which the speakers' intents are unknown or vary widely, as in individualistic cultures. Because the individual speaker's intent is unclear, the speaker has a variety of linguistic options available from which to choose. The speaker must expand and elaborate so that his or her intentions are clearly communicated. Any language will allow the speaker to do that, but the social system regulates it. The social structure of elaborated-code users is such that considerable flexibility exists in role prescriptions. To communicate his or her intent, the speaker must be given much linguistic latitude. In this way, it is very difficult to predict the vocabulary and syntax of a speaker using an elaborated code. Students in the United States, for example, may have no idea what kinds of things a new professor will say on the first day of class. Students in China, on the other hand, can probably quite accurately predict the kinds of messages their professors will send. In the United States, the culture generally uses an elaborated code, whereas in China the code is restricted.[33]

Cross-Cultural Communication Styles

Although the capacity for language is universal, the language of a particular culture must be learned by its members. Moreover, cultures seem to have a predominant manner, fashion, or style in which they use their language. Communication theorists William Gudykunst and Stella Ting-Toomey argue that at different language acquisition stages, children learn not only the structure and vocabulary of their culture's language but also the various styles of language interaction unique to their culture. Such language styles reflect the affective, moral, and aesthetic patterns of a culture. Gudykunst and Ting-Toomey describe a culture's verbal style as its tonal coloring of a message that is communicated through shades of tonal qualities. Gudykunst and Ting-Toomey describe four verbal communication styles that have been identified by intercultural theorists: (1) *direct/indirect*, (2) *elaborate/succinct*, (3) *personal/contextual*, and (4) *instrumental/affective*. Variations of these styles may exist in any culture, but typically one style dominates within a culture.[34]

DIRECT AND INDIRECT STYLES

According to Gudykunst and Ting-Toomey, cultures differ in the degree to which speakers disclose their intentions through precise and candid verbal communication. Persons using a direct communication style employ overt expressions of intention. Such messages clearly articulate the speaker's desires and needs. Direct styles are often used in low-context, individualistic cultures. Conversely, in an indirect communication style, which is often seen in high-context and collectivistic cultures, the speaker's intentions are hidden or only hinted at during interaction. Ambiguity and vagueness are characteristic of an indirect style. In high-context cultures, there is no need to articulate every message. True understanding is implicit, coming not from words but from actions in the environment. Moreover, indirect communication prevents potentially embarrassing moments that might threaten the "face" of either speaker.[35]

The direct style is preferred in cultures such as the United States, England, Australia, Germany, and Israel. In the United States, we frequently use such phrases as "for sure," "no question," "without a doubt." We value verbal precision and self-expression. Americans are encouraged to "speak their mind." We are so direct and candid that we will even announce to an entire room when we are going to use the bathroom, as in "I'll be right back—I have to use the restroom." Gudykunst and Ting-Toomey allege that Israel is also considered a direct culture, perhaps even more so than the United States. Fedarko points out that many Israelis use the direct style of *dugri* (straight talk) that is quintessentially Israeli. Israelis value communication that is simple, direct, and honest. A speaker displaying *dugri* places substance before style and makes no attempt at pretense or deception. Some have referred to Israel as an "in your face" culture when it comes to interacting.[36] Germans, too, value frankness and directness in their interaction with others and are especially fond of the use of examples. Along with their direct style is an absence of small talk. Hall and Hall maintain that in their quest for direct and candid talk, Germans despise social chit-chat. Sometimes Germans are perceived by their European counterparts as brutally frank.[37]

The use of an indirect style of language is seen in many Asian cultures. Indirectness is valued in these cultures because saving face and harmony in social relationships is highly valued. Directness threatens both of these goals. According to Gudykunst and Ting-Toomey, Japanese speakers limit themselves to implicit and even ambiguous use of words such as *maybe* and *perhaps*. Children in Japan are taught not to be self-centered, and those who take the initiative are generally not rewarded. Japanese mothers typically use rhetorical questions and tone of voice and context to express disapproval. Sumiko Iwao argues that there is an unspoken belief among Japanese that verbalizing deep feelings spoils their value. To the Japanese, being understood without words is far more cherished than precise articulation. Iwao asserts that in Japan, interpersonal communication is based on a great deal of guessing and reading between the lines. Directness is disagreeable

Intercultural Conversation

An Intercultural Conversation: Direct and Indirect Communication Styles

To some extent, direct and indirect modes of communication are universal. Indirect modes, for example, are often used out of simple politeness. However, most often, direct modes of communication are seen in cultures such as the United States, whereas indirect modes are seen in many Asian cultures, such as Japan, Korea, and China. The following conversation takes place between a young couple who have been dating for a short time. The man is an American student, and the woman is from an Asian culture. Note the misunderstanding that results from the collision of direct and indirect modes of communication.

Jim: Ya know, Michiko, I really enjoy the time we spend together. I really like you. I've been so happy since we met.

Michiko: Hmmm . . . thank you.

Jim: I mean, I feel like I've learned so much about you and your culture.

Michiko: Yeah, it's very interesting.

Jim: I'm so glad you came to the United States. Do you like it here? What is your favorite thing about us?

Michiko: Well, it's pretty big. It's very nice here.

Jim: What do you think about Americans?

Michiko: I don't know. Maybe I haven't been here long enough to know.

Jim: You must think something!

Michiko: Well, I'd probably have to think about it.

Jim: I mean, do you like us?

Michiko: Well, I don't really know that many Americans yet.

In all likelihood, Jim is not going to get much of an answer from Michiko. She continually gives rather general answers to Jim's very specific and direct questions about her feelings toward the United States. Michiko might believe that Jim is being far too direct and invading her privacy. Besides, the fact that she has traveled halfway around the world should be indicative of her desire to be here. Right? There must be something about the United States that attracted her. Michiko cannot possibly say something critical about the United States since she would lose face, as would Jim as a native. She relies on imprecise and indefinite answers.

SOURCE: The dialogue in this example is loosely adapted from C. Storti, *Cross-Cultural Dialogues: 74 Brief Encounters with Cultural Difference* (Yarmouth, Maine: Intercultural Press, 1994).

and repugnant. The ability to correctly grasp what a person thinks and feels without verbal expression is considered a sign of closeness between two persons. In marital relationships, verbal communication is thought to be unnecessary. Iwao calls Japan "a culture of no words." She alleges that this phenomenon may be due to the high value placed on masculinity. According to Japanese ideals, the most masculine of men is a man of few words who does not disclose personal weakness by complaints or expose his innermost thoughts and feelings, especially to his wife.[38] To a certain degree, the French are indirect. Hall and Hall argue that the French often indulge in small talk and prefer some mystery in interactions with others. They maintain that the French will often talk around the point they wish to make.[39]

ELABORATE, EXACTING, AND SUCCINCT STYLES

According to Gudykunst and Ting-Toomey, the elaborate, exacting, and succinct communication styles deal with the quantity and/or volume of talk that is preferred across cultural groups. There are three levels: (1) an *elaborate style* that emphasizes flashy and embellished language; (2) an *exacting style* in which persons say no more or less than is needed; and (3) a succinct style characterized by the use of concise statements, understatements, and even silence.[40] An elaborate style of communication can be seen in many Arab, Middle Eastern, and African American cultures. Many Middle Easterners tend to use metaphors, similes, and adjectives in everyday conversation. African Americans, too, prefer personalized, often exaggerated, spontaneous styles of interaction. Kochman writes:

> Stylistic self-expression within black culture is characterized by dramatic self-conscious flair. . . . Black stylistic self-expression is also characterized by inventive (humorously ironic) exaggeration as in the self-promotion of demonstrably capable aspects of self ("If you've got it, flaunt it") or even by less demonstrably positive capabilities ("If you don't have it, flaunt it, anyway"), which is all part of Afro-American boasting: the "making of one's noise." As Hollywood Henderson said, "I put a lot of pressure on myself to see if I can play up to my mouth." But exaggeration also serves to characterize (and neutralize the impact of) negative situations, such as poverty ("The soles on my shoes are so thin, I can step on a dime and tell you whether it's heads or tails").[41]

Americans tend to prefer an exacting style of interaction consistent with a "just the facts" mentality popularized by the *Dragnet* television series of the 1960s.

A succinct style can be found in Japan, China, and some Native American cultures (for example, Apache or Navajo). These cultures value the use of concise talk and silence. To the Chinese, silence is a means to maintain social control in a situation. Stowell points out that the Chinese, in general, do not value verbal skills. In fact, speaking skills are considered immoral. The skilled speaker may be labeled as "having a flattering mouth," "an oil-mouth," or a "honey-mouth." Chinese children are taught to be cautious about the use of words. The Chinese say, "One should use the eyes and ears, not the mouth," and "Disaster emanates from careless talk." The Chinese consider the wisest and most trustworthy person to be the one who talks the least, the one who listens, watches, and restricts his or her verbal communication.[42]

The Navajo and Apache American Indian tribes also value the use of silence as a way to deal with ambiguity. Steven Pratt, an actively participating member of the Osage tribe, and Lawrence Weider, a professor of communication, argue:

> To the real Indian, it appears that White Americans who are strangers to each other may freely engage in conversation in such places as the supermarket check-out line. Commercial airlines provide an even more intense opportunity

for easy conversation between strangers. Seatmates often disclose their life histories to each other. In the culture of real Indians, these are extraordinary and improper ways to behave, especially when both parties are real Indians. When real Indians who are strangers to one another pass each other in a public space, wait in line, occupy adjoining seats, and so forth, they take it that it is proper to remain silent and to not initiate conversation. Being silent at this point is a constituent part of the real Indian's mode of communicating with others, especially other Indians.[43]

The use of an elaborated, exacting, or succinct style is closely related to Hall's high- and low-context communication and Bernstein's classification of restricted and elaborated codes. Gudykunst and Kim contend that restricted codes resemble jargon or shorthand speech in which speakers are almost telegraphic. This seems to correlate with a succinct style. Conversely, Bernstein asserts that elaborate codes rely heavily on verbal amplification for message transmission, with much less emphasis on the nonverbal code or environmental cues. This seems to correspond with the elaborate style.[44]

PERSONAL AND CONTEXTUAL STYLES

Gudykunst and Ting-Toomey define the *personal communication style* as one that amplifies the individual identity of the speaker. Such a style stresses and underscores "personhood." This style is often seen in individualistic cultures. A personal style relies on the use of first-person pronouns in sentence construction. Person-oriented language stresses informality and symmetrical power relationships. For example, English has only one form for the second person—that is, *you*. Regardless of whether they are speaking to someone of higher, equal, or lower status, English speakers use the same form for the second person. For example, if we were to meet the head of the local chamber of commerce, we might say "It's nice to meet you." If we were to meet a new colleague or neighbor, we could say, "It's nice to meet you." If we meet our new colleague's first-grade daughter, we might say, "It's nice to meet you." The personal nature of our language does not distinguish status or rank via pronoun usage. Moreover, in the United States, we tend to treat each other with informality and forgo the use of formal titles and strict manners. These cultural attitudes are reflected in our personal verbal style. As Condon notes, two of the most frequently used words in English are *I* and *you*. He points out that for many Americans, it is difficult to talk for any length of time without using pronouns. In Japan, however, there are at least ten words that might be equivalent to the English *I*.[45] In addition, Storti notes that the Thai language has twelve forms of the pronoun *you*.[46]

In contrast, assert Gudykunst and Ting-Toomey, a *contextual style* accentuates and highlights one's "role" identity and status. In cultures that employ a contextual style, the social context dictates word choice, especially of personal pronouns. For example, when using Thai language, one must look carefully at the situation, including the status and intimacy level among the interactants in order to decide

Many Native American tribes have unique ways of communicating verbally and nonverbally. *(Robert Daemmrich/TSI)*

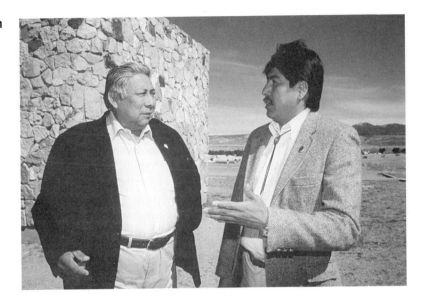

what form of pronoun to use. Unlike a personal style, where pronoun usage is consistent across situations, contextual-style language varies across situations. The correct form of pronoun is contingent on the context. Storti notes that German and French, for example, have familiar and formal forms of the pronoun *you*. The decision to use one form over another is based on the context of the interactants.[47] To use the familiar form with an unfamiliar interactant would be inappropriate. Germans are well known for their formality and strict use of titles, even among friends. Male German neighbors who have known each other for years still use the title *Herr* when addressing each other. June Ock Yum maintains that a fundamental function of many East Asian languages is to recognize the social status, degree of intimacy, age, and sex of the interactants. These types of demographics will influence the degree of formality and the use of honorifics in the language code. Many Asian languages highlight status differences and asymmetrical power relationships. According to Samuel Martin, Korean and Japanese have what he calls two "axes of distinction," including the *axis of address* and the *axis of reference*. In the axis of address, the speaker carefully chooses language based on the status role of the speakers. With the axis of reference, the speaker chooses language based on the speaker's attitude about the subject of communication. Yum provides the example of the phrase "to eat." In English "to eat" is "to eat" regardless of with whom one is eating (e.g., a friend, a parent, or the president of the United States). In Korean, however, there are at least three different ways to say "to eat," depending on the role of the speakers: *muka-da* (plain), *du-shin-da* (polite), and *chap-soo-shin-da* (honorific).[48]

The Japanese use a contextual style, and their language includes an elaborate system of honorifics. *Honorifics* are linguistic forms that communicate respect according to one's rank and the rank of those to whom one is speaking. Honorifics take the form of suffixes to nouns, adjectives, and verbs. For example, the informal form of the verb *to go, iku,* is used when speaking with someone to whom one is intimate. If the person with whom one is interacting is a stranger or is older, then the politeness marker, *-masu,* appears, as in *iki-masu.* If the person with whom one is interacting is socially superior, the honorific form of the verb *to go, irassyaru,* is used.[49] Hooker notes that one cannot learn to speak Japanese without learning the honorific language forms, including syntax and grammar, for defining one's social status. According to Hooker, throughout most of Japanese history, learning the language meant experiencing and reinforcing the social differences that ordered society. Hooker points out that there was a time in Japanese history when one literally could not construct a sentence without defining one's own social class and the social class to whom one was speaking. In addition, Hooker notes, Japanese honorifics is a gendered system. Women's speech tends to be filled with honorifics and a sense of deference toward males.[50]

Intercultural Conversation

Personal and Contextual Styles

In the following interaction, Jim is a student at a local university. He was born and raised in the United States. Akira is an exchange student from Japan. Jim and Akira are eating dinner together in a local restaurant. They have known each other for only a short time. Not only is Jim's style of communication overtly personal; he's also quite direct.

Jim is trying to involve Akira in the conversation by relating to him his personal experiences and preferences. Jim uses the first-person pronoun *I* no fewer than eleven times and even refers to Akira as a "buddy." Akira never refers to himself in the first person. Akira generally defers to Jim, even addressing him as "Mr. Jim," and says little. As a foreigner, Akira probably sees Jim as socially superior and therefore uses a formal title. Moreover, rather than talking about his own personal preferences, Akira mentions that Japanese people enjoy restaurants.

Jim: Hey buddy, what do you think of this American restaurant? I really like it.

Akira: Yes, Mr. Jim. This is very nice.

Jim: I always prefer restaurants like this, kinda casual but good food. I come here a lot. Do you go out to each much in Japan?

Akira: Japanese restaurants are nice, too.

Jim: Yeah, but do you go out to each much?

Akira: Sure, Japanese people like restaurants.

Jim: Whenever I come here, I usually order the same thing. It's kinda funny, but since I like it, I figure I may as well eat it. I have a lot of friends that do that.

Akira: Sure.

Jim: Yeah, I was thinking the other day that since the dorm food sucks so bad, I should go out to eat more often.

Akira: Yes, that's a good idea.

INSTRUMENTAL AND AFFECTIVE STYLES

Gudykunst and Ting-Toomey define an *instrumental verbal style* as sender based and goal-outcome based. The instrumental speaker "uses" communication to achieve some goal or outcome. Instrumental messages are often constructed to persuade and influence others and to maintain one's face. Yum maintains that instrumental-style users believe that communication should end after some goal has been attained and outcomes can be assessed, such as friends gained, opponent defeated, or some form of self-fulfillment reached.[51] Julia Wood reports that men in the United States engage an instrumental style more often than American women, who, in contrast, use collaborative and cooperative talk.[52]

An *affective communication style* is receiver and process oriented. The affective speaker is concerned not so much with the outcome of the communication but with the process. In cultures in which instrumental style predominates, the burden of understanding often rests with the speaker. The speaker carefully chooses and organizes his or her messages so as to be understood by the audience. In cultures in which an affective style is used, the responsibility of understanding rests with both parties—that is, the speaker and the listener. Affective speakers carefully watch for the reactions of their listener. Verbal expressions are insinuated and quite subtle. Affective speakers often operate on an intuitive sense and are nonverbally expressive. Hall and Hall assert that before getting down to business, the French prefer to establish a mood or a feeling and that a certain amount of intuition is required on the part of the listener in order to discover the meaning.[53] Condon argues that whereas Americans like to talk about themselves, Japanese people talk about each other. The Japanese are very conscious of the other person with whom they are interacting. Unlike the American concern for independence, the Japanese concern is for interdependence. Condon notes:

> The difference in orientations is apparent when friends who have not seen each other for a while happen to meet. Americans are likely to ask about each other and tell each other about where they have been or what they have been doing. Who speaks first does not seem to matter very much. When Japanese friends meet, one is likely to begin by thanking the other for some previous favor or gift or letter that was sent. Most often, a reference to the last time they were together is part of this greeting. Thus, they re-establish a particular continuing relationship.[54]

Samuel Martin contends that the Japanese language has a complex array of polite formulas, or stock phrases, that have a leveling effect in just about any social situation. Martin argues that foreigners traveling in Japan can increase their effectiveness if they memorize these twenty or thirty polite formulas. According to Martin, to some extent, Japanese conversation is all formula and no content.[55] Perhaps the affective style of the Japanese is best reflected in haiku, a very short form of poetry popular in Japan. Haiku poems always deal with some aspect of the season, and the writer is required to communicate a vivid impression using only seventeen

Intercultural Conversation

An Intercultural Conversation: Instrumental and Affective Communication Styles

In the following conversation, Mr. Benton has traveled to China to introduce Mr. Yeh-Ching to a new operating system. Mr. Benton, coming from a culture that values an instrumental style of speaking, wants to get right down to business. Mr. Yeh-Ching, on the other hand, wants to establish a relationship before discussing any business possibilities. Mr. Benton and Mr. Yeh-Ching are meeting at a local restaurant in Beijing.

Mr. Benton: Ah, Mr. Yeh-Ching. I've been waiting awhile. Had you forgotten about our meeting?

Mr. Yeh-Ching: Good morning, Jerry, it is so nice to see you.

Mr. Benton: Well . . . I'm glad you're finally here. I have all the material you need to see about the new computers we're installing. Here's our plan . . .

Mr. Yeh-Ching: Jerry, have you seen much of our city?

Mr. Benton: Well . . . I really don't have much time for sightseeing. This isn't a vacation, ya know. Business, business, business. My boss expects me to close this deal today and be back in New York by the weekend. So, here's my idea for installation.

Mr. Yeh-Ching: Our city is so beautiful and full of history. Please allow me to arrange a tour for you. We can go together.

Mr. Benton: I'd love to, but ya know . . . business is business.

Mr. Yeh-Ching: Can I arrange a tour for you? My staff would be happy to meet you.

Mr. Benton: No, thanks, but I'd like to show you something. Look at these new configurations for the computers we're installing. Now . . . notice that . . .

Mr. Yeh-Ching: Here is a menu. This restaurant has some very interesting Chinese dishes that I would like you to try.

Mr. Benton: Oh, I grabbed a bite to eat at the Hilton. Go ahead and eat, though. I can show you the production schedule.

Chances are pretty good that Mr. Yeh-Ching will not buy Mr. Benton's new computer system. To an affective speaker like Mr. Yeh-Ching, Mr. Benton is too concerned about his business and not concerned enough about the personal side of business—that is, relationships. Affective speakers are sometimes suspicious of people who refuse to get to know each other before striking a deal.

SOURCE: Dialogue adapted from L. Copeland, producer, *Managing the Overseas Assignment* [videorecording] (San Francisco: Copeland Griggs Productions, 1983).

Japanese characters. The haiku poem is concise while simultaneously communicating a deep spiritual understanding. Much effort is required of the reader. One of the most popular haiku poets was Basho, who lived some three hundred years ago, but whose poetry is still used as the definitive model for contemporary haiku poets.

> Waterjar cracks:
> I lie awake
> This icy night.

Lightning:
Heron's cry
Stabs the darkness.

Sick on a journey:
Over parched fields
Dreams wander on.[56]

SOURCE: "Waterjar Cracks," "Lightning," and "Sick on a Journey" from *On Love and Barley: Haiku of Basho* by Basho, translated by Lucien Stryk, illustrated by Taiga (Penguin Classics, 1985). Copyright © Lucien Stryk, 1985. Used by permission from the publisher.

Chinese communication is also said to be more affective than instrumental. Becker argues that Chinese people reject debate and argumentation during the process of communication.[57] June Ock Yum believes Confucianism has a large impact on Chinese communication and asserts that the Chinese emphasize a process and receiver orientation. According to Confucian philosophy, the primary function of communication is to initiate, develop, and maintain social relationships. Yum states that in China, it is important to engage in small talk before initiating business and to communicate personalized information. The Chinese view communication as a never-ending interpretive process. During a conversation, Chinese do not calculate what they "give" or "receive." To do so, states Yum, would be to think about immediate personal profits, which conflicts with the Confucian notion of mutual faithfulness. The Chinese are disgusted by purely businesslike transactions that are carefully planned and orchestrated.[58] Echoing Yum's seminal work, Stowell contends that Chinese is a listener-responsible language, rather than a speaker-responsible language like English. In a listener-responsible language, the listener is required to construct the meaning on the basis of his or her relationship with the speaker. The Chinese view communication as an interdependent process in which both speaker and listener are active participants who, together, create meaning.[59]

Language and Ethnic Identity

As we saw in Chapter 6, a fundamental way groups distinguish themselves from other groups, and thereby maintain their group identity, is through the language they speak. Within groups, status and hierarchy are recognized primarily through the use of language. Often immigrant groups maintain their cultural heritage and identity by using their native language in their host culture and by teaching it to their children. Other immigrant groups may discourage the use of their native tongue so as to establish themselves as legitimate members of their new culture. McNamara argues that immigrants entering into a new culture may have to redefine their former social identity. In a study of Hebrew-speaking Israeli immigrants in Australia, McNamara found that as the Israelis changed their social identities, there was a corresponding change toward favoring English over Hebrew. The subjects in McNamara's study were considered *yordin,* a term with negative connotations referring to Israelis living abroad. Among other things, their Hebrew language identified the *yordin* as an out-group in Australia. As with most migrant languages used in Australia, Hebrew had low status. By learning and speaking English and teaching it to their children, the *yordin* were able, to some extent, to manage their negative social identities in their new host culture.[60]

Patricia SanAntonio conducted research on the language practices of an American computer company based in Japan. This particular company required its employees to speak English. However, because they wanted to hire native Japanese with business expertise and English skills, they had trouble attracting high-quality candidates. In order to compete with other Japanese companies, they hired new college graduates who lacked proficient English skills. The result was that they had a work force with a wide range of ability in English; some were quite competent, whereas others struggled considerably. Because English was so important to the company, the ability to speak English and to interact with American managers became a real source of power within the company. SanAntonio argues that within the Japanese context, language and identity are inextricably linked and that the ability and willingness of Japanese employees to use English identified their desire to become integrated into the organization. SanAntonio concluded that the English-only policy created a boundary between the Japanese and Americans such that Japanese input was reduced. The policy essentially circumvented the Japanese hierarchy and allowed the Americans to maintain control within the organization.[61]

Intraculturally, the use of language can mark a person as a member of a particular group. In their analysis, Weider and Pratt argue that among some Native Americans, being silent is fundamental in the "real" Indian's mode of communicating. Moreover, the topic of one's "Indianness" is forbidden; "real" Indians do not discuss it. Real Indians do not engage in casual conversation or idle chitchat with other Indians. Weider and Pratt note that individuals who initiate small talk or openly discuss their Indianness are disqualified from the group of "real" Indians.[62] In Gerry Philipsen's seminal research on speaking "like a man" in Teamsterville, he argued that to present oneself as a man requires an implicit understanding of the communication rules of the particular speech community of real men. "Real" men in Teamsterville engage in a variety of communicative strategies that signal their membership in the group. Real "men" do not rely on speech as their primary mode of self-expression. Only in situations in which the interactants are equal (for example, two "men") is speaking allowed. Here, speaking serves as a means of solidarity. Speaking is restricted when the communicants are unequal, as when a man is interacting with someone of higher status, such as a boss, or of lower status, such as a wife, a girlfriend, or children. Moreover, speaking is discouraged when a "man" must assert his power or influence over others, as when he is responding to an insult to himself or his wife or girlfriend, disciplining children, or asserting himself in political or economic discussions. In these types of contexts, nonverbal communication is preferred. In some situations, "men" may be silent, but in others they may react physically, as when responding to an insult. As Philipsen argues:

In critical symbolic ways, as protector and as master of a house the Teamsterville man disvalues speech as a resource for male role enactment . . . speech is not an integral part of earning a living or other aspects of economic life. . . . For the Teamsterville man, minimal emphasis of talk in work settings is one part of a pattern of minimal talk with outsiders to the neighborhood, with persons in positions of authority who are not long-time associates, and with white collar persons, with whom there is a perceived status difference.[63]

As any other microcultural group in the United States, African Americans are identified by their use of language; specifically, Ebonics. Moreover, they clearly identify themselves in terms of their use of Ebonics. Smitherman estimates that 80 to 90 percent of all African Americans use some form of Ebonics in certain situations. Weber asserts that Ebonics is critical in fostering black identity in the United States for at least three reasons. First, Weber maintains that because blacks experience life differently than other groups, they need a language to express their unique experience. Secondly, black language bridges the economic, educational, and social gap among blacks. Weber states that Ebonics "is the language that binds, that creates community for blacks, so that the brother in the three-piece Brooks Brothers suit can go to the local corner where folks 'hang out' and say, 'Hey blood, what it is?' and be one with them." Finally, Ebonics expresses a political statement that blacks have not relinquished a vital part of themselves—that is, language—and that they can maintain control over at least one part of their lives.[64]

The controversy over Ebonics is both political and linguistic. Linguists disagree as to whether Ebonics is a dialect (of English) or a language by itself. If a language is defined as a set of sounds, combined with a set of rules, for the purpose of communicating, then Ebonics should be considered a language. A dialect is typically thought of as a regional variety, or subset, of a language. Dialects are distinguished by their variations in vocabulary, grammar, and pronunciation from other regional varieties. As Smitherman notes, the labels "language" and "dialect" are equally respectable among linguists. The term *dialect,* however, has taken on negative connotations among the public.[65] Politically, the debate centers on the appropriateness of Ebonics in various social settings, such as schools. Politically, some factions argue that Ebonics is appropriate and should be taught in schools. For example, in December of 1996, the Oakland, California, school board wrote:

> BE IT RESOLVED that the Board of Education officially recognizes the existence, and the cultural and historic bases of West and Niger-Congo African Language Systems, and each language as the predominantly primary language of African-American students. . . . BE IT FURTHER RESOLVED that the Superintendent in conjunction with her staff shall immediately devise and implement the best possible academic program for imparting instruction to African-American students in their primary language for the combined purposes of maintaining the legitimacy and richness of . . . 'Ebonics' . . . and to facilitate their acquisition and mastery of English language skills.[66]

The resolution prompted an Anti-Ebonics movement spearheaded by Peter King (New York), member of the United States House of Representatives. On January 9,

1997, King introduced House Resolution 28, which said in part that no federal funds should be used to pay for or support any program based on the premise that Ebonics is a legitimate language.[67] Linguistic and political arguments notwithstanding, Ebonics is clearly a medium of expression for many African Americans. Ebonics not only serves as a vehicle for communication but fosters a sense of identity and community among those who speak it.

Language has an immense impact on how individuals see themselves and others within any cultural milieu. Language is perhaps the major marker that people use to categorize and group others.

Chapter Summary

All human languages are made up of a system of sounds, syntax, and semantics. The sole purpose of language is to communicate. Historically, linguists once believed that language was tied to race and culture. Contemporary linguists have discounted that notion in favor of the idea that languages are essentially human and are not unique to any particular race or culture. As humans, regardless of culture, we are born with a universal grammar that allows us to learn the particular language of our culture. Any individual language is simply a subset of the universal grammar that is embedded in our brains. Considerable evidence shows that children (even those who are deaf or blind) acquire language in the same way at about the same time. Moreover, children are able to construct grammatically correct sentences without ever having been formally taught.

Language is a guide to social reality, helping people to observe events around them and to organize their thoughts. Moreover, language is so powerful that speakers can generate an infinite number of never-before-spoken sentences that are completely comprehensible by speakers of the same language. Although the universal grammar of all languages is similar, persons from different cultures use different styles of language, ranging from direct to indirect, personal to contextual, instrumental to affective, and from elaborate to succinct. Direct/indirect style refers to how speakers reveal their intentions. Personal/contextual style refers to the degree to which speakers focus on themselves or on their partner. Instrumental style is goal oriented, whereas affective style is process oriented. Elaborate/succinct style refers to the actual quantity or volume of talk that is preferred. These different styles probably reflect cultural values and beliefs.

GLOSSARY OF TERMS

Affective style: Manner of speaking in which the process of interaction is emphasized, placing the burden of understanding on both the speaker and the listener. Affective style relies heavily on nonverbal cues.

Conceptual symbols: Specific stimuli that refer to concepts that have no physical referent and exist only in the mind of the user, such as "liberty" or "democracy."

Contextual style: Role-centered mode of speaking in which one's choice of messages is influenced by one's relative status in the conversation.

Direct style: Manner of speaking in which one employs overt expressions of intention.

Elaborated code: A cultural context in which the speakers of a language have a variety of linguistic options open to them to explicitly communicate their intent through verbal messages.

Elaborate style: Mode of speaking that emphasizes rich, expressive language.

Ethnic identity: The degree to which a person identifies, associates, and empathizes with his or her ethnic group. Ethnic identity is often achieved and recognized through language.

Exacting style: Manner of speaking in which persons say no more or less than is needed to communicate a point.

Generative grammar: The idea that from a finite set of rules, a speaker of any language can create or generate a countably infinite number of sentences, many of which have never before been uttered.

Iconic semblances: Signs that visually represent their referent to some degree, as in a map or photograph.

Indirect style: Manner of speaking in which the intentions of the speakers are hidden or only hinted at during interaction.

Instrumental style: Sender-focused manner of speaking that is goal and outcome oriented. Instrumental speakers "use" communication to achieve some goal or purpose.

Language: A systematic set of sounds, combined with a set of rules, for the sole purpose of communicating.

Linguistic determinism: How humans think about the world is determined by the language they speak.

Linguistic relativity: Differences in language are reflected in the differences in the worldview of the speakers of the language.

Morpheme: Smallest meaningful unit of sound: a combination of phonemes.

Personal style: Manner of speaking relying on the use of personal pronouns and stressing informality and symmetrical power relationships.

Phoneme: Smallest unit of sound, as in a consonant or vowel.

Proper symbols: Specific stimuli that name reality—for example, the word *cat* is a proper symbol for a specific type of animal.

Restricted code: A cultural context in which the speakers of a language are limited as to what they can say or do verbally. A restricted code is a status-oriented system.

Ritual semblances: Exaggerated symptoms, such as begging or acts of submission.

Succinct style: Manner of very concise speaking, often accompanied by silence.

Symbol: Arbitrarily selected and learned stimulus representing something else.

Symptoms: Fixed, hard-wired reactions to environmental stimuli, such as pupil dilation, blushing, or piloerection.

Syntactic symbols: Symbols that express grammatical relationships between other symbols, such as possession or tense.

Universal grammar: The idea that all languages share a common rule structure or grammar that is innate in human beings, regardless of culture.

REFERENCES

1. G. Searchinger, director and producer, *The Human Language Series: Part I: Colorless Green Ideas* [Film] (1996; available from Ways of Knowing, Inc., 200 West 72nd Street, New York, NY 10023).

2. Z. Salzmann, *Language, Culture, and Society* (Boulder, Colo.: Westview Press, 1993).

3. E. Sapir, "The Status of Linguistics as a Science," *Language*, 5 (1929), 209.

4. Salzmann, *Language, Culture, and Society.*

5. B. Whorf, "Science and Linguistics," *Technology Review*, 42 (1940), 231.

6. B. Whorf, "Linguistics as an Exact Science," *Technology Review*, 43 (1940), 61–63, 80–83.

7. Salzmann, *Language, Culture, and Society.*

8. J. B. Carroll, "Linguistic Relativity, Contrastive Linguistics, and Language Learning," *International Review of Applied Linguistics in Language Teaching*, 1 (1963), 1–20.

9. N. Chomsky, *Aspects of the Theory of Syntax* (Cambridge: MIT Press, 1965); B. Goss and D. O'Hair, *Communicating in Interpersonal Relationships* (New York: Macmillan, 1988).

10. K. Katzner, *Languages of the World* (New York: Funk & Wagnalls, 1975).

11. C. K. Tohsaku, "Japanese 'Kanji'" (1997) (http://edweb.sdsu.edu/courses/edtec670/cardboard/card/k/kanji.html).

12. J. Liska, "Bee Dances, Birdsongs, Monkey Calls, and Cetacean Sonar: Is Speech Unique?" *Western Journal of Speech Communication*, 57 (1993), 1–26.

13. Ibid.

14. Liska, "Bee Dances, Birdsongs, Monkey Calls, and Cetacean Sonar."

15. Chomsky, *Syntactic Structures* (The Hague: Mouton & Company, 1957).

16. Much of this discussion of language is based on interviews with Chomsky and other linguists in Searchinger, *The Human Language Series.*

17. L. R. Gleitman "A Human Universal: The Capacity to Learn Language," *Modern Philology*, 90 (1993), s13–s33.

18. Searchinger, *The Human Language Series.*

19. Gleitman, "A Human Universal."

20. S. Pinker, "Language Acquisition," in *An Invitation to Cognitive Science*, 2nd ed., ed. L. R. Gleitman and M. Liberman, vol. 1, *Language* (Cambridge: MIT Press, 1995).

21. Gleitman, "A Human Universal."

22. Searchinger, *The Human Language Series.*

23. Pinker, "Language Acquisition"; some of these examples are from an interview with Pinker in Searchinger, *The Human Language Series.*

24. J. Heath, "Super-Quick Overview of Characteristics of the Japanese Language" (1997) (http://stripe.colorado.edu/-jheath/faq4.html).

25. Katzner, *Languages of the World.*

26. Searchinger, *The Human Language Series*; D. Kulick, *Language Shift and Cultural Reproduction, Socialization, Self, and Syncretism in a Papua New Guinea Village* (Cambridge: Cambridge University Press, 1992).

27. Ibid.

28. Salzmann, *Language, Culture, and Society.*

29. Searchinger, *The Human Language Series.*

30. Ibid.

31. B. Bernstein, "Elaborated and Restricted Codes: Their Social Origins and Some Consequences," in *Communication and Culture*, ed. A. G. Smith (New York: Holt, Rinehart and Winston, 1966), pp. 427–441.

32. Ibid.

33. Ibid.

34. W. B. Gudykunst and S. Ting-Toomey, "Verbal Communication Styles," in *Culture and Interpersonal Communication*, ed. W. B. Gudykunst and S. Ting-Toomey (Newbury Park, Calif.: Sage, 1988), pp. 99–115.

35. Ibid.

36. K. Fedarko, "Man of Israel: Rabin's Stirring Life Story Marks Out the Mileposts in the History of His Nation," *Time*, 146, no. 20 (1995), 68–72.

37. E. T. Hall and M. R. Hall, *Understanding Cultural Differences: Germans, French, and Americans* (Yarmouth, Maine: Intercultural Press, 1990).

38. S. Iwao, *The Japanese Woman: Traditional Image and Changing Reality* (Cambridge: Harvard University Press, 1993).

39. Hall and Hall, *Understanding Cultural Differences*.

40. Gudykunst and Ting-Toomey, "Verbal Communication Styles," pp. 99–115.

41. T. Kochman, "Cultural Pluralism: Black and White Styles," in *Cultural Communication and Intercultural Contact*, ed. D. Carbaugh (Hillsdale, N.J.: Erlbaum, 1990), pp. 220–221.

42. J. Stowell, "The Changing Face of Chinese Communication: A Synthesis of Interpersonal Communication Concepts" (paper presented at the annual convention of the Speech Communication Association, San Diego, Calif., 1996).

43. D. L. Weider and S. Pratt, "On Being a Recognizable Indian Among Indians," in *Cultural Communication and Intercultural Contact*, p. 51.

44. Bernstein, "Elaborated and Restricted Codes"; Gudykunst and Kim, *Communicating with Strangers*.

45. J. C. Condon, *With Respect to the Japanese: A Guide for Americans* (Yarmouth, Maine: Intercultural Press, 1984); Gudykunst and Ting-Toomey, *Culture and Interpersonal Communication*.

46. C. Storti, *Cross-Cultural Dialogues: 74 Brief Encounters with Cultural Differences*, (Yarmouth, Maine: Intercultural Press, 1994).

47. Ibid.

48. J. O. Yum, "The Impact of Confucianism on Interpersonal Relationships and Communication Patterns in East Asia," in *Intercultural Communication: A Reader*, ed. L. A. Samovar and R. E. Porter (Belmont, Calif.: Wadsworth, 1997), pp. 78–88; S. E. Martin, "Speech Levels in Japan and Korea," in *Language in Culture and Society*, ed. D. Hymes (New York: Harper and Row, 1964), pp. 407–415.

49. S. Miyagawa, "The Japanese Language" (© Massachusetts Institute of Technology, 1995) (www.japan.mit.edu/articles/JapaneseLanguage.html).

50. R. Hooker, "The Japanese Language" (1999) (www.wsu.edu:8080/~dee/ANCJAPAN/language.htm).

51. Gudykunst and Ting-Toomey, "Verbal Communication Styles"; Yum, "The Impact of Confucianism."

52. J. T. Wood, *Gendered Lives: Communication, Gender, and Culture* (Belmont, Calif.: Wadsworth, 1997).

53. Hall and Hall, *Understanding Cultural Differences*.

54. Condon, *With Respect to the Japanese*, p. 50.

55. Martin, "Speech Levels in Japan and Korea."

56. "A Haiku Homepage" (www.dmu.ac.uk/~pkal/haiku.html); "The Shiki Internet Salon" (http://mikan.cc.matsuyama.u.acjp/~shiki/).

57. C. B. Becker, "Reasons for the Lack of Argumentation and Debate in the Far East," *International Journal of Intercultural Relations*, 10 (1986), 75–92.

58. Yum, "The Impact of Confucianism on Interpersonal Relationships and Communication Patterns in East Asia."

59. Stowell, "The Changing Face of Chinese Communication"; M. W. Lustig and J. Koester, *Intercultural Competence: Interpersonal Communication Across Cultures* (New York: HarperCollins, 1996).

60. T. F. McNamara, "Language and Social Identity: Israelis Abroad," in *Language and Ethnic Identity*, ed. W. B. Gudykunst (Clevedon, UK: Multilingual Matters, Ltd., 1988), pp. 59–72.

61. P. M. SanAntonio, "Social Mobility and Language Use in an American Company in Japan," in *Language and Ethnic Identity*, pp. 35–44.

62. Weider and Pratt, "On Being a Recognizable Indian Among Indians."

63. G. Philipsen, "Speaking 'Like a Man' in Teamsterville: Culture Patterns of Role Enactment in an Urban Neighborhood," in *Cultural Communication and Intercultural Contact*, p. 17.

64. G. Smitherman, *Talkin That Talk: Language, Culture and Education in African America* (New York: Routledge, 2000); S. Weber, "The Need to Be: The Socio-Cultural Significance of Black Language," in *Intercultural Communication: A Reader*, ed. L. A. Samovar and R. E. Porter (Belmont, Calif: Wadsworth, 1994), pp. 221–226.

65. G. Smitherman, *Talkin That Talk*.

66. Ibid. (Quote on page xi).

67. E. Richardson, "The Anti-Ebonics Movement: 'Standard' English Only," *Journal of English Linguistics*, 26 (1998), 156–170.

Nonverbal Language

*Speakers of
every language
accompany
their words
with
nonverbal
signals that
serve to mark
the structure of
their
utterances.*

—Peter Farb[1]

CHAPTER OBJECTIVES

After reading this chapter, you should be able to

- Define nonverbal communication.
- Compare and contrast verbal and nonverbal codes.
- Define kinesics and provide examples of kinesic behavior across cultures.
- Define paralanguage and provide cross-cultural examples of paralinguistic differences.
- Define proxemics and provide cross-cultural examples of proxemic differences.
- Define haptics and provide cross-cultural examples of haptic differences.
- Define olfactics and discuss how smell is perceived across cultures.
- Define chronemics and discuss how time is perceived across cultures.
- Discuss the fundamental assumptions of the nonverbal expectancy violations theory.

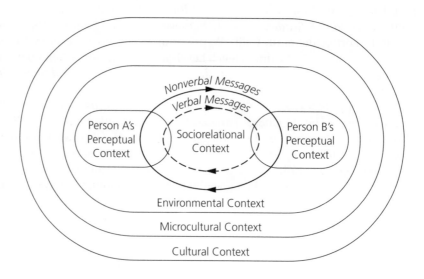

Many linguists, psychologists, and sociologists believe that human language evolved from a system of nonlinguistic (nonverbal) communication. To these scholars, language and communication are not the same. Humans possess a host of nonlinguistic ways to communicate with each other through the use of their hands, arms, face, and personal space. When we combine verbal and nonverbal language, we create an intricate communication system through which humans come to know and understand each other.[2] All animals communicate nonlinguistically—that is, nonverbally—through sight, sound, smell, or touch. Moths, for example, communicate by smell and color. Through smell, some species of male moths can detect female moths miles away. Elephants communicate with low-frequency sound waves undetectable by humans. Felines are well known for rubbing their scent on ("marking") people and objects to communicate their ownership of such property. This kind of animal or nonlinguistic communication is probably innate and invariant within a particular species. Most scholars also recognize that a significant portion of our nonverbal behavior, such as the expression of emotion, is innate and varies little across cultures. Like verbal language, however, much of our nonverbal communication is learned and varies across cultures.

This chapter investigates nonverbal communication and how it differs across cultures. It begins with some definitions of nonverbal communication and a discussion of how verbal and nonverbal codes differ. The chapter then outlines the various channels of nonverbal communication and how cultures differ regarding their use. These channels include kinesics, paralanguage, proxemics, haptics, olfactics, physical appearance and dress, and chronemics. The chapter closes with a discussion of nonverbal expectancy violations theory.

Definitions of Nonverbal Communication

The study of nonverbal communication focuses on the messages people send to each other that do not contain words, such as messages sent through body motions, vocal qualities, and the use of time, space, artifacts, dress, and even smell. Communication with the body, called *kinesics*, consists of the use of the hands, arms, legs, and face to send messages. Through *haptics*, or touch, people communicate intimacy. A handshake, hug, or kiss can be very meaningful in a relationship. How much people touch, and what it means, varies dramatically across cultures. *Paralanguage*, or the use of the voice, refers to vocal characteristics such as volume, pitch, rate, and so forth. Through paralanguage, people communicate their emotional state, veracity, and sincerity. Most of us can identify when speakers are confident or nervous through their vocal pitch, rate, and pace. Through *chronemics*, the use of time, people can communicate status and punctuality. We saw in Chapter 3 that cultures differ widely in their monochronic or polychronic orientation. By studying space, or *proxemics*, we can learn how people express intimacy and power. In the United States, for example, people tend to prefer an "arm's length" distance from others during communication. Through smell, called *olfactics,* a person's eth-nicity, social class, and status are communicated. Many cultures establish norms for acceptable and unacceptable scents associated with the human body. To other cultures, for example, people raised in the United States seem obsessed with de-odorants, perfumes, soaps, and shampoos that mask natural body odors.

Linguist Deborah Tannen estimates that as much as 90 percent of all human communication is nonverbal, though other scholars argue that the percentage is much lower.[3] During intercultural communication, verbal and nonverbal mes-sages are sent simultaneously. Verbal communication represents the literal con-tent of a message, whereas the nonverbal component communicates the style or "how" the message is to be interpreted. Hence, the nonverbal code often *comple-ments, accents, substitutes, repeats,* or even *contradicts* the verbal message.[4] For ex-ample, a speaker might complement the verbal message "This dinner is delicious" with a smile and increased vocal volume. Politicians often accent their speeches by pounding their fists on podiums. When asked how many minutes are left to complete an exam, the professor might simply raise five fingers to substitute for the words "five minutes." Persons often repeat their verbal message "Yes" with af-firmative head nodding.

Sometimes a person's verbal and nonverbal messages contradict each other, however. When this happens, we usually believe the nonverbal message. For ex-ample, your roommate has been very quiet and reserved for a couple of days. Fi-nally, you ask what is wrong. Your roommate replies with a long sigh and says, "Oh . . . nothing." Which do you believe, the verbal or the nonverbal message? Most people believe the nonverbal message because, unlike the verbal message, which requires conscious effort to encode, nonverbal messages are often less con-scious and therefore are perceived as more honest. Psychologist David McNeill ar-gues that our nonverbal behavior is partly unconscious and represents a sort of visual metaphor or analogue of conscious thought. McNeill states that gestures and other body motions are primitive forms of speech. Whereas verbal language takes thought and puts it into linear digital form—that is, a sentence—gestures and body movements show the instantaneous thought itself as an analogue of the thought.[5] This is why verbal communication is often called *digital communication* and nonverbal communication is called *analogic communication.* Because we have less control over our nonverbal behavior, it tends to be perceived as more honest than our verbal behavior.

In addition to complementing, accenting, substituting, repeating, and contra-dicting verbal communication, nonverbal communication also regulates and man-ages our conversations with others. Professors delivering lectures can monitor the reactions of their students through their eye contact, body posture, and other non-verbal behaviors (for example, yawning) and adapt their lectures accordingly. Stu-dents who raise their hands are signaling the professor that they have questions or comments. Such behavior manages the flow of communication in the classroom. Individually we can regulate the flow and pace of a conversation by engaging in di-rect eye contact, affirmative head nodding, and stance, thus signaling our conver-sational partner to continue or stop the communication.

The Relationship Between Verbal and Nonverbal Codes

By comparing and contrasting the human verbal and nonverbal codes, many linguists have concluded that verbal language evolved from its nonlinguistic predecessor. Noam Chomksy argues that verbal language is an advanced and refined form of an inherited nonlinguistic (nonverbal) system.[6] A key distinction between the two is that the verbal language system is based primarily on symbols, whereas the nonverbal system is signal based. The difference between a symbol and a signal is that a *symbol* is an arbitrarily selected and *learned* stimulus representing something else. A *sign*, or *signal*, however, is a natural and constituent part of that which it represents. For example, when we hear thunder in the distance, it signals us that a storm is approaching. The thunder is a sign of a storm. But the thunder is also an intrinsic part of the storm. Sweating, for example, signals that one may be hot, but sweating is a natural part of being hot, as is shivering of being cold. Humans do not learn to sweat or shiver. Unlike signals, symbols have no natural relationship with that which they represent; therefore they are arbitrary abstractions and must be learned. For example, the symbols *cat* have no intrinsic connection with a feline animal. Speakers of any language learn to associate symbols with referents.

Another difference between the verbal and nonverbal codes is that the nonverbal signal system is much more restrictive in sending capacity than the verbal code. For example, it is virtually impossible to communicate about the past or future through nonverbal communication. You might be able to signal a friend of impending danger by waving your hands, but you cannot warn your friend of danger that might occur tomorrow or recall danger that occurred yesterday with nonverbal signals. In addition, communication of negation is practically impossible with the nonverbal code system. Try communicating to a friend nonverbally that you are not going to the grocery store tomorrow. The same task is relatively easy through the linguistic system, however.[7]

FORMAL VERSUS INFORMAL CODE SYSTEMS

In Chapter 7, verbal language was defined as a systematic set of sounds combined with a set of rules for the sole purpose of communication. All verbal languages have a formal set of sounds, syntax, and semantics. The degree of formality of verbal language is not found in the nonverbal code, however. The alphabets of most verbal languages in the world represent about forty sounds. No such formalized alphabet exists for nonverbal codes. Different types of nonverbal behavior can be categorized, but these categories are much more loosely defined than in the verbal code. All verbal languages have a set of rules, called grammar or syntax, that prescribe how to combine the various sounds of the language into meaningful units, such as words and sentences. Although there are rules governing the use of nonverbal communication, a formal grammar or syntax does not exist. Nowhere is there a book or guide prescribing exactly what nonverbal behavior should be used when or where. There is no doubt that certain social contexts prescribe certain nonverbal behaviors, such as a handshake when greeting someone in the United States, but no systematic rule book on the same level of formality as an English grammar book exists for nonverbal communication. The rules for nonverbal communication are learned informally through socialization and vary considerably even intraculturally. Finally, the verbal code, when used with the correct syntax, takes on *denotative meaning*. When using verbal language, if we hear a word that we do not understand, we can quickly go to a dictionary that will define the word for us. The dictionary tells us what the language means. No such device exists for our nonverbal communication. If someone touches us, or stands too close, or engages in prolonged eye contact, we can only surmise its meaning. Popular psychology notwithstanding, we have no dictionary for nonverbal communication. To be sure, nonverbal communication is meaningful, perhaps even more meaningful than verbal communication, but the denotative meaning of the nonverbal act must be inferred.[8]

Channels of Nonverbal Communication

The closest thing the nonverbal code has to an alphabet is a gross classification system of the various channels through which nonverbal communication is sent. These channels include kinesics, paralanguage, proxemics, haptics, olfactics, physical appearance and dress, and chronemics. As we will see later in this chapter, some nonverbal expressions, particularly some facial expressions of emotion, seem to be universal, but much of our nonverbal behavior is learned, and is therefore culturally unique.

KINESICS

Kinesic behavior, or body movement, includes gestures, hand and arm movements, leg movements, facial expressions, eye gaze and blinking, and stance or posture. Although just about any part of the body can be used for communicating nonverbally, the face, hands, and arms are the primary kinesic channels through which nonverbal messages are sent. Relative to other body parts, they have a high sending capacity, especially the face.

The most widely recognized system for classifying kinesic channels was developed by Paul Ekman and Wallace Friesen. Together, they organized kinesic behavior into five broad categories: (1) *emblems*, (2) *illustrators*, (3) *affect displays*, (4) *regulators*, and (5) *adaptors*. The meaning behind most of these kinesic behaviors varies across cultures.[9]

Emblems and Illustrators.   Emblems are primarily (though not exclusively) hand gestures that have a direct literal verbal translation. In the United States, the hand gesture used to represent "peace" is an example of a widely recognized emblem. Dane Archer asserts that emblems are a rich channel of communication. Moreover, he maintains that emblems are often subtle yet filled with precise meaning. People in different cultures use different emblems, yet within any culture there is usually a high level of agreement on a particular emblem's meaning. To a stranger, however, a culture's favorite emblem is probably meaningless.[10]

Whereas emblems are primarily hand gestures that have a direct verbal translation, *illustrators* are typically hand and arm movements that accompany speech or function to accent or complement what is being said. Pounding your fist on the podium during a speech is an illustrator. Illustrators serve a *metacommunicative function*—that is, they are messages about messages. They are nonverbal messages that tell us how to interpret verbal messages. Shaking your fist at someone while expressing anger is an illustrator.

For the most part, emblems and illustrators are not taught in school but are learned informally through a child's socialization in his or her culture. By six months, babies in all cultures begin to use gestures to communicate to their parents.

Dane Archer maintains that emblems and illustrators are at least 2,500 years old and can be seen in the ancient art work of various cultures. Archer asserts that the systematic study of gestures began about 400 years ago, during Shakespeare's time. Although cultures differ widely in their use of emblems and illustrators, people in most cultures tend to use them for the same kinds of communication situations. For example, most cultures use emblems and illustrators during greetings and departures, to insult or to utter obscenities to others, to indicate fight or flight, and to designate friendly or romantic relationships.[11]

Greeting rituals are an important component in any person's communicative repertoire. To know the greetings of different cultures when interacting outside your own culture is a first step toward developing intercultural communication competence. In high-context and collectivistic cultures, greeting rituals often differ according to one's social status. Moreover, in some cultures, men and women have different rules for how to greet someone. Bowing is the customary greeting in Korea and other Asian cultures, such as Japan and Vietnam. When Koreans greet elders, professors, persons of power, and persons of higher status than themselves, they bow lower and longer and divert eye contact. When businesspeople or friends meet, the bow is generally shorter and quicker.[12] In Japan, the appropriate bow is with the hands sliding down toward the knees, back and neck stiff, and eyes averted. As in other Asian cultures, bowing recognizes social stratification. Social subordinates should bow lower and longer than their superiors. Persons of equal status match bows unless one is younger, in which case the younger person should bow a shade lower and longer. The eyes should always be lowered.[13]

In addition to bowing as a greeting, Japanese businesspeople typically exchange business cards. The exchange is indispensable in order to commence formal communication with each other. The business card communicates the group to which the person belongs and the rank of the person. Great care and time should be spent examining another's card, and only when a meeting is finished can the card be put away into a shirt or coat pocket (but never into a pants pocket,

Bowing is a traditional Japanese greeting. Social subordinates bow longer and lower than their superiors.
(Robert A. Isaacs/ Photo Researchers)

as that shows disrespect). When receiving the card of a Japanese businessperson, one should take the card with both hands, as a sign of respect.[14]

Microcultural groups in the United States have unique greetings as well. Moellendorf notes that although most Amish generally will not initiate greetings with strangers or non-Amish persons, many Amish will respond to an outsider's wave by pointing their index finger toward the sky. The raised finger points to heaven and shows respect to non-Amish while revealing the Amish people's strong religious beliefs.[15]

As in the United States, the handshake is a common gesture/illustrator during a greeting in most parts of developed Kenya. In this case, however, when greeting a person of higher status, such as a teacher, the person of lower status should take the left hand (the hand not being used in the handshake) and grasp his or her own right arm somewhere in the proximity of the forearm during the shake. According to Axtell, the handshake is a common greeting in China as well. The traditional Chinese greeting is to cup one's hands (left over right), place them about chest high, and raise them while bowing.[16] According to Bishop, when greeting a holy man or priest, East Indians bow slightly or kneel with their hands pressed together palm to palm in front of their chests. This shows ultimate respect for the higher castes.[17] Harris and Moran report that when greeting male friends in Saudi Arabia, Saudi men kiss both cheeks of the friend. They prefer to get very close during the greeting. The cheek-kissing ritual is practiced in other Middle Eastern cultures as well. The Arab handshake feels loose compared with the firm handshake practiced in many Western cultures.[18] In traditional Sri Lanka greetings, the hands are placed together, palms touching at the chin level, and the person bows slightly and says, *"Namaste,"* which means "I salute the Godlike qualities in you."[19]

Archer has observed that many cultures have emblems and illustrators for insulting others and for communicating obscenities. According to Archer, some cultures may have as many as six or seven obscene gestures, whereas some northern European cultures like the Netherlands and Norway do not have any native obscene gestures.[20] Giving someone "the finger" (making a fist with the hand and extending the middle finger upward) is a widely recognized obscene gesture in many parts of the world, including the United States, Mexico, and much of Europe. Forming a "V" with the index finger and middle fingers with the palm facing in is vulgar in Australia and England, communicating the same intent as "the finger." Creating the very same gesture with the palm facing out is completely acceptable, however, and represents "V for victory." In the Ladino culture of Guatemala, a hand gesture called *la mano caliente* ("the hot hand") is equivalent to "the finger" and is created by placing the thumb between the first and middle fingers, then squeezing the hand to make a fist. This gesture is considered obscene in other Central and South American cultures as well. In the Ladino culture, however, this gesture is very offensive, and anyone using it should be prepared to fight. If a person were to use the *mano caliente* to a military or police officer, the offender could expect to spend time in jail or doing hard labor in the army.[21] The same hand gesture is used in Hmong culture to belittle or insult someone. In the Hmong culture, only males use this gesture.[22] In Jamaica, this gesture is called "the fig" and is considered obscene there also.[23]

In Peru, making a pistol gesture with each hand and then pointing the "pistols" at someone from about waist level is considered obscene and may evoke a fight. In Iran, putting an open hand directly in front of and horizontal to one's face with the palm facing in and rubbing the hand down over the face from about the eyes to the chin, almost as if stroking a beard, is considered obscene and is equivalent to "Fuck you." An obscene gesture recognized in many European cultures, especially France, is taking either hand, palm down, and putting it on the biceps of the opposite arm while quickly raising the opposite arm and making a fist in one fluid

"Mano caliente," the "hot hand" gesture, is seen in some Central American cultures.
(Marianne Stepanian)

In Peru, this gesture is considered obscene and may provoke a fight. *(Marianne Stepanian)*

motion. This gesture is basically equivalent to "the finger" and to the verbal designate "Up yours" or "Fuck you."[24]

Archer points out that in addition to obscene emblems and illustrators, many cultures have gestures indicating that someone is homosexual or an adulterer. These gestures are strongly linked to one's sex role. Most gestures indicating that someone is a homosexual almost always apply to men, whereas gestures indicating that someone is unfaithful usually apply to women. In Japan, putting the hand,

In Iran, this gesture is considered obscene. *(Marianne Stepanian)*

In many European cultures, this gesture is roughly equivalent to giving someone "the finger."
(Marianne Stepanian)

palm out, against the cheek while turning the face away, almost as if to pretend to be telling a secret, is a sign that someone is homosexual. In Colombia, making a circle with the index finger and thumb (like the "OK" gesture in the United States), and then placing the circle around the nose, is a sign for homosexual. The limp-wrist gesture, or slight variations of it, for homosexual is recognized in the United States, China, Mexico, and Thailand, among other countries. In Uruguay, four or five quick claps of the hands indicate that a woman is a lesbian.[25]

Archer contends that gestures communicating "I am afraid" or "I want to fight you" (that is, fight or flight) are uncommon in the United States but occur with some regularity across cultures. In Mexico and Nepal, placing the hand with the palm up, fingers extended upward while moving in and out touching the thumb is an invitation to fight. In Japan, putting the index fingers on the temples of the head as in making horns is a sign that one is angry. In China, pretending to pull up one's sleeve with the hand of the opposite arm designates that one is ready to fight.[26] In Hmong culture, clapping one's hands during an argument is a signal to the opponent that it is time to fight. The gesture is usually reserved for very intense situations in which someone intends to harm the other.[27]

Most cultures use emblems and illustrators to designate friendly and/or romantic relationships. In the United States, for example, crossing the index and middle fingers of the same hand designates closeness and communicates, "We're close" or "We're tight." In China, clasping the index fingers from each hand together signals love or romance. In Thailand, pressing the palms of both hands together and placing them against a cheek (as in a "Sleeping Beauty" gesture) is indicative of romance. Tapping the tips of the index fingers together in Japan, or extending both index fingers parallel at waist level in Mexico, communicates that someone is in love.[28]

Affect Displays: Facial Expressions of Emotion.   Knapp and Hall point out that perhaps more than any other part of the body, the face has the highest nonverbal sending capacity. Through facial expressions, we can communicate our personality, open and close channels of communication, complement or qualify other nonverbal behavior, and perhaps more than anything, communicate emotional states.[29]

Many linguists believe that our verbal language evolved from a system of nonlinguistic communication that was inherited from our animal past. If this is a valid assumption, then we should expect that some forms of our nonverbal communication would be invariant across cultures. Current evidence suggests that some facial expressions of emotion, called *affect displays,* are universal. Paul Ekman alleges that humans can make more than ten thousand facial expressions and that two or three thousand of them have to do with emotion. Ekman is careful to point out that by studying faces, we cannot tell what people are thinking, only what they are feeling about what they are thinking.[30] Initially, Ekman believed that affect displays, like so many other forms of communication, were the result of learning and were culturally unique. He originally agreed with sociologist Ray Birdwhistell, who wrote that

> just as there are no universal words, no sound complexes, which carry the same meaning the world over, there are no body movements, facial expressions, or gestures which provoke *identical* responses the world over.[31]

In contrast to Birdwhistell, other scholars hypothesized that because they were inherited, human nonverbal expressions would be similar, if not universal, the world over. The basis of this argument can be found in the writings of evolutionary scholar Charles Darwin, who wrote:

> We can thus also understand the fact that the young and the old of widely different races, both with man and animals, express the same state of mind by the same movements. . . . I have endeavoured to show in considerable detail that all the chief expressions exhibited by man are the same throughout the world. This fact is interesting, as it affords a new argument in favour of the several races being descended from a single parent-stock, which must have been almost completely human in structure, and to a large extent in mind, before the period at which the races diverged from each other.[32]

Harvard University Professor Stephen Jay Gould, well known for his stance on evolution, agreed with Darwin and argued that although universal facial expressions may have been functional for the animals from whom we inherited them, they are not functional for us today. Take, for example, a facial expression of anger, in which a person snarls, grits his or her teeth, and displays the canine teeth. This facial expression is remarkably similar to expressions of anger in several animal species. The fact that there is no need for us to display our teeth in order to express

Certain facial expressions of emotion are thought to be inherited from our animal past.
(Jon Feingersh/Stock Market)
(Steve Ayres/TSI)

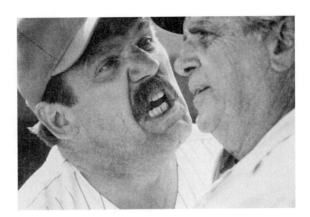

anger (we can simply say how angry we are) suggests that such a gesture must have been inherited.[33]

Ekman was determined to find whether certain elements of facial behavior are universal or culturally specific. He and his colleagues believed that there may be distinctive movements of the face for the primary emotions of surprise, fear, anger, disgust, happiness, and sadness that are probably universal. They further argued that while people from divergent cultures may express emotions similarly, what stimulates the emotion and the intensity with which it is expressed is probably culturally specific. In other words, although Germans and Japanese may express fear, surprise, anger, happiness, disgust, and sadness similarly in terms of muscular facial expressions, what *elicits* fear in Germans may be different from what elicits fear in Japanese. Moreover, cultures may differ in how they manage and regulate facial expressions of emotion, particularly in the presence of others.[34]

Ekman and Friesen (among others) have conducted numerous studies testing their hypotheses. In one study, Ekman, Friesen, and a number of their associates had over five hundred participants from ten different countries look at slides of people expressing the six emotions of fear, anger, happiness, disgust, sadness, and surprise. The participants in the study came from a variety of cultures the world over, including Estonia, Italy, Germany, Japan, Hong Kong, Scotland, Sumatra, Turkey, Greece, and the United States. Participants were shown photographs of Caucasians in posed facial expressions of the six different emotions, one at a time for ten seconds each, and were instructed to indicate which of the six emotions was presented. The participants were also asked to rate the intensity of the presented emotion on a scale of 1 to 8. The results showed that in the overwhelming number of trials, the emotion rated strongest by the largest number of observers in each culture was the predicted emotion. Where cultures differed was in their ratings of intensity of the emotion. Ekman reasoned that perhaps people judge a foreigner's expressions to be less intense than expressions shown by members of their own culture or that attributions of less intense emotions to foreigners might be due to more uncertainty about the emotional state of a person from an unfamiliar culture. In interpreting these results, Izard claims that there appears to be an evolutionary and biological relationship between facial expressions and certain emotional states, but that this connection can be uncoupled by the human capacity to exercise voluntary control over innate emotional expressions.[35]

Although Ekman's studies provide evidence that facial expressions of primary emotions appear to be universal, other data suggest that cultural influences, such as individualism and collectivism, play a role in the expression of emotion. Stephan, Stephan, and De Vargas found that persons from individualistic cultures express emotions affirming independent self-conceptions, such as self-actualized, capable, self-satisfied, and proud of oneself. They also found that persons from collectivistic cultures were less comfortable expressing negative emotions (for example, indignation, annoyance, distrust) than persons from individualistic cultures.[36]

In related research, Schimmack found that persons from individualistic cultures are better able to recognize happiness than collectivists and that persons from high-uncertainty-avoidant cultures were less accurate in the recognition of facial expressions of fear and sadness than persons with low uncertainty avoidance.[37] Matsumoto alleges that high-uncertainty-avoidant cultures create social institutions to deal with fear and therefore recognize this emotion less well.[38] Along similar lines, Pittam, Kroonenberg, Gallois, and Iwawaki found that Australians were rated as more expressive by Japanese and that Japanese may conceptualize emotions as less intense.[39]

Cross-Racial Recognition of Faces.   Most of us have heard statements such as "I can't tell one Japanese from another . . . they all look alike!" Although this statement smacks of racism and ignorance, scientific evidence indicates that "own-race" identifications tend to be more accurate, by as much as 10 percent to 15 percent, than "cross-race" identifications. Own-race identifications are those in which we identify someone of the same race as our own. Cross-race identifications are those in which we identify people from a race different from our own.[40] Legal scholars have expressed a concern over an "own-race" recognition bias in eyewitness identification for some time. In fact, Feingold argued nearly ninety years ago that

> it is well known that, other things being equal, individuals of a given race are distinguishable from each other in proportion to our familiarity, to our contact with the race as a whole. Thus, to the uninitiated American, all Asiatics look alike, while to the Asiatic all White men look alike.[41]

Experts in the field of eyewitness memory and about half of potential jurors endorse the belief that cross-racial identifications are less reliable than same-race identifications. This presumption is based on the belief in the existence of an own-race bias—that is, that people recognize people of their own race better than people of another race. Brigham and Malpass note that the own-race recognition bias has been demonstrated among whites, blacks, Asians, Latinos, and Hispanics. Explanations for this phenomenon vary. Some evidence shows that persons who have close friends of the other race show less of an own-race recognition bias.[42] Moreover, Ferman and Entwistle found that children living in mixed-race environments show less of an own-race recognition bias than children living in a segregated environment.[43] Conversely, other research indicates that the own-race recognition bias is not reduced by frequent contact with the other race and that prejudiced persons are no more likely to exhibit an own-race recognition bias than nonprejudiced persons.[44] There is some evidence indicating that persons who view other-race faces tend to focus on the constituent (individual) features of the face, whereas observers of same-race faces focus on configural features of the face.[45]

Regulators. Nonverbal regulators include those behaviors and actions that govern, direct, and/or manage conversation. During conversations in the United States, for example, direct eye contact and affirmative head nodding typically communicate agreement or that a conversant understands what is being communicated. How close one stands to another during a conversation can also signal to the conversant whether to continue the communication. Rules for direct eye contact and distance during communication vary considerably across cultures. In many Asian cultures, such as South Korea, Vietnam, and Japan, direct eye contact is prohibited between persons of differing status. In these cultures, the person of lower status avoids making direct eye contact with his or her superior as a sign of respect. Direct eye contact in these cultures can communicate insolence or signal a challenge to the person of higher status. In South Korea, when people of higher status hand something to a person of lower status (for example, a professor handing something to a student), the person of lower status accepts whatever is handed with both hands, gives a slight nod of the head, and averts eye contact during the act, all as a sign of recognizing the status differential.

Communicator distance during conversation can also govern the flow of communication. According to Almaney and Alwan, in some Middle Eastern cultures, people stand very close together during interaction to smell each other's breath. To smell one another is considered desirable. In fact, to deny someone your breath communicates shame.[46] Harris and Moran point out that in many Arab cultures, men hold hands as they converse to demonstrate their trust in each other. During conversation, a raising of the eyebrows or a clicking of the tongue signifies a negative response and a disruption in the flow of communication.[47]

Adaptors. Adaptors are kinesic actions that satisfy physiological or psychological needs. Scratching an itch satisfies a physiological need, whereas tapping the tip of your pen on the desk while waiting for the professor to deliver a final exam satisfies a psychological need. Very little, if any, cross-cultural research on adaptors has been conducted. For the most part, adaptors are not learned and probably do not vary much across cultures.

PARALANGUAGE

Paralanguage refers to vocal qualities that usually, though not necessarily, accompany speech. Knapp and Hall divide paralanguage into two broad categories: *voice qualities* and *vocalizations*. Paralinguistic voice qualities include pitch, rhythm,

In some Arab cultures, men hold hands as a sign of trust, not homosexuality.
(Tim Gibson/Envision)

tempo, articulation, and resonance of the voice. Paralinguistic vocalizations include laughing, crying, sighing, belching, swallowing, clearing of the throat, snoring, and so forth. Other paralinguistic vocalizations include intensity and *nonfluencies,* such as *um, ah,* and *uh.* Silence is also considered within the domain of paralanguage.[48]

Often paralinguistic qualities, vocalizations, and nonfluencies reveal a speaker's emotional state and/or veracity. Audiences can discern when speakers are nervous or confident by listening to their tone of voice, rhythm, pace, and number of nonfluencies. Parents often detect a child's deception not so much by what the child says but by how it is said. Through paralanguage we can tell whether speakers are being genuine, cynical, or sarcastic. Moreover, a person's geographical origin can be determined by listening closely to his or her paralanguage.[49]

In all spoken languages, vocal sounds are carried by vowels; it is impossible to speak words without them. Consonants, on the other hand, function to stop and start sound. Linguist Peter Ladefoged has observed that although there are perhaps as many as nine hundred consonants and two hundred vowels in all the world's languages, many languages tend to use only five vowel sounds. In fact, one in five languages uses the same vowel sounds as are used in Spanish and English— *a, e, i, o,* and *u*—though there are variations on their pronunciation. According to Ladefoged, although there are literally thousands of speech sounds that any human is capable of making, only a few hundred sounds have ever been observed among the world's spoken languages. The average language uses only about forty sounds, and all babies are capable of making all of them. All babies, the world over, make the same sounds during infancy. Linguists believe that these sounds are the building blocks by which infants construct mature sounds. Although infants have not yet learned the specific language of their culture and have not yet spoken a single word, they practice the sounds of all human languages. All babies regularly produce a small subset of universal syllable types that occur in all of the world's languages. This is strong evidence that human language was not invented by humans but rather evolved. To be sure, unusual sounds show up in some languages. Clicking sounds, for example, can be heard in South Africa's Zulu and Xhosa languages, and nasal sounds are heard in Eskimo languages. And although these sounds may be unique components of these languages, all human babies, regardless of culture, can be heard making them at some time prior to learning their culture's formal verbal language.[50]

Some languages, called tonal languages, rely on vocalized tones to communicate meaning. In these languages, a rising or falling tone changes the meaning of a word. Thai is a pentatonal language that uses five tones: monotone, low, falling, high, and rising. Modern Vietnamese is a monosyllabic language, meaning that all words are only one syllable long. Like the Thai language, Vietnamese is tonal, and the meaning of the syllable changes with tone. The Chinese language is tonal also. Mandarin Chinese, the most common language in China, is based on four or five tones. Every syllable in Mandarin has its definite tone. The first tone, called *yinping*, is a high-pitched tone without variation from beginning to end. The syllable is spoken with an even tone, using the highest pitch of the speaker's voice. The second tone, *yangping*, starts from a lower pitch and ends high. The syllable is spoken with a rising tone, not unlike speakers of English asking a question. The third tone, *shangsheng*, is perhaps the most difficult to master. It begins as a middle-level tone, goes down, bounds up, and ends with a relatively higher pitch. The fourth tone, *chyusheng*, is a falling tone that starts high and ends at the lowest range of the speaker's voice. The fifth tone, *chingsheng*, is often left out of descriptions of Mandarin. This tone is spoken very quickly and lightly, as if it has no tone. *Chingsheng* is often called the neutral tone.[51]

To be sure, English and other languages have inflections—that is, a change in pitch on certain words and sentences. English speakers can communicate anger or sadness by changing the pitch of their voice. Without the appropriate inflection, the meaning of an English speaker's sentence can be misinterpreted. In Chinese, however, tones completely change the meaning of a word. Take, for example, the word *ma*. In the first tone, *ma* is "mother." In the second tone, *ma* becomes "hemp" or "grass." In the third tone, *ma* becomes "horse," and in the fourth tone *ma* becomes "to scold" or "to nag." In Mandarin Chinese, the meanings of words are strictly based on the tones, which remain constant in whispering, yelling, or even singing. Mandarin tones are relative to the natural pitch of the speaker. A deep-voiced man's high note may be much lower than the high note of a woman.[52]

As with any other form of communication, some paralinguistic devices are learned and vary across cultures. South Koreans are taught to avoid talking or laughing loudly in any situation; such behavior is seen as rude and unbecoming since it tends to draw attention. Many Koreans, especially women, cover their mouths when laughing.[53]

In their study of paralanguage, Zukerman and Miyake introduce the idea of a vocal attractiveness stereotype. They contend that like one's physical attractiveness, individuals perceived to be vocally attractive elicit more favorable impressions than those not perceived to be vocally attractive. The results of their study indicate that attractive voices are those that are relatively loud, resonant, and articulate. Unattractive voices are squeaky, nasal, monotone, and off-pitched. Zukerman and Miyake found some sex differences in vocal attractiveness. For example, throatiness was more negatively perceived among female voices than among male voices.[54]

Silence is a part of the paralinguistic channel. Hasegawa and Gudykunst maintain that silence is the lack of verbal communication or the absence of sound and assert that culture influences the meaning and use of silence. In their research, Hasegawa and Gudykunst compared the use of silence among Japanese and Americans. According to their findings, in the United States, silence is defined as a pause, break, empty space, or lack of verbal communication. Hasegawa and Gudykunst maintain that silence is generally not a part of Americans' everyday communication routines. They argue that silence is acceptable among intimate others but that when meeting strangers, Americans are very conscious of silence and find it quite awkward. In Japan, however, silence is a space or pause that has important meaning during verbal communication. Pauses, or silence, are to be interpreted carefully. Stylistically, Japanese are taught to be indirect and sometimes ambiguous to maintain harmony. Silence, then, can be used to avoid directness, such as bluntly saying "No" to a request.[55]

Charles Braithwaite has studied silence across cultures and argues that silence is a central nonverbal component in any speech community. Braithwaite argues that some communicative functions of silence may be universal and do not vary across cultures. For example, Braithwaite maintains that among Native American groups, Japanese, Japanese-Americans in Hawaii, and people in rural Appalachia, the use of silence as a communicative act is associated with communication situations where the status of the interactants is uncertain, unpredictable, or ambiguous. In addition, Braithwaite argues that silence as a communicative act is associated with communication situations where there is a known and unequal distribution of power among interactants. In others words, when interactants consciously recognize their differential status, they consciously use silence. Braithwaite cites evidence of this in many cultures, including the Anang of southwestern Nigeria, the Wolof of Senegal, the Maori of New Zealand, the Malagasy in Madagascar, urban African American women, and some white working-class Americans.[56]

PROXEMICS

Proxemics refers to the perception and use of space, including territoriality and personal space. Territoriality refers to physical geographical space; personal space refers to perceptual or psychological space—sometimes thought of as the "bubble" of space that humans carry with them in their day-to-day activities. In cultures whose population density is high, personal space and territoriality are highly valued. Privacy in densely populated locations is often accomplished psychologically rather than physiologically. In Calcutta, India, for example, there are nearly eighty thousand persons per square mile. There is literally not enough room in the city to claim any personal space. Touching and bumping into others while walking through the streets of Calcutta is quite common and to be expected.[57]

Socioeconomic factors can also affect a culture's perception of space. Cramped and insufficient housing is common in much of Sri Lanka. In the 1980s most housing units were quite small. Thirty-three percent of the homes had only one room, 33 percent had two rooms, and only 20 percent had three rooms. Moreover, the average number of persons per home was five. (Overcrowding in Sri Lanka is declining, however, since the government initiated intensive housing programs in the 1990s.)[58]

The Moroccan perception of space reflects the culture's valuing of community. Personal space during a conversation is typically less than an arm's length. In mosques, worshipers line up shoulder to shoulder to pray. Houses typically have very little space between them as well.[59] Because Kenyan culture values harmony and sharing, Kenyans tend to be less aware of personal territory than people in the United States. For example, many Kenyans do not designate specific rooms in the home for specific activities, such as a living room or a dining room. In addition, the personal space distance between interactants is much closer than in the United States.[60] Saudi Arabians, too, are known to have closer personal space than Americans. Saudis typically enjoy getting very close, face to face, and engaging in direct eye contact.[61] Many other studies support the link between culture and proxemic behavior in comparing Americans with Arabs, Latin Americans, Pakistanis, Germans, Italians, Japanese, and Venezuelans. These examples suggest that culture plays a decisive role in how spatial distances are maintained during communication. There are other variables besides culture that affect proxemic distances, however, such as the age and sex of the interactants, the nature of the relationship, the environment, and ethnicity. Several studies have documented that in most cultures, the need for personal space increases with age. In addition, the use of space as influenced by sex seems to significantly vary by culture.[62]

HAPTICS

Haptics, or tactile communication, refers to the use of touch. Mark Knapp argues that touch may be the most primitive form of communication. In the United States, much research has been conducted to examine the impact of touching during the first few years of life.[63] Haptic communication varies widely across cultures, and the amount and kind of touch varies with the age, sex, situation, and relationship of the people involved. In his theorizing about culture and nonverbal communication, Edward Hall distinguishes between contact and noncontact cultures.[64] Contact cultures are those that tend to encourage touching and engage in touching more frequently than either moderate-contact or noncontact cultures, in which touching occurs less frequently and is generally discouraged. Many South and Central American cultures are considered contact countries, as are many southern European countries. The United States is regarded as a moderate-contact culture, whereas many Asian countries are considered noncontact. Many Asian cultures have established norms that forbid public displays of affection and intimacy that involve touch. One of the five central tenets of Confucian philosophy is the division between the sexes. Because Confucianism is so central to many Asian cultures, engaging in touch with the opposite sex is considered uncivil.[65] In their field study of touch patterns among cross-sex couples, McDaniel and Andersen observed the touch behavior of couples in airports. They found that couples from the United States touched most, followed by (in order from most to least) couples from northern Europe, Carribbean, Southeast Asia, and northeast Asia.[66] Psychologist Sidney Jourard conducted a study that counted the frequency of body contact between couples as they sat in cafés in different cities and countries. He found that the average number of touches per hour in San Juan, Puerto Rico, was 180; in Paris, 110; in Gainesville, Florida, 2; and in London, 0.[67]

Since we are often taught not to touch others, some people develop touch avoidance. These people feel uncomfortable in situations requiring touch and generally avoid touching when possible. In her study of Americans, Japanese, Puerto Ricans, and Koreans, Beth Casteel found no touch avoidance differences in same-sex dyads for the Japanese and Americans in that both were significantly more touch-avoidant than same-sex dyads in Puerto Rico and Korea. In opposite-sex dyads, however, Japanese and Koreans showed much higher levels of touch avoidance than Americans and Puerto Ricans. Casteel concluded that the Japanese and Americans allow women to touch other women, but men should not touch men. Koreans and Puerto Ricans are just the reverse.[68]

In their comparison of high-contact cultures of southern Europe and low-contact cultures of northern Europe, psychologists Remland, Jones, and Brinkman found that more touch was observed among Italian and Greek dyads than among English, French, and Dutch dyads.[69] The people of northern Italy have few inhibitions about personal space and touch. Heterosexual men are often seen kissing each other on both cheeks and walking together arm in arm, as are women. East Indians are very expressive with touch. To touch the feet of elders is a sign of respect. Indians demonstrate their trust for one another by holding hands briefly during a conversation or religious activity. When a Hindu priest blesses others at religious gatherings, he gently touches the palms of their outstretched hands.[70] Saudi Arabians tend to value touching also. Saudi businessmen often hold hands as a sign of trust, a form of touch behavior that some Americans often misunderstand. Saudi women, however, are never to be touched in public.[71]

Most cultures prohibit some forms of touch. Harris and Moran observe that in Thailand, Sri Lanka, and some other cultures, the head is considered sacred and should not be touched by others. Americans sometimes make the mistake of patting children of other cultures on the top of the head as a sign of affection or endearment. In some cultures, this is seen as a serious breach of etiquette.[72]

In many African and Middle Eastern cultures, the use of the left hand is forbidden in certain social situations. In Kenya, Indonesia, and Pakistan, for example, the left hand should not be used in eating or serving food. Harris and Moran report that

Many Arabs prefer very close personal space and touch during communication.
(Jean Higgins/Envision)

in Kenya, the left hand is considered weak and unimportant. Sometimes Kenyans intentionally use the left hand when serving food to someone they disrespect. In other cultures, such as Iraq and Iran, the left hand is used for cleaning and bodily functions and should never be used to give or receive gifts or other objects.[73]

Like proxemics, the nature of touch is often mediated by more than culture. The relationship between the interactants, the location and duration of touch, the relative pressure of the touch, the environment in which the touch occurs (public or private), and whether the touch is intentional or accidental influence touch across cultures.

OLFACTICS

Probably the least understood, yet most fascinating, of all human sensations is olfactics—that is, our sense of smell. Our lack of understanding is certainly not because we lack a sense of smell. According to Gibbons, humans can detect as many as ten thousand different compounds by smell. Moreover, approximately 1 percent of our genes are devoted to detecting odors. Although this may not seem like much, humans have more olfactory genes than any other type of gene identified in human and mammalian DNA. Gibbons suggests that our lack of understanding may exist because we lack a vocabulary for smell and are discouraged from talking about smell. Particularly in the United States, we have become obsessed with masking certain smells, especially those of the human body. According to Gibbons, the biggest users of fragrance in the world are U.S.-based companies like Procter & Gamble, Lever Bros., and Colgate. Some brands of soap use more than 2 million pounds of fragrance a year. In many Western cultures, body odor is regarded as unpleasant and distasteful, and we go to great efforts to mask or remove it.[74]

David Stoddart asserts that in addition to their ability to detect odors, humans are even more adept at producing odors. According to Stoddart, evidence from anatomy, chemistry, and psychology indicates that humans are the most highly scented of all the apes. Human scent comes from two types of glands that lie beneath the skin, the sebaceous glands and the apocrine glands. Sebaceous glands are all over the body wherever there are hair follicles. They produce an odorous oily fluid whose original purpose was to protect hair. The apocrine glands are a type of sweat gland. They are most dense in our armpits but are also found in the pubic and anal regions, the face, the scalp, and the umbilical region of the abdomen (the "belly button"). Women appear to have more apocrine glands than men, but some evidence suggests that their glands are less active than those in men. The most distasteful odors come from the apocrine glands, which are activated when we are frightened, excited, or aroused. Human saliva and urine also produce human scent.[75]

According to Kohl and Francoeur, research has repeatedly shown that women perceive odors differently at various phases of their menstrual cycles. They tend to be the most sensitive to odors during ovulation. Other studies indicate that when in close proximity to each other over time, as in dormitory living, women synchronize their menstrual cycles. Scientists believe that axillary organ secretions function as odor cues to stimulate their cycles. On a related note, studies have shown that vaginal secretions during ovulation are minimally unpleasant, whereas such secretions before and after ovulation are described as distinctly unpleasant.[76]

Kohl and Francoeur suggest that although preferences for certain smells seem to vary across cultures, there appears to be a universal preference for some kinds of scents that may have biological and evolutionary roots. These preferences are probably mediated by culture to some extent, however. For example, the finest perfumes in the world contain olfactory hints of urine. Scientists allege that these scents function as sex attractants. We know, for example, that sex-attractant pheromones are expelled from the body in urine. These two kinds of smell may mirror those of our humanoid ancestors and unconsciously stimulate the deepest parts of the brain.[77]

In addition to functioning as a sex attractant, smell is also used politically for marking social class distinctions. Classen, Howes, and Synnott contend that smell plays a signficant role in the construction of power relations in many societies.[78] Le Guerer comments, for example, that idiomatic expressions often employ smell-related terms to voice antagonism and repugnance toward others. People refer to persons they dislike as "stinkers." When we are suspicious of someone, we say we "smell a rat." When something seems wrong or amiss, we comment that "it doesn't smell right" or "smells fishy." Dishonest politicians may "reek of hypocrisy."[79]

Anthony Synnott claims that odor is often used to categorize groups of people into status, power, and moral classes. To be sure, the smells themselves are not intrinsically moral or immoral, but the qualities or thoughts attributed to the specific scents are what give them their moral significance. Synott argues that a person's scent is not only an individual emission and a moral statement, but also a perceived social attribute that is significant especially for members of subordinate groups, who are often labeled "smelly." Such labels often foster racal, ethnic, and religious prejudice and hatred. Subordinate and microcultural groups are often described as possessing negative olfactory characteristics. In fact, Synnott argues that perceived foul odors legitimize inequalities and are one of the criteria by which a negative identity is imposed on a particular class or race.[80] Many cultures establish norms for acceptable and unacceptable scents associated with the human body. When individuals or groups of people fail to fit into the realm of acceptability, their odor signals that something is "wrong" with them, either physically or mentally. Kohl and Francoeur note that the American Puritan tradition of "cleanliness is next to godliness" may explain the American obsession with deodorants, perfumes, soaps, and shampoos.[81] Muslims believe that cleanliness of the body and purity of the soul are related. Muslim women are told to purify themselves after menstruation. Cleanliness is prescribed before and after meals. The Koran specifies that all five daily prayers must be preceded by washing of the hands, arms, and feet.[82]

Social class distinctions based on smells are the cultural product of education, religion, parenting, and social pressure from peers. With the exception of those scents that appeal to everyone, people are conditioned to find certain scents attractive and others dirty or foul. Moreover, such distinctions sustain social barriers between groups and even justify a dominant group's persecution of subordinate groups.[83] In the Middle Ages, wealthy people bought perfumes to diminish the scent of the lower classes. Nineteenth-century Japanese described European traders as *bata-kusai*—"stinks of butter."[84] Adolf Hitler's hatred of Jews was based partially on olfactics; he claimed that they had a foul odor that was representative of their "moral mildew" and reflected their outer and inner foulness, therefore their immorality.[85] Gibbons reports that during World Wars I and II, German and English soldiers claimed they could identify the enemy by their smell. Similar claims have been made by North Vietnamese and United States troops.[86] Baker reports that in U.S. history, Thomas Jefferson is purported to have said that blacks have "a very strong and disagreeable odour."[87] Dollard claims that many white racists used the "disagreeable scent" of blacks as a final proof of the impossibility of close association between the races.[88] In 1912, sociologist Georg Simmel wrote, "It would appear impossible for the Negro ever to be accepted into high society in North America because of his bodily odor."[89] Indeed, Simmel concluded that "the moral ideal of harmony and equality between the different classes and races runs up against the brick wall of an invincible disgust inspired by the sense of smell."[90]

Classen, Howes, and Synnott maintain that more than any other group, women are stereotyped and classified by their scent. Historically, in many cultures women were considered the fragrant sex, unless they were prostitutes or suffragettes or challenged the male-dominated social order. The role of fragrance was primarily to entice men. In general, the Western cultural axiom has been that unless perfumed, women stink. Jonathan Swift's poem "The Lady's Dressing Room" expresses this belief:

His foul imagination links
Each Dame he sees with all her Stinks:
And, if unsav'ry Odours fly,
Conceives a Lady standing by.[91]

Although it may be the least studied of all the senses, social scientists are discovering that olfactory sensation is a potent influence on social interaction. Survey data indicate that a significant percentage of adults are conscious of and influenced by smells in their environment. In their poll of over 350 American adults, the Olfactory Research Fund found that 64 percent of respondents indicated that smell greatly influenced the quality of their lives. Specifically, 76 percent of the respondents reported that the sense of smell was "very important" in their daily relationships with persons of the opposite sex, and 20 percent indicated that it was "somewhat important." Seventy-four percent indicated that smell was "very important," and 22 percent said that it was "somewhat important" in their relationships with their spouses. Although the percentages dropped somewhat, 36 percent of the respondents indicated that smell was "very important" in their relationships with friends, and 40 percent agreed that smell was "very important" in their relationships with coworkers. Eighty percent of the respondents reported using environmental fragrances, such as potpourri, room sprays, and scented candles. Well over 60 percent of respondents believed that particular aromas enhance the quality of life, relieve stress, and help retrieve memories. Of those respondents who used cologne, perfume, or after-shave, 83 percent said they did so because they liked the scent, 68 percent said it made them feel better about themselves, 56 percent said it enhanced their sense of well-being, 51 percent said they used fragrances to make themselves more romantically attractive to others, and 46 percent said they used fragrances to make a fashion statement.[92]

This emphasis on smell is often motivated by the pivotal role olfactics play in the maintenance of social relationships. Todrank, Byrnes, Wrzesniewski, and Rozin assert that most cultures assign meanings to odors that are often displaced onto the people wearing them.[93] This is especially evident in relationships with members of the opposite sex. While it is widely recognized that odors play a determinant role in the mating practices of many animal species, Kohl and Francoeur argue that odors are also an important ingredient in human mating and bonding and cite empirical evidence showing that odors hasten puberty, mediate women's menstrual cycles, and even influence sexual orientation.[94] Extant research indicates that odors help people identify their family members, facilitate the bond between parents and children, and influence how often and with whom individuals mate.

Kate Fox is a social anthropologist and the Director of the Social Issues Research Center in Oxford, England. She has studied cultural differences in olfactics, with a special emphasis on non-Western cultures. Fox maintains that unlike most Western cultures, smell is "the emperor of the senses" in many other cultures. For example, she describes the importance of smell among the Ongee people of the Andaman Islands, a group of islands off the southeast coast of India. According to

Fox, much of Ongee cultural life revolves around smell. For example, their calendar is based on the smell of flowers which bloom at different times of the year. One's personal identity is defined by smell. Fox writes that to refer to him- or herself, an Ongee touches the tip of his or her nose, which is a gesture meaning both "me" and "my smell." Fox also reports that during greetings, Ongee routinely ask, "How is your nose?" rather than "How are you?" Ongee etiquette prescribes that if a person responds that he or she feels "heavy with smell," the greeter should inhale deeply to remove the excess smell. Conversely, if the greeted person indicates that he or she is short of smell energy, Ongee etiquette prescribes that the greeter contribute some extra scent by blowing on him or her.[95]

Fox also describes smell rituals among the Bororo peoples of Brazil and the Serer Ndut of Senegal (western Africa). Among the Bororo, personal body smell indicates the life force of the individual, while one's breath odor indicates the state of one's soul. The Ndut believe that individuals possess a physical smell, defined by one's body and breath odor, and a spiritual smell. The spiritual smell is thought to be a reincarnated smell. For example, the Ndut can tell which ancestor has been reincarnated by associating the smell of a child with that of a deceased person.[96]

In her olfactic research, Fox has discovered that among those cultures where smell is so closely associated with one's personal identity, the exchange or mixing of odors among people is carefully prescribed. For example, among the Amazonian Desana, members of a particular tribal group are thought to share a similar odor. Marriage is allowed only between people of different odors; that is, between members of different tribal groups. Similarly, among the Batek Negrito of the Malay Peninsula, people of similar odor groups are prohibited from engaging in sexual intercourse and even from sitting too close to one another. The Batek Negrito believe that the prolonged mixing of similar odors causes illness in the people themselves and in any children they may conceive.[97]

Fox also writes that Western smell preferences are not universal. For example, the Dassanetch, a tribal cattle-raising group in Ethiopia, believe that the smell of cows is the most pleasing of all smells. Dassanetch men routinely wash their hands in cattle urine and smear their bodies with cattle manure. Such smells are associated with status and fertility. The Dogon people of Mali find the scent of onions very attractive, especially for young men and women who rub fried onions all over their bodies.[98]

PHYSICAL APPEARANCE AND DRESS

Often we can identify a person's culture by the person's physical appearance and dress. Communication with another is often preceded by visual observations of the other's physical appearance. Moreover, in most cultures, people consciously manipulate their physical appearance to communicate their identity. Most cultures have strict rules for how their members should present themselves. To violate a culture's prescriptions for appearance may result in negative sanctions. In many cultures, a person's physical appearance and dress communicate his or her age, sex, and status within the culture.

Self-Assessment 8-1

Personal Report of Olfactory Perception and Sensitivity (PROPS)

The following instrument is designed to assess your level of olfactory perception and sensitivity. On a scale of 1 to 7, indicate the degree to which each statement applies to you. 1 = strongly disagree, 2 = disagree, 3 = slightly disagree, 4 = undecided, 5 = slightly agree, 6 = agree, and 7 = strongly agree.

1. _____ When interacting with a stranger of the opposite sex, I am typically conscious of the scent of his or her breath.

2. _____ When interacting with a stranger of the opposite sex, I am typically conscious of the scent of his or her body.

3. _____ When interacting with a stranger of the opposite sex, I am typically conscious of the scent of his or her cologne or perfume.

4. _____ When interacting with a stranger of the same sex, I am typically conscious of the scent of his or her breath.

5. _____ When interacting with a stranger of the same sex, I am typically conscious of the scent of his or her body.

6. _____ When interacting with a stranger of the same sex, I am typically conscious of the scent of his or her cologne or perfume.

7. _____ When interacting with a close friend of the opposite sex, I am typically conscious of the scent of his or her breath.

8. _____ When interacting with a close friend of the opposite sex, I am typically conscious of the scent of his or her body.

9. _____ When interacting with a close friend of the opposite sex, I am typically conscious of the scent of his or her cologne or perfume.

10. _____ When interacting with a close friend of the same sex, I am typically conscious of the scent of his or her breath.

11. _____ When interacting with a close friend of the same sex, I am typically conscious of the scent of his or her body.

12. _____ When interacting with a close friend of the same sex, I am typically conscious of the scent of his or her cologne or perfume.

13. _____ When interacting with a stranger of the opposite sex, I am typically conscious of the scent of my breath.

—Continued

14. _____ When interacting with a stranger of the opposite sex, I am typically conscious of the scent of my body.

15. _____ When interacting with a stranger of the opposite sex, I am typically conscious of the scent of my cologne or perfume.

16. _____ When interacting with a stranger of the same sex, I am typically conscious of the scent of my breath.

17. _____ When interacting with a stranger of the same sex, I am typically conscious of the scent of my body.

18. _____ When interacting with a stranger of the same sex, I am typically conscious of the scent of my cologne or perfume.

19. _____ When interacting with a close friend of the opposite sex, I am typically conscious of the scent of my breath.

20. _____ When interacting with a close friend of the opposite sex, I am typically conscious of the scent of my body.

21. _____ When interacting with a close friend of the opposite sex, I am typically conscious of the scent of my cologne or perfume.

22. _____ When interacting with a close friend of the same sex, I am typically conscious of the scent of my breath.

23. _____ When interacting with a close friend of the same sex, I am typically conscious of the scent of my body.

24. _____ When interacting with a close friend of the same sex, I am typically conscious of the scent of my cologne or perfume.

25. _____ When interacting with someone from a different culture or ethnicity, I am typically conscious of the scent of his or her breath.

26. _____ When interacting with someone from a different culture or ethnicity, I am typically conscious of the scent of his or her cologne or perfume.

27. _____ When interacting with someone from a different culture or ethnicity, I am typically conscious of the scent of his or her body.

28. _____ When interacting with someone in a private environment, I am typically conscious of the scent of the immediate surroundings.

—Continued

29. _____ When interacting with someone in a private environment, I am typically conscious of the scent of the furniture.

30. _____ When interacting with someone in a public environment, I am typically conscious of the scent of the immediate surroundings.

To calculate your PROPS score, sum your responses as follows:

1. Perception and sensitivity to others: add items 1–12 (range = 12–84).
2. Perception and sensitivity to self: add items 13–24 (range = 12–84).
3. Perception and sensitivity to different cultures: add items 25–27 (range = 3–21).
4. Perception and sensitivity to environment: add items 28–30 (range = 3–21).

Higher scores indicate more sensitivity to the particular contexts. For example, scores of above 50 for perception and sensitivity to others and/or self would be high, whereas scores below 30 would be considered low sensitivity. Scores above 15 for perception and sensitivity to persons from different cultures would be considered high, whereas scores below 7 would be considered low sensitivity.

SOURCE: J. W. Neuliep and E. L. Groshkopf, *Toward a Communication Theory of Olfactics: Explication, Development of the Personal Report of Olfactic Perception and Sensation and Some Initial Tests.* Paper presented at the 2001 annual convention of the National Communication Association, Atlanta, Georgia.

In virtually every culture, men and women dress differently, and in many cultures the differences begin at birth. In the United States, for example, male infants are traditionally dressed in blue and female infants are dressed in pink. In the Masai culture of Kenya, the distinction between young girls and women is communicated through body artifacts. According to Vandehey, Buerger, and Krueger, Masai woman wear specific necklaces and earrings to designate their marital status. For a married women to be seen without her earrings may bring harsh physical punishment from her husband. Masai men wear earrings and arm rings that designate social status. The specific earring distinguishes the man as an elder or a warrior. Other body ornaments communicate whether a Masai (male or female) has been circumcised.[99]

In most Islamic cultures, Muslim women are often easily recognized by their headscarfs, or turbans, which are important symbols of religious faith among Muslims. Smucker maintains that the scarfs are often perceived by Westerners as a sign of male subjugation of women. In Turkey, however, many young Muslim women believe that rather than being a symbol of subservience to men, the headscarf, or veil, serves as a guard against the eyes of men and as a symbol of women's allegiance to God, rather than to their husbands or fathers.[100] Harris and Moran note that in many Middle Eastern cultures, such as Saudi Arabia, Islamic law decrees that women dress conservatively and cover their hair in public. Although women are not required to wear the traditional full-length *abaya* (black cloak) over

Variations of traditional Saudi dress habits for women (left) and men (right).
(Peter Carmichael/TSI) (David Austen/Stock Boston)

their clothing, they are encouraged to wear a knee-length tunic/dress over slacks and a scarf on their heads. Moreover, they should avoid explicit makeup in the presence of Saudi men. The idea behind these dictates is to avoid sexually arousing men. Saudi men may wear either Saudi dress or their normal Western dress but should not wear shorts or open shirts. Long hair for men is discouraged.[101]

Harris and Moran observe that in India, businessmen wear a *dhoti,* a single piece of white cloth about five yards long and three feet wide that wraps around their lower body. Long shirts are worn on the upper part of the body. Most Indian women wear a *sari* and blouse. A *sari* consists of several yards of lightweight cloth draped so that one end forms a skirt and the other a head and shoulder covering. It is not acceptable for women to show skin above the knees or a large portion of the back. Wearing clothes that are in any way revealing is discouraged since it may unintentionally communicate "a loose woman."[102]

In Japan, the kimono—a long robe with wide sleeves—is the traditional clothing for both men and women; it is traditionally worn with a broad sash, or *obi,* as an outer garment. The specific design of the kimono varies according to one's sex, age, and marital status, the time of year, and the occasion. In the ancient past, there was no distinction between a man's and a woman's kimono. Today, there are several types of kimonos worn by men, women, and children. Men typically wear kimonos of blue, black, brown, gray, or white. Women's kimonos are the most elaborate and varied in style and design. The fabric, cut, color, and sleeve length, and the details of the *obi,* vary according to a woman's age, social status and marital status, and the season. During the summer months, women wear *yukata*s, lightweight cotton kimonos. Many Japanese hotels provide *yukata*s for guests to wear in their rooms. In Japan, on "7-5-3 Day" (November 15), boys who are three or five years old and girls who are three or seven years old dress up in kimonos to pray at the temples. There is also a special day for all girls and all boys to go to the temple: March 3 is Girls' Day and May 5 is Boys' Day. Kimonos are worn on these days as well.[103]

CHRONEMICS

Chronemics refers to the nonverbal channel of time. Recall (from Chapter 4) Hall's description of monochronic and polychronic time oriented cultures. According to Hall, monochronic (M-time) orientations emphasize schedules, the compartmentalization and segmentation of measurable units of time. Many M-time cultures are low-context, including the United States, Germany, Scandinavia, Canada, France, and most of northern Europe. Conversely, polychronic (P-time) orientations see time as much less tangible and stress multiple activities with little emphasis on scheduling. P-time cultures focus on involvement of people and the completion of tasks as opposed to a strict adherence to schedules. Many P-time cultures are high-context, including southern Europe, Latin America, and many African and Middle Eastern countries.[104]

The primary system for organizing time, in just about every culture, is the calendar. According to L. E. Doggett, one of the world's leading authorities on calendars, cultures create and use calendars as a way of organizing units of time to satisfy the needs of the society. Doggett maintains that calendars give people a sense that they can control time. Calendars also provide a link between people and the cosmos, or the supernatural. Doggett asserts that in many cultures, calendars are considered nearly sacred and serve as a source of social order and cultural identity. In many ways, calendars dictate human communication patterns. When people eat, work, celebrate, worship, enjoy being at leisure, attend school, hunt, rest, and fight wars is often prescribed by the calendar. Social contracts of just about every kind are typically determined by calendars. For example, marriages are deemed successful by the number of years they have lasted. Prison terms are defined as a number of months or years. In most cultures an individual's age, which is measured by a calendar, is the primary criterion for social and cultural privileges and responsibilities.[105]

According to Doggett, there are about forty calendars used in the world today. Most of these calendars are astronomically based. The primary astronomical cycles include the day, month, and year. Days are defined by the rotation of the planet Earth on its axis. The month is based on the revolution of the moon around Earth. The year is based on the revolution of Earth around the sun. Most cultures use either a solar, a lunar, or a lunisolar calendar. Many Western cultures, such as the United States, use a solar calendar. Islamic cultures use a lunar calendar. The Israelis and Chinese use a lunisolar calendar.[106] Doggett points out that the Gregorian calendar (a solar calendar) serves as the international standard. The United

States functions under the Gregorian calendar. An ordinary year has 365 days; a leap year has 366. Months have either 30 or 31 days except for February, which has 28 or 29, depending on whether or not the year is a leap year. The Hebrew calendar is lunisolar and is the official calendar of Israel. Each year consists of either 12 or 13 months. Months consist of either 29 or 30 days. The beginning of each month is determined by a new moon. Traditionally, days of the week are designated by number, except for the seventh day, the Sabbath. Days begin and end at sunset. In the Islamic calendar, months correspond to the lunar cycle. On the basis of religious principles, Muslims begin each month upon the first visibility of the moon's crescent. Like the Hebrew calendar, days begin at sunset. In China, the Gregorian calendar is used for governmental purposes, but the traditional Chinese calendar is used for scheduling cultural festivals and for timing agricultural activities. The Chinese calendar is lunisolar; months have either 29 or 30 days.[107]

Hall has pointed out that perceptions of time differ considerably across cultures. In the United States, for example, time is tangible (i.e., concrete, perceptible). Hall notes that to Americans, time can be bought, sold, saved, spent, wasted, lost, made up, and measured. Americans are also future oriented, in that we make great efforts to plan and schedule what we expect (or want) to happen. Conversely, to many Arabs a person who tries to look into the future appears to be irreligious or insane. To many Arabs, only God can decree what will or will not occur. Hall also notes that duration is an important component of one's perception of time. According to Hall, duration is what happens between two points. Most Americans view time in this manner and carefully schedule and evaluate cultural events according to their duration (e.g., minutes, hours, days), as in "Oh, that movie was way too long," "This won't take but a minute," or "When will you get here?" In some Native American groups, time is not thought of as measurable; rather, time is a sequence of events that differs for each set of circumstances.[108]

Nonverbal Expectancy Violations Theory

Judee Burgoon has formalized a theory of nonverbal communication called the nonverbal expectancy violations theory (NEV).[109] The basic premise of the theory is that people hold expectancies about the appropriateness of the nonverbal behaviors of others. These expectations are learned and culturally driven. For example, in the United States, people expect to shake hands when they are introduced to someone. Burgoon posits that occasionally people violate nonverbal expectations. When this happens, the violation produces arousal, which can be physiological or cognitive and either positive or negative. Burgoon maintains that once a violation has been committed and arousal is triggered, the recipient evaluates the violation and the violator. Violations initiated by highly attractive sources may be evaluated positively, whereas those initiated by unattractive sources may be evaluated negatively.[110] The very same violation may produce very different evaluations, depending on who has committed it. The evaluation of the violation depends on (1) the evaluation of the communicator, (2) implicit messages associated with the violation, and (3) evaluations of the act itself. In presenting the theory, Burgoon outlines several key assumptions, as listed in the accompanying box.

Burgoon bases assumption 1 on literature from anthropology, sociology, and psychology indicating that humans are a social species with a biological/survival instinct to be with other humans. Conversely, humans cannot tolerate extended physical contact with, or excessive closeness with, others; that is, humans have a basic need to insulate themselves from others and a need for privacy. Although this first assumption appears to be universal, the degree to which a person feels the need to be with others or insulated from them is probably culturally driven. Individualists may be more comfortable alone in the same situations in which a collectivist feels uncomfortable. Moreover, the way in which a person satisfies the need for privacy or affiliation certainly varies across cultures. In the United States and Germany, for example, privacy is often satisfied by physical separation from others (for example, closed doors), whereas in densely populated cultures such as India, privacy may be fulfilled psychologically.

Assumption 2 indicates that affiliation for others is triggered by rewards within the communicative context. These rewards may be biological (food, sex, safety) or social (belonging, esteem, status). Biological needs are no doubt universal, but social needs are often learned and vary across cultures. Belonging needs are felt much more strongly in collectivistic cultures than in individualistic ones. Conversely, esteem needs are more strongly felt in individualistic cultures than in collectivistic ones. Assumption 3 extends assumption 2 by stating that humans are attracted to rewarding situations and repelled by punishing situations. This phenomenon is probably universal, but it should be noted that what people deem rewarding and punishing varies across cultures.

Assumption 4 asserts that humans have the perceptual ability to discern differences in spatial relationships. We can tell when someone is standing close to us or far away from us. Assumption 5 deals with the establishment of normative nonverbal behaviors. Normative behavior is that which is usual or typical, or which follows a regular pattern. For example, the lecture style of your professor is probably consistent day after day. The professor has established a normative way of delivering his or her material. Many normative behaviors are established by society and culture. In the United States, for example, saying "good-bye" is a normative way of terminating a telephone conversation.

Assumption 6 recognizes that even though most of us follow similar normative rules and regulations for our verbal and nonverbal behavior, we also develop our own personal style of interaction that is unique in some way. Assumption 7 states that norms operate as a function of the interactants, the interaction, and the environment. Characteristics of the interactants might include their sex, age, personality, and race. Characteristics of the interaction itself might include status differences or degree of intimacy between the interactants. Finally, characteristics of the environment may include the physical features of the setting, such as furniture arrangement, lighting, or even temperature.

Assumption 8 deals with the notion of expectancies, a key element of the theory. Burgoon argues that during interaction, interactants develop expectancies

Fundamental Assumptions of the Nonverbal Expectancy Violations Theory

Assumption 1: Humans have two competing needs, a need for affiliation and a need for personal space (or distance). These two needs cannot be satisfied at once.

Assumption 2: The desire for affiliation may be elicited or magnified by the presence of rewards in the communication context. The rewards may be biological or social.

Assumption 3: The greater the degree to which a person or situation is defined as rewarding, the greater the tendency for others to approach that person or situation; the greater the degree to which a person or situation is defined as punishing, the greater the tendency for others to avoid that person or situation.

Assumption 4: Humans are able to perceive gradations in distance.

Assumption 5: Human interaction patterns, including personal space or distance patterns, are normative.

Assumption 6: Humans may develop idiosyncratic behavior patterns that differ from the social norms.

Assumption 7: In any communication context, the norms are a function of three classes of factors: (a) characteristics of the interactants, (b) features of the interaction itself, and (c) features of the immediate physical environment.

Assumption 8: Interactants develop expectations about the communication behavior of others. Consequently, they are able to recognize or at least respond differently to normative versus deviant behaviors on the part of others.

Assumption 9: Deviations from expectations have arousal value.

Assumption 10: Interactants make evaluations of others.

Assumption 11: Evaluations are influenced by the degree to which the other is perceived as rewarding such that a positively valued message is only rewarding if the source is highly regarded and a negatively valued message is only punishing if the source is not highly regarded.

SOURCE: J. K. Burgoon, "A Communication Model of Personal Space Violations: Explication and an Initial Test," *Human Communication Research*, 4 (1978), 129–142.

and preferences about the behaviors of others. These expectancies are anticipations of others' behaviors that are perceived to be appropriate for the situation. Typically, expectancies are based on a combination of societal and cultural norms. For example, students expect that their professors will behave in an appropriate and consistent manner. In certain cases, however, students might expect idiosyncratic deviations from the norms from particular professors (for example, a certain professor frequently tells jokes in class).

Assumption 9 focuses on two other key ingredients in the theory, violations of expectancies and arousal. Burgoon subscribes to the notion that when a person's nonverbal expectancies are violated, the person becomes aroused. The violation tends to stimulate the receiver/communicator's attention and to arouse either adaptive or defensive reactions. For example, we learned earlier in this chapter that in some cultures (for example, Korea), touching the top of a child's head is prohibited. To do so would be a violation of expectancy, and the child or the parents might respond negatively or defensively. In some situations, however, some violations are perceived positively. A shaman may be allowed to touch the top of a child's head, and such behavior may be perceived positively.

Assumption 10 states that people make value judgments about others. Assumption 11 extends this notion by specifying how evaluations are made. Burgoon contends that the first factor influencing the positive or negative evaluation of a violation is the communicator reward valence—that is, how much the violator is perceived as someone with whom it is desirable to interact. Thus, communicator reward valence is based on communicator and relationship characteristics (age, sex, personality, status, reputation, anticipated future interaction) and interactional behaviors (style, positive feedback). Communicator reward valence influences how one will evaluate the violation of expectancies. Burgoon's theory holds that more favorable evaluations will be given when the violation is committed by a high-reward person than when it is committed by a low-reward person. If someone to whom you are attracted stands very close to you at a party, much closer than is normative, you may interpret this violation positively as a sign of mutual attraction or affiliation. Conversely, if someone by whom you are repulsed stands too close to you at a party, you may evaluate this violation quite negatively.

Burgoon asserts that positively evaluated violations produce favorable communication patterns and consequences, whereas negatively evaluated violations produce unfavorable communication patterns. In addition, Burgoon contends that even extreme violations, if committed by a high-reward person, can be evaluated positively and produce reciprocal communication patterns. Although a significant number of studies support the assumptions of Burgoon's theory, very few, if any, have investigated its cross-cultural applicability.

CULTURAL CONTEXTS AND NONVERBAL EXPECTANCIES

As we have seen throughout this book, the cultures of Japan and the United States differ significantly. Japan is a collectivistic, high-context culture, whereas the United States is an individualistic, low-context culture. Individualistic cultures stress the importance of an individual's unique identity. Emphasis is placed on individual goals over group goals. From an early age, American children are taught that they are individuals with unique abilities and talents. People are rewarded for being "the best," "the one and only," and "number one" in whatever they do. The goal of Americans is to be the best that they can be and to strive for the top. A well-known cliché in the United States states that "the squeaky wheel gets the grease," meaning that in order to get attention or to have one's needs met, one must draw attention to oneself.

In contrast, collectivistic cultures place precedence on group goals over individual goals. Such cultures emphasize values that serve the in-group by subordinating personal goals for the sake of the in-group. Group activities are dominant and pervasive. Responsibility is shared, and accountability is collective.[111] Japan has an unofficial motto that reads *"Deru kugi wa utareru,"* or "The tallest nail gets hammered down." Children are taught at a young age that their identity is based on their relationship within the group (family or business). Group leadership, rather than individual initiative, is valued. However, especially among Japanese youth, a new sense of individualism is growing in Japan.[112]

A high-context culture, such as Japan, is one whose members are highly sensitive to the perceptual, sociorelational, and environmental contexts for information. High-context cultures have a restricted-code system (language). Members do not rely on verbal communication as their main source of information. Silence and nonverbal behavior are most informative. Statements or actions of affection are rare. Members are quite adept at decoding nonverbal behavior. Japanese, for example, expect others (that is, Japanese) to understand the unarticulated communication. Cultural members are expected to know how to perform in various situations where the guidelines are implicit.[113]

Members of a low-context culture, such as the United States, are less sensitive to the perceptual, sociorelational, and environmental contexts. That is not to say that they ignore the environment—they are simply less aware of it than are members of a high-context culture. A low-context communication is one in which the mass of information is found in the explicit code. Hence low-context cultures have an elaborated-code system. Verbal messages are extremely important when information to be shared with others is coded in the verbal message. Members of low-context cultures do not perceive the environment as a source of information. Guidelines and expectations are frequently explained explicitly.[114] In addition to high-context/low-context distinctions between the two countries, Japan is considered a low-contact culture, whereas the United States is considered a moderate-contact culture.

Many of the communicative behaviors of high/low-context, individualistic/collectivistic, and high/low-contact cultures are different, and the interactants will inevitably violate each other's expectations regarding appropriate nonverbal behavior (see Intercultural Conversation box).

Intercultural Conversation

An Intercultural Conversation: Violation of Nonverbal Expectancies

In the following scenario, Jim, Akira, and Mitsuko interact. Akira and Mitsuko are exchange students from Japan who are spending a semester studying at an American college. Jim is an American student at the same college. Notice how each violates the others' expectations without realizing it. When reading the scenes, keep in mind the different cultural orientations and the assumptions of the nonverbal expectancy violations theory.

Jim and Akira are at a party.

1. *Jim:* *(Nudges Akira and says loudly)* This is a great party, eh?
2. *Akira:* *(Is startled—stands back—tries to put some distance between himself and Jim)* Yes, thank you.
3. *Jim:* *(Leaning forward toward Akira, with direct eye contact)* If you wanted to meet some girls, I could introduce you.
4. *Akira:* *(Shocked by such an offer, he backs away)* But I don't know them. They might be upset.
5. *Jim:* Well, how else are you going to meet them?
6. *Akira:* *(Uncomfortable)* Maybe during a class or something.

Mitsuko, another Japanese exchange student, approaches Jim and Akira. She knows Akira, but not Jim.

7. *Mitsuko:* Hello, Akira *(Bows slightly and looks down)*
8. *Akira:* Ah, Mitsuko, this is my friend Jim.
9. *Jim:* Hi! *(Leaning forward into her space)*
10. *Mitsuko:* Hi, Jim. *(Bows slightly and does not make direct eye contact)*
11. *Jim:* Are you two friends? *(Wonders why she won't look at him, thinks to himself, "Well, I'm not one of them. She probably thinks I'm ugly.")*
12. *Akira:* Yes, we know each other.

A long pause ensues.

13. *Jim:* *(Thinks to himself, "This is going nowhere—I've got to think of something to say." He speaks rather loudly)* Great party, hey guys?

Akira and Mitsuko both jump back.

14. *Akira:* *(Thinks to himself, "This guy is too weird.")* Yeah, this is fun.

During this scenario, Jim violates Akira's kinesic, proxemic, paralinguistic, and haptic expectations. Several of the axioms and propositions from Burgoon's NEV theory can be applied to this interaction. Notice in lines 1 through 4 that Akira perceives that Jim is standing too close and talking too loudly and thus Akira backs away. From Akira's point of view, Jim violated his proxemic and paralinguistic expectations. In line 1 Jim touches Akira, which probably violated Akira's nonverbal expectations regarding haptics. From Jim's vantage point, Akira violated his expectations as well, by not looking at him and not responding to his offer to introduce him to women.

According to the NEV theory, violations have arousal value (assumption 9). Throughout the dialogue we can see how Akira and Jim became aroused (shocked, uncomfortable, startled, annoyed) by each other's violations. Both Mitsuko and Akira jump when Jim says loudly, "Great party, hey guys?" In lines 13 and 14 we can see how Burgoon's assumption 10 applies in that the arousal leads to evaluations ("This is going nowhere"; "This guy is too weird"). In this case, the evaluations are negative.

According to the theory, the greater the degree to which a person is perceived as rewarding, the greater the tendency for others to approach that person. Likewise, the greater the degree to which a person is perceived as punishing, the greater the tendency for others to avoid that person. Unfortunately for Akira, since he is in a "foreign" country, he will be the more likely of the two to change his behavior to conform to the expectations of others.

Chapter Summary

Many social scientists believe that our verbal language evolved from a system of nonlinguistic communication that we inherited from our animal predecessors. As humans we possess a host of nonlinguistic ways to communicate with one another through the use of kinesics, proxemics, chronemics, paralanguage, haptics, olfactics, and physical appearance. Our nonverbal communication, when combined with verbal language, creates a very complicated communication system through which humans come to know and understand one another.

Our nonverbal behavior is innate and learned. Many of our unconscious behaviors, such as the expression of emotions, are universal. People from all cultures express anger, happiness, and sadness the very same way. Yet other forms of nonverbal communication, such as gestures, are unique manifestations of our culture's distinctive cosmos. We learn how to communicate with our bodies (kinesics), through the use of space (proxemics), by touching others (haptics), with our voice (paralanguage), with smell (olfactics), and through the way we dress and present ourselves. Sometimes our nonverbal behaviors violate the expectations of others. Sometimes we stand too close or touch too much. When this happens, the other person evaluates the violation as positive or negative depending on whether we are perceived as attractive or unattractive. If we are thought of as attractive, our violation may be welcome. If we are perceived as unattractive, the same violation may be evaluated quite negatively.

GLOSSARY OF TERMS

Adaptors: Mostly unconscious nonverbal actions that satisfy physiological or psychological needs, such as scratching an itch.

Affect displays: Nonverbal presentations of emotion, primarily communicated through facial expressions.

Analogic communication: Nonverbal communication.

Chronomics: The use of time.

Denotative meaning: The literal meaning of a word; the dictionary meaning.

Digital communication: Verbal communication.

Emblems: Primarily hand gestures that have a direct verbal translation. Can be used to repeat or to substitute for verbal communication.

Haptics: Nonverbal communication through physical contact or touch.

Illustrators: Primarily hand and arm movements that function to accent or complement speech.

Kinesics: General category of body motion, including emblems, illustrators, affect displays, and adaptors.

Nonverbal expectancy violations theory: Theory that posits that people hold expectations about the nonverbal behavior of others. When these expectations are violated, people evaluate the violation positively or negatively, depending on the source of the violation.

Olfactics: The perception and use of smell, scent, and odor.

Paralanguage: Characteristics of the voice, such as pitch, rhythm, intensity, volume, and rate.

Proxemics: The perception and use of space, including territoriality and personal space.

Regulators: Nonverbal acts that manage and govern communication between people, such as stance, distance, and eye contact.

REFERENCES

1. P. Farb, *Word Play: What Happens When People Talk* (New York: Bantam, 1973), p. 234.
2. G. Searchinger, director and producer, *The Human Language Series: Part III: With and Without Words* [film] (1996; available from Ways of Knowing, Inc., 200 West 72nd Street, New York, NY 10023).
3. Ibid.
4. M. L. Knapp and J. A. Hall, *Nonverbal Communication in Human Interaction,* 3rd ed. (Fort Worth: Holt, Rinehart and Winston, 1992).
5. Searchinger, *The Human Language Series.*
6. Ibid.
7. Ibid.
8. S. W. Littlejohn, *Theories of Human Communication,* 5th ed. (Belmont, Calif.: Wadsworth, 1996); J. C. Conden and F. Yousef, *An Approach to Intercultural Communication* (Indianapolis: Bobbs-Merrill, 1975).
9. P. Ekman and W. V. Friesen, "The Repertoire of Nonverbal Behavior: Categories, Origins, Usage, and Coding," *Semiotica,* 1 (1969), 49–98.
10. D. Archer, producer, and J. Silver, director, *A World of Gestures: Culture and Nonverbal Communication* [film] (1991; available from University of California Extension, Center for Media and Independent Learning, 2000 Center Street, Fourth Floor, Berkeley, CA 94704).
11. Ibid.
12. M. Choi, "Cultural Profile of South Korea" (unpublished student manuscript, St. Norbert College, De Pere, Wisc., 1995).
13. P. R. Harris and R. T. Moran, *Managing Cultural Differences,* 4th ed. (Houston: Gulf Publishing, 1996).
14. D. Schug and M. Sturino, "The Japanese Cultural Profile" (unpublished student manuscript, St. Norbert College, De Pere, Wisc., 1995).
15. S. Moellendorf, H. Warsh, and K. Yoshimaru, "The Amish Culture: A Closer Look at the People of Lancaster County" (unpublished manuscript, St. Norbert College, De Pere, Wisc., 1996).
16. R. E. Axtell, *Gestures: The Do's and Taboos of Gestures and Body Language Around the World* (New York: Wiley, 1991).
17. R. J. Bishop, "Cultural Profile, Examination of Value Orientations and Sociocultural Influences, and Verbal and Nonverbal Language Aspects of the East Indian Culture" (unpublished student manuscript, St. Norbert College, De Pere, Wisc., 1995).
18. Harris and Moran, *Managing Cultural Differences*; A. Wolter, "Saudi Arabia and Its Culture" (unpublished manuscript, St. Norbert College, De Pere, Wisc., 1994).
19. S. Rieck and M. Ogura, "Sri Lanka: The Pearl of the Indian Ocean" (unpublished manuscript, St. Norbert College, De Pere, Wisc., 1996).
20. Archer and Silver, *A World of Gestures.*
21. M. C. Keberlein, "A Cultural Profile of the Guatemalan Ladinos" (unpublished manuscript, St. Norbert College, De Pere, Wisc., 1993).
22. K. Thao, "The Hmong Culture" (unpublished student manuscript, St. Norbert College, De Pere, Wisc., 1995).
23. A. G. Penasa, M. Peters, and S. Smits, "Jamaica: Out of Many, One People" (unpublished manuscript, St. Norbert College, De Pere, Wisc., 1996).
24. These examples are shown in Archer and Silver, *A World of Gestures.*
25. Ibid.
26. Ibid.
27. K. Thao, "The Hmong Culture."
28. Archer and Silver, *A World of Gestures.*
29. Knapp and Hall, *Nonverbal Communication in Human Interaction.*
30. Searchinger, *The Human Language Series.*
31. R. L. Birdwhistell, *Kinesics and Context: Essays on Body Motion Communication* (New York: Ballantine, 1970), p. 42.
32. C. Darwin, *The Expression of the Emotions in Man and Animals* (London: J. Murray, 1872), p. 361.
33. Searchinger, *The Human Language Series.*

34. P. Ekman, W. Friesen, M. O'Sullivan, et al., "Universals and Cultural Differences in the Judgment of Facial Expressions of Emotions," *Journal of Personality and Social Psychology,* 53 (1987), 712–717.

35. C. E. Izard, "Innate and Universal Facial Expressions: Evidence from Developmental and Cross-Cultural Research," *Psychological Bulletin,* 115 (1994), 288–299.

36. W. G. Stephan, C. W. Stephan, and M. C. De-Vargas, "Emotional Expressions in Costa Rica and the United States," *Journal of Cross-Cultural Psychology,* 27 (1996), 147–160.

37. U. Schimmack, "Cultural Influences on the Recognition of Emotion by Facial Expressions," *Journal of Cross-Cultural Psychology,* 27 (1996), 37–51.

38. D. Matsumoto, "Cultural Influences on the Perception of Emotion," *Journal of Cross-Cultural Psychology,* 20 (1989), 92–105.

39. J. Pittan, P. Kroonenberg, C. Gallois, and S. Iwawaki, "Australian and Japanese Concepts of Expressive Behavior," *Journal of Cross-Cultural Psychology,* 26 (1995), 451–464.

40. R. K. Bothwell, J. C. Brigham, and R. S. Malpass, "Cross-Racial Identification," *Personality and Psychology Bulletin,* 15 (1989), 19–25; R. S. Malpass and J. Kravitz, "Recognition for Faces of Own and Other Race," *Journal of Personality and Social Psychology,* 13 (1969), 330–354.

41. C. A. Feingold, "The Influence of Environment on Identification of Persons and Things," *Journal of Criminal Law and Police Science,* 5 (1914), 50.

42. J. C. Brigham and R. S. Malpass, "The Role of Experience and Contact in the Recognition of Faces of Own- and Other-Race Persons," *Journal of Social Issues,* 41 (1985), 139–155.

43. S. Ferman and D. R. Entwistle, "Children's Ability to Recognize Other Children's Faces," *Child Development,* 47 (1976), 506–510.

44. J. C. Brigham and P. Barkowitz, "Do 'They All Look Alike'? The Effect of Race, Sex, Experience, and Attitudes on the Ability to Recognize Faces," *Journal of Applied Social Psychology,* 8 (1978),

306–318; Malpass and Kravitz, "Recognition for Faces of Own and Other Race"; S. Teitelbaum and R. E. Geiselman, "Observer Mood and Cross-Racial Recognition of Faces," *Journal of Cross-Cultural Psychology,* 28 (1997), 93–106.

45. G. Rhodes, S. Tan, S. Brake, and K. Taylor, "Expertise and Configural Coding in Face Recognition," *British Journal of Psychology,* 80 (1989), 313–331.

46. A. Almaney and A. Alwan, *Communicating with the Arabs* (Prospect Heights, Ill.: Waveland, 1982).

47. Harris and Moran, *Managing Cultural Differences.*

48. Knapp and Hall, *Nonverbal Communication in Human Interaction.*

49. Ibid.

50. Searchinger, *The Human Language Series.*

51. Y. Hsin-Yun, "The Four Tones in Mandarin Chinese" (1998) (www.wellgot.ca/english-fm.html); "Mandarin Tones," *QI: The Journal of Traditional Eastern Health and Fitness* (www.qi-journal.com/tones.html).

52. Ibid.

53. Choi, "Cultural Profile of South Korea."

54. M. Zuckerman and K. Miyake, "The Attractive Voice: What Makes It So?" *Journal of Nonverbal Behavior,* 17 (1993), 119–135.

55. T. Hasegawa and W. B. Gudykunst, "Silence in Japan and the United States," *Journal of Cross-Cultural Psychology,* 29 (1998), 668–684.

54. C. A. Braithwaite, "Cultural Uses and Interpretations of Silence," in *The Nonverbal Communication Reader,* 2nd ed., ed. L. K. Guerrero, J. A. DeVito, and M. L. Hecht (Prospect Heights, Ill.: Waveland, 1999), pp. 163–172.

57. Bishop, "Cultural Profile, Examination of Value Orientations and Sociocultural Influences, and Verbal and Nonverbal Language Aspects of the East Indian Culture."

58. Rieck and Ogura, "Sri Lanka: The Pearl of the Indian Ocean."

59. R. C. Hesselink, R. T. Mullen, and J. M. Rouse, "Moroccan Culture: An In-Depth Study" (un-

published manuscript, St. Norbert College, De Pere, Wisc., 1996).

60. Y. Ishikawa and M. Hashimoto, "The Kenyan Culture" (unpublished student manuscript, St. Norbert College, De Pere, Wisc., 1996).

61. Wolter, "Saudi Arabia and Its Culture"; M. Argyle, *Bodily Communication* (New York: International Universities Press, 1975).

62. C. Z. Dolphin, "Variables in the Use of Personal Space in Intercultural Transactions," in *Intercultural Communication: A Reader,* 8th ed., ed. L. A. Samovar and R. E. Porter (Belmont, Calif.: Wadsworth, 1997), pp. 266–276.

63. Knapp and Hall, *Nonverbal Communication in Human Interaction.*

64. E. T. Hall, "A System for the Notation of Proxemic Behavior," *American Anthropologist,* 65 (1963), 1003–1026.

65. M. S. Kim, "A Comparative Analysis of Nonverbal Expressions as Portrayed by Korean and American Print-Media Advertising," in *Readings in Cultural Contexts,* ed. J. N. Martin, T. K. Nakayama, and L. A. Flores (Mountain View, Calif.: Mayfield, 1998), pp. 206–216.

66. E. McDaniel and P. A. Andersen, "International Patterns of Interpersonal Tactile Communication: A Field Study," *Journal of Nonverbal Behavior,* 22 (1998), 59–76.

67. S. M. Jourard, "An Exploratory Study of Body Accessibility," *British Journal of Social and Clinical Psychology,* 5 (1966), 221–231.

68. B. Casteel, "A Cross-Cultural Study of Touch Avoidance" (unpublished master's thesis, West Virginia University, cited in D. W. Klopf, *Intercultural Encounters: The Fundamentals of Intercultural Communication* (Englewood, Colo.: Morton, 1995).

69. M. S. Remland, T. S. Jones, and H. Brinkman, "Interpersonal Distance, Body Orientation, and Touch: Effects of Culture, Gender, and Age," *Journal of Social Psychology,* 135 (1995), 281–298.

70. Bishop, "Cultural Profile, Examination of Value Orientations and Sociocultural Influences, and Verbal and Nonverbal Language Aspects of the East Indian Culture."

71. Wolter, "Saudi Arabia and Its Culture."

72. Harris and Moran, *Managing Cultural Differences.*

73. Ibid.

74. B. Gibbons, "The Intimate Sense of Smell," *National Geographic,* 170 (1987), 324–361.

75. D. M. Stoddart, *The Scented Ape: The Biology and Culture of Human Odour* (Cambridge: Cambridge University Press, 1990).

76. J. V. Kohl and R. T. Francoeur, *The Scent of Eros* (New York: Continuum, 1995).

77. Ibid.

78. C. Classen, D. Howes, and A. Synnott, *Aroma: The Cultural History of Smell* (New York: Routledge, 1994).

79. A. Le Guerer, *Scent: The Mysterious and Essential Powers of Smell* (New York: Turtle Bay Books, 1992).

80. A. Synnott, "A Sociology of Smell," *Canadian Review of Sociology and Anthropology,* 28, no. 4 (1996), 437–460; D. Howes, A. Synnott, and C. Classen, "The Anthropology of Odour," in *Compendium of Olfactory Research,* ed. A. N. Gilbert (Dubuque, Iowa: Kendall-Hunt, 1995), pp. 111–116.

81. Kohl and Francoeur, *The Scent of Eros.*

82. E. Fernea and R. Fernea, "Cleanliness and Culture," in *Psychology and Culture,* ed. W. J. Lonner and R. Malpass (Boston: Allyn and Bacon, 1994), pp. 65–70.

83. Classen, Howes, and Synnott, *Aroma: A Cultural History of Smell.*

84. Gibbons, "The Intimate Sense of Smell."

85. Synnott, "A Sociology of Smell."

86. Gibbons, "The Intimate Sense of Smell."

87. R. L. Baker, *Race* (New York: Oxford University Press, 1974).

88. J. Dollard, *Caste and Class in a Southern Town* (New York: Doubleday, 1957); Classen, Howes, and Synnott, *Aroma: The Cultural History of Smell.*

89. G. Simmel, *Mélanges de philosophie relativiste*

(Paris: F. Alcon, 1912), p. 12; Classen, Howes, and Synnott, *Aroma: The Cultural History of Smell*; A. Le Guerer, *Scent: The Mysterious and Essential Powers of Smell*.

90. G. Simmel, *Mélanges de philosophie relativiste*, p. 34; Classen, Howes, and Synnott, *Aroma: The Cultural History of Smell*; A. Le Guerer, *Scent: The Mysterious and Essential Powers of Smell*.

91. This poem was cited in Classen, Howes, and Synnott, *Aroma: The Cultural History of Smell*. Four lines from "His Foul Imagination Links" from THE POEMS OF JONATHAN SWIFT, edited by Harold Williams. Copyright © 1937 Oxford University Press. Used with permission.

92. Olfactory Research Fund, "Enthusiastic Response to Website Sense of Smell Survey" (©1996–1997) (www.olfactory.org/response.html).

93. J. Todrank, D. Byrnes, A. Wrzesniewski, and P. Rozin, "Odors Can Change Preferences for People in Photographs: A Cross-Modal Evaluative Conditioning Study with Olfactory Uss and Visual Css," *Learning and Motivation*, 26 (1995), 116–140.

94. Kohl and Francoeur, *The Scent of Eros*.

95. K. Fox, *The Smell Report* (Oxford: Social Issues Research Centre, 2001).

96. Ibid.

97. Ibid.

98. Ibid.

99. K. Vandehey, C. Buerger, and K. Krueger, "Traditional Aspects and Struggles of the Masai Culture" (unpublished manuscript, St. Norbert College, De Pere, Wisc., 1996).

100. P. G. Smucker, "The Meaning of a Scarf: Turkish Students Fight to Wear Islamic Head Coverings," *US News and World Report* (March 16, 1998), 31–33.

101. Harris and Moran, *Managing Cultural Differences*; K. M. Batarfi, "Welcome to Saudi Arabia: The Land of Islam" (1998) (darkwing.uoregon.edu:80/~kbatarfi/saudi.html).

102. Harris and Moran, *Managing Cultural Differences*; "Recreational Travel Guide to India" (1993) (www.solutions.mb.ca/rec-traqvel/asia/india/india-guide.html).

103. "A History of Kimono" (www.japan.mit.edu/kimono/intro.html). This site is part of the Japanese Language and Culture Network.

104. E. T. Hall, *The Silent Language* (New York: Doubleday, 1959).

105. L. E. Doggett, "Calendars," in *Explanatory Supplement to the Astronomical Almanac*, ed. P. K. Seidelmann (Sausalito, Calif: University Science Books, 1992).

106. Ibid.

107. Ibid.

108. Hall, *The Silent Language*.

109. J. K. Burgoon, "A Communication Model of Personal Space Violations: Explication and an Initial Test," *Human Communication Research*, 4 (1978), 129–142; J. K. Burgoon and S. B. Jones, "Toward a Theory of Personal Space Expectations and Their Violations," *Human Communication Research*, 2 (1976), 131–146.

110. An excellent review of research associated with NEV can be found in J. K. Burgoon and J. L. Hale, "Nonverbal Expectancy Violations: Model Elaboration and Application to Immediacy Behaviors," *Communication Monographs*, 55 (1988), 58–79.

111. S. H. Schwartz, "Individualism-Collectivism: Critique and Proposed Refinements," *Journal of Cross-Cultural Psychology*, 21 (1990), 139–157.

112. Harris and Moran, *Managing Cultural Differences*.

113. Schwartz, "Individualism-Collectivism."

114. W. B. Gudykunst, ed., *Intercultural Communication Theory: Current Perspectives* (Beverly Hills, Calif.: Sage, 1983).

Developing Intercultural Relationships

> *Without others, there is no self.*
>
> —Kenneth J. Gergen[1]

CHAPTER OBJECTIVES

After reading this chapter, you should be able to:

- Recount the fundamental assumptions of the Uncertainty Reduction Theory.
- Discuss the relationship between uncertainty reduction and intercultural communication apprehension.
- Identify assertive and responsive sociocommunicative styles.
- Define relational empathy and third-culture building.
- Compare ratings of relational intimacy across cultures.
- Describe differences in relationships between Eastern and Western cultures.
- Compare marital types across cultures.
- Compare divorce rates across cultures.

I nitiating and maintaining relationships with others is one of the most necessary and challenging functions of human survival. Our self-concept and self-esteem are sustained largely by the substance of our relationships with others. From our relational partners we receive feedback that we use to assess ourselves. In essence, the only way we know ourselves is through our relationships with others. Our existence is relative to other people. Take a moment and think of three terms that describe you. Perhaps you see yourself as a good student, a loyal good friend, and a fast runner. How do you know that these descriptions are accurate? For example, if you describe yourself as a "good student," the only way you know that is because of your relationships with teachers who have provided you with feedback. If you describe yourself as a "fast runner," the only way you know that is by comparing your running with that of other runners. You can describe yourself only in relation to others. A person cannot be tall unless someone else is short. A person cannot be fast unless someone else is slow. As the quote at the beginning of the chapter states, without others, there is no self.

Regardless of one's cultural origins, relationships provide the substance of life. Several variables affect the initiation and maintenance of personal relationships. Much of our communication behavior during the first stage of a relationship is designed to reduce uncertainty about our relational partner. One factor that affects our ability to do that is the degree to which we experience intercultural communication apprehension. Another variable that affects the uncertainty process is our sociocommunicative style—that is, the extent to which we are assertive and responsive with our relational partners. Two other variables that impact our relations with others are the degree to which we can empathize with others and how similar we perceive ourselves to be to others. Uncertainty reduction, intercultural communication apprehension, sociocommunicative style, empathy, and similarity are experienced differently by each interactant in a relationship. The relationship established by any two people is the result of a complex combination of these factors, as is depicted in Figure 9-1.

FIGURE 9-1   Factors That Affect Relationships

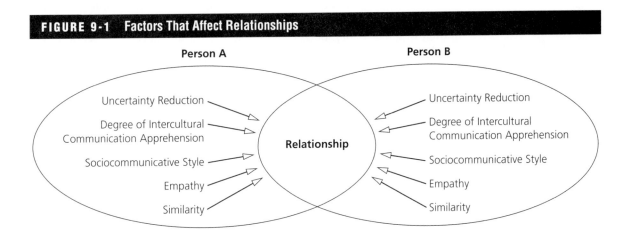

This chapter explores a variety of topics associated with relationships. The first section deals with uncertainty reduction and factors that affect how people go about reducing uncertainty, including intercultural communication apprehension and sociocommunicative style. The next part of the chapter focuses on empathy, third-culture building, and similarity. The third part of the chapter examines how perceptions about relationships vary across cultures, with particular emphasis on how relationships are perceived in Eastern and Western cultures. The final part of the chapter looks at marital relationships, including mate selection across cultures, arranged marriages, and divorce.

Communication and Uncertainty

All relationships must begin somewhere. The people with whom we are now intimate were at one time strangers. Initiating communication with a stranger, particularly a person from a different culture, can be frightening. Many people experience anxiety when interacting with others for the first time. Moreover, interacting with a person from a different culture may be even more anxiety producing. In an attempt to explain our communication behavior during initial communication encounters with others, Charles Berger and Richard Calabrese have developed a communication theory called the Uncertainty Reduction Theory (URT). The major premise of this theory is that when strangers first meet, their primary goal is to reduce uncertainty and increase predictability in their own and the other person's behavior.[2] According to the theory, uncertainty can be both a proactive and a retroactive process. That is, we can experience and reduce uncertainty both before and after interacting with someone. We can proactively reduce uncertainty when we weigh alternative behavioral options prior to interacting with another. We try to figure out ways the other might interact and then select our own communication strategies on the basis of this prediction. For example, if you are about to interact with a person from a different culture, you might anticipate that the other person does not speak English and adjust your speech accordingly. Retroactively, uncertainty is reduced by attempting to explain behavior after it has been enacted. For example, having interacted with a South Korean, we may be able to explain why the person did not engage in direct eye contact.

In their original theory, Berger and Calabrese posited seven axioms outlining the fundamental assumptions of their theory (see the next page).

Although people in any culture seek to reduce uncertainty, Berger and Calabrese's seven axioms are based on communication patterns of people in the United States and may not be generalizable across cultures. Many researchers believe that the verbal and nonverbal communication strategies people use to reduce uncertainty vary from culture to culture. For example, William Gudykunst and his associates have begun a research program investigating cross-cultural differences in uncertainty reduction communication. Gudykunst maintains that people may be more motivated to reduce uncertainty during initial intercultural communication than during communication with someone who is familiar.[3] Gudykunst argues that several factors may influence the amount of uncertainty

The Seven Axioms of Uncertainty Reduction Theory

Axiom 1: Given the high level of uncertainty present at the onset of the entry phase, as the amount of verbal communication between strangers increases, the level of uncertainty for each interactant in the relationship will decrease. As uncertainty is further reduced, the amount of verbal communication will increase.

Axiom 2: As nonverbal affiliative expressiveness increases, uncertainty levels will decrease in an initial interaction situation. In addition, decreases in uncertainty level will cause increases in nonverbal affiliative expressiveness.

Axiom 3: High levels of uncertainty cause increases in information-seeking behavior. As uncertainty levels decline, information-seeking behavior decreases.

Axiom 4: High levels of uncertainty in a relationship cause decreases in the intimacy level of communication content. Low levels of uncertainty produce high levels of intimacy.

Axiom 5: High levels of uncertainty produce high rates of reciprocity. Low levels of uncertainty produce low reciprocity rates.

Axiom 6: Similarities between persons reduce uncertainty, whereas dissimilarities produce increases in uncertainty.

Axiom 7: Increases in uncertainty level produce decreases in liking; decreases in uncertainty level produce increases in liking.

SOURCE: C. R. Berger and R. J. Calabrese, "Some Explorations in Initial Interaction and Beyond: Toward a Developmental Theory of Interpersonal Communication," *Human Communication Research*, 1 (1975), 99–112. Used by permission of International Communication Association and Charles R. Berger.

experienced by people during an intercultural encounter, including the interactants' expectations about communicating, individual social identities, the degree of similarity between interactants, shared communication networks, and the interpersonal salience of the contact with strangers. For example, Gudykunst points out that like others, people from high-context cultures try to reduce uncertainty in initial encounters, but the nature of the information they seek seems to be different than that sought by persons from low-context cultures. Because much of the information resides in the context as opposed to the individual, persons from high-context cultures are more cautious concerning what they talk about with strangers. In addition, certain types of information are more important sources of uncertainty to persons in high-context cultures than to people in low-context cultures, including the other's social background, knowing whether others will behave in a socially appropriate manner, knowing that others understand individuals' feelings, knowing what others mean when they communicate, and knowing whether others will make allowances for individuals when they communicate.[4] So when interacting together for the first time, people from high- and low-context cultures are each trying to reduce uncertainty, but they use different kinds of communication. The low-context person asks a lot of questions, whereas the high-context person focuses on nonverbal aspects.

Axioms 1 and 2 deal with the quantity of verbal and nonverbal communication and its effect on uncertainty—that is, as communication increases, uncertainty decreases. Gudykunst and Nishida found that the frequency of communication predicts uncertainty reduction in individualistic low-context cultures but not in collectivistic high-context cultures.[5] In axiom 2, "nonverbal affiliative expressiveness" refers to nonverbal behaviors that reduce the physiological and psychological distance between interactants. In the United States, eye contact, pleasantness of vocal expressions, affirmative head nods, head and arm gestures per minute, and closer physical distance between interactants are considered affiliative. In other cultures, these same behaviors may actually increase uncertainty and anxiety. In South Korea, for example, children and people of lower status do not engage in direct eye contact with parents or people of higher status because to do so communicates a challenge. Sanders and Wiseman found that positive nonverbal expressiveness predicts uncertainty reduction for whites, Hispanics, and Asian-Americans, but not for African Americans.[6] These studies indicate that the specific nonverbal behaviors that constitute affiliative expressiveness may vary across cultures.

Axiom 3 is closely related to the first two insofar as information-seeking behavior is defined as the number of questions asked by each interactant. In the United States, people seek information from others by asking questions. In other cultures, particularly high-context cultures, people may seek information through nonverbal means, perhaps through silence or by observing the other's cultural and sociorelational background. In fact, Gudykunst, Sodetani, and Sonoda suggest that question asking as a form of uncertainty reduction may be limited to whites.[7]

Axiom 4 refers not to the quantity of communication, as in the case of the preceding axioms, but to the quality of communication. In this case, the lower the level of uncertainty, the more intimate the communication. Intimate communication may be defined as interaction based on issues related to the interactants' attitudes, beliefs, motivations, and dispositions. There is limited cross-cultural research in this area.

Axiom 5 deals with the concept of communication reciprocity, or the mutual exchange of information between interactants. Berger and Calabrese contend that at early stages in a relationship, the interactants are compelled to ask for and give the same kinds of information at the same rate so that neither person gains information power over the other. As the relationship develops, and uncertainty is reduced, there is less felt need to reciprocate since the interactants are more com-

Self-Assessment 9-1

Assessing Attributional Confidence

Please answer the following questions with respect to your ability to predict selected aspects of the behavior of the person with whom you have just interacted. Answer each question using a scale from zero (0) to one hundred (100). If you have to make a total guess about the person's behavior or feelings, you should answer "0"; if you have total certainty about the other person's behavior, your answer should be "100." Feel free to use any number between 0 and 100.

1. How confident are you in your general ability to predict how he or she will behave? _____ %

2. How confident are you that he or she likes you? _____ %

3. How accurate are you at predicting his or her attitudes? _____ %

4. How accurate are you at predicting the values he or she holds? _____ %

5. How well can you predict his or her feelings? _____ %

6. How much can you empathize with (share) the way he or she feels about himself or herself? _____ %

7. How well do you know him or her? _____ %

8. How certain are you of his or her background? _____ %

9. How certain are you that he or she will behave in a socially appropriate way when this is important? _____ %

10. How certain are you that he or she can understand your feelings when you do not verbally express them? _____ %

11. How certain are you that you understand what this person means when you communicate? _____ %

12. How confident are you that this person will make allowances for you when you communicate? _____ %

SCORING: Sum the percentages and divide by 12. This is your average confidence level, by which comparisons with others can be made.

SOURCE: "Attributional Confidence Items" from W. B. Gudykunst and T. Nishida, "Attributional Confidence in Low- and High-Context Cultures," *Human Communication Research*, Vol. 12 (1986), 525–549. Copyright © 1986 International Communication Association. Reprinted by permission of the publisher.

fortable with the relationship.[8] To date, there is little or no cross-cultural research that has examined this hypothesis outside the United States.

Axiom 6 centers around the notion of similarity. Berger and Calabrese argue that as similarity between interactants increases, uncertainty decreases. Likewise, the more dissimilarity, the more uncertainty. Berger and Calabrese assert that knowledge of dissimilar attitudes leads to a greater number of attributions about why another may hold such attitudes, thus increasing uncertainty about the other.[9] Cross-cultural research about Germany, Norway, Canada, and Japan seems to validate this axiom. There are a number of ways people can be similar to one another. Two people may share race, language, age, sex, or occupation. Linguistic similarity is of particular importance here. Uncertainty can be very difficult to reduce if two people speak different languages and have little knowledge of the other's linguistic code.[10]

Finally, axiom 7 focuses on the concept of liking. This axiom is based on research that indicates a positive relationship between similarity and liking—that is, the more similar two people are, the more they tend to like each other. Thus, if similarity decreases uncertainty, it is likely to increase liking simultaneously. The research on this axiom, even within the United States, is mixed. In some cases, the more we know about another, the less we may like the person.

In many of the communication studies reported above, uncertainty is assessed using some form of variation of an instrument called the CL7 (a seven-item scale designed to measure "confidence level"—hence, CL7).[11] The scale is designed to assess the degree of attributional confidence (that is, how much uncertainty) a person has about another person after initial interactions. In a typical cross-cultural communication study, participants are asked to interact with (or think about) someone from another culture and then complete the CL7 instrument. Other variables play a role in many of these studies. For example, people from high- and low-context cultures might be asked to interact for a few minutes, then complete the CL7. Researchers then compare the scores on the CL7 across the two cultures. Other researchers may have participants from individualistic and collectivistic cultures engage in certain types of uncertainty reduction behaviors (for example, nonverbal affiliative gestures or verbal information seeking) to see how CL7 scores are affected. There are a variety of ways in which this scale can be used in cross-cultural communication research. Think about the last time you interacted with someone for the first time; then complete the attributional confidence assessment in Self-Assessment 9-1 (see page 279). The scale is designed to assess how much uncertainty you experienced during that initial encounter.

UNCERTAINTY REDUCTION AND INTERCULTURAL COMMUNICATION APPREHENSION

As mentioned above, persons from different cultures reduce uncertainty during initial interaction in various ways. One factor that may affect how persons reduce uncertainty is whether they experience intercultural communication apprehension. Communication researchers Jim Neuliep and Dan Ryan investigated the relationship between intercultural communication apprehension and uncertainty reduction during initial cross-cultural interaction. Imagine that you have just been introduced to someone from a different culture. You have never met this person before and know very little about his or her culture. Chances are good that you will experience a bit of anxiety and apprehension. This is a very common response, and you need not feel bad about yourself for having felt it. Neuliep and Ryan argue that because intercultural communication is loaded with novelty and dissimilarity, people may experience inordinate amounts of anxiety, which inhibit the ability to reduce uncertainty.[12] For example, Gudykunst argues that competent intercultural communication is partly based on the ability to manage anxiety and uncertainty.[13] Mark Leary argues that anxiety is typically experienced as an unpleasant emotional state marked by feelings of tension, apprehension, and worry regarding potentially negative outcomes.[14] Many people, regardless of culture, experience anxiety when communicating, or when they anticipate communicating, with persons from different cultures or ethnic groups. Often we tend to avoid situations that make us feel anxious. In this case, if intercultural communication causes us to feel anxious, we may avoid initiating interaction with people from different cultures. However, unless we interact, we cannot reduce much uncertainty, and therefore our anxiety levels remain high.

Gudykunst and Kim suggest that all of us experience maximum and minimum tolerance levels of uncertainty. If uncertainty is above our maximum tolerance level, we may feel uncomfortable communicating. For example, assume that you have just been introduced to a person who is from a culture that you have never heard of and who speaks a language of which you know nothing. In such a situation you may not be able to predict how this person will behave. Uncertainty is very high, and you may feel uncomfortable. On the other hand, if uncertainty is below your minimum tolerance level, you may find the interaction dull and uninteresting. Believe it or not, most of us like at least a little uncertainty to make the communication refreshing.

Uncertainty and anxiety are related: as uncertainty increases, so does anxiety. As with uncertainty, you have maximum and minimum thresholds for anxiety. When anxiety is above your maximum tolerance level, you will experience so much anxiety that you may even avoid interacting with others or withdraw from communication. When anxiety is below your minimum level, you may feel unmotivated to reduce uncertainty. In such cases, predictability may be high. You probably communicate most effectively when your level of anxiety is somewhere between your maximum and minimum thresholds.[15]

Berger and Calabrese maintain that the principal way people reduce uncertainty during initial interaction is through verbal and nonverbal communication.[16] To the extent that people can reduce uncertainty and anxiety during communication, they can increase their communication effectiveness. In their study, Neuliep and Ryan found a direct relationship between intercultural communication apprehension (ICA) and uncertainty reduction. Specifically, they found that during initial intercultural communication, people who experienced high ICA also experienced high uncertainty. Neuliep and Ryan reasoned that because persons with high ICA may avoid or withdraw from communication with persons from different cultures, they are less likely to engage in communication tactics that reduce uncertainty. Persons who generally do not experience apprehension interacting with persons from other cultures communicate comfortably, thereby facilitating uncertainty reduction. A lesson here is that by increasing our interaction with persons from different cultures we can reduce our uncertainty about them and reduce our anxiety. In fact, in related research Neuliep and Grohskopf found that as individuals reduce uncertainty, their satisfaction with communication increases. Hence, by engaging in intercultural communication, we can reduce uncertainty, which will reduce anxiety, and result in more satisfying communication with others. It is a "win-win" situation![17]

Although an individual may be faced with large amounts of uncertainty and anxiety during initial intercultural communication, Neuliep and Ryan reasoned that the person's communication style may enable him or her to effectively reduce uncertainty. Jim McCroskey and Virginia Richmond have outlined two types of *communication style,* what they call sociocommunication orientation, that affect how one communicates in different situations: (1) *assertiveness* and (2) *responsiveness.*[18] Assertiveness refers to one's ability to make requests, actively disagree, express positive or negative personal rights and feelings, initiate, sustain, and terminate conversations, and defend oneself without attacking others. Responsiveness refers to one's ability to be sensitive to the communication of others, be a good listener, engage in comforting communication, and recognize the needs and wants of relevant others. McCroskey and Richmond note that assertiveness and responsiveness are inversely related to communication apprehension. In other words, persons high in communication apprehension are not likely to engage in assertive or responsive communication behaviors. Because apprehensive persons tend to avoid communication, they are not likely to initiate conversation or advance their position on a topic of communication during a conversation.[19] Likewise, a responsive communicator is one who invites others to engage in conversation. In their research, Neuliep and Ryan argued that these tendencies may be highlighted during initial intercultural interaction, in which situational novelty, unfamiliarity, and dissimilarity are prominent. Indeed, in their study, Neuliep and Ryan found that people who were assertive and responsive reported experiencing less intercultural communication apprehension.[20]

Neuliep and Ryan contend that the fundamental components of assertiveness and responsiveness are consistent with those behaviors associated with reduced uncertainty. For example, a characteristic of assertiveness is the ability to make requests. In axiom 3, Berger and Calabrese point out that as information-seeking behavior (question asking) increases, uncertainty decreases. In addition, assertiveness is associated with initiation and maintenance of conversations. In axiom 1, Berger and Calabrese maintain that as verbal communication increases, uncertainty decreases. Responsive communicators invite others to interact, thus increasing verbal communication. Likewise, responsive communicators are nonverbally sensitive to others. Responsiveness is communicated through eye contact, smiling, forward leaning, and touching. Axiom 2 states that as nonverbal affiliative expressiveness increases, uncertainty decreases. From the association of assertiveness and responsiveness with behaviors designed to reduce uncertainty, Neuliep and Ryan predicted that assertive and responsive communicators may be better able to reduce uncertainty. Their results supported their prediction. Persons scoring

Intercultural Conversation

Intercultural Conversation: Uncertainty Reduction and Sociocommunicative Style

In the following intercultural conversations, we see how an individual's sociocommunicative style affects uncertainty reduction during initial intercultural communication. In the first conversation, we see Dan, who is from the United States, interacting with Natasha, who is from Ukraine. Dan seems unassertive and unresponsive. In the second conversation, we see Jim, who is from the United States, interacting with Foday, who is from Sierra Leone. In comparison to Dan, Jim seems assertive and responsive. Jim's assertiveness and responsiveness help him reduce uncertainty about Foday and Sierra Leone.

Natasha: Hi, I'm Natasha.
Dan: Oh, hi.
Natasha: What's your name?
Dan: Dan.
Natasha: Hi, Dan.
Dan: Hi.
Natasha: I'm not from here. I'm from Ukraine.
Dan: Oh.
Natasha: You've heard of it?
Dan: Ah, yeah, I think so.
Natasha: Ukraine is in Eastern Europe, between Poland and Russia.
Dan: Oh.
Natasha: Yeah. Have you ever been to Europe?
Dan: Yeah, but I was pretty young.
Natasha: It must have been quite an experience, though.
Dan: Ah . . . do you know what time it is?
Natasha: It's about 3 o'clock.
Dan: I have to go now. Bye.
Natasha: Bye, Dan, nice meeting you.

Jim: Hi, I'm Jim. I don't believe we've met.
Foday: Hello, Jim, I'm Foday.
Jim: Hi, Foday, where are you from?
Foday: I'm from Sierra Leone.

Jim: Oh really? Where is Sierra Leone? I know it's on the African continent, but I'm not sure where.
Foday: It's on the western coast between Guinea and Liberia.
Jim: Oh, toward the north? How big is it?
Foday: Yes, that's right. We're about the size of your South Carolina.
Jim: That's interesting. What kind of government do you have in Sierra Leone?
Foday: We have a constitutional democracy.
Jim: Is that based on English law?
Foday: Yes.
Jim: Who's the president, and how long a term does he serve?
Foday: His name is Ahmad Tejan Kabbah. He is elected for a five-year term.
Jim: Oh yeah . . . I think I've heard of him. By the way, you speak English very well. Is that your official language?
Foday: English is the official language of my country, but it is only spoken by a literate minority of about 20 percent of the population.
Jim: Really? What language does the other 80 percent speak?
Foday: People in the north speak a vernacular language called Temme, while those in the south speak Mende.
Jim: That's fascinating. I suspect that most citizens are Muslim?
Foday: About 60 percent are Muslim, with about 20 percent Christian. The other 20 percent or so vary.
Jim: I understand that mining is a major industry in Sierra Leone. I hear you mine diamonds.
Foday: Yes, they are a big export. But many people live by simple subsistence farming like my father.

—Continued

Jim: Foday, it has been really nice meeting you. I'd like to introduce you to my wife. She's over there.

Foday: Thank you, I'd like to meet her.

In comparing the two conversations, notice how much more uncertainty Jim reduces in his short conversation with Foday than Dan does with Natasha. Jim is assertive in initiating conversation with Foday and asking him questions about his country. Jim also appears responsive to Foday, using such comments as "That's interesting." Dan, on the other hand, says very little, even when prompted by Natasha. Natasha is probably more uncertain about Dan after the conversation than before. His lack of assertiveness and responsiveness probably leaves a negative impression with her.

high on assertiveness and responsiveness instruments reported experiencing less uncertainty during initial cross-cultural interaction.[21]

ASSESSING SOCIOCOMMUNICATIVE ORIENTATION/STYLE

In their study of uncertainty reduction during initial intercultural communication, Neuliep and Ryan measured assertiveness and responsiveness using scales developed by McCroskey and Richmond (see Self-Assessment 9-2 on the next page). These scales have been used successfully in other cultures, including China, Finland, Japan, Korea, and Russia. Note, however, that these scales were designed to measure assertiveness and responsiveness as defined in the United States and may not be generalizable across all cultures. In fact, studies examining assertiveness and responsiveness across cultures have reported differences. American men and women, for example, score higher on the assertiveness dimension than Finnish and Japanese men and women. Generally, American women score higher on the responsiveness scale than men and women from other cultures. Within most cultures, however, men generally score higher on the assertiveness scale, whereas women score higher on the responsiveness scale.[22]

Empathy and Similarity in Relationship Development

The majority of uncertainty reduction occurs during the initial stages of a relationship. To the extent that relational partners are able to reduce uncertainty, they learn more about each other and can further develop their relationship. Two factors (among others) that have a significant influence on communication and relational development are empathy and similarity. Empathy and similarity are important in any relationship, but they take on added importance in intercultural relationships. Due to their cultural differences, persons in intercultural relationships may find it difficult to empathize with their relational partners because they are dissimilar.

Self-Assessment 9-2

Assessing Sociocommunicative Orientation/Style

The following questionnaire lists twenty personality traits. Indicate the degree to which you believe each of these characteristics applies to you, as you normally communicate with others, by marking whether you (5) strongly agree that it applies, (4) agree that it applies, (3) are undecided, (2) disagree that it applies, or (1) strongly disagree that it applies. There are no right or wrong answers. Work quickly; record your first impression.

1. _____ Helpful

2. _____ Defends own beliefs

3. _____ Independent

4. _____ Responsive to others

5. _____ Forceful

6. _____ Has strong personality

7. _____ Sympathetic

8. _____ Compassionate

9. _____ Assertive

10. _____ Sensitive to the needs of others

11. _____ Dominant

12. _____ Sincere

13. _____ Gentle

14. _____ Willing to take a stand

15. _____ Warm

16. _____ Tender

17. _____ Friendly

18. _____ Acts as a leader

19. _____ Aggressive

20. _____ Competitive

SCORING: Items 2, 3, 5, 6, 9, 11, 14, 18, 19, and 20 measure assertiveness. Add the scores on these items to get your assertiveness score. Scores above 40 indicate that

—Continued

you see yourself as assertive. Items 1, 4, 7, 8, 10, 12, 13, 15, 16, and 17 measure responsiveness. Add the scores on these items to get your responsiveness score. Scores above 40 suggest that you see yourself as responsive. Being assertive and responsive is not necessarily "good" or "bad." Your sociocommunicative style is a barometer of how you interact with others, not whether you are a good or bad person.

Empathy

As uncertainty is reduced, people get to know each other more and can work on developing their relationship. The ability to empathize with someone is a crucial ingredient in any relationship. Empathy takes on added importance in intercultural relationships, however. Because persons from other cultures are different from us, it may be difficult for us to empathize with them, their ideas, and their style of communication. In these types of relationships, reducing uncertainty becomes essential. In fact, some communication scholars maintain that empathy may be impossible in intercultural communication. However, in general, communication scholars believe that because empathy motivates communication behavior, it is an essential ingredient in effective interpersonal communication.[23]

Empathy is often defined as the degree to which we can accurately infer another's thoughts or feelings. Benjamin Broome contends that this definition is inadequate for the study of intercultural communication and offers what he calls a model of *relational empathy* (see Figure 9-2).[24] Broome argues that because our thoughts and perceptions are based on our unique personal, cultural, sociocultural, and individual past experiences, we can never completely comprehend or directly know what another is thinking or feeling. As Broome argues, "While we can never become another person, it is possible to erect a structure within the framework of which the other's interpretation of the world or us takes shape or assumes meaning."[25] The model of relational empathy is based on the idea that whenever two people come together and interact, they create a *third culture* of shared meaning and relational empathy.[26] Broome argues that mutual understanding and shared meaning are a product of the meeting between individuals. Relational empathy is conceptualized not as the ability to accurately reproduce another's perceptions or emotions, but rather that which is created by two people interacting. This third culture of relational empathy and shared meaning is the outcome or harmonization of communication in which unique values, beliefs, norms, and symbols are shared by the interactants. Broome asserts that the third culture emerges when the interactants are open and willing to communicate with others and expose themselves to new meanings.

FIGURE 9-2   Model of Relational Empathy

Third Culture

Shared Meaning and
Relational Empathy

- Interdependent Meaning
- Interdependent Worldview
- Interdependent Interpretations
- Interdependent Reality

Messages   *Messages*

Person from Culture A   **Person from Culture B**

- Objective and Subjective Meanings   - Objective and Subjective Meanings
- Worldview   - Worldview
- Interpretation   - Interpretation

Approximation of Reality   Approximation of Reality

SOURCE: *This model is based on a combination of Broome's ideas and F. L. Casmir, "Third Culture Building: A Paradigm Shift for International and Intercultural Communication," in* Communication Yearbook, *ed. S. A. Deetz (Newbury Park, Calif.: Sage, 1993), vol. 16, pp. 407–428.*

According to the model, persons cannot possess direct, firsthand knowledge of the emotional states or cognitive processes of another person. Instead, people possess objective and subjective meanings. Objective meaning, according to Broome, is one's interpretation of one's own personal experiences to oneself. For example, your interpretation of what it meant to grow up in your hometown with your family is a part of your own objective meaning. Subjective meaning, on the other hand, is one's interpretation of the other person's experiences in relation to one's own. For example, a friend's description of what it meant to grow up in his or her hometown and of his or her family experiences would be a part of your subjective meaning.

When two people come together and interact, a product of the third culture is interdependent meaning—that is, new meaning based on the combining of each individual's objective and subjective meanings. People also bring with them a personal worldview largely based on cultural orientation. Hence, a Japanese person brings a collectivistic, high-context worldview, and an American brings an individualistic, low-context worldview. In a relationship, these two different worldviews merge into an interdependent worldview. Because of the individuals' objective

Through intercultural communication, people can develop a third culture of relational empathy.
(D. Wells/Image Works)

and subjective knowledge and worldviews, they have different interpretations of what is real. Through the establishment of relational empathy, an interdependent interpretation and approximation of reality materializes.

Broome asserts that similarity among individuals is not necessary to achieve relational empathy and shared meaning. Instead, Broome's model assumes that the emergence of a third culture creates a medium in which the interactants can relate and one in which similarity becomes moot. Because a third culture has evolved through the verbal and nonverbal messages of the interactants, each is an active participant in its creation. Hence, neither person has to re-create anything since each is an integral part of its existence.[27]

Intercultural researcher Donald Klopf maintains that we can approach empathy with others by developing empathic listening skills. Empathic listening means listening more to the meanings than to the words of another person. According to Klopf, empathic listening involves (1) *paraphrasing*, the rewording of what the other person has said; (2) *reflecting feelings*, relating back to the other the feelings we believe the other is experiencing, (3) *reflecting meanings*, the restating of what we heard to confirm its meaning, and (4) *summarizing*, briefly restating the major topics the other has communicated.[28]

Although complete empathy cannot be experienced by anyone, taking Broome's model of relational empathy and Klopf's prescription for empathic listening into account and practice, we can develop and enhance our relationships with persons from cultures different from our own.

Similarity

Although Broome's model of relational empathy discounts the importance of similarity, a great deal of research (mostly conducted in the United States) has demonstrated that similarity plays a key role in the establishment and development of relationships. As communication researcher Steve Duck states, "All communication and all relationships are likewise founded on a necessary base of similarity of understanding or similarity of meaning that facilitates the development of each."[29] This topic is important for communication researchers because of the belief that we are attracted to those people we perceive as similar to ourselves. Intercultural researchers have found that the more we perceive another as similar to ourselves, the more we are able to reduce uncertainty about the person and to form accurate categories of him or her. Thus similarity may be particularly important during initial encounters with another person.

One of the pioneers in the study of similarity is Donn Byrne. Though similarity may come in many forms, Byrne's efforts have focused mainly on attitude similarity and attraction. Byrne's fundamental postulate is that attitude similarity between persons leads to positive affect, which in turn leads to attraction (see Figure 9-3).[30] Byrne has become well known for his "bogus stranger" experiments, which have relevance for intercultural communication. In these experiments, Byrne asks research participants to indicate their attitudes on a variety of topics and issues. The participants are then paired with a "stranger," who is portrayed as a research participant whose attitudes on the same topics and issues were assessed at an earlier time. Prior to the pairing of the research participants and the stranger, the research participants are shown the stranger's attitude responses. In actuality, however, the stranger is "bogus" because his or her attitude responses are manufactured to

FIGURE 9-3 Relationship Between Attitudinal Similarity and Attraction

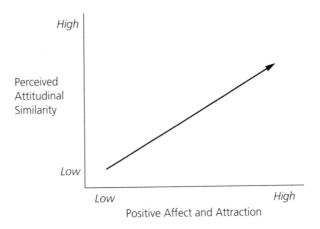

either match or conflict with the research participants' attitude responses. After interacting with the stranger, the research participants then rate the stranger's level of attractiveness. Consistently, those research participants paired with an attitudinally similar stranger provide higher attractiveness ratings than those paired with an attitudinally dissimilar stranger. Yet in each case, the stranger is the same person.[31]

Attitude similarity is only one way in which people label themselves as like or unlike others. A white student once commented that similarity was not a factor in her relationship with her boyfriend, explaining that her boyfriend was black. Upon further questioning, it was discovered that she and her boyfriend were the same age, were studying at the same college, were pursuing the same major, enjoyed similar tastes in music and food, and had very similar attitudes on a variety of topics. The point here is that although we may have dissimilarities with others, the people with whom we develop and maintain interpersonal relationships are typically very much like ourselves. Perceived similarity is perhaps the most dominant force in our motivations to interact with others. But similarity can come in many shapes and sizes. We can be similar to others culturally, attitudinally, linguistically, racially, behaviorally, affectively, and/or physically. The more we find ourselves like someone else, the more likely we are to initiate and sustain communication with that person. Although it facilitates interaction and attraction, cultural similarity (which is only one kind of similarity) may not be a necessary ingredient in forming meaningful and lasting relationships. Two persons from radically different cultures may find a great deal of similarity with each other.

Perceptions of Relational Intimacy Across Cultures

Although the same types of relationships exist across cultures, the level of intimacy varies considerably. In other words, what it means to be a student in your culture is probably not the same as what it means to be a student in another culture. Moreover, the relationship between student and teacher varies widely across cultures. In the United States, for example, student/teacher relationships at the college level might be perceived as relatively informal and personal compared with student/teacher relationships in China or Korea. William Gudykunst and Tsukasa Nishida studied the influence of culture on perceptions of intimacy and communication behavior in the United States and Japan.[32] In each culture, students were asked to rate the level of intimacy (on a scale of 1 to 9, where 1 = intimate, 9 = nonintimate) for thirty different relationships. Gudykunst and Nishida reasoned that because of their collectivistic tendencies, the Japanese students would perceive in-group relationships as more intimate than would the American students, who are individualistic. Gudykunst and Nishida also maintained that because Japan is considered a masculine-oriented culture in which sex roles are clearly differentiated, male/female relationships (lover, spouse, boy/girlfriend) would be perceived as less intimate than in the United States. Gudykunst and

Nishida argue that in cultures such as Japan, where sex roles are strictly distinguished, there is not much informal interaction between males and females. Moreover, when interaction does occur, assert Gudykunst and Nishida, the content of it is relatively superficial. The results of their survey are shown in Table 9-1.

TABLE 9-1 Perception of Relational Intimacy in the United States and Japan		
Relationship Type	U.S.	Japan
Family		
Spouse (*haigusha*)	1.33	4.32
Father (*chichioya*)	2.75	2.57
Mother (*hahaoya*)	2.35	2.06
Son (*musuko*)	2.59	4.76
Daughter (*musume*)	2.55	4.87
Brother (*kyodai*)	3.12	3.51
Sister (*shimai*)	2.88	3.78
Aunt (*oba*)	4.53	4.99
Cousin (*itoko*)	4.67	4.66
Grandparent (*sofubo*)	3.75	4.15
Uncle (*oji*)	4.55	5.21
Social		
Fiancé (*konyakusha*)	1.29	4.32
Lover (*koibito*)	1.25	2.81
Boy/Girlfriend (*otoko/onna tomodachi*)	1.70	3.32
Best friend (*ichiban no shinyu*)	2.51	1.73
Mate (*tsureai*)	1.75	4.45
Steady (*kosai shiteiru hito*)	2.27	2.92
Close friend (*shinyu*)	2.85	1.83
Friend (*tomo*)	3.67	3.42
Date (*detonoaite*)	4.02	3.48
Companion (*tomodachi*)	3.08	3.05
Neighbor (*kinjo no hito*)	5.72	5.92
Acquaintance (*chijin*)	6.79	4.95

—Continued

TABLE 9-1 Perception of Relational Intimacy in the United States and Japan (continued)		
Relationship Type	**U.S.**	**Japan**
Professional/Work		
Cohort (*nakama*)	5.40	2.85
Coworker (*shigato-makama*)	5.76	5.27
Employer (*koyosha*)	6.39	6.86
Colleague (*doryo*)	5.33	4.76
Roommate (*doshukusha*)	3.85	4.88
Classmate (*dokyusei*)	5.72	3.84
Other		
Stranger (*shiranai hito*)	8.35	7.99

SOURCE: *"Perceived Intimacy Ratios"* from W. B. Gudykunst and T. Nishida, *"The Influence of Cultural Variability on Perceptions of Communication Behavior Associated with Relationship Terms,"* Human Communication Research, *Vol. 13 (1986), 147–166. Copyright © 1986 International Communication Association. Reprinted by permission of the publisher.*

When comparing the ratings, American students are often surprised to see that Japanese rate close friend and best friend as the most intimate of their relationships. In Japan, even classmates are rated as more intimate than spouses. These results confirm the notion that when you travel to cultures different from your own, your relationships in that culture (as student, friend, employee) could be perceived very differently than when you occupy the same role in the United States.

EASTERN AND WESTERN CULTURES AND RELATIONSHIPS

As demonstrated by Gudykunst and Nishida, perceptions of relationships differ widely across cultures. In individualistic cultures such as the United States, relationships are typically viewed from the perspective of the self. As June Ock Yum asserts, individualists see themselves as distinct individuals who participate in relationships to maximize their own self-interests.[33] In many collectivistic cultures, like China, relationships are guided by Confucianism. According to Yum, the fundamental theme of Confucianism is that proper relationships form the cornerstone of society. Moreover, an individual's conduct in society should be guided by four principles: (1) *humanism:* treating others as one wishes to be treated; (2) *faithfulness:* loyalty rather than personal interest or profit; (3) *propriety:* social decorum and etiquette; and (4) *wisdom.*[34] Yum points out that three of these four principles have direct implications for how relationships are perceived in East Asian cultures like China, as compared with Western cultures like the United States. First, in contrasting Eastern and Western relationships, Yum alleges that many East Asian cultures practice *particularism*—that is, the belief that there are particular or unique rules and guidelines that apply to each individual relationship. Relational partners are to be sensitive to differences in such things as status when interacting with others. Most East Asian cultures believe in strict and well-defined social hierarchies in which people are perceived as higher or lower. In contrast, persons in Western cultures practice what Yum calls a *universalistic orientation* to relationships. Yum alleges that most Westerners try to treat others as equally as possible, regardless of status or intimacy level of the partners.[35]

Yum also contends that relational partners in Eastern cultures engage in *long-term and asymmetrical reciprocity*. You may recall from Chapter 3 that reciprocity refers to the give and take or mutual exchange in interpersonal encounters. According to Yum, in Confucian philosophy, dependency on others is an inevitable and accepted part of relations with others. People will always be indebted to others who help or assist them in some way. Yum states that "under this system of reciprocity, the individual does not calculate what he or she gives and receives. To calculate would be to think about immediate personal profits, which is the opposite of the principle of faithfulness."[36] Western relationships, on the other hand, are characterized by short-term and symmetrical reciprocity or even contractual reciprocity. In the United States, for example, some marital relationships begin with premarital legal agreements that carefully spell out expectations, possessions, and obligations that are to be followed.

Another difference between Eastern and Western relationships is that in many Eastern cultures, there is a clear difference between who is and is not a member of the in-group or the out-group. Yum maintains that Confucian philosophy prescribes that people associate and identify with relatively few, yet very cohesive, groups. Moreover, one's affiliation with in-groups is long-lived, perhaps even life-long. Group associations in most Western cultures are, for the most part, optional and voluntary. Many of the groups with whom one associates in the United States, for example, are designed to somehow facilitate one's individual development (for example, "self-help" groups), and one's association with the group lasts only as long as one benefits from membership.[37]

A fourth difference between relationships in Eastern and Western cultures is the use of intermediaries (go-betweens). For the most part, persons in Western cultures prefer direct face-to-face contact in interpersonal relationships, including relationships with business associates. In the United States, for example, the use of intermediaries is typically reserved for very formal and/or legal situations and is usually contractual (as with lawyers or realtors). Yum points out that in Eastern cultures, because the distinction between in-groups and out-groups is so well defined, intermediaries are essential and are used even in informal situations, such as in introductions, dating, marital arrangements, and even relatively small business transactions. The principle behind the use of intermediaries is to save face.[38]

A fifth difference in interpersonal relations in Eastern and Western cultures, according to Yum, is that Confucianism's emphasis on faithfulness and loyalty in relationships leads to blending of personal and public relationships. In the United States, people can maintain "strictly business" relationships, whereas many Eastern cultures prefer to do business with trusted associates with whom they have established a strong interpersonal bond. Many United States businesses would be well served by initiating frequent contact, establishing mutual interests, and developing shared experiences with their Eastern culture counterparts.[39]

Marital Relationships

Marital relationships exist in virtually every culture. According to anthropologist Michael Howard, the most common type of marriage practice in the United States and most Western industrialized nations is monogamy—that is, marriage between one man and one woman.

In most cases, monogamy is prescribed legally, and acquiring multiple spouses is illegal. In cultures in which marriage is governed legally, people are allowed, by law, to enter into and leave marriages—that is, people can marry, divorce, and marry again. This is called *serial monogamy.* Howard asserts that most cultures prefer not to limit the number of spouses available to a person. These cultures practice *polygamy*—that is, marriage to more than one spouse. Contrary to popular belief, polygamy is not the practice of a husband's having multiple wives. Actually, there are two types of polygamy: *polygyny,* in which a man has multiple wives, and *polyandry,* in which a woman has more than one husband. According to Howard, polygyny is permitted in the majority of societies.[40] Indeed, in their study of cross-cultural differences in family and sexual life among sixty-eight cultures, Becker and Posner report that only two cultures did not practice polygyny.[41]

INTERCULTURAL AND INTERRACIAL MARRIAGES

The number of intercultural and/or interracial marriages is growing, but according to the United States Census Bureau, over 97 percent of married couples in the United States are of the same race. Nearly 95 percent of unmarried couples living together are of the same race. Interracial couples account for less than 2 percent of the population of married couples and just over 4 percent of unmarried couples living together.[42] It is important to note, however, that these percentages take into account only interracial marriages and couples living together. The number of intercultural, or cross-cultural, marriages may be much higher. For example, the Census Bureau does not consider Hispanics as a racial group. Thus, white-hispanic couples are considered same-race couples. Renowned sociologist Amitai Etzioni argues that nearly 9 percent of all marriages are interracial or interethnic. He also reports that the proportion of marriages among people of different racial or ethnic origin has increased by 72 percent since 1970.[43]

In addition to the growing number of cross-cultural marriages, American attitudes about these relationships are changing. A recent national survey conducted by the *Washington Post,* the Henry J. Kaiser Family Foundation, and Harvard University found that 86 percent of black respondents said their families would welcome a white, Asian, or Hispanic person to their family. Among whites, 66 percent would accept Hispanics or Asians, but only 55 percent would accept a black person. Among Hispanics, 86 percent would accept whites, 79 percent would accept Asians, and 74 percent would accept blacks. Among Asians, 77 percent would accept whites, 71 percent would accept Hispanics, and 66 percent would accept blacks.[44]

Although the percentage of cross-cultural marriages is growing and the attitudes about such relationships are improving, cross-cultural (i.e., racial or ethnic) relationships are susceptible to pressures and strains not experienced in same-race or same-ethnic marriages or relationships. For example, additional results from the survey reported above indicate that 65 percent of white-black couples said they experienced problems within their families at the start of their relationship; 24 percent of white-Asian and white-Hispanic couples reported problems.[45]

Communication plays a principal role in any marriage, but it may play an even more important role in intercultural marriages and relationships. In his book on intercultural marriage, Dugan Romano argues that there are many communication obstacles facing intercultural couples. For example, regarding verbal language, Romano points out that usually one of the two members of the intercultural marriage is not speaking his or her native language. This means that his or her relational messages might have a higher likelihood of being distorted or misinterpreted. Moreover, one member of the couple may have an accent, misuse words, or not understand all of the words used. Romano notes, for example, that to an American woman, the "mother" is the person who nurtures her children into adulthood and then lets them go. To East Indians, "mother" is the eternal presence in children, one who dictates their life and demands overt expressions of their loyalty. Hence, American–East Indian couples may experience trouble defining the appropriate role of the mother.[46]

Romano argues that since one member typically is speaking in his or her native language, language can affect the balance of power. Thus, because language is power, the more fluent partner has the upper hand. According to Romano, superior linguistic facility, speed, and vocabulary not only direct conversation but can be used to manipulate the conversation to serve personal needs. In interviewing persons from intercultural marriages, Romano noted that several persons felt they had lost their personalities by having to speak in a second language. Romano also points out that humor is often the most difficult aspect of learning a language since neither the words nor the concepts translate well. Humor is often a key component of successful relationships, and many intercultural couples have difficulty using it.[47]

Nonverbal communication between members of intercultural marriages can be problematic too. In the United States and similar cultures, relational intimacy is often communicated nonverbally through close physical contact, intimate touching, increased eye contact, and so on. In many other cultures, such as Japan, these behaviors are seen as rude and intrusive and can be easily misinterpreted. As with their verbal communication, intercultural couples need to be very conscious of the nonverbal differences.

Romano maintains that there are generally four different types of intercultural marriages, including submission, compromise, obliteration, and consensus. Each type is defined by how the couple manages its cultural differences and communication. Submission-type marriages are characterized by one member's virtually abandoning or denying his or her native culture. Theoretically, this model may be the most successful because, in a way, it annuls the cultural differences. This style is difficult to implement, however, because it may be impossible for a person to completely ignore his or her cultural upbringing. For this reason, the submission type may not work in the long run. In the compromising type of marriage, each partner relinquishes certain features of his or her culture. One benefit of this type of marriage is that it stresses negotiating between partners and a willingness to recognize that each partner has to "give" something. Sometimes, however, partners feel as if they have lost something, and neither is truly satisfied. In the obliteration model, couples try to wipe out any cultural differences and create a third culture (such as was described earlier in this chapter) that has no "baggage" attached (e.g., traditions, language). For example, a couple may move to a third "neutral" culture to raise their children. For many couples, this is the only satisfactory solution. Often this strategy does not work because having a cultural tradition is a basic human need. Finally, the consensus type of marriage is one where neither partner sacrifices any basic culturally derived needs. This requires that each member be very strong and secure enough to be different and not feel threatened by such differences.

Finally, Romano points out several factors for successful intercultural marriages. Many of these factors are communication based. Some include sensitivity to each other's needs, flexibility, ability to communicate, sense of humor, and a solid, secure self-image.[48]

MATE SELECTION ACROSS CULTURES

When you think about getting married, what are the characteristics you look for in a potential mate? Are you looking for someone who is good looking? Is educated? Has a sense of humor? Is wealthy? David Buss has been interested in the answers to these questions and has investigated mate preferences across cultures for decades. Before looking at his findings, take a moment to complete the survey.

For over ten years, Buss has led the International Mate Selection Project, consisting of forty-nine research collaborators from thirty-three countries located on six continents and five islands.[49] The focus of Buss's work has been to identify people's preferences in choosing a mate. According to Buss, scholars from myriad academic fields are interested in mating practices and mate selection. Evolutionary biologists, for example, believe that mate preference is a central evolutionary force. Sociologists study mating practices because they affect the distribution of wealth in society (for example, when the rich prefer to mate with the rich). Geneticists understand that mate preferences can affect genetic inheritability estimates. Social psychologists see mate preference as a psychological phenomenon related to interpersonal attraction. Yet despite all of the interest, Buss alleges that very little is known about the types of characteristics people value in potential mates and how these values might vary across cultures. Hence, Buss initiated the International Mate Selection Project. The purpose of his research was (1) to identify which characteristics individuals value in potential mates; (2) to identify similarities and differences among countries in their values; (3) to identify clusters of countries that are similar to each other; and (4) to identify sex differences in the degree of variation in mate selection within each country. Buss and his research collaborators surveyed over ten thousand people from thirty-three different countries. In Africa, subjects were from Nigeria, South Africa, and Zambia. Asian countries sampled were China, India, Japan, and Taiwan. In the Middle East, Israel (Jewish

Self-Assessment 9-3

Selecting a Mate: Factors in Choosing a Mate

Below are 18 characteristics of people that you may find either desirable or undesirable. On a scale of 0 to 3, rate each of the characteristics on how important or desirable it is in choosing a mate. A score of 0 = irrelevant or unimportant, 1 = somewhat important, 2 = important, and 3 = indispensable.

1. _____ Sociability

2. _____ Similar education

3. _____ Pleasing disposition

4. _____ Refinement, neatness

5. _____ Similar religious background

6. _____ Good looks

7. _____ Education and intelligence

8. _____ Mutual attraction—love

9. _____ Good cook and housekeeper

10. _____ Good financial prospect

11. _____ Desire for home and children

12. _____ Chastity (no previous experience in sexual intercourse)

13. _____ Dependable character

14. _____ Good health

15. _____ Favorable social status or rating

—Continued

16. _____ Similar political background

17. _____ Emotional stability and maturity

18. _____ Ambitious and industrious

Preferences Concerning Potential Mates

Below is a set of 13 characteristics. Please rank them on their desirability in someone you might marry. Give a "1" to the most desirable characteristic in a potential mate; a "2" to the second most desirable characteristic in a potential mate; a "3" to the third most desirable characteristic in a potential mate, and so on until you have ranked all 13 characteristics. No characteristic can receive the same ranking as another.

1. _____ Easygoing

2. _____ Healthy

3. _____ Physically attractive

4. _____ Good heredity

5. _____ College graduate

6. _____ Exciting personality

7. _____ Intelligent

8. _____ Creative and artistic

9. _____ Good housekeeper

10. _____ Good earning capacity

11. _____ Religious

12. _____ Wants children

13. _____ Kind and understanding

SOURCE: "Factors in Choosing a Mate and Preferences Concerning Potential Mates," David Buss, *Journal of Cross-Cultural Psychology,* Vol. 21, No. 1, pp. 5–47.

and Palestinian) and Iran were surveyed. European countries studied were Belgium, Bulgaria, Estonia, Finland, France, Germany, Great Britain, Greece, Ireland, Italy, the Netherlands, Norway, Poland, Spain, Sweden, and the former Yugoslavia. In North America, the United States (including Hawaii) and Canada were sampled. South American countries surveyed were Brazil, Colombia, and Venezuela. Oceanic countries were Australia and New Zealand. Participants from Indonesia were also sampled.[50]

In the study, individuals were asked to complete the "Factors in Choosing a Mate" and the "Preferences Concerning Potential Mates" instruments (see Self-Assessment 9-3). After analyzing the completed surveys, Buss found that in spite of the unique cultural variability associated with each sample, there were substantial commonalities among all the samples. Table 9-2 outlines the top-four-rated variables.

Some of the least preferred characteristics from the rating instruments were chastity, similar religious background, similar political background, and favorable social status. The lowest-ranked characteristics were college graduate, good earning capacity, and religious. Buss noted that although there were some overall commonalities among the cultures, each country displayed some unique mate preferences. For example, the highest-rated characteristic for Iranian men and women was refinement and neatness. On the other hand, Chinese men rated good health as most important. Chinese women chose emotional stability as their top-rated characteristic. Nigerian men rated good health the highest, while Nigerian women rated emotional stability the highest. Buss reported that the largest effect of culture was seen in the variable of chastity. China, India, Indonesia, Iran, Taiwan, and Palestinian Israel placed the most importance on this characteristic, whereas Sweden, Finland, Norway, the Netherlands, and West Germany gave it the least importance.[51]

Probably the greatest difference among cultures occurred between men and women. In some countries, the sexes differed little in their rankings, whereas in

Across cultures, people have very similar mate preferences. (© James Neuliep)

TABLE 9-2   Universally Preferred Characteristics

Universally Preferred Characteristics: Ranking Instrument = Preferences Concerning Potential Mates

1. Kind and understanding
2. Intelligent
3. Exciting personality
4. Healthy

Universally Preferred Characteristics: Rating Instrument = Factors in Choosing a Mate

1. Mutual attraction—love
2. Emotional stability and maturity
3. Good health
4. Pleasing disposition

SOURCE: *D. M. Buss, "Mate Preferences in Thirty-Seven Cultures," in* Psychology and Culture, *ed. W. J. Lonner and R. Malpass (Boston: Allyn & Bacon, 1994), pp. 197–202; D. M. Buss, "Sex Differences in Human Mate Preference: Evolutionary Hypotheses Tested in Thirty-Seven Cultures,"* Behavioral and Brain Sciences, *12 (1989), 1–49.*

others the sexes differed greatly. The two countries with the highest degree of sexual dimorphism, Nigeria and Zambia, were also the two that practice polygyny. Moreover, there was more similarity between men and women from the same culture than between men and men or women and women from different cultures. The largest sex difference occurred for the variables of "good financial prospect" and "good earning capacity." Women generally valued these traits more than men. Men across the globe valued physical attractiveness in marriage partners more than women. Buss states:

> The importance of good looks is not limited to Western Europe or North America; nor is it limited to cultures saturated with visual media such as television, movies, and videos; nor is it limited to particular racial, ethnic, religious, or political groups. In all known cultures worldwide, from the inner-continental tribal societies of Africa and South America to the big cities of Madrid, London, and Paris, men place a premium on the physical appearance of a potential mate.[52]

Women, on the other hand, place somewhat greater value than do men on "emotional stability and maturity," "favorable social status," "education and intelligence," and "college graduate." In another sex difference, men, worldwide, prefer wives who are younger than themselves. In polygynic cultures such as Zambia and Nigeria, where men may have multiple wives, men prefer brides who are much younger than themselves. Conversely, women prefer men who are older. In his conclusion, Buss notes that culture appears to exert substantial effects on mate preferences and that, in general, the effects of sex on mate preferences are small compared with those of culture.[53]

ARRANGED MARRIAGES

In some cultures, an individual's preference in selecting a mate becomes moot because marriage is arranged by parents or a trusted family friend and/or mediator. In many instances, the bride and groom of an arranged marriage do not even meet until the day of the wedding. In many cultures, a bride price similar to that of a dowry is an essential ingredient of the arranged marriage. Although not as common as they once were, arranged marriages are still practiced in a variety of cultures and within some microcultural groups in the United States, such as the Hmong. Many young persons in the United States find the prospect of an arranged marriage quite frightening and unnerving. Yet Katie Thao, a Hmong woman who emigrated from Laos to the United States when she was young, indicates that the arranged marriage in which she participated was one of the most satisfying events of her life.[54] To Katie, the time and effort associated with searching for a mate represented considerable uncertainty and anxiety. In traditional Hmong culture, arranged marriages are negotiated by the parents. Because Katie had faith and trust in her parents to select for her the ideal spouse, she had little to worry about and very little uncertainty. Although she admits to being nervous on her wedding day, Thao says she very much loves the man she married, and they have three children. Although it happens only infrequently, the woman can reject the match. As Lor notes, however, there are certain situations in which the match cannot be refused. According to Lor, if the groom's family clan has high status, is unusually wealthy, or is related to the bride's family in some way, the match is essentially permanent.[55]

Almost 90 percent of all marriages in Pakistan are arranged. Jill Hoffman estimates that as many as 95 percent of marriages in India are arranged. As in other cultures with arranged marriages, in India there is a certain amount of bargaining and negotiation. Hoffman notes that family status and wealth play key roles in the process. Although it is illegal, in southern India, according to Hoffman, the groom's family often pays a bride price, especially if the bride is exceptionally beautiful or if the groom himself is flawed or impaired in some way. In most cases, the bride and groom do not meet before the wedding.[56] In her analysis of marriage in Iran, Kelly Pretty found that in traditional Iranian families, a marriage is arranged by the parents and a bride price is negotiated. In some instances, arranged marriages are between cousins, although this trend is changing.[57] In traditional Pakistani families, marriages are arranged by the fathers. According to Rebecca Sinnen, Pakistanis place a great deal of importance on status and wealth and so are careful to arrange marriages between a bride and groom of the same caste. Typically, the fathers negotiate through intermediaries. Sinnen notes that parents consider this the most important of all parental duties.[58] In Japan, as many as 25 percent of all marriages are arranged through an intermediary called a *pro nakodo.* The *pro nakodo* serves as a kind of dating service in that he interacts with other *nakodo*s in order to find an appropriate match. Prospective brides and grooms begin the procedure by completing a lengthy registration process. Their applications are then kept on file and can be reviewed by other *pro nakodo*s looking for a match. When a possible match is made, the clients meet to become acquainted. If the match is successful, the *pro nakodo* receives a substantial payment for his services. Another payment is then made to the bride's family. For the groom's family, the process can be very expensive. Renkens notes that the success rate is rather low at about 20 percent.[59]

In China, a grotesque form of arranged marriage has been rekindled: bride trafficking. *Newsweek* correspondent Dorinda Elliot reports that in many of the rural communities of China, crooked marriage brokers offer kidnapped women and girls for sale to prospective buyers. According to Elliot, from 1991 through 1996, Chinese authorities freed almost 100,000 kidnapped women and children and arrested almost 150,000 bride traffickers for participating in what she calls a virtual slave trade. Ironically, writes Elliot, local Chinese peasants sympathize with men who buy their wives, believing that if a woman takes the bride price and sends it to her parents, the man deserves to have her as his wife.[60]

Recall from earlier in this chapter that a primary motive of people interacting with others for the first few times is to reduce uncertainty. Recall also that many of our communication strategies during initial interaction are designed specifically to reduce uncertainty and increase the predictability about the other. In arranged marriages, the bride and groom have had virtually no time to engage in uncertainty-reducing communication. Unlike couples in most Western cultures, where considerable courtship time has passed, persons in arranged marriages do not know each other. Communication early in an arranged marriage likely consists of messages designed to reduce uncertainty.

MARITAL DISSOLUTION AND DIVORCE ACROSS CULTURES

A fact of life for all of us is that some of our relationships will end. Like marriage practices, divorce customs vary across cultures. Although it is relatively easy to calculate the divorce rate in any given culture, to understand why people divorce is a much more difficult task. In many cultures, social and economic issues often play a role in divorce decisions. Factors such as income, sexual dissatisfaction, childlessness, women's equality issues, religion, and the ease with which one can obtain a divorce all vary across cultures. In general, monogamy is correlated with lower divorce rates than polygyny.[61] A 1979 survey of marriage counselors in the United States indicated that a breakdown in communication was the most frequently cited reason for relational dissolution in this country. Other reasons included loss of shared goals, sexual incompatibility, infidelity, and the loss of excitement (in that order).[62] Although the reasons for divorce vary, one trend that seems to be consistent across most cultures is that the overall divorce rate is on the rise. For example, since the passage of legislative reforms in the early 1980s, divorce has become much simpler in China, and divorce rates are soaring. In urban areas, such as Beijing, the divorce rate increased from 2 percent in 1981 to almost 20 percent of all marriages in 1992.[63] Similarly, Hall reports that in Canada, both cohabitation and divorce rates have increased considerably in the past quarter century. Approximately 30 percent of Canadian marriages now end in divorce.[64] Great Britain has the second highest divorce rate in Europe (Denmark's is the highest), with two out of five new marriages ending in divorce. The rise in Britain's divorce rates correlates with the rise of married women's employment.[65] Avner Gidron of the *World Press Review* reports that over twenty years of civil war are partially responsible for the rise in divorce in Lebanon. Not only has divorce risen some 30 percent since the outbreak of civil war; the marriage rate has fallen 25 percent. According to Gidron, between 30 to 40 percent of Christian marriages now end in divorce. The divorce rate among Shiite Moslems has risen about 26 percent.[66] Citing increased opportunities for women, the *Women's International Network News* reports that the divorce rate in Russia is rising quickly. Because they are able to find new apartments and support themselves financially, more and more Russian women are seeking divorce. The divorce rate in Russia has plateaued at about 40 percent.[67]

Though there is an upward trend, Japan has a relatively low divorce rate. According to sociologist Steve Stack, Japan is characterized by a low divorce rate, high family integration, cultural conformism, and low couple-centeredness. Stack argues that Japan's low divorce rate may be attributable to the degree of role segregation in Japan. Japanese women tend to remain in marriages because of their financial dependence on their husbands. Furthermore, asserts Stack, Japan emphasizes cultural conformity, in which the individual is subordinate to larger cultural institutions, such as marriage.[68] Ho writes that divorce in traditional Asian cultures, such as Japan, is discouraged because it disrupts familial harmony.[69] Although higher than many European countries, the divorce rate in Sweden is declining. A part of the reason for the declining divorce rate in Sweden is that the rate of cohabitation is rising significantly. According to David Popenoe, about 15 percent of all couples in Sweden are cohabiting (compared with about 5 percent in the United States). Hence, over 50 percent of all Swedish children are born out of wedlock, the highest percentage in the industrialized world. As Popenoe points out, "In order to divorce, one must marry, and that is precisely what Swedes in large numbers are not doing."[70]

Second only to that of the United States, the divorce rate in Puerto Rico is very high, at about 46 percent since the early 1980s.[71] But as most people know, the United States has the highest divorce rate in the world, at about 48 percent. The number of U.S. citizens who are currently divorced has quadrupled since 1970 and now numbers at about 17 million. Divorced persons make up nearly 40 percent of the adult population.[72] Although they have the lowest out-group interracial marriage rate (that is, exogamy) of any microcultural group, blacks have the highest divorce rate of any microcultural group in America. Research by Oggins, Veroff, and Leber suggests that there may be more affective intensity in African American marriages than in Caucasian marriages, which can lead to more open, direct interaction and is therefore more likely to erupt in marital difficulties.[73] Table 9-3 lists divorce rate percentage for twenty different countries.

TABLE 9-3 Divorce Rates in 20 Countries (1993)	
Country	**Divorce Rate (%)**
United States	48
Sweden	44
Canada	43
Russia	42
Britain	41
New Zealand	37
Australia	34
Switzerland	33
France	31
Hungary	31
Germany	30
Japan	22
Israel	18
Bahamas	13
Hong Kong	12
South Korea	11
Mexico	8
Spain	8
Italy	8
India	1

SOURCE: *"Divorce Rates in 20 Countries (1993)"* from *"Nirvana by Numbers,"* The Economist, *Vol. 329, 1993, pp. 39–43. © 1993 The Economist Newspaper Group, Inc. Reprinted with permission. Further reproduction prohibited. www.economist.com.*

Chapter Summary

The purpose of this chapter was to introduce you to the theories of relationship that affect intercultural communication. People across the world, in all cultures, initiate, maintain, and dissolve relationships. We've learned that reducing uncertainty is a major component to initiating relationships. When people meet for the first time, they have very little information about each other and one of their primary motives is to reduce uncertainty. In this chapter we've also learned that one's level of intercultural communication apprehension and one's sociocommunicative style affect the uncertainty reduction communicative process. In addition, this chapter discussed the idea that empathy and similarity are important in maintaining relationships. In fact, perceived similarity may be the most powerful attractant in others. We have seen that developing empathy for others can be a key factor in maintaining intercultural relationships. Another important point discussed in this chapter is the idea that perceptions of relationships differ significantly across cultures, particularly between Eastern and Western cultures. Finally, this chapter has discussed one of the most important types of relationships—that is, marriage. We've seen that intercultural marriages pose unique obstacles, many of which are communication oriented. Moreover, marriage varies across cultures in terms of the different types of marriage, mate selection, arranged marriage, and marital dissolution.

GLOSSARY OF TERMS

Arranged marriages: Marriages that are initiated and negotiated by a third party rather than by the bride and groom.

Assertiveness: An individual's ability to make requests, actively disagree, and express positive or negative personal rights and feelings.

Polyandry: The practice of having multiple husbands.

Polygamy: The practice of having multiple spouses.

Polygyny: The practice of having multiple wives.

Relational empathy: Shared meaning and harmonization that is the result of the interaction of two people.

Responsiveness: An individual's ability to be sensitive to the communication of others, including providing feedback, comforting communication, and listening.

Sociocommunicative style: Degree of assertiveness and responsiveness during communication.

Third culture: That which is created when a dyad consisting of persons from different cultures come together and establish relational empathy.

Uncertainty: The amount of predictability in a communication situation.

Uncertainty reduction theory: Theory whose major premise is that when strangers first meet, their primary goal is to reduce uncertainty.

REFERENCES

1. K. J. Gergen, *The Saturated Self: Dilemmas of Identity in Contemporary Life* (New York: Basic Books). 1991 (Quote on page 178.)

2. C. R. Berger and R. J. Calabrese, "Some Explorations in Initial Interaction and Beyond: Toward a Developmental Theory of Interpersonal Communication," *Human Communication Research,* 1 (1975), 99–112.

3. W. B. Gudykunst and Y. Y. Kim, *Communicating with Strangers: An Approach to Intercultural Communication* (New York: McGraw-Hill, 1997).

4. W. B. Gudykunst, "Uncertainty Reduction and Predictability of Behavior in Low- and High-Context Cultures," *Communication Quarterly,* 31 (1983), 49–55; Gudykunst, "Uncertainty and Anxiety," in *Theories of Intercultural Communication,* ed. Y. Y. Kim and W. B. Gudykunst (Newbury Park, Calif.: Sage, 1988), pp. 123–156; Gudykunst, "Anxiety/Uncertainty Management (AUM) Theory," in *Intercultural Communication Theory,* ed. R. Wiseman (Thousand Oaks, Calif.: Sage, 1995), pp. 8–58.

5. W. B. Gudykunst and T. Nishida, "Individual and Cultural Influences on Uncertainty Reduction," *Communication Monographs,* 51 (1984), 23–36.

6. J. Sanders and R. Wiseman, "Uncertainty Reduction Among Ethnicities in the United States" (paper presented at the annual convention of the International Communication Association, Chicago, Ill., 1991).

7. W. B. Gudykunst, L. L. Sodetani, and K. T. Sonoda, "Uncertainty Reduction in Japanese-American-Caucasian Relationships in Hawaii," *Western Journal of Speech Communication,* 51 (1987), 256–278.

8. Berger and Calabrese, "Some Explorations in Initial Interaction and Beyond," 99–112.

9. Ibid.

10. Gudykunst and Kim, *Communicating with Strangers.*

11. G. W. Clatterbuck, "Attributional Confidence and Uncertainty in Initial Interaction," *Human Communication Research,* 5 (1979), 147–157.

12. J. W. Neuliep and D. J. Ryan, "The Influence of Intercultural Communication Apprehension and Socio-Communicative Orientation on Uncertainty Reduction During Initial Cross-Cultural Interaction," *Communication Quarterly,* 46 (1998), 88–99.

13. Gudykunst, "Anxiety/Uncertainty Management (AUM) Theory."

14. M. Leary, "Anxiety, Cognition, and Behavior: In Search of a Broader Perspective," in *Communication, Cognition, and Anxiety,* ed. M. Booth-Butterfield, [special issue] *Journal of Social Behavior and Personality,* 5 (1990), 39–44.

15. Gudykunst and Kim, *Communicating with Strangers.*

16. Berger and Calabrese, "Some Explorations in Initial Interaction and Beyond."

17. Neuliep and Ryan, "The Influence of Intercultural Communication Apprehension and Socio-Communicative Orientation on Uncertainty Reduction During Initial Cross-Cultural Interaction"; J. W. Neuliep and E. L. Grohskopf, "Uncertainty Reduction and Communication Satisfaction During Initial Interaction: An Initial Test and Replication of a New Axiom," *Communication Reports,* 13, (2000), 67–78.

18. J. C. McCroskey and V. P. Richmond, *Fundamentals of Human Communication* (Prospect Heights, Ill.: Waveland, 1996).

19. Ibid.

20. Neuliep and Ryan, "The Influence of Intercultural Communication Apprehension and Socio-Communicative Orientation on Uncertainty Reduction During Initial Cross-Cultural Interaction."

21. Ibid; Berger and Calabrese, "Some Explorations in Initial Interaction and Beyond."

22. C. M. Anderson, M. M. Martin, M. Zhong, and D. West, "Reliability, Separation of Factors, and Sex Difference on the Assertiveness-Responsiveness Measure: A Chinese Sample" (paper presented at the annual convention of the International Communication Association, Montreal, Quebec, Canada, 1997); C. A. Thompson and D. W. Klopf, "An Analysis of Social Style Among Disparate Cultures," *Communication Research Reports,* 8 (1991), 65–72; C. A. Thompson, S. Ishii, and D. W. Klopf, "Japanese and Americans Compared on Assertiveness/Responsiveness," *Psychological Reports,* 66 (1990), 829–830.

23. B. J. Broome, "Building Shared Meaning: Implications of a Relational Approach to Empathy for Teaching Intercultural Communication," *Communication Education,* 40 (1991), 235–249.

24. Ibid., 240.

25. Ibid., 241.

26. The concept of third-culture building was initially articulated by Fred Casmir. Broome's approach is based on Casmir's work in this area.

27. Broome, "Building Shared Meaning."

28. D. W. Klopf, *Intercultural Encounters: The Fundamentals of Intercultural Communication* (Englewood, Colo.: Morton, 1998).

29. S. Duck and M. K. Barnes, "Disagreeing About Agreement: Reconciling Differences About Similarity," *Communication Monographs,* 59 (1992), 199–208.

30. D. Byrne, "The Transition from Controlled Laboratory Experimentation to Less Controlled Settings: Surprise! Additional Variables Are Operative," *Communication Monographs,* 59 (1992), 190–198.

31. Ibid.
32. W. B. Gudykunst and T. Nishida, "The Influence of Cultural Variability on Perceptions of Communication Behavior Associated with Relationship Terms," *Human Communication Research,* 13 (1986), 147–166.
33. J. O. Yum, "The Impact of Confucianism on Interpersonal Relationships and Communication Patterns in East Asia," in *Intercultural Communication: A Reader,* 8th ed., ed. L. A. Samovar and R. E. Porter (Belmont, Calif.: Wadsworth, 1997), pp. 78–88.
34. Ibid.
35. Ibid.
36. Ibid., p. 81.
37. Ibid.
38. Ibid.
39. Ibid.
40. M. C. Howard, *Contemporary Cultural Anthropology* (Glenview, Ill.: Scott, Foresman, 1989).
41. G. S. Becker and R. A. Posner, "Cross-Cultural Differences in Family and Sexual Life," *Rationality and Society,* 5 (1993), 421–432.
42. J. Fields and L. M. Casper, "American Families and Living Arrangements: March 2000" *Current Population Reports* (Washington, D.C.: United States Bureau of the Census).
43. A. Etzioni, "Some Diversity," *Society,* 35 (1998), 59–62.
44. *Race and Ethnicity in 2001: Attitudes, Perceptions, and Experiences.* Survey conducted by the *Washington Post,* the Kaiser Family Foundation, and Harvard University (Henry J. Kaiser Family Foundation, Menlo Park, Calif.: 2001).
45. Ibid.
46. D. Romano, *Intercultural Marriage: Promises and Pitfalls* (Yarmouth, Maine: Intercultural Press, 1997).
47. Ibid.
48. Ibid.
49. D. M. Buss, "Mate Preferences in Thirty-Seven Cultures," in *Psychology and Culture,* ed. W. J. Lonner and R. Malpass (Boston: Allyn & Bacon, 1994), pp. 197–202; Buss, "Sex Differences in Human Mate Preference: Evolutionary Hypotheses Tested in Thirty-seven Cultures," *Behavioral and Brain Sciences,* 12 (1989), 1–49.
50. Ibid.
51. Ibid.
52. Ibid, p. 200.
53. Ibid.
54. The account was provided by Katie Thao in a personal communication in the summer of 1995.
55. H. Lor, "The Hmong" (unpublished student manuscript, St. Norbert College, De Pere, Wisc., 1997).
56. J. Hoffman, "Arranged Marriage in India: Rules Governing the Process" (unpublished student manuscript, St. Norbert College, De Pere, Wisc., 1997).
57. K. Pretty, "Marriage in Iran: A Changing Way of Life" (unpublished student manuscript, St. Norbert College, De Pere, Wisc., 1997).
58. R. Sinnen, "Arranged Marriage in Traditional Pakistani Culture" (unpublished student manuscript, St. Norbert College, De Pere, Wisc., 1997).
59. S. Renkens, "Pro Nakodo Arranged Marriages" (unpublished student manuscript, St. Norbert College, De Pere, Wisc., 1997).
60. D. Elliot, "Trying to Stand on Two Feet," *Newsweek,* 313 (1998), 48–50.
61. A. J. Gage-Brandon, "The Polygyny-Divorce Relationship: A Case Study of Nigeria," *Journal of Marriage and the Family,* 54 (1992), 285–293.
62. C. Safran, "Troubles That Pull Couples Apart," *Redbook,* 83 (1979), 138–141.
63. "China: Divorce Increase and Change Affect Women," *Women's International Network News,* 20 (1994), 59.
64. D. R. Hall, "Marriage as a Pure Relationship: Exploring the Link between Premarital Cohabitation and Divorce in Canada," *Journal of Comparative Family Studies,* 27 (1996), 1–12.
65. "Not Such a Family Affair," *The Economist,* 321 (1991), 69–71.
66. A. Gidron, "War on Families," *World Press Review,* 40 (1993), 35.
67. "Russian Business Women Are Moving Up Slowly," *Women's International Network News,* 24 (1998), 75.

68. S. Stack, "The Effect of Divorce on Suicide in Japan: A Time Series Analysis, 1950–1980," *Journal of Marriage and the Family,* 54 (1992), 327–335.

69. M. K. Ho, *Family Therapy with Ethnic Minorities* (Beverly Hills, Calif.: Sage, 1987).

70. D. Popenoe, "Family Decline in the Swedish Welfare State," *Public Interest,* 102 (1991), 65–78.

71. M. E. Canabal, "An Economic Approach to Marital Dissolution in Puerto Rico," *Journal of Marriage and the Family,* 52 (1990), 515–531.

72. P. Grier, "New Census Bureau Portrait of the American Landscape," *Christian Science Monitor,* 88 (1996), 69 (March 6, 1996).

73. J. Oggins, J. Veroff, and D. Leber, "Perceptions of Marital Interaction Among Black and White Newlyweds," *Journal of Personality and Social Psychology,* 65 (1993), 494–511.

Intercultural Communication in Organizations

However objective and uniform we try to make organizations, they will not have the same meaning for individuals from different cultures.

—Fons Trompenaars[1]

CHAPTER OBJECTIVES

After reading this chapter, you should be able to:

- Discuss how dimensions of the cultural context affect organizations across cultures.
- Identify how the environmental context affects doing business in other cultures.
- Identify variables in the perceptual context and how they influence business with other cultures.
- Compare and contrast sociorelational contexts on the job across cultures.
- Discuss some verbal and nonverbal differences across cultures.
- Compare and contrast managerial practices in Japan, Germany, and Mexico.
- Identify the individual, intermediary, and societal factors that facilitate conflict.

Coordinating and managing people from different cultures within an organizational context represents one of the greatest challenges for the corporate world in the new millennium. Businesses and organizations from virtually every culture have entered into the global marketplace. The expansion of world trade has increased astronomically in the past thirty years. For example, between 1970 and 1990, world trade expanded more than ten times. Global output of goods and services increased from about $15.5 trillion in 1980 to about $20 trillion in 1990. In the year 2000, the expansion of merchandise output was 4.5 percent and for trade 12 percent, the strongest in more than a decade.[2] According to the U.S. Department of Commerce, in 1997 more than 200,000 U.S. companies exported more than $560 billion in merchandise to more than two hundred foreign countries. Our top export partners included Canada, the United Kingdom, Japan, Germany, and Mexico. Interestingly, over 95 percent of all exporters were small- or medium-sized companies (those employing fewer than five hundred workers). Large companies, with more than five hundred employees, represented only about 4 percent of all exporters.[3]

In early 1994, the United States, Canada, and Mexico set in motion the North American Free Trade Agreement (NAFTA), which generated the largest free-trade area in the world. In 2001, the agreement linked over 400 million people producing more than $11 trillion worth of goods and services. From 1994 to 2000, the total volume of trade between Canada, Mexico, and the United States expanded from $300 billion to $676 billion.[4]

Within our borders as well, the face of U.S. business is becoming more and more diverse. According to the U.S. Census Bureau, in 1997 over 3 million American businesses were owned by minorities (i.e., microcultural groups), employing over 4.5 million workers and generating nearly $600 billion in revenues. Hispanics owned the largest number (1.2 million) of businesses and held the largest share of businesses owned by minority men and minority women. Blacks owned just over 800,000 businesses, of which 54 percent were owned by black men and 38 percent were owned by black women. While Hispanics owned the largest share of businesses, Asian and Pacific Islander–owned businesses accounted for the largest share (52 percent) of all revenues collected by microcultural-group business owners.[5]

Given the dramatic cultural transformation in today's marketplace, the relevance of intercultural communication competence cannot be overstated. To compete in the global and U.S. markets, today's managers must possess the skills to interact with people who are different from themselves. Today, there are over 300,000 persons from the United States working abroad. Approximately 57 percent of companies that send employees abroad provide cross-cultural training. Forty-three percent provide no training at all. Of those employees receiving training, 97 percent believe the training is valuable.[6]

Intercultural Management

The purpose of this chapter is to introduce some of the salient issues affecting intercultural management. The chapter will take each component of the model of intercultural communication introduced in Chapter 1 and apply it to intercultural management. First, the cultural context within organizations will be explored, prior to a discussion of the environmental context. Next, the chapter will identify the variables in the perceptual context and how they affect business in other cultures. The chapter will then compare and contrast sociorelational job contexts across cultures, along with some verbal and nonverbal differences. The chapter then examines managerial practices among Japanese, German, and Mexican managers. Finally, the chapter concludes with a model of intercultural conflict.

There is no culture-free theory of management. Managing other people is the responsibility of people (i.e., managers) who, like everyone else, have been enculturated and socialized into a cultural set of values and beliefs that govern their thinking, emotions, and behaviors. Like communication, management is culture bound. Moreover, managerial perceptions regarding the factors that lead to organizational success vary across cultures. For example, in her survey of over 12,000 managers, Rosabeth Moss Kanter asked managers to rate factors they considered important for their organizations' success. The top-rated factors varied considerably across cultures. Table 10-1 shows ratings by managers in the United States, Japan, and Germany (Japan and Germany are two of our biggest trading partners).[7] The numbers in parentheses refer to the percentage of managers checking each item.

Unfortunately, many U.S. managers are ill equipped to handle overseas assignments. For example, 20 percent of U.S. managers sent abroad are asked to return home because of poor performance. Moreover, only 11 percent of managers receive promotions after completion of an overseas assignment, and nearly 80 percent are demoted. Although fostering competent intercultural communication managerial skills represents an enormous challenge, the rewards of successful international commerce are extraordinary. Managers are receiving a different message than they did only a few years ago: now, to be promoted to top levels of the organization, an overseas assignment is virtually a prerequisite. Gayle Kosterman, a vice president for S. C. Johnson & Son (makers of Pledge and Windex), states that the top managers must have a sense of the global marketplace, particularly of how it differs from the U.S. market. Each year Johnson selects its best new employees and devises for them a five-year career plan that includes a one- or two-year overseas assignment. Many corporations simply expect that to advance in the ranks, one must have international experience. Seventy-five percent of Citicorp's top officers have completed assignments outside the United States. Major businesses such as AT&T, G.E. Medical Systems, and Motorola have initiated cross-cultural

TABLE 10-1 Top Three Organizational Success Factors		
Japan	**Germany**	**United States**
1. Product development (54)	1. Work force skills (63)	1. Customer service (52)
2. Management (41)	2. Problem-solving (47)	2. Product quality (40)
3. Product quality (36)	3. Management (44)	3. Technology (36)

development programs for their overseas managers. The managers, along with their families, engage in intense cultural and language programs designed to increase the probability of success.[8]

Professor Philip Rosenzweig of Harvard University argues that successful cross-cultural management depends on the abilities of managers to communicate effectively. Rosenzweig points out that communication is especially important during the initial stages of a business relationship. Depending on the culture, the process of building trust among business partners may take days, weeks, or even months. Moreover, Rosenzweig asserts, this process cannot be accelerated. Rosenzweig recognizes that many American managers prefer to "get down to business" without spending much time getting to know their business partners. In fact, according to Rosenzweig, many American managers view such relationship building as a waste of valuable time. Rosenzweig argues that investing the time and energy in building trust and developing relationships may pay huge benefits in terms of confidence and trust.[9]

Perceptions of time and timing are also important considerations in cross-cultural business exchanges. Rosenzweig recommends that American managers allow the pace of negotiations to develop on its own. He cautions managers not to impose artificial deadlines for the sake of efficiency. How agreement and disagreement are communicated is another important factor during cross-cultural negotiations. Rosenzweig points out that American managers tend to favor forthrightness during negotiations. In many other cultures, such directness may be seen as rude and discourteous. Finally, Rosenzweig points out that the specificity with which a contract is written may vary considerably across cultures. In the United States, we tend to favor explicit contracts that include a great deal of precise wording covering all aspects of the agreement. In some cultures this may be interpreted as a sign of distrust. Many cultures prefer very general contracts. Such cultures place significance on trust and mutual obligation rather than on formalized agreements.[10]

Much of what you have been exposed to in this textbook can be applied to your role in organizational settings across cultures. The topics and issues discussed in each chapter can guide you in becoming a successful multicultural manager. Most businesses and organizations can be thought of as minicultures, each representing a pattern of values held by a recognizable group of people with a common goal pursued by means of a collective verbal and nonverbal symbol system. Like cultures themselves, organizations possess value systems, exist in some environmental context, process information from a unique perceptual perspective, develop sociorelations with others, and communicate using distinctive verbal and nonverbal codes. As you prepare to conduct business with persons in organizations from different cultures or microcultures, you cannot assume that your business practices will be understood or accepted by your counterpart. Figure 10-1 outlines some of the more salient issues that affect the development of organizational cultures in any culture.

Prior to entering into a business transaction with an organization from a different culture or microculture, you should conduct an extensive organizational analysis. The model in Figure 10-1 can help. In your analysis, take into account your foreign partner's cultural, environmental, perceptual, and sociorelational

FIGURE 10-1   Contexts Affecting Organizational Culture

contexts as well as the verbal and nonverbal code system and the nature of the relationships you are about to initiate.

CULTURAL CONTEXT

First, consider the cultural context of an organization. Organizational culture often parallels country culture. Hence, if values differ significantly across cultures, then the management practices of those cultures are also likely to differ. In their study of twelve countries, Bass and Burger found that cultural differences accounted for differences in managers' goals, risk taking, pragmatism, interpersonal competence, emotional stability, and leadership style. In similar research Adler, Campbell, and Laurent found that cultural values, beliefs, and norms affected managers' leadership style and organizational strategies.[11]

When managing people from other cultures, try to ascertain where on the individualism/collectivism continuum an organization falls. Organizations in collectivistic cultures are more likely to emphasize group harmony and teamwork. For example, Mitsui Group of Japan, one of the largest cross-ownership companies in Japan, with nearly one thousand subsidiaries and associates worldwide, including Toyota and Toshiba, employs almost eight thousand people and lists group harmony as its number one corporate value. Similarly, Apple Computer workers in

Intercultural Conversation

Intercultural Conversation: Clashing Cultural Concepts on the Job

In the following conversation, American businessman Jim Neumouth is applying for a job in Japanese businessman Kietaro Matsumoto's corporation, located in Kyoto, Japan.

Kietaro: So, Mr. Neumouth, why would you like to work for our corporation?

Jim: I believe I have the necessary skills and experience for this position. I'm very independent, I set very high goals for myself, and I believe your company will allow me to pursue them.

Kietaro: What do you mean by "goals"?

Jim: I have very high sales objectives. I try to reach the top in whatever I do. One of my goals is to become your leading salesperson.

For example, I had the highest percentage of sales of anyone in the company I worked for in the United States. I was named salesperson of the year in 1998.

Kietaro: I see. That's very impressive.

Jim: Thanks. Now I'd like to expand into an international market, and I'd like to bring my experience and motivation to your company. I think I can be the best here, too.

In the above conversation, Mr. Neumouth does a good job of expressing his talents and experiences. In the United States, he might appear like the ideal candidate. However, to Mr. Matsumoto, he does not appear to be a team player.

Singapore listed teamwork and reserve as their number one and two (respectively) corporate values. However, these same employees indicated that individualism was the number one value of Apple Computer workers in the United States.[12] Therefore, when doing business with companies in collective cultures, it may be wise to formulate strategies that are consistent with group unity. Strategies that are perceived to promote the individual within the organization may be frowned upon (see box). Also keep in mind that reaching a decision in collectivistic organizations sometimes takes much longer than in individualistic organizations. Often collectivists go to great pains to win everyone over in order to achieve consensus.

Power distance is another important cultural influence to assess when dealing with organizations across cultures. Recall from Chapter 2 that Malaysia ranked at the top of the power distance index (indicating high power distance). A recent survey indicated that the highest-rated values of middle-level managers of Petronas Corporation, the Malaysian state-owned oil company, included status consciousness (position, degree), top-down communication, and welfare of the employees. Petronas owns Petronas Towers, which in 1996 became the world's tallest office building, surpassing Chicago's Sears Tower, which had held that record since 1974. Hence, when planning business with Petronas or other Malaysian companies, be prepared to treat your counterpart with more humility and formality than you might expect from your U.S. partners.[13]

Uncertainty avoidance is another important consideration. Because the United States is a low-uncertainty-avoidant culture, the U.S. marketplace is associated with a great deal of risk. In fact, middle-line managers at Advance Mico Devices, a U.S.-based company, indicate that aggressiveness and risk taking are the top two values guiding their company. Risky business propositions are likely to be rejected by cultures high in uncertainty avoidance, however.[14]

Detelin Elenkov has investigated cultural differences between Russia and the United States. He argues that Russia is more collectivistic and has a higher power distance and higher uncertainty avoidance than the United States. In his comparison of managers and business students from Russia and the United States, Elenkov found that the Russians scored higher than the persons from the United States on measures of collectivism, power distance, and uncertainty avoidance. In discussing his research Elenkov argues that the results of his study support the contention that managerial values closely parallel cultural values.[15]

ENVIRONMENTAL CONTEXT

Consider the following scenario:

> You have traveled to Korea to meet with your Korean counterpart, whom you have never met in person but with whom you have communicated through letters, e-mail, and so forth. You arrive at his office building at the appointed time. The weather in Seoul today is incredibly hot and humid. As you enter the floor of your partner's office, you notice that there are no walls separating the various desks. The scene appears very relaxed to you. Most of the men are sitting around in their undershirts. When you locate your partner, you find him sitting with his feet up on the desk, in his undershirt, fanning himself. When you introduce yourself, your Korean partner acts as if nothing has happened and puts on a shirt, tie, and jacket in a very matter-of-fact way. Your meeting now begins.

In addition to assessing an organization's cultural context, it is important to assess its perspective on the environment, including such issues as information load, privacy, and the company's overall orientation to nature. Recall from Chapter 4 that some cultures believe they can master nature, whereas others attempt to live in harmony with it, and still others believe they are subjugated by it. International business expert Fons Trompenaars suggests that a culture's perspective on nature often translates into its organizational practices. Paralleling their culture's attitude toward nature, some organizations believe they can control market forces and create new markets where none exist. Others attempt a balancing act with the market, sometimes trying to influence and at other times adjusting to its fluctuations. Still others believe that the market is in control, and they simply react to it. Trompenaars points to Indonesia as a culture that sees itself as controlled by external forces (e.g., nature, the marketplace). In Indonesia, incentive programs designed to motivate employees may fail because they consider market changes to be natural and arbitrary. To them it makes no sense to attribute blame or lack of incentive to those who are caught in a market downturn. Moreover, it makes even less sense to reward those who have the fortune of being in a market upturn. As Trompenaars notes, to either blame or reward may deplete the morale of the team by simply adding to the randomness of events.[16]

A culture's tolerance of, and comfort with, varying information rates should also be ascertained. In cultures such as the United States, managers often prefer to have as much factual information as possible before making decisions. Statistics, sales projections, historical trends, and so forth all help them with decision making. In some Arab cultures, however, decision making is fairly inexact and rests on the manager's personal position in the organization, his intuition, and his religious beliefs.[17]

Assumptions about privacy are also important considerations to take into account. In collectivistic cultures, for example, in which group harmony is paramount, employees may prefer to work together in the same physical location, not isolated by office walls and doors. Many U.S. corporations have borrowed the Japanese model of an open working environment devoid of private offices. Imagine what the reaction might be if a U.S. corporation hired a group of Japanese managers and put each in his or her own private office, or if a U.S. manager in Japan requested a private space. The scenario presented at the beginning of this section is based on a fascinating discussion of privacy in Korea by Philip Harris and Robert Moran. They report that in Korea, privacy is a luxury that few possess or can afford. Because privacy may be impossible to obtain physically, Koreans build imaginary and/or psychological walls around themselves. A client calling on a Korean on a typically hot and humid day may actually find this person in his undershirt with his feet on his desk, fanning himself. Because there are no physical walls, the informed visitor coughs to announce his arrival. Harris and Moran allege that although the person he has come to visit is in clear view, the visitor pretends not to "see" him. Moreover, the Korean does not "see" the visitor. Only after he has risen, put on his shirt, coat, and tie and adjusted himself, do they "see" each other and introduce themselves. According to Harris and Moran, in order to secure some level of privacy, Koreans retreat behind a psychological curtain and do what they have to do, not being seen by those who are in plain view. To violate the screen of privacy once it has been created is rude and discourteous.[18]

PERCEPTUAL CONTEXT

The perceptual context of the individual, learned through enculturation, is often manifest in the organization. Understanding how the organization processes information is crucial to establishing and maintaining effective communication. One information-processing strategy that people from all cultures engage in is categorizing and stereotyping. Before embarking on a business venture with a foreign culture, it may be useful to know of the culture's stereotypes of U.S. business practices. Harris and Moran surveyed what Arab business managers thought of U.S. managers working in the Middle East. The results shed light on why so many U.S. managers have difficulty working in Arab countries.[19] Arab managers believe:

1. Americans think they are superior.
2. Americans take credit for everything, even in joint efforts.
3. Americans do not adjust to or respect the local customs.

4. Americans do not innovate relative to the local customs.

5. Americans refuse to work through normal administrative channels.

6. Americans lose their democratic ways when working in foreign cultures.

Most Americans have been brought up to think in very logical, linear, and rational terms. We prefer to make decisions on the basis of empirical (verifiable through direct observation) data. Many of our business decisions are based on the logic that the shortest distance between two points is a straight line. Such thinking permeates our business transactions. Asian employers, however, may be guided by their intuition and base their decisions on trial and error. They may get sidetracked or take multiple paths to get to the same point. Chinese, for example, are known to be very patient and to take their time in making decisions, a characteristic that sometimes frustrates their American business counterparts. Remember, the way a person processes information is very much influenced by his or her enculturation.

SOCIORELATIONAL CONTEXT

An organization's emphasis on group membership is clearly something that U.S. managers should know about their foreign counterparts. As mentioned in Chapter 6, all people of all cultures belong to groups. One of the primary groups to which all people belong is the family. Recall that Chapter 6 profiled family life across a variety of cultures. Trompenaars employs a family metaphor in describing a particular type of ideal corporate culture seen often in Turkey, Venezuela, Hong Kong, Malaysia, India, Singapore, and Spain. This does not mean that all corporations in these countries are family-like; it simply means that this prototype is seen more frequently in these cultures than in others.

According to Trompenaars, the family corporation culture is simultaneously personal, with close face-to-face relationships, and hierarchical in the sense that everyone knows his or her place in the rank order. At the top of the hierarchy are the parents (the chief executives), who are regarded as caring and as knowing better than the children (the subordinates). The power at the top is perceived not as threatening, but as intimate and benign. The philosophy of the employees is to do more than is required contractually to please the older brother or father (the person of higher rank). Trompenaars notes that the primary reason for working hard and performing well in this type of corporate culture is the pleasure derived from familial relations. To please one's elders is reward in itself. The main sanction for poor performance is loss of affection and place in the family. In the family corporate culture, pressures to perform are moral and social rather than financial and/or legal.

Trompenaars argues that family corporate cultures sometimes experience difficulty with project-group organization, in which authority is divided. Moreover, U.S. businesses dealing with family-oriented cultures often see them as nepotistic (that is, as practicing favoritism or patronage, usually with family members). In many instances, such corporations literally hire and promote bona fide family

Many U. S. managers experience difficulty working in the Middle East.
(David Austen/Stock Boston)

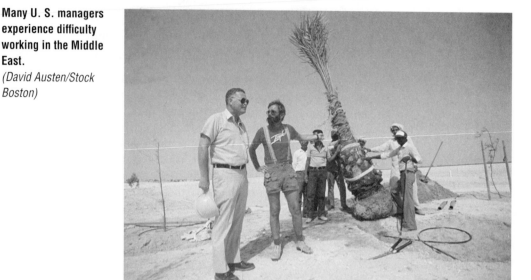

members over other candidates who may be more qualified. Trompenaars notes that the strict hierarchy in family corporations is akin (metaphorically) to the gradient angle of a triangle. The steeper the angle, the stricter the hierarchy. The hierarchy in the family-oriented corporation is analogous to the steep triangles depicted in Figure 10-2.[20]

VERBAL AND NONVERBAL CODES

Obviously, understanding the verbal and nonverbal codes of your foreign counterpart is an essential part of a successful business venture. Although it is true that most of your foreign business partners will speak some English, your knowledge and use of their language demonstrates your willingness to meet them halfway and will be very much appreciated. International business expert Roger Axtell argues that although most of the representatives of international corporations speak English, the English spoken in the United States is of such a type that it is not understood by foreigners. In a survey of persons doing business overseas with a foreign corporation, Axtell found that 80 percent had difficulties interacting with foreigners because of the latter's misunderstanding of American English. However, the same respondents reported that the problem lay with them, not their foreign counterparts. The type of English spoken in the United States is so laden with jargon, colloquialisms, and slang that English-speaking foreigners have a very difficult time understanding us. Most foreigners learn "standard" English and are unfamiliar with how Americans actually "use" the language. As Axtell notes, American business is perhaps the worst offender in language proliferation.

Axtell points out what he calls the "seven deadliest sins" of international mis-

FIGURE 10-2   Organizational Hierarchies Across Cultures

Turkey
Pakistan
Singapore
China
Malaysia
Hong Kong

France
Greece
Philippines
Thailand
Indonesia

Denmark
Canada
USA

SOURCE: *Adapted from F. Trompenaars,* Riding the Waves of Culture: Understanding Diversity in Global Business *(Burr Ridge, Ill.: Irwin, 1994).*

understanding: local color, jargon, slang, officialese, humor, vocabulary, and grammar.[21] When conducting business with your foreign counterpart, be very conscious of terms and phrases that may be well understood within your corporation but which may be misunderstood by an outsider. At St. Norbert College, for example, women's groups such as sororities annually select an "Ugly Man" to represent their group in homecoming activities. An "Ugly Man" is analogous to a homecoming king. Imagine how a foreigner might respond to seeing "Ugly Man" on a potential client's resume! Axtell recalls a U.S. firm that lost an international client by using the phrase "This is a whole new ballgame" during sensitive renegotiations of a contract. Apparently the client did not consider the negotiations a "game" and terminated their relationship. Consider the slang, jargon, and colloquialisms listed in the box on page 320 and how they might be misinterpreted across cultures.

Axtell recommends that when verbally communicating with your foreign host, you should not speak too quickly or too slowly. Fast is difficult to comprehend, whereas slow is offensive and condescending. Finally, Axtell remembers a piece of advice given to him by a well-traveled vice president, who recommended talking with your foreign host as if answering a somewhat hard-of-hearing, wealthy old aunt who just asked you how much money to leave you in her will.[22]

Another important consideration here is the use of a mediator. Unlike U.S. businesspeople, who enjoy face-to-face encounters and direct bargaining, some Asian cultures, such as China, save face by negotiating through the use of a mediator. In addition, because of their emphasis on the group, the overuse of personal pronouns (for example, *I*) is perceived negatively.

One's verbal style is of utmost importance in situations where managers need to resolve conflicts with coworkers from different cultures. For example, American managers often misinterpret silence used by their Asian (e.g., Chinese, Japanese, Korean) coworkers. Asians characteristically express objection with silence. U.S. managers often interpret the silence as an expression of consent. Similarly, many Asian

Intercultural Conversation

Intercultural Conversation: Misinterpretation of Common U.S. Phrases

American Phrase	Foreign Interpretation
"See ya later."	To schedule a definite future contact.
"Y'all come for another visit."	Bring more people next time. "Y'all" interpreted to mean "more."
"You're on a roll."	I look like a hot dog or hamburger?
"Let's use a shotgun approach."	Shoot our competition?
"Let's organize this like a Chinese menu."	Very offensive to Chinese counterparts.
"Send me your response ASAP."	Have no idea what you're talking about.
"I have to find a bathroom."	You're going to take a bath now?
"It'll take me the better part of the day to finish this report."	Which is the better part? Morning, midday, or evening?
"We need to cover all the bases."	Do we need a blanket?

managers misread U.S. managers' directness in communication. Asians often see directness as unreasonable and disrespectful. Morris and his colleagues point out that Asian managers typically use an avoiding style of conflict resolution character-ized as low levels of assertiveness and cooperativeness. The avoiding manager tends to evade conflict. Conversely, U.S. managers favor a competing style of conflict res-olution, characterized as high levels of assertiveness and low levels of cooperative-ness. The competing manager confronts conflict directly and forcefully.[23]

Although your knowing your foreign partner's language (and his or her knowing yours) is certainly an advantage, there are other communication considerations, independent of verbal language, that can affect your business propositions—most notably nonverbal communication. As discussed in Chapter 8, nonverbal commu-nication varies a great deal across cultures. One's kinesic, paralinguistic, olfactory, haptic, and proxemic behaviors can be interpreted differently depending on with whom one is interacting. For example, greetings occur in all cultures and are typi-cally ritualized to that culture. In the United States, businesspersons typically greet each other with a firm handshake and direct eye contact. In the Middle East, how-ever, a limp handshake is preferred. Moreover, many Middle Eastern men will hold hands with their male counterparts as a display of trust in the business deal. Most U.S. businessmen would find such behavior disquieting, to say the least. Direct eye contact should also be avoided during greetings in many Asian cultures, where it is interpreted as a challenge or as an instigation of conflict. In what may seem like un-usual rituals, some East African tribesmen greet each other by spitting at each other's feet, and Tibetan men greet each other by sticking out their tongues.[24]

In addition to kinesics, Trompenaars notes that one's tone of voice may prove crucial during cross-cultural business transactions. Tone of voice can communi-

FIGURE 10-3   Vocal Patterns Across Cultures

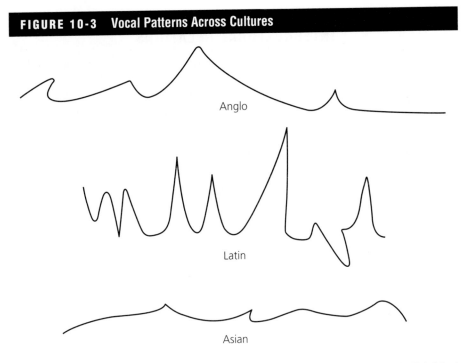

Anglo

Latin

Asian

SOURCE: *Adapted from F. Trompenaars,* Riding the Waves of Culture: Understanding Diversity in Global Business *(Burr Ridge, Ill.: Irwin, 1994).*

cate much about the person speaking. Figure 10-3 shows characteristic paralinguistic patterns for Anglo, Latin, and Asian cultures.

Trompenaars suggests that fluctuations and variations in vocal pitch carry different meanings across cultures. For example, in Latin-American cultures, exaggerated ups and downs in pitch communicate that the individual is actively involved in what is being said. Many Asian cultures, however, prefer a more monotonous style, which communicates self-control and respect for the person with whom one is communicating. Most Anglo speakers are in between the Latin and Asian models. Trompenaars recalls the story of a British manager in Nigeria who raised his voice during meetings and presentations. The Nigerians perceived his way of speaking as positive and as demonstrative of his concern for the issues. The same manager was relocated to Malaysia, where he employed the same vocal style, but in Malaysia he was perceived negatively and was quickly transferred out.[25] Other channels of nonverbal communication are equally important in the cross-cultural business exchange but are often overlooked—for example, olfactics, or smell. Most Americans are taught to bathe frequently and to mask as much of the natural odor of the human body as possible. To other cultures we smell antiseptic. Koreans, for example, have been known to call American businesspersons "butter-breath." Apparently our use of dairy products is evident in our breath.

INTERCULTURAL RELATIONS

As mentioned throughout this textbook, especially in Chapters 6 and 9, perceptions of relationships vary dramatically across cultures. Especially important are male/female relations within corporations. Although women have made great strides in the U.S. corporate world, in many cultures women still occupy a subordinate role and are treated as second-class citizens. Because of this situation, more than half (54 percent) of multinational corporations in North America say they are hesitant to send women managers abroad for fear that the host culture's perspective on women will negatively impact their effectiveness. According to Nancy Adler, many countries simply do not promote women into management positions. In Japan, reports Adler, women are encouraged to obtain the level of education that will enable them to *marry* managers rather than attain management positions for themselves. In fact, according to Adler, many large Japanese corporations encourage women employees to marry male employees, then use the company's antinepotism policies to force the women to retire. Moreover, one-third of Japanese companies indicate that they will not promote women college graduates even if they are as qualified as their male counterparts. Even in Europe, reports Adler, opposition to women in high-level management is quite strong. In one survey, nearly 70 percent of British managers said they preferred male applicants for executive positions. Likewise, two-thirds of Italian managers said they did not want to receive orders from female managers. In Germany, nearly 95 percent of job advertisements for top executives use the masculine noun form, thereby discouraging women from even applying for the position. There are encouraging signs, however, especially for American women entering the international market. According to Adler, in many cultures, foreign women (for example, Americans) are much better received in management positions than local women. Moreover, many women managing abroad have achieved excellent results, thereby encouraging U.S. corporations to continue sending women abroad. In addition, the success of U.S. women abroad encourages the local community to hire more of their own women into management positions.[26]

Management Practices Across Cultures

As more and more U.S. businesses enter into the intensely competitive global marketplace, they will be confronted with myriad management styles, especially within those cultures with whom we do much business. In 2001, three of the United States' top five trading partners were Mexico, Japan, and the Federal Republic of Germany. In the month of November 2001, the U.S.-Mexico trade totaled nearly $20 billion, U.S.-Japan trade totaled $14.5 billion, and U.S.-Germany trade totaled nearly $7 billion.[27] Because Mexico, Japan, and Germany represent such important trading partners, their cultures and management practices will be profiled next.

JAPANESE MANAGEMENT PRACTICES

Japan is a country of nearly 130 million people including a work force of 64 million. According to the United States Department of State, per capita income is just over $25,000 a year. Japan is considered an urban culture because only about 7 percent of the work force is engaged in agriculture. Japan's $4.7 trillion economy is the second largest in the world. After maintaining one of the highest economic growth rates in the world from the 1960s through the 1980s, the Japanese economy slowed significantly in the 1990s. Although Japan's long-term economic prospects are considered good, Japan was in its worst recession since the 1940s. For example, Japan's gross domestic product grew at an average of only 1 percent annually between 1991 and 1998. In 2001, Japan's forecast growth was expected to be 1.7 percent. According to the State Department, the economic relationship between Japan and the United States is quite healthy. Although it has taken time and patience, American businesses are competing successfully in Japanese markets.[28]

As American/Japanese business relationships continue to develop, managers and workers from both countries will be expected to communicate with each other. In so doing, they may find very different work ethics and managerial styles. First, the Japanese corporation is very paternalistic (i.e., fatherly, patriarchal). Most Japanese corporations furnish their workers with a host of services and social activities designed to foster allegiance and group harmony. A typical Japanese worker may spend as many as four hours a day commuting to and from work in Tokyo. It is not at all uncommon for a Japanese worker to spend as many as fifteen hours a day on the job. He (they are mostly men) is expected to be at work early and to remain there until late at night, six days a week. Many Japanese work groups begin their day by exercising together, called *taiso*. Interestingly, the primary purpose of the *taiso* is not for physical benefits, but to get the group members engaging in coordinated activity. After the day's work is finished, businesses encourage their employees to eat and drink together to maintain harmonious group relationships. Though it may appear that such activity is for purely social reasons, the underlying motivation is to continue work. According to Brown, Lubove, and Kwalwasser, the typical Japanese worker spends over 2,500 hours on the job every year, compared with about 1,900 hours for the typical U.S. worker. In their interviews of Japanese managers, Brown, Lubove, and Kwalwasser found that because many Japanese workers spend their entire working careers with one company, maintaining harmony with their colleagues is considered a prime motive. Brown and his colleagues also found that, on average, Japanese managers are less satisfied with their jobs, perhaps because of the stress of long hours.[29]

Robert Bolda of the University of Michigan asked Japanese and American managers to list the skills, behaviors, traits, or other attributes that they thought were characteristic of productive supervisors. Although there was a broad range of agreement between the Japanese and American managers, there were some interesting disagreements, as outlined in the box on page 324.

In reviewing the results of this survey, Bolda concluded that Japanese managers

INTERCULTURAL COMMUNICATION IN PRACTICE IN THE REAL WORLD

Traits Characteristic of Productive Supervisors

Traits Endorsed by Japanese and American Managers	Traits Endorsed by American Managers	Traits Endorsed by Japanese Managers
Prioritizes tasks	Works well with people	Open to innovation
Motivates employees	Delegates	Good listener
Communicates clearly	Considers alternatives	Puts right person in right job
Leadership	States expectations	Thinks in future tense
Makes good use of resources	Good speaker	Thinks about the "big picture"
Decision-making ability	Can shift attention	Helps other departments get job done
	Knowledgeable of company	Monitors employee progress

Traits Where Japanese and American Managers Differed the Most

Believes in his or her ability to get job done (Americans agreed/Japanese disagreed)

Helps other departments get their job done (Americans disagreed/Japanese agreed)

Delegates (Americans agreed/Japanese disagreed)

Reprimands and disciplines employees (Americans agreed/Japanese disagreed)

Monitors employees (Americans disagreed/Japanese agreed)

SOURCE: Data from R. A. Bolda, "Correlates of Personal Productivity of Supervisors: Perceptions of American and Japanese Managers," *Current Psychology*, 9 (1990), 339–346.

endorsed behaviors that were other oriented and principle oriented. For example, Japanese managers preferred traits that dealt with innovations, employee selection, and performance monitoring. The American managers, on the other hand, supported behaviors that were more instrumental—that is, goal oriented—such as individual supervisory skills, belief in one's own ability, and decision making.[30]

Although the Japanese and American managers in Bolda's survey agreed on many of the traits that constitute good management, the differences expressed by the two groups of managers may lead to communication problems on the job. Neil Abramson and his colleagues maintain that contract negotiations between Japanese and American firms are often difficult and frustrating. Abramson points out that the American preference for individualistic rational decision making often clashes with the Japanese tendency toward relationships and group harmony. Moreover, Abramson points out that American and Japanese managers may require different kinds of information to solve problems or negotiate contracts. Americans, for example, tend to negotiate by exchanging information with the expectation that the other side will reciprocate. Furthermore, Americans have a tendency to focus on efficiency and quick closure to negotiations by pinpointing disagreements and attempting to resolve them promptly. Additionally, Americans

Assumptions about what constitutes good management differ across cultures.
(Charles Gupton/Stock Market)

do not highly value interpersonal relationships with their negotiation partners, instead allowing legal contracts to define future alliances. On the other hand, contends Abramson, Japanese negotiate by trying to foster steady relationships with their partners with the ultimate goal of consensus. Whereas Americans negotiate a contractual agreement, Japanese think of it as negotiating a relationship. During initial stages of a negotiation, Japanese are more interested in interpersonal attraction and deference toward their partner (as opposed to clearly defining any disagreements). Instead of quickly reaching closure, Japanese prefer to take their time in order to establish relationships built on trust and deliberate negotiations.

In their comparison of North American and Japanese management students, Abramson and his colleagues found that the North Americans preferred a thinking-based cognitive style that is logical, impersonal, and objective. Abramson claims that such a style may lead to quick, impersonal, and analytically based decisions. In such cases, there may be a tendency to subordinate human relationships by discounting some kinds of information (for example, affiliation with partner) in favor of theoretically based models of decision making. The Japanese management students, on the other hand, preferred a feeling-based cognitive style that emphasizes the human element in decision making. Such a style, according to Abramson, expresses a concern for group harmony and a preference for friendly relations with one's partner. In decision making and in contract negotiations, Japanese may resist fast decisions and remain open to new information.[31]

In related research, Brett and Okumura studied the negotiation styles of U.S. and Japanese managers. They reasoned that because U.S. culture is individualistic and egalitarian and Japanese culture is collectivistic and hierarchical, managers from the two cultures would exercise different styles of negotiation. Their results

INTERCULTURAL COMMUNICATION IN PRACTICE IN THE REAL WORLD

Negotiating with the Japanese

A recent edition of *Manager's Intelligence Report* listed several recommendations for negotiating with the Japanese. The recommendations are based on case study analyses of a variety of U.S. firms doing business in Japan.

1. **Stay in the game.** Be prepared for long negotiations. The Japanese take their time to get to know you and your business. They want to establish a relationship before signing any deal.

2. **Understand the "need" principle.** The Japanese will try to create and count on the idea that you "need" their deal. Once you start believing that you might lose the much-needed deal, you lose face to them.

3. **Communicate with their top decision makers.** Too much time is wasted interacting with people who can't and won't make decisions.

4. **Suspend assumptions and expectations.** The deal isn't done until it's done. Do not assume that once you have an agreement it's a done deal.

5. **Focus on the Japanese rather than yourself.** Attend to what the Japanese need from you and demonstrate how you can accommodate them.

6. **Instead of telling them, let the Japanese discover what you want.** Negotiations in the United States are often characterized by one side explicitly telling the other side what it wants and needs. But to the Japanese the skill of negotiating is to allow your position to surface on its own.

SOURCE: "What You Can Learn from Japanese Negotiation," *Manager's Intelligence Report, N* (1996), 8–10.

showed that Japanese negotiators paid significantly more attention to power during negotiations than did U.S. negotiators. Brett and Okumura also found a difference in the two cultures' focus on self-interest during negotiations. The American negotiators were much more focused on self-interest than were the Japanese. The two researchers also found that joint gains in negotiations were significantly higher in intracultural negotiations than in intercultural ones. In other words, when U.S. managers negotiated with other U.S. managers, there were higher gains than when U.S. managers negotiated with Japanese managers. The same result was found among Japanese managers.[32]

In most organizations across cultures, managers are in positions of power and influence. As such, managers engage in a variety of behavioral strategies to influence the attitudes and behaviors of their subordinates. In a recent study, Rao, Hashimoto, and Rao surveyed Japanese managers regarding their preferences for a variety of influence strategies. Although some of the Japanese managers preferred influence tactics similar to those preferred by U.S. managers, Rao, Hashimoto, and Rao identified several strategies that appear to be unique to the Japanese. One strategy is labeled *firm's authority*. In contrast to American managers, who may appeal to "higher-ups" to influence their employees, Japanese managers do not appeal to a specific person in the organizational hierarchy, but to the entire organization itself, independent of their superiors. This strategy is probably linked to the Japanese concept of business organization as a family. A second type of strategy, called *personal development,* occurs when a Japanese manager convinces his (most managers are men) employees to comply with a request to enhance their careers within the organization. This tactic may be effective because many Japanese remain with a single company for their entire lives. American managers, on the other hand, convince employees that by complying with a request, the employees will develop skills they can take with them when they leave the organization.

Another strategy is labeled *socializing.* With this strategy, Japanese managers ask to spend time with their employees after hours. According to Rao, Hashimoto, and Rao, such a strategy allows for informal interaction between managers and subordinates that is impossible in the context of the formal work environment. Interestingly, Rao, Hashimoto, and Rao report that Japanese managers in Canada were disappointed when their subordinates rejected their requests to socialize after work. The Japanese managers felt that this severely limited their influence potential and had to resort to using assertive tactics on the job. Rao, Hashimoto, and Rao report that Japanese managers use a variety of tactics outside the work environment to influence their subordinates.

In general, Rao, Hashimoto, and Rao indicate that compared with American managers, Japanese managers use influence tactics that are subtle and indirect. For example, if a Japanese manager wants a subordinate to focus on the Canadian market for a specific product, the manager, rather than telling him directly, might funnel information about that market to the employee, hoping that the employee would sense his intent. In addition, Japanese managers use strategies that rely on the influence of the organization and group harmony. Such strategies are associated with the three main principles of Japanese management practices: (1) lifetime employment, (2) promotion through seniority, and (3) consensus decision making.[33] The promotion system in Japanese companies is based almost exclusively on seniority. In contrast to the norm in many U.S. companies, the older employees get, the more enthused they become about their corporation and the more effectively they communicate their enthusiasm to the other employees. According to William Drake and Associates, work attitudes within an organization evolve from the senior members of the organization, who are ensured promotion and lifetime employment. One reason the older employees are so satisfied with their jobs is that they know that they are secure; they do not have to worry about the younger, more energetic employees' jeopardizing their jobs.[34]

While interacting with Japanese businesspersons, Americans often notice behaviors that are widely misunderstood by non-Japanese.

To be sure, the Japanese businessperson has perceptions of American behavior that may be misinterpreted as well. For example, Japanese are astonished by the typical American's informality and spontaneity. The quick pace of conversation and what are perceived to be ostentatious—that is, flashy or showy—nonverbal mannerisms are off-putting to most Japanese. In fact, many Japanese believe that Americans are inclined to make mistakes because of the fast pace with which they conduct

INTERCULTURAL COMMUNICATION IN PRACTICE IN THE REAL WORLD

American Misinterpretations of Japanese Behaviors

American Perception	Japanese Reality
1. The Japanese are really shy; they don't talk much.	As a high-context culture, the Japanese obtain much of their information from the social context and do not feel a need to talk. They are comfortable with silence.
2. Japanese fall asleep a lot during class or presentations.	Many Japanese close their eyes when they are deeply concentrating.
3. Japanese say yes even when they mean no. Why can't they just say what they mean?	To save face (yours and theirs), Japanese will agree with you in principle.
4. It takes Japanese forever to make decisions or even to respond to a fax or written correspondence.	Japanese will not make a decision without first consulting relevant others to reach a consensus.
5. Japanese will never look you in the eye.	Indirect eye contact is a sign of deference in Japan.
6. When Japanese talk, they seem so ambiguous. I never know what they're trying to say or what they really mean.	Japanese language is vague. But even more, to the Japanese, communication is a two-way process. The burden of understanding rests with the speaker AND the listener. Often the speaker will only hint at what is meant. The listener must be an active participant.

SOURCE: Table adapted from pages 410–412 of *When Cultures Collide* by R. D. Lewis. Copyright © 2000 Nicholas Brealey Publishing. Used by permission. (London: Nicholas Brealey, 1997). British linguist Richard Lewis is well known for his work on cross-cultural differences in organizations, especially in Japan, where he spent a number of years as a tutor to the Japanese Imperial Family.

business dealings. The "don't take it personally—it's just business" attitude portrayed by most American businesspersons intimidates Japanese because to them it disrupts the harmony of the business relationship. The Japanese tend to view conversations and negotiations as formalized rituals rather than as a meeting of minds.[35]

GERMAN MANAGEMENT PRACTICES

Although there have been fluctuations in the German economy since reunification, in 1997 the German economy was slowly growing at about a 2.5 percent rate;

it is now the fourth largest economy in the world. The U.S. Department of State maintains that the German market, the largest in Europe, is attractive to many U.S. businesses. Germans are attracted to innovative products that display high quality and contemporary styling. They are especially interested in high-tech products, particularly those that assist them in entering the age of the Internet.[36]

Like the United States and Europe in general, Germany is a decentralized collection of states and regions. Many are quite diverse, with unique customs and conventions. The northern and the southern regions are particularly different, so generalizing about Germany is difficult and should be approached with some degree of caution. According to intercultural consultants William Drake and Associates, most Germans believe that people are controlled by their own actions, that facts are more important than face (in sharp contrast to the Japanese), and that factual honesty is more important than politeness (again, clashing with Japanese conventions). According to Drake, German children are taught that useless people amount to nothing and that they are to be quiet and respectful. Children are also taught to "save for a rainy day."[37]

Focusing their analysis primarily on West Germans, anthropologists Edward and Mildred Hall contend that compartmentalization is the most prominent structural feature of German culture—that is, that Germans have a tendency to isolate and divide many aspects of their lives into discrete, independent units. Germans are known to compartmentalize their daily schedules, their educational system, their office buildings, corporations, homes, and even lines of communication. In fact, Hall and Hall argue that on the job, Germans will not share information with others except within their own working groups. Hall and Hall maintain that such a restricted flow of information may be the biggest obstacle in doing business with the Germans. One result of German compartmentalization is a culture in which significant events and changes can take place without people knowing about them. Even informal information networks that connect public and private organizational boundaries are rare in Germany.[38] Given this condition, U.S. companies wishing to do business in Germany would be wise to understand that they may not be able to operate out of a centralized location. Instead, they may have to set up multiple sites from which to conduct commerce.

German emphasis on compartmentalization manifests itself in many areas of German life and business, particularly in respect to privacy and specialization. Germans are a very private (and formal) people. Most German managers isolate themselves in their offices behind closed doors, contrasting sharply with open-door policies exercised by American managers. Doors are an important cultural symbol to the Germans. According to Hall and Hall, doors provide a protective shield between the individual and outsiders. When encountering a closed door in German businesses or homes, an "intruder" should always knock. As Hall and Hall note, closed doors uphold the honor of the space, afford a boundary between people, and eliminate the possibility of eavesdropping, interruptions, and accidental intrusions. Moreover, according to Hall and Hall, within corporations, the closed door indicates that a manager respects the privacy of subordinates and is not looking over their shoulders.[39]

German compartmentalization can also be seen in the overall market strategy

of many very successful German corporations. Unlike many U.S. or Japanese corporate conglomerates whose global market success is attributable to diversifica-
tion, many German firms concentrate on specialization—that is, doing one thing
and doing it right. German corporations with large shares of specialized markets
can focus on design, quality, and service rather than on competing with price.
Such corporations manufacture a smaller and narrower class of products, sell to
fewer consumers, and contract with fewer suppliers than their less successful
competition. To be sure, many of these exclusive products are expensive. But the
Germans believe that specialization leads to quality and profit. German products
are known worldwide for their high caliber and workmanship (for example, Mer-
cedes, BMW). Steiner Optik maintains 80 percent of the global market for military
field glasses. Krones manufactures over 70 percent of the world's bottling labeling
machines. The Germans seem to be teaching the rest of the world that, at least for
them, specialization works.[40]

Like the United States, Germany is considered a low-context, monochronic culture, except even more so. According to Hall and Hall, the German language is quite
literal, individual German words having exact and precise meaning. For example,
the Germans have no fewer than eight words for "comfort," each reflecting a slightly
different type of comfort.[41] Having been conditioned by their language, Germans
are fairly formal, nitpicky about precision, punctual, and fanatic about facts. All of
these characteristics carry over into their business relations. On the job and in business dealings, Germans are absolutely obsessed with facts and precision. Lines of
authority are carefully observed. Interactions between business partners and
friends are reserved and formalized. Germans are very conscious of rank and will
always refer to someone by the person's appropriate title. Even neighbors who may
have lived next door to one another for years address each other with their last
names, as in "Herr (Mr.) Schmidt." If a person also carries a degree, such as a Ph.D.
or an M.D., he will be called "Herr Doktor Neuleib," and so forth.[42] Women, however, are typically addressed with their first names, as in "Frau Batina Neulieb."
Even in social situations, Germans often appear unfriendly. They generally will not
smile during a greeting and are intolerant of small talk. On the job, German workers expect that their managers will respect their privacy and that procedures will be
executed precisely. The box on page 331 outlines some features of doing business
with the Germans that may help Americans transacting business in Germany.

Although to many Americans the outward appearance and demeanor of the
typical German is aloof, intense, humorless, and quite formal and rigid, on the inside, Germans desire meaningful interpersonal relationships. As intercultural expert Richard Lewis asserts:

> Anglo-Saxons do not always see the way towards making quick friends with them,
> but when they succeed in entering into the somewhat complicated structure of a
> German friendship, they find rich rewards. A German is generally a loyal and true
> friend of incredible durability. Outwardly glum and cautious, they are inwardly
> desperate for affection and popularity. They want to be cherished just as the rest
> of us do. . . . A German friendship is indeed a very worthwhile investment.[43]

INTERCULTURAL COMMUNICATION IN PRACTICE IN THE REAL WORLD

Interacting Effectively with Germans

1. Be prepared. In business, the Germans will be very informed and will expect that you are too.

2. Engage in only minimal small talk.

3. Be informed about, and use, appropriate titles.

4. Avoid emotional appeals. Emphasize facts and figures. Germans respect quantitative reports.

5. Observe hierarchical seating and order of speaking.

6. Organize your presentation in compartments, and have your specialists present their own areas separately and as distinct parts of the presentation.

7. Be very punctual; start and stop as you planned. Follow your agenda closely.

8. Avoid humor. Be frank, direct, and honest. Demonstrate that you have done your homework.

SOURCE: Based on E. T. Hall and M. R. Hall, *Understanding Cultural Differences* (Yarmouth, Maine: Intercultural Press, 1990); William Drake and Associates, "Managing Business Relationships in Germany" (1997) (www.culturebank.com/demo/demogermany/sld001.htm); R. D. Lewis, *When Cultures Collide* (London: Nicholas Brealey, 1997); P. R. Harris and R. T. Moran, *Managing Cultural Differences,* 4th ed. (Houston: Gulf Publishing, 1996).

MANAGEMENT PRACTICES IN MEXICO

In 1994, Canada, Mexico, and the United States entered into the North American Free Trade Agreement (NAFTA). In 2001, the United States accounted for over 80 percent of Mexico's total trade. Mexico is the United States' second most important trading partner following Canada. In 2001, the Mexican peso was one of the strongest currencies in the world against the U.S. dollar. In addition to its economic development, the Mexican political climate has improved dramatically too. Elections have become more free and fair, and in 2000, the National Action Party won the presidency, the first opposition party to win in years. Many U.S. government officials believe that Mexico's stabilizing political system and economic development represent a unique opportunity for U.S. businesses.[44]

As mentioned earlier, a country's cultural orientation and values are typically reflected in the business practices of that culture. Three dimensions of cultural variability discussed in Chapter 2 are closely associated with Mexican business practices. These three include individualism-collectivism, power distance, and uncertainty avoidance. Generally, in comparison with the United States, Mexico is more collectivistic, and is considered a high-power-distance and high-uncertainty-avoidant culture.[45] Mexican collectivism is evident in the Mexican workplace. Generally, Mexican organizations do not emphasize self-determination on the job. Unlike workers in the United States, Mexicans generally are not rewarded for initiative. Pelled and Xin point out that Mexicans see work as a "necessary evil." To many Mexicans, work is required to appreciate the more important things in life, such as family and friends. Pelled and Xin maintain that Mexicans who are too eager to spend long hours at work or who are preoccupied with their careers are seen as odd and unusual. De Forest asserts that Mexican employers seek employees who are agreeable, respectful, and obedient rather than innovative and independent.[46]

In the United States, people often change jobs and switch organizations in order to get ahead and be promoted. U.S. workers are generally in charge of their own careers and strive to succeed individually. Schuler and his colleagues argue that under Mexican law, Mexican organizations are responsible for the life, health, and dignity of their workers. In this way, Mexican organizations are considered paternalistic. Consistent with a collectivistic orientation, Mexican workers value harmonious relations between union and management. Conversely, in the United States, union and management interactions are often antagonistic. De Forest points out that traditional Mexican ideals stress employee/employer interdependence, mutual responsibilities, loyalty between superiors and subordinates, belongingness, cooperation (rather than competition), and not exceeding boundaries. According to De Forest, Mexican employers rebuff employees who criticize to higher authorities and are competitive on the job. Such behaviors disrupt the harmony of the organization.[47]

Mexico is considered a high-power-distance culture. Recall that in high-power-distance cultures, people expect and accept that the power within the culture and its institutions will be distributed unequally. De Forest contends that Mexico's high power distance can be seen in the government, in the church, and throughout Mexican society. According to De Forest, most Mexican businesses have a rigid hierarchy where the power is centralized in the person or people at the top. Often the top positions are not gained through hard work and initiative but are inherited or acquired through friendships or mutual favors. De Forest has observed that Mexican managers reward submission, direction, and loyalty to the person with power.[48]

Relationships among Mexican managers and their subordinates are generally distant and communication is rather formal. For example, managers and subordinates are usually not on a first-name basis. Unlike U.S. manager/subordinate communication, interactive strategies that promote equality, participative decision making, open communication, and employee ownership are not considered necessary—or even desirable—in Mexican organizations. When interacting with Mexican employees, managers need not explain the reasoning behind a decision because employees may perceive this as a sign of weakness. In fact, Mexican workers expect to be given orders. They accept their unequal status and prefer that those in power protect their interests, give clear direction, and treat them with civility. Communication channels should follow the hierarchical structure of the business.[49]

In low- (or weak) uncertainty-avoidant cultures like the United States, employees are encouraged to innovate and take risks. In high (or strong) uncertainty-avoidant cultures like Mexico, innovative or risk-taking behavior is inappropriate. Mexican workers generally prefer close supervision. Likewise, compensation based on incentive is eschewed. Mexican workers prefer to know exactly what they are supposed to do, and they want to be rewarded for doing it.[50]

De Forest maintains that one of the most frustrating aspects for Americans doing business in Mexico is the Mexican perception of time. American managers should be advised to be patient. According to De Forest, life is simply slower in Mexico than in the U.S. She points out that in Mexico, time does not advance: it tends to be either right now or some other time. American managers should be prepared for delays. De Forest says that phone service may take months to be installed or repaired; obtaining a post office box can take weeks or months; people frequently show up late for meetings; businesses and government offices open and close at all hours, as if at random; electricity shuts down for no apparent reason and may be off for days.[51]

Since the start of NAFTA, the United States and Mexico have become active trading partners. If American managers can adjust to the culturally influenced business environment in Mexico, they can make great strides. The key to being successful in Mexico is adjusting and adapting to the cultural environment.

Conflict in Organizations

Conflict is an inevitable part of life. Attempts to eliminate conflict are futile. Conflict can, however, be reduced and managed. In fact, effective conflict management can have many positive outcomes. As U.S. businesses increase their interactions with different cultures, intercultural conflict will be inescapable. Young Kim has developed a model of intercultural conflict: it points out several variables that facilitate or promote conflict.[52] According to Kim, there are three levels of intercultural conflict, including individual, intermediary, and societal levels. At each level, there are factors that increase the probability that conflict will ignite.

The *individual level of intercultural conflict* refers to factors that the individual personally brings to the interaction. An individual's attitudes, dispositions, and beliefs are included here. Cognitive simplicity/rigidity refers to the degree of

RECAP

Factors Facilitating Intercultural Conflict		
Individual Level	**Intermediary Level**	**Societal Level**
Cognitive simplicity/ rigidity	Segregation and contact	History of subjugation
Ingroup bias	Intergroup salience	Ideological/Structural inequities
Insecurity/frustration	Status discrepancy	Minority group strength
Divergent behavior		

inflexibility in the way that the individual thinks about people from different cultures. Rigid, simplistic thinking would include gross stereotyping (e.g., all blacks are lazy; all whites are rich; all Japanese are sneaky). In-group bias refers to the degree to which the individual is ethnocentric. (Recall from Chapter 1 that ethnocentrism is defined as viewing one's own group as at the center of everything and using the standards of one's own group to measure or gauge the worth of all other groups.) Insecurity/frustration refers to the degree to which the individual has a high level of uncertainty about, and fear of, out-group members. Divergent behavior refers to the behavioral patterns of the individual that clearly differentiate and distance him or her from out-group members. For example, obviously different speech patterns or accents may ostensibly separate groups from one another. Sometimes people even exaggerate their mannerisms and speech to accentuate their differences from out-groups. Imagine two employees working together, each from a different culture, who have gross stereotypes of each other, are both ethnocentric, fear each other, and have highly divergent behavioral patterns. The model predicts that such a situation is likely to engender conflict.

The *intermediary level of intercultural conflict* refers to the actual location and context of the interaction. Some business environments may be more likely than others to facilitate conflict. Segregation and contact refer to the extent to which the cultural groups of the individuals interact on a daily basis. Perhaps the most basic condition for intercultural conflict is contact between diverse cultures or ethnicities on a day-to-day basis. Segregated workplaces do not allow for much interaction, and components at the individual level (e.g., cognitive rigidity, in-group bias, etc.) tend to escalate to intolerable levels that facilitate intercultural conflict. Intergroup salience refers to the observable physical and social differences between the conflicting individuals. Such cultural markers include distinct physical and behavioral differences, such as race, language, and speech patterns. As Kim notes, to the extent that the groups are culturally distinct, the communicative skills of the less powerful cultural group will clash with those of the majority group members. The majority group's symbol system is dominant. Status discrepancy refers to the degree to which conflicting parties differ in status along cultural lines. For example, blacks often argue that American culture practices an asymmetrical power structure. Blacks may feel that the American corporate culture reflects the same asymmetry. On the job, managers and supervisors have more power than workers. If all the managers in a business are white and all the workers are black (or Hispanic, etc.), then the status discrepancy is heightened.

The *societal level of intercultural conflict* includes factors that probably are out of the control of the interactants. These conditions include any history of subjugation, ideological/structural inequality, and minority group strength. The history of subjugation of one group by another is a key environmental factor in many intercultural conflicts. For example, blacks have long been subjugated by whites in America. Historically, African Americans were slaves. Even upon emancipation, they were not allowed to vote. As late as the 1960s, restaurants in the South had separate bathrooms, seating areas, and drinking fountains for blacks and whites. Often the tensions expressed today are rooted in the history of the subjugation of one group over another. Ideological and structural inequity refers to societal differences regarding power, prestige, and economic reward. Historically, in the United States, whites have held most of the power positions and gained most of the economic reward. Hence, there is a vast ideological and structural difference between whites and other groups. Blacks and Hispanics have much higher levels of unemployment, for example. Minority (i.e., microcultural) group strength refers to the amount of power (e.g., legal, political, economic) a particular group possesses. Microcultural groups vary in their ability to rally their members against structural inequalities. Minority group strength varies as a function of the status of the group's language within the society, the sheer numbers of members in the group, and forms of societal support (e.g., governmental services designed specifically for the group). Relative to other microcultural groups, blacks, for example, are economically and politically quite powerful. Political scientists argue, for instance, that presidential elections are swung by the African American voting block. According to Kim, the stronger the ethnic group strength, the more likely will the individual take action in intercultural conflict situations.[53]

Chapter Summary

Doing business and managing people in a culture other than one's own is a daunting task indeed. In order to be an effective business partner, one needs to have a knowledge and understanding of the culture in which one is doing business. This chapter has discussed how the principles presented throughout the text can be applied to the business world across cultures. The corporate culture usually mirrors the national culture. An understanding of the cultural, microcultural, environmental, perceptual, sociorelational, verbal, nonverbal, and relational contexts of the host culture increases the probability of being an effective and productive manager across cultures. Three diverse cultures—Japan, Germany, and Mexico—are active participants in the global marketplace, each with its own unique way of doing business. Managers who understand the cultural contexts of these cultures are in a much better position to do business there. As we have seen in this chapter, the Japanese are subtle and indirect, Germans are forthright and direct, while Mexicans are collective and hierarchical. Finally, we have seen that there are several factors that affect and facilitate intercultural conflict. Although conflict can never be eliminated, identifying these factors can help us reduce and manage conflict in our professional lives.

GLOSSARY OF TERMS

Cultural context: An accumulated pattern of values, beliefs, and behavior held by an identifiable group of people with a common verbal and nonverbal symbol system.

Environmental context: The geographical and psychological location of communication within some cultural context.

Individual-level factors that facilitate conflict: These include cognitive simplicity/rigidity, in-group bias, insecurity/frustration, and divergent behavior.

Intermediary-level factors that facilitate conflict: These include segregation and contact, intergroup salience, and status discrepancy.

Organizational culture: An organized pattern of values, beliefs, behaviors, and communication channels held by the members of an organization.

Perceptual context: The cognitive process by which persons gather, store, and retrieve information.

Power distance: The extent to which less powerful members of a particular culture accept and expect that power within the culture will be distributed unequally.

Societal-level factors that facilitate conflict: These include a history of subjugation, structural inequities, and minority group strength.

Sociorelational context: The roles that one assumes within a culture; roles are defined by verbal and nonverbal messages.

REFERENCES

1. F. Trompenaars, *Riding the Waves of Culture: Understanding Diversity in Global Business* (Burr Ridge, Ill.: Irwin, 1994), p. 14.

2. A. F. Alkhafaji, *Competitive Global Management: Principles and Strategies* (Delray Beach, Fla.: St. Lucie Press, 1995). *International Trade Statistics, 2001* (Geneva, Switzerland: World Trade Organization, 2001).

3. United States Department of Commerce, "A Profile of U.S. Exporting Companies: 1996–1997" (1999) (www.census.gov/foreign-trade/misc/edbrel.html).

4. Office of the United States Trade Representative, "NAFTA at Seven" (2001) (www.ustr.gov/idex.html).

5. United States Department of Commerce, U.S. Census Bureau, "Summary: 1997 Economic Census, Survey of Minority-Owned Business Enterprises" (Washington, D.C.: 2001) (www.census.gov/prod/ec97cs-7.pdf).

6. "Global Relocation Trends 2000 Survey Report" (New York: © 2000 by GMAC Global Relocation Services/Windham International).

7. R. M. Kanter, "Transcending Business Boundaries: 12,000 World Managers View Change," *Harvard Business Review* (May–June, 1991).

8. K. Hannon, "The Fast Track Now Leads Overseas," *US News and World Report,* 117 (1994), 94–96.

9. P. M. Rosenzweig, "National Culture and Management," (Cambridge: © Harvard Business School, President and Fellows of Harvard College, 1994).

10. Ibid.

11. B. M. Bass and P. C. Burger, *Assessment of Managers: An International Comparison* (New York: Free Press, 1979); N. J. Adler, N. Campbell, and A. Laurent, "In Search of Appropriate Methodology: From Outside the People's Republic of China Looking In," *Journal of International Business Studies,* 20 (1989), 61–74.

12. F. Elashmawi and R. R. Harris, *Multicultural Management: New Skills for Global Success* (Houston: Gulf Publishing, 1993).

13. Ibid.

14. Ibid.

15. D. S. Elenkov, "Differences and Similarities in Managerial Values Between U.S. and Russian Managers," *International Studies of Management & Organization,* 27 (1997), 85–107.

16. Trompenaars, *Riding the Waves of Culture.*

17. Elashmawi and Harris, *Multicultural Management.*

18. P. R. Harris and R. T. Moran, *Managing Cultural Differences* (Houston: Gulf Publishing, 1991).

19. Ibid.

20. Trompenaars, *Riding the Waves of Culture.*

21. R. E. Axtell, *Do's and Taboos Around the World: A Guide to International Behavior* (New York: Wiley, 1987).

22. Ibid.

23. M. W. Morris, K. Y. Williams, K. Leung, R. Larrick, M. T. Mendoza, D. Bhatnagar, J. Li, M. Kondo, J. Luo, and J. Hu, "Conflict Management Style: Accounting for Cross-National Differences," *Journal of International Business Studies,* 29 (1998), 729–748.

24. Some of these examples are from R. E. Axtell, *Gestures: The Do's and Taboos of Gestures and Body Language Around the World* (New York: Wiley, 1991).

25. Trompenaars, *Riding the Waves of Culture.*

26. N. J. Adler, "Competitive Frontiers: Women Managers in the Triad," *International Studies of Management and Organization,* 23 (1993), 3–24.

27. "Top Ten Countries with Which the U.S. Trades," (Washington, D.C.: United States Bureau of the Census, 2000) (www.census.gov/foreign-trade/top/dst/current/balance.html).

28. United States Department of State, "Background Notes: Japan" (Washington, D.C.: Bureau of Public Affairs, 2001).

29. W. S. Brown, R. E. Lubove, and J. Kwalwasser, "Karoshi: Alternative Perspectives of Japanese Management Styles," *Business Horizons,* 37 (1994), 58–61.

30. R. A. Bolda, "Correlates of Personal Productivity of Supervisors: Perceptions of American and Japanese Managers," *Current Psychology,* 9 (1990), 339–346.

31. N. R. Abramson, H. W. Lane, H. Nagai, and H. Takagi, "A Comparison of Canadian and Japanese Cognitive Styles: Implications for Management Interaction," *Journal of International Business Studies,* 24 (1993), 575–588.

32. J. M. Brett and T. Okumura, "Inter- and Intracultural Negotiation: U.S. and Japanese Negotiators," *Academy of Management Journal,* 41 (1998), 495–510.

33. A. Rao, K. Hashimoto, and A. Rao, "Universal and Culturally Specific Aspects of Influence: A Study of Japanese Managers," *The Leadership Quarterly,* 8 (1997), 295–313.

34. William Drake & Associates, "The Japanese Seniority System" (1997) (www.culturebank.com/jpn043.html).

35. William Drake & Associates, "Japanese and Americans: Sources of Mutual Misunderstandings" (1997) (www.culturebank.com/jpn027.html).

36. United States Department of Commerce, "Country Commercial Guide: Germany Fiscal Year 1998" (1997) (www.ita.doc.gov/uscs/ccg98/ccgogerm.html).

37. William Drake and Associates, "Managing Business Relationships in Germany" (1997) (www.culturebank.com/demo/demogermany/sld001.htm).

38. E. T. Hall and M. R. Hall, *Understanding Cultural Differences* (Yarmouth, Maine: Intercultural Press, 1990).

39. Ibid.

40. "German Lessons," *The Economist,* 340 (1996), 59.

41. Hall and Hall, *Understanding Cultural Differences.*

42. Ibid.; Drake and Associates, "Managing Business Relationships in Germany."

43. R. D. Lewis, *When Cultures Collide* (London: Nicholas Brealey, 1997), p. 212.

44. "Mexico: Country Commercial Guide" (Washington, D.C.: © United States & Foreign Commercial Service and the United States Department of State, 2001).

45. R. S. Schuler, S. E. Jackson, E. Jackofsky, and J. W. Slocum, "Managing Human Resources in Mexico: A Cultural Understanding," *Business Horizons,* 39 (1996), 55–62; L. H. Pelled and K. R. Xin, "Work Values and the Human Resource Management Implications: A Theoretical Comparison of China, Mexico, and the United States," *Journal of Applied Management Studies,* 6 (1997), 185–199.

46. Ibid; M. E. De Forest, "Hecho en Mexico: Tips for Success," *Apparel Industry,* 59 (1998), 98–104.

47. Schuler, Jackson, Jackofsky, and Slocum, "Managing Human Resources in Mexico"; De Forest, "Hecho en Mexico."

48. De Forest, "Hecho en Mexico."

49. Schuler, Jackson, Jackofsky, and Slocum, "Managing Human Resources in Mexico"; De Forest, "Hecho en Mexico."

50. Schuler, Jackson, Jackofsky, and Slocum, "Managing Human Resources in Mexico."

51. De Forest, "Hecho en Mexico."

52. Y. Y. Kim, "Interethnic Conflict: An Interdisciplinary Overview," in *Annual Review of Conflict Knowledge and Conflict Resolution, vol. 1,* ed. J. B. Gittler (New York: Garland, 1989); Y. Y. Kim, "Explaining Interethnic Conflict: An Interdisciplinary Overview" (paper presented at the annual convention of the Speech Communication Association, Chicago, Ill., 1990).

53. Ibid.

Acculturation and Culture Shock

Nothing so sensitizes us to our own culture as living outside it and then trying to return.

—John Condon and Fathi Yousef[1]

CHAPTER OBJECTIVES

After reading this chapter, you should be able to

- Define acculturation.
- Identify and discuss the factors that facilitate or hinder acculturation.
- Define culture shock.
- Identify and name the stages of culture shock.
- Recognize and discuss the causes of culture shock.
- Identify and discuss strategies for managing culture shock.
- Assess your level of culture shock.

H aving read the previous ten chapters of this book, you may well be motivated to go out and interact with people from different cultures. Perhaps you are even ready to travel abroad! In either case, remember that intercultural communication assumes the principle of difference. Not all intercultural communication is successful. This chapter focuses on two important features associated with intercultural communication as they relate to traveling abroad to foreign cultures: (1) acculturation and (2) culture shock. *Acculturation* is the process whereby you adapt to a new culture by adopting its values, attitudes, and practices. *Culture shock* is a multifaceted experience resulting from the stress associated with entering a new culture. Each of these variables affects the success rate of your intercultural communication experiences.

Acculturation

When individuals or groups of individuals enter into a new culture, they are faced with a different set of values, different behavioral patterns, and a different verbal and nonverbal communication system. In most (perhaps all) cases, such people are affected by their new cultural surroundings. *Acculturation* is the term used to describe what happens when people from one culture enter into a different culture. Acculturation was first defined by Redfield, Linton, and Herskovits as "those phenomena which result when groups of individuals having different cultures come into continuous first-hand contact with subsequent changes in the original culture pattern of either or both groups."[2] John Berry, well known for his work on acculturation, argues that in practice, when two different cultural groups engage in continuous contact, one of the two groups will induce more change than the other. For example, when immigrants enter the United States, they are probably going to experience more change than the people already living here. Berry also distinguishes between acculturation at the group level and acculturation at the individual level. He contends that the distinction is important because not all members of the group experience the same levels of acculturation.[3]

According to Berry, in pluralistic, diverse societies like the United States, there are three factors that bring cultural groups together, including mobility, voluntariness, and permanence. For example, regarding mobility, some groups experience acculturation because they have moved into a new culture, as do immigrants and refugees like the Hmong people of Laos who came to the United States. Other groups experience acculturation because they have had a new culture thrust upon them, as did indigenous peoples like Native Americans. Some groups enter into acculturation voluntarily, like the Mexican immigrants entering the United States, while others experience acculturation involuntarily, as did African slaves brought to the United States. Finally, some groups will experience a relatively permanent acculturation change, like African Americans and Mexican Americans, while others face only temporary acculturation, as do exchange students studying abroad or expatriates in temporary job transfers. Berry maintains that despite the some-

Acculturation depends on the degree to which people interact with their host culture while simultaneously maintaining or relinquishing attributes of their native culture.
(Lawrence Migdale/ Stock Boston)

times dramatic differences in the circumstances of acculturating groups, the overall acculturation process is universal across groups.[4]

ACCULTURATIVE STRESS

Most people experience a degree of stress and strain when they enter into a culture different from their own. Acculturation is often marked by physical and psychological changes that occur as a result of the adaptation required to function in a new and different cultural context. People adapting to new cultures face changes in their diet, climate, housing, communication, role prescriptions, media consumption, and the myriad rules, norms, and values of a new and (relatively) dissimilar culture. Moreover, such persons are isolated from familiar social networks and may experience problems with language, unemployment, and discrimination. The stress associated with such changes, known as *acculturative stress,* is marked by a reduction in one's physical and mental health.[5]

Many immigrant groups in the United States experience acculturative stress. A rather substantial body of research has documented the effects of acculturative stress on America's largest microcultural group, Hispanics. Miranda and Matheny point out that among Hispanics, acculturative stress is related to decreased self-efficacy expectations, decreased career aspirations, depression, and suicidal ideation (especially in Hispanic adolescents).[6] In their work with Hispanics, Julie and David Smart have observed that acculturative stress is associated with fatalistic thinking. Smart and Smart argue that acculturative stress has a lifelong effect on Hispanics' psychological well-being, decision-making abilities, occupational effectiveness, and physical health. Smart and Smart contend that for Hispanic immigrants, the most significant aspect of acculturative stress is the loss of social support from the family. They maintain that the loss of social support is particularly intense for Hispanics because of their collectivistic orientation. In fact, Hispanic women may be more likely than men to suffer from acculturative stress because in their native culture their roles were very clearly prescribed. In the United States, an individualistic, equality-based society, women's roles are more open and unspecified.[7] In his work, Hovey found that family dysfunction, separation from family, negative expectations for the future, and low income levels were significantly related to higher levels of acculturative stress.[8]

In an interesting line of research, Nwadiora and McAdoo investigated acculturative stress among Amerasian refugees in the United States. Amerasians are individuals born of American servicemen and Vietnamese or Cambodian women during the Vietnam war. Because of their mixed racial background, these children were considered half-breeds and social outcasts in their homeland. In 1987, Congress passed the Amerasian Homecoming Act permitting all Amerasians and their immediate families (including wives, half-siblings, and mothers) to immigrate to the United States. Nwadiora and McAdoo report that Amerasians have faced pervasive prejudice in the United States, often by Asian, European, and especially African Americans. In their research they found that the Amerasians experienced acculturative stress in the areas of spoken English, employment, and limited formal education. They also report that gender and race had no significant impact on acculturative stress.[9]

In addition to the above factors, Berry argues that the degree of acculturative stress experienced by people adapting to new cultures varies according to the similarities and dissimilarities between the host culture and the native culture of the immigrants. To the extent that the cultures are more similar than different, less stress is experienced. Individual personal traits also play a role in the manifestation of acculturative stress. Berry notes that such characteristics as the amount of exposure one has had to the new culture; one's level of education; one's sex, age, language, race, and income; and one's psychological and spiritual strength all affect acculturative stress.[10] A well-educated woman from the United States may experience more acculturative stress than a well-educated man from the United States when entering a culture that does not recognize sexual equality (either socially or legally).

A MODEL OF ACCULTURATION

Acculturation is not unilateral; it is an interactive process between a culture and groups of people. When individuals or groups of individuals enter a new culture, they are often changed by the culture, but they also have an impact on the culture. For example, while Mexican immigrants face challenges imposed on them by the dominant culture, their presence has changed the United States cultural milieu, especially in places such as Texas and California. Young Kim's model of cultural adaptation takes into account both individual and cultural factors that affect ac-

Factors Affecting Cultural Adaptation and Acculturation

The Role of Communication	The Role of the Environment	The Role of Predisposition
Personal communication	Host receptivity	Preparedness
Social communication	Host conformity pressure	Ethnicity
	Ethnic group strength	Personality

culturation. Kim argues that acculturation is not a linear one-way process; rather, there is an interaction between the stranger and the host culture. Kim argues that the role of communication, the role of the host environment, and the role of predisposition best explain the acculturation process. [11]

In terms of the role of communication, personal communication refers to the individual's host communication competence—that is, the degree to which the newcomer can encode and decode verbal and nonverbal messages within the host environment. Kim argues that natives acquire this competence early in life, so it comes to them automatically. Host communication competence also refers to the degree to which the newcomer understands the host's language rules and norms, understands effective and appropriate conflict resolution strategies, and is motivated to initiate and develop host culture relationships. Social communication refers to the actual interaction between the newcomer and host persons. The actual participation in relationships, engaging in conflict resolution, and exposing oneself to the mass communication of the host culture can enhance and facilitate the acculturation process. [12]

Kim argues that the environment plays a key role in the acculturation process. The degree to which the host culture is receptive to strangers is important. There are certain factions in the United States, for example, that believe the country should close its borders to immigrants. Given the tensions in the Middle East, Americans sometimes face hostilities when they enter certain countries. Host conformity pressure is another factor. The extent to which natives within the host culture exert pressure on newcomers to conform to their culture's values, beliefs, and practices can facilitate or alienate the newcomers. In the United States, for example, people expect that newcomers will speak English. In fact, some members of the United States Congress have introduced legislation that would make English the "official" language of the United States. Ethnic group strength refers to the amount of influence the newcomer's group wields in the host culture. Clearly some ethnic groups are more powerful in terms of political, economic, and social power than others. Because of their numbers, blacks and Hispanics have become powerful ethnic groups in the United States. Kim notes that as ethnic group strength increases, members of the ethnic group may encourage newcomers to maintain their native ethnic heritage and pressure them not to conform to the host culture. Hence, newcomers may feel pressure from the host culture to adapt while simultaneously facing pressure from their native ethnic group to preserve their ethnic heritage.[13]

Predisposition factors also affect acculturation. Kim argues that newcomers enter into their new culture with varying degrees of readiness. How much people know about their new culture, their ability to speak the language, the probability of employment, and their understanding of the cultural institutions will have a dramatic effect on their acculturation process. Newcomers' ethnicity will also play a role in the pace of their acculturation. Kim uses the term *ethnicity* to refer to the inherited characteristics that newcomers have as members of distinct ethnic groups. Such characteristics include race and language. For example, because of their ethnicity, Japanese may have a more difficult time acculturating to the United States than a person from Great Britain. Finally, Kim argues that there are certain personality characteristics that affect the individual's acculturation process. Age, for example, has been shown to affect acculturation. Generally, young persons more quickly adapt to new and different modes of behavior than do older persons, who may be set in their ways. Karmela Liebkind found that among Vietnamese refugees in Finland, younger generations maintained much more positive attitudes about acculturation than did older generations. Liebkind explains that the Finnish values and practices of gender equality and egalitarian parent/child relationships contrasted sharply with Southeast Asian values of hierarchical familial relationships and filial piety. In the traditional Southeast Asian family, children are taught to be loyal. They are obligated to show respect and obedience to their parents. Wives are expected to rear the children and serve their husbands. Not having been completely enculturated into Vietnamese society, the younger generations of the refugee Vietnamese families found it much easier than their parents to acculturate into Finnish society.[14]

MODES OF ACCULTURATION

In order for acculturation to occur, there must be contact between the members of the host culture and the newcomers. Berry argues that such contact needs to be continuous and direct. He maintains that short-term accidental contact does not generally lead to much acculturation. Moreover, the purpose of contact between the two groups is an important consideration. Berry points out that acculturation effects may vary according to whether the purpose of contact is colonization, enslavement, trade, military control, evangelization, or education. The length of contact is also a factor, as are the social or political policies of the mainstream culture as they relate to the immigrant group (that is, political representation, citizenship criteria, language requirements, employment opportunities, and so forth).[15]

Berry points out that an individual's level of acculturation depends in part on two independent processes depicted in Figure 11-1. These processes include the degree to which the person approaches or avoids interaction with the host culture

FIGURE 11-1   Modes of Acculturation

SOURCE: *Adapted from J. W. Berry, "Psychology of Acculturation," in* Nebraska Symposium on Motivation 1989, *ed. R. A. Dienstbier (Lincoln: University of Nebraska Press, 1990), pp. 201–234.*

(that is, out-group contact and relations) and the degree to which the individual maintains or relinquishes his or her native culture's attributes (in-group identity and maintenance). On the basis of these two factors, Berry has identified four modes of acculturation: (1) *assimiliation,* (2) *integration,* (3) *separation,* and (4) *marginalization.* The relationships among these modes is depicted in Figure 11-1. To the extent that the individual desires contact with the host culture (and the various microcultures) while not necessarily maintaining an identity with his or her native culture, *assimilation* occurs. In this case, the individual loses his or her original cultural identity as he or she acquires a new identity in the host culture. During assimilation, the individual takes on the behaviors and language habits and practices the basic rules and norms of the host culture. There is an ongoing effort to approach the dominant culture while discontinuing the values, beliefs, and behaviors associated with the native culture. The defining property of the assimilation mode is that the individual endeavors to acquire the values and beliefs of a single cultural group with the ultimate goal of becoming indistinguishable from other members of the host culture. The individual will seek interaction with members of the host culture and build social networks with them.[16]

On the other hand, some people desire a high level of interaction with the host culture while maintaining identity with their native culture. This kind of acculturation is called *integration.* In this mode, the individual develops a kind of bicultural orientation that successfully blends and synthesizes cultural dimensions from both groups while maintaining an identity in each group. People practicing this mode of acculturation take part in activities that allow individuals from different groups to interact without the obstacle of social hierarchies. Presumably, integration is associated with less acculturative stress and conflict. To be sure, an individual's successful integration of cultural skills and norms does not mean that the person relinquishes his or her native cultural identity. In fact, many researchers contend that it is the development of the bicultural identity that leads to a successful life in a bicultural context. In other models of acculturation, this mode is called *pluralism* and/or *multiculturalism*. This mode of acculturation guides many of the social and legislative efforts in the United States' educational and affirmative-action statutes.[17]

When individuals prefer low levels of interaction with the host culture and associated microcultural groups while desiring a close connection with, and reaffirmation of, their native culture, the mode of acculturation is called *separation*. Here the individual resists acculturation with the dominant culture and chooses not to identify with the host cultural group. At the same time, the person retains his or her native cultural identity. People choosing separation may harbor animosity toward the host culture as a result of social or historical factors. Such persons generally focus on the perceived incompatibility between their native culture and the host culture. Although the values and beliefs of the host culture are eschewed, the individual may take on selected behaviors of the host culture for purely functional reasons (such as to get a job). Separated persons communicate almost exclusively with their own group while actively avoiding participation in situations with members of the host culture. Some African Americans and Native Americans, for example, prefer not to identify with the dominant white culture because of past racism and the country's history of slavery. In some models, the separation mode is labeled the segregation mode.[18]

The fourth type of acculturation is *marginalization*. Marginalization occurs when the individual chooses not to identify with his or her native culture or with the host culture. In many instances, marginalized people give up their native culture only to find that they are not accepted by the host culture, to which they would choose to acculturate if given the opportunity. These persons experience alienation from both cultures. Often they feel a sense of abandonment. Dysfunctional behaviors (for example, alcoholism or drug abuse) are often seen in marginalized people. African Americans, Asian Americans, and Hispanic Americans often feel marginalized in U.S. culture. Acculturative stress is often found among marginalized groups.[19]

Another possible acculturation mode, articulated by Richard Mendoza, is *cultural transmutation*. In this mode, the individual chooses to identify with a third cultural group (microculture) that materializes out of the native and host cultural groups. For example, a youth may choose to join a gang or some other kind of microcultural outlet. Although similar to separation, cultural transmutation is different in that a new cultural identity is created. In other models of acculturation, this is called *fusion*. Gay and lesbian groups are a good example of the cultural transmutation mode of acculturation. In this mode, individuals have left their native heterosexual groups and have immigrated into homosexual contexts. Religious groups are another example of acculturative transmutation. Many religious communities merge the values, beliefs, and behaviors of diverse religions into a new religion.[20]

ACCULTURATION IN THE UNITED STATES

The two largest ethnic populations in the United States are Hispanics and blacks. For these groups, acculturation refers to the degree to which they participate in the cultural traditions, values, beliefs, and norms of the dominant white society, remain immersed in their own unique cultural customs and conventions, or participate in both. As Hope Landrine comments, some microcultural groups remain highly traditional, whereas others are highly acculturated. Highly traditional Hispanics and blacks differ significantly from whites in a variety of values and behaviors, whereas highly acculturated Hispanics and blacks do not.[21]

Social scientists are beginning to understand that the degree of acculturation for microcultural groups within the United States is associated with a variety of social and medical problems, such as alcoholism, cigarette smoking, drug abuse, and HIV/AIDS-related knowledge, attitudes, and behaviors.[22] Moreover, microcultural group acculturation is associated with methods of conflict resolution (for example, belligerent behaviors), willingness to use counseling, career development and work habits, and educational achievement—that is, increased absences, lower grades. The more marginalized or segregated the group, the more likely they are to experience physical and mental health problems and the less likely they are to seek out appropriate avenues to handle them. Landrine maintains that ethnic differences observed in the United States might be better understood as degrees of acculturation. According to Landrine, understanding a microcultural group's level of acculturation has the potential to diminish racist beliefs about ethnic differences and to increase our knowledge of such differences as a symptom and/or an exhibition of culture.[23]

In an effort to better understand maladaptive attitudes and behaviors among the various microcultural groups in the United States, researchers have devoted considerable effort to assessing levels of acculturation. The Acculturation Rating Scale for Mexican Americans (ARSMA) was first published in 1980.[24] The scale was recently revised and is designed to assess Mexican American acculturation according to Berry's four modes of acculturation—namely, integration, assimilation, separation, and marginalization.[25] It is designed to be completed by persons of Mexican or Hispanic origin.

Approximately 13 percent of the population in the United States is African American. As with other microcultural groups, some African Americans are more acculturated than others. Hope Landrine and Elizabeth Klonoff have developed an instrument designed to measure levels of African American acculturation (see box on pages 351–352). Landrine and Klonoff argue that within the microcultural context, acculturation refers to the degree to which microcultural groups (for example, African Americans, Asian Americans, Native Americans) participate in the traditional values, beliefs, and practices of the dominant white culture, remain immersed in their own cultural traditions, or blend the two traditions.[26]

Self-Assessment 11-1

Acculturation Rating Scale for Mexican-Americans II

In the blank space to the left of each item, place a number between 1 and 5 that best applies to you. 1 = not at all, 2 = very little or not very often, 3 = moderately, 4 = much or very often, and 5 = extremely often or almost always.

1. _____ I speak Spanish.

2. _____ I speak English.

3. _____ I enjoy speaking Spanish.

4. _____ I associate with Anglos.

5. _____ I associate with Mexicans and/or Mexican-Americans.

6. _____ I enjoy listening to Spanish music.

7. _____ I enjoy listening to English-language music.

8. _____ I enjoy Spanish-language TV.

9. _____ I enjoy English-language TV.

10. _____ I enjoy English-language movies.

11. _____ I enjoy Spanish-language movies.

12. _____ I enjoy reading books in Spanish.

13. _____ I enjoy reading books in English.

14. _____ I write letters in Spanish.

15. _____ I write letters in English.

16. _____ My thinking is done in English.

17. _____ My thinking is done in Spanish.

18. _____ My contact with Mexico has been . . .

19. _____ My contact with the U.S.A. has been . . .

20. _____ My father identifies or identified himself as "Mexicano."

21. _____ My mother identifies or identified herself as "Mexicana."

22. _____ My friends while I was growing up were of Mexican origin.

23. _____ My friends while I was growing up were of Anglo origin.

24. _____ My family cooks Mexican food.

—Continued

25. _____ My friends now are of Anglo origin.

26. _____ My friends now are of Mexican origin.

27. _____ I like to identify myself as an Anglo.

28. _____ I like to identify myself as a Mexican-American.

29. _____ I like to identify myself as a Mexican.

30. _____ I like to identify myself as an American.

31. _____ I have difficulty accepting some ideas held by Anglos.

32. _____ I have difficulty accepting certain attitudes held by Anglos.

33. _____ I have difficulty accepting some behaviors exhibited by Anglos.

34. _____ I have difficulty accepting some values held by some Anglos.

35. _____ I have difficulty accepting certain practices and customs commonly found in some Anglos.

36. _____ I have, or think I would have, difficulty accepting Anglos as close personal friends.

37. _____ I have difficulty accepting some ideas held by some Mexicans.

38. _____ I have difficulty accepting certain attitudes held by Mexicans.

39. _____ I have difficulty accepting some behaviors exhibited by Mexicans.

40. _____ I have difficulty accepting some values held by some Mexicans.

41. _____ I have difficulty accepting certain practices and customs commonly found in some Mexicans.

42. _____ I have, or think I would have, difficulty accepting Mexicans as close personal friends.

43. _____ I have difficulty accepting ideas held by some Mexican-Americans.

44. _____ I have difficulty accepting certain attitudes held by Mexican-Americans.

45. _____ I have difficulty accepting some behaviors exhibited by Mexican-Americans.

46. _____ I have difficulty accepting some values held by Mexican-Americans.

47. _____ I have difficulty accepting certain practices and customs commonly found in some Mexican-Americans.

—*Continued*

48. _____ I have, or think I would have, difficulty accepting Mexican-Americans as close personal friends.

SCORING:

Sum your responses to the following items: 2, 4, 7, 9, 10, 13, 15, 16, 19, 23, 25, 27, and 30. Divide the sum by 13. This is your Anglo Orientation Score (AOS).

Sum your responses to the following items: 1, 3, 5, 6, 8, 11, 12, 14, 17, 18, 20, 21, 22, 24, 26, 28, and 29. Divide the sum by 17. This is your Mexican Orientation Score (MOS).

Sum your responses to the following items: 31, 32, 33, 34, 35, and 36. This is your Anglo Marginality (ANGMAR).

Sum your responses to the following items: 37, 38, 39, 40, 41, and 42. This is your Mexican Marginality (MEXMAR).

Sum your responses to the following items: 43, 44, 45, 46, 47, and 48. This is your Mexican-American Marginality (MAMARG).

Acculturative Types Generated by ARSMA-II

Traditional Mexican = MOS scores >/= 3.7 and AOS scores </= to 3.24.

Integrated = AOS >/= 3.5 and MOS >/= 2.8.

Marginal = ANGMAR >/= 17.34, MEXMAR >/= 17, and MAMARG >/= 15.

Separation = MEXMAR </= 11, ANGMAR >/= 15, and MAMARG >/= 15.

Assimilated = MOS </= 2.4 and AOS >/= 4.

African Americans who complete the instrument are asked to indicate their preference for things African American, their religious beliefs and practices, their experience with traditional African American foods, childhood experiences, superstitions, interracial attitudes and cultural mistrust of the white majority, "falling out," traditional African American games, black family values, and family practices. This scale is designed for African Americans in the United States and is not applicable to other microcultural groups.

The two scales discussed here are valid indices of acculturation for Hispanics and African Americans and indicate that cultural diversity can be reliably measured. Such measurements give us a better understanding of an individual's perceptual context. The more we know about a person's individual level of acculturation, the better able we are to provide culturally competent services to him or her.

Self-Assessment 11-2

African-American Acculturation Scale

On a scale ranging from 1 to 7, indicate the extent to which you agree or disagree with the statement. 1 = totally disagree, 2 = disagree, 3 = slightly disagree, 4 = don't know, 5 = slightly agree, 6 = agree, and 7 = totally agree.

1. _____ Most of the music I listen to is by black artists.

2. _____ I like black music more than white music.

3. _____ The person I admire most is black.

4. _____ I listen to black radio stations.

5. _____ I try to watch all the black shows on TV.

6. _____ Most of my friends are black.

7. _____ I believe in the Holy Ghost.

8. _____ I believe in heaven and hell.

9. _____ I like gospel music.

10. _____ I am currently a member of a black church.

11. _____ Prayer can cure disease.

12. _____ The church is the heart of the black community.

13. _____ I know how to cook chitlins.

14. _____ I eat chitlins once in a while.

15. _____ Sometimes I cook ham hocks.

16. _____ I know how long you're supposed to cook collard greens.

17. _____ I went to a mostly black elementary school.

18. _____ I went (or go) to a mostly black high school.

19. _____ I grew up in a mostly black neighborhood.

20. _____ I avoid splitting a pole.

21. _____ When the palm of your hand itches, you'll receive some money.

22. _____ There's some truth to many old superstitions.

23. _____ IQ tests were set up purposefully to discriminate against black people.

—Continued

24. _____ Most tests (like the SAT and tests to get a job) are set up to make sure blacks don't get high scores on them.

25. _____ Deep in their hearts, most white people are racists.

26. _____ I have seen people "fall out."

27. _____ I know what "falling out" means.

28. _____ When I was a child, I used to play tonk.

29. _____ I know how to play bid whist.

30. _____ It's better to move your whole family ahead in this world than it is to be out for only yourself.

31. _____ Old people are wise.

32. _____ When I was young, my parent(s) sent me to stay with a relative (aunt, uncle, grandmother) for a few days or weeks, and then I went back home again.

33. _____ When I was young, I took a bath with my sister, brother, or some other relative.

SCORING: Sum your responses to the above 33 items. Your score must range between 33 and 231.

Scores 33–60 = Acculturated.

Scores 66–85 = Mostly acculturated.

Scores 99–130 = Bicultural (slightly acculturated).

Scores 165–185 = Bicultural (slightly traditional).

Scores 198–200 = Mostly traditional.

Scores 200–231 Traditional.

SOURCE: "The African American Acculturation Scale II" from H. Landrine & E. A. Klonoff, "The African American Acculturation Scale II," *Journal of Black Psychology,* Vol. 21, 1995, pp. 124–153. Copyright © 1995 Association of Black Psychologists. Used by permission of Sage Publications.

Culture Shock

When people move to a new culture, they take with them the values, beliefs, customs, and behaviors of their old culture. Often, depending on the degree of similarity between the old and the new culture, the values, beliefs, customs, and behaviors of the native culture clash with those of the new culture. This can result in disorientation, misunderstandings, conflict, stress, and anxiety. Researchers call this phenomenon *culture shock*. Winkelman defines culture shock as a multi-faceted experience that results from the numerous stressors that occur when coming into contact with a different culture.[27] Anyone can experience culture shock, though some are more prone to it than others. Winkelman maintains that culture shock can occur with immigrant groups, such as foreign students and refugees, international business exchanges, Peace Corps volunteers, and social workers entering new communities during crises, as well as for members of microcultural groups within their own culture and society. Expatriate professors teaching abroad often describe their experiences using the term *education shock*.

Anthropologist Kalervo Oberg was the first to apply the term *culture shock* to the effects associated with the tension and anxiety of entering into a new culture combined with the sensations of loss, confusion, and powerlessness resulting from the forfeiture of cultural norms and social rituals.[28] Likewise, Winkelman points out that culture shock stems from the challenges associated with new cultural surroundings in addition to the loss of a familiar cultural environment.[29]

Culture shock appears to be a psychological and social process that progresses in stages, usually lasting as long as a year. Most models of culture shock include four stages. The first model of culture shock, developed by Oberg nearly fifty years ago, incorporates a medical metaphor and terminology, beginning with the incubation stage, followed by crisis, leading to recovery, and finishing with full recovery.[30] Smalley's model begins with a fascination stage, then hostility, adjustment, and biculturalism. Richardson's four-stage model includes elation, depression, recovery, and acculturation. Kealey's model incorporates exploration, frustration, coping, and adjustment phases.[31]

Most models of culture shock describe the process curvilinearly, or by what Lysgaard called the "U curve hypothesis."[32] Elaborating on the "U curve," Professor Kim Zapf asserts that culture shock begins with feelings of optimism and even elation that eventually give way to frustration, tension, and anxiety as individuals are

RECAP

Culture Shock Models

Oberg (1954)	Smalley (1963)	Richardson (1974)	Kealey (1978)
1. Incubation	1. Fascination	1. Elation	1. Exploration
2. Crisis	2. Hostility	2. Depression	2. Frustration
3. Recovery	3. Adjustment	3. Recovery	3. Coping
4. Full recovery	4. Biculturalism	4. Acculturation	4. Adjustment

FIGURE 11-2 The "U Curve" Model of Culture Shock

Tourist Phase
- Interest in culture
- Honeymoon
- Euphoria and elation
- Positive reaction to stress
- Photographs

Culture Shock
- Confusion
- Frustration
- Preoccupation with cleanliness
- Lack of control
- Fatigue
- Stress and anxiety
- Depression
- Paranoia

Adjustment
- Problem-solving skills
- Conflict-resolution strategies
- Appreciation of host culture
- Intercultural relationships

Adaptation/Acculturation
- Stable adaptations
- Personal growth
- Bicultural identity
- Constructive response to stress

SOURCE: *Based on Winkelman's discussion of culture shock and his delineation of the stages in M. Winkelman, "Cultural Shock and Adaptation,"* Journal of Counseling and Development, *73 (1994), 121–127.*

unable to effectively interact with their new environment. As they develop strategies for resolving conflict, people begin to restore their confidence and eventually recover and reach some level of acculturation.[33] The "U curve" model is depicted in Figure 11-2.

The initial stage of culture shock, usually called something like the *tourist* or *honeymoon stage,* is characterized by intense excitement and euphoria associated with being somewhere different and unusual. Winkelman asserts that this stage is typical of that experienced by people who enter other cultures temporarily during honeymoons, vacations, or brief business trips.[34] The stresses associated with cultural differences are tolerated and may even seem fun and humorous. During the tourist phase, the newcomers' primary interaction with their new cultural environment is through major cultural institutions, such as museums, hotels, Western restaurants, and so forth. This phase may last weeks or months but is temporary. In some instances, the tourist phase may be very short, as when newcomers are confronted with drastic changes in climate or hostile political environments.

Eventually, the fun and excitement associated with the tourist phase gives way to frustration and real stress, or active *culture shock.* Failure events once considered minor and funny are now perceived as stressful. Winkelman maintains that culture shock is partially based on the simultaneous effects of cognitive overload and behavioral inadequacy that are rooted in the psychological and physical stresses associated with confronting a new environment. The new environment requires a great deal of conscious energy that was not required in the old environ-

The "honeymoon" or "tourist" phase of culture shock is often filled with great enthusiasm and excitement. *(Strauss/Curtis/Stock Market)*

ment, which leads to cognitive overload and fatigue. People also experience role shock in that the behaviors associated with their role in their native culture may be dramatically different in the new culture. Finally, people may experience personal shock in the form of a loss of intimacy with interpersonal partners. In describing the second phase of culture shock, Winkelman notes:

> Things start to go wrong, minor issues become major problems, and cultural differences become irritating. Excessive preoccupation with cleanliness of food, drinking water, bedding, and surroundings begins. One experiences increasing disappointments, frustrations, impatience, and tension. Life does not make sense and one may feel helpless, confused, disliked by others, or treated like a child.[35]

Rinesmith notes that during the culture shock phase, people feel helpless, isolated, and depressed. Paranoia—in which newcomers are convinced that their troubles are deliberate attempts by the natives to disrupt their lives—is also a typical response to culture shock. In this phase, people may develop irrational fears of being cheated, robbed, or even assaulted.[36]

The degree to which one experiences culture shock varies from person to person. Walt Lonner has identified six factors that affect the nature of culture shock experienced: (1) control factors, (2) interpersonal factors, (3) organismic/biological factors, (4) interpersonal factors, (5) spatial/temporal factors, and (6) geopolitical factors. Churchman and Mitrani have added three additional factors: (1) the degree of similarity between one's native and new culture, including the physical environment, (2) the degree and quality of information about the new environment, and (3) the host culture's attitude and policies toward immigrants.[37] These

FIGURE 11-3   Factors Affecting Degree of Culture Shock

SOURCE: *Based on W. Lonner, "Foreword," in* Culture Shock: Psychological Reactions to Unfamiliar Environment, *ed. A. Furnham and S. Bochner (London: Methuen, 1986), pp. xv–xx; A. Churchman and M. Mitrani, "The Role of the Physical Environment in Culture Shock,"* Environment & Behavior, *29 (1997), 64–87.*

nine factors are depicted in Figure 11-3. Some people never recuperate from the crisis stage of culture shock and return home or isolate themselves from the host culture by restricting their interaction with it, such as by fostering only intracultural relationships (for example, in a military base or university setting). When the lines of communication with the host culture are severed, there is little hope of acculturation or recovery from the crisis stage.

The third phase of culture shock is typically called the *adjustment or reorientation phase.* Here people eventually realize that the problems associated with the host culture are due not to deliberate attempts by the natives, but to a real difference in values, beliefs, and behaviors. At this stage, people actively seek out effective problem-solving and conflict-resolution strategies. They begin to develop a positive attitude about solving their problems. As Winkelman notes, the host culture begins to make sense, and pessimistic reactions and responses to it are lessened as people recognize that their problems are due largely to their inability to understand, accept, and adapt.[38] Typically the adjustment phase is gradual and slow, and often people relapse into minicrisis stages.

The final stage of culture shock is labeled the *adaptation or acculturation stage*. At this point, individuals actively engage the culture with their new problem-solving and conflict-resolution tools with some degree of success. Young Kim argues that to the extent that people acculturate to their new culture, they experience cultural transformation. They possess a degree of functional fitness in which the external demands of the host culture are met with appropriate and consistent internal responses. Moreover, they develop a level of competency in communicating with the natives. As a result of their successes, people also acquire psychological health, take on an intercultural identity, and foster a sense of integration with their host environment.[39]

"W CURVE" MODELS OF REENTRY CULTURE SHOCK

As mentioned above, most models of culture shock contain four phases in the "U curve" tradition. But many people who have lived outside of their native culture argue that they experience a kind of reentry shock when they return to their native culture. Furnham and Bochner's "W curve" model of culture shock contains two "U curves," including the initial culture shock experienced when the traveler en-

FIGURE 11-4   "W Curve" Model of Reentry Culture Shock

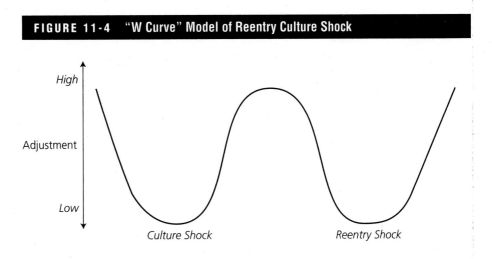

SOURCE: *A. Furnham and S. Bochner,* Culture Shock: Psychological Reactions to Unfamiliar Environments *(London, 1986, Methuen).*

ters a new culture and a reentry shock "U curve." In other words, when people return home after an extended stay in a foreign culture, they experience another round of culture shock, this time in their native culture.

Furnham and Bochner note that students returning from study abroad often report a reentry shock phenomenon. Some students fear that they will be treated differently by their "stay-at-home" peers, friends, and parents when they return. In addition, because they have successfully acculturated themselves to a foreign culture, they essentially have to "re-acculturate" to their native culture. Students frequently report that the nature of long-term international travel transforms them. When they return home, they are different and have taken on new perspectives and see the world with a different outlook. Students lament that communicating their experiences abroad to their friends and families is often very difficult.

STRATEGIES FOR MANAGING CULTURE SHOCK

If you are traveling to a new culture for the first time, it is likely that you will experience some kind of culture shock. The level of intensity you experience will vary. In addition, the duration of your culture shock will depend on your ability to manage it. Probably the best piece of commonsense advice is to do your homework and be prepared.

ASSESSING CULTURE SHOCK

Successful management of culture shock depends on an awareness of its symptoms and the degree of its severity. Winkelman maintains that sometimes people falsely attribute their problems to sources other than culture shock. He argues that there is a tendency to deny that one is experiencing it. His advice is that one should accept the fact that virtually all atypical problems that occur during acculturation are caused by or exacerbated by culture shock.[40] Professor Kim Zapf has developed a questionnaire, called the Culture Shock Profile, that is designed to assess the intensity of culture shock you are experiencing. A modified version of the questionnaire is presented in Self-Assessment 11-3.

Please keep in mind that everyone experiences some degree of culture shock when entering into a new culture for some length of time. Zapf recommends that the Culture Shock Profile should be taken several times during the first year of your move—specifically, after the first month, then sometime during about your fourth or fifth month, and then after one year. If managed appropriately, most culture shock is significantly reduced after a year.[41]

Managing Culture Shock

Study the Host Culture. Read about your new culture, attend seminars, rent films, and socialize with host nationals about their culture. Popular "Hollywood" films may distort the reality of the culture, so be careful interpreting them. Most embassies have web pages that include information about the geography, population, climate, government, and education system of their country. If possible, interview friends or colleagues who have traveled or lived in the culture.

Study the Local Environment. In addition to studying about the general culture, try to learn as much as you can about the local environment in which you will live—such as where to buy favorite foods, where to find physicians trained in the United States, where schools are located, how public transportation operates (if there is any), or how to fill prescriptions. Taken-for-granted operations that we unconsciously perform in our day-to-day lives will be different in your host culture.

Learn Basic Verbal and Nonverbal Language Skills. If you are not fluent in the language of your host culture, or even if they speak English, it is a good idea to familiarize yourself with their verbal and nonverbal language. Attach labels to the various items of your home in the language of the host culture. Practice functional and frequently used phrases that will help you perform basic survival tactics. Keep in mind that common verbal colloquialisms can be wildly misinterpreted across cultures. Find out nonverbal mannerisms and expectations for personal space, time, paralanguage, kinesics, haptics, and so forth. Learn some appropriate verbal and nonverbal formalities of greeting rituals.

Develop Intercultural Relationships. A common mistake made by many expatriots is remaining within a network of intracultural relationships. The best way to get to know and understand another culture is to establish relationships with host nationals. You will learn more about another culture by initiating and developing relationships with host nationals in your own country than you will by traveling to their country and staying in Western hotels and seeing the countryside on a tour bus with a translator. Host nationals know the norms and subtleties of their culture and can be of immense help in assisting you to learn and understand them.

Maintain an Intimate Social Network. Although this may sound contradictory to the above recommendation, if possible, maintain your intimate intracultural relational network. Close interpersonal relations can provide positive feedback on matters related to one's self-esteem and emotional needs. Venting your problems to understanding and empathetic others can be an effective outlet for stress and frustration.

Assume the Principle of Difference/Remember Your Perceptual Context. Try to understand that things are simply going to be different in your new culture and that the way you are accustomed to doing things is not the only way. Remember that your perceptual context is biased in favor of your culture and your in-group. How you perceive your host culture is not objective or neutral. All the verbal and nonverbal messages encoded and decoded are filtered through your cultural, microcultural, environmental, sociorelational, and perceptual filters. These filters bias and color your expectations, which will certainly be violated as you interact with your host culture.

Anticipate Failure Events. Regardless of how well you prepare for your journey, there will be moments when you are unsuccessful at accomplishing your goals. Before you depart, anticipate failure events. No doubt you will engage in acts that are unintentional and/or intentionally performed but inappropriate for the situation or incorrectly executed.

Self-Assessment 11-3

Culture Shock Profile

Below is a list of 33 terms that may or may not describe how you feel about your experiences in your new culture. On a scale of 0 to 3, indicate the frequency with which you experience the feeling. 0 = none, 1 = slight, 2 = moderate, and 3 = great.

I feel:

1. _____ Enthusiastic

2. _____ Impatient/irritable

3. _____ A desire to resign

4. _____ Happy/content

5. _____ Energetic

6. _____ Rejected

7. _____ Purposeful/directed

8. _____ Pessimistic/hopeless

9. _____ Contemptuous of others (natives)

10. _____ Angry/resentful

11. _____ A need to complain

12. _____ Creative

13. _____ Confident/self-assured

14. _____ Ready to cry

15. _____ Challenged

16. _____ Cynical

17. _____ A sense of discovery

18. _____ Helpless/vulnerable

19. _____ Optimistic/hopeful

20. _____ Inadequate/self-doubt

21. _____ Isolated/homesick

22. _____ Physically ill

—Continued

23. _____ A need to "get out"

24. _____ Confused/disoriented

25. _____ Excited/stimulated

26. _____ Accepted

27. _____ A sense of loss

28. _____ Overwhelmed/bewildered

29. _____ Afraid/panic

30. _____ Depressed/withdrawn

31. _____ Frustrated/thwarted

32. _____ Exhausted/sleep difficulty

33. _____ Apathetic/"I don't care"

SCORING: To determine your level of culture shock, reverse your score for items 1, 4, 5, 7, 12, 13, 17, 19, 25, and 26. If your original score was a 0, reverse it to a 3. If your original score was a 1, reverse it to a 2. If your original score was a 2, reverse it to a 1, and if your original score was a 3, reverse it to a 0. After reversing the score for those 10 items, sum the entire 33 items. Scores must range from 0 to 99. The higher your score, the more culture shock you are experiencing, and you should engage in some of the strategies listed in this section.

SOURCE: M. K. Zapf, "Remote Practice and Culture Shock: Social Workers Moving to Isolated Northern Regions," *Social Work*, 38 (1993), 694–705.

Chapter Summary

Leaving your native culture for a new one can be one of the most rewarding yet challenging experiences of a lifetime. Having relocated to a new culture, everyone goes through a process of acculturation—that is, a process of cultural change that results from ongoing contact between two or more culturally different groups. For some, this process can be particularly difficult, whereas for others it is relatively easy. Acculturation is in large part a function of how much interaction one chooses to have with members of the new culture and how much of the old culture one desires to maintain.

Virtually everyone experiences some degree of culture shock when entering a new culture for an extended period of time. Culture shock results in feelings of disorientation, misunderstandings, conflict, stress, and anxiety. Often the very same feelings are experienced when a traveler returns home. In addition to discussing its causes and symptoms, this chapter has offered several strategies for assessing and managing culture shock. Although culture shock sounds awful, having an understanding of its causes, symptoms, and effects is the first step in alleviating the severity you might experience. Generally speaking, most students who travel abroad experience only minor levels of culture shock.

GLOSSARY OF TERMS

Acculturation: The process of cultural change that results from ongoing contact between two or more culturally different groups.

Acculturative stress: The anxiety and tension associated with acculturation.

Adjustment phase: Third stage of culture shock, in which people actively seek out effective problem-solving and conflict-resolution strategies.

Assimilation: The degree to which an individual takes on the behaviors and language habits and practices the basic rules and norms of the host culture while relinquishing ties with the native culture.

Cultural transmutation: Mode of acculturation in which the individual chooses to identify with a third cultural group (microculture) that materializes out of the native and host cultural groups.

Culture shock: The effects associated with the tension and anxiety of entering into a new culture, combined with the sensations of loss, confusion, and powerlessness resulting from the forfeiture of cultural norms and social rituals.

Integration: Mode of acculturation in which the individual develops a kind of bicultural orientation that successfully blends and synthesizes cultural dimensions from both groups while maintaining an identity in each group.

Reentry Shock: The effects associated with the tension and anxiety of returning to one's native culture after an extended stay in a foreign culture.

REFERENCES

1. J. C. Condon and F. Yousef, *An Introduction to Intercultural Communication* (Indianapolis, Ind.: Bobbs-Merrill, 1975). (Quote on page 270.)
2. R. Redfield, R. Linton, and M. Herskovits, "Memorandum on the Study of Acculturation," *American Anthropologist,* 38 (1936), 149–152.
3. J. W. Berry and D. L. Sam, "Acculturation and Adaption," in *Handbook of Cross-Cultural Psychology: Social Behavior and Applications,* vol. 3, ed. J. W. Berry, M. H. Segall, and C. Kagitcibasa (Boston, 1997, Allyn & Bacon), 291–326.
4. Ibid.
5. E. Nwadiora and H. McAdoo, "Acculturative Stress Among Amerasian Refugees: Gender and Racial Differences," *Adolescence,* 31 (1996), 477–488.
6. A. O. Miranda and K. B. Matheny, "Socio-Psychological Predictors and Acculturative Stress Among Latino Adults," *Journal of Mental Health Counseling,* 22 (2000), 306–318.
7. J. F. Smart and D. W. Smart, "Acculturative Stress of Hispanics: Loss and Challenge," *Journal of Counseling & Development,* 73 (1995), 390–397.
8. J. D. Hovey, "Psychosocial Predictors of Acculturative Stress in Mexican Immigrants," *Journal of Psychology,* 134 (2000), 490–502.
9. E. Nwadiora and H. McAdoo, "Acculturative Stress Among Amerasian Refugees."
10. J. W. Berry, "Understanding the Process of Acculturation for Primary Intervention" (unpublished manuscript, Department of Psychology, Queen's College, Kingston, Ontario, 1987), cited in Nwadiora and McAdoo, "Acculturative Stress Among Amerasian Refugees."
11. Y. Y. Kim, "Adapting to a New Culture," in *Intercultural Communication: A Reader,* 8th ed., ed. L. A. Samovar and R. E. Porter (Belmont, Calif.: Wadsworth, 1997), pp. 404–417.
12. Ibid.
13. Ibid.
14. Ibid.; K. Liebkind, "Acculturation and Stress:

Vietnamese Refugees in Finland," *Journal of Cross-Cultural Psychology,* 27 (1996), 161–180.

15. J. W. Berry, "Psychology of Acculturation," in *Nebraska Symposium on Motivation 1989,* ed. R. A. Dienstbier (Lincoln: University of Nebraska Press, 1990), pp. 201–234.

16. Berry, "Psychology of Acculturation"; H. L. K. Coleman, "Strategies for Coping with Cultural Diversity," *Counseling Psychology,* 23 (1995), 722–741.

17. Coleman, "Strategies for Coping with Cultural Diversity"; I. Cuellar, B. Arnold, and R. Maldonado, "Acculturation Rating Scale for Mexican-Americans II: A Revision of the Original ARSMA," *Hispanic Journal of Behavioral Science,* 17 (1995), 275–305.

18. Ibid.

19. Cuellar, Arnold, and Maldonado, "Acculturation Rating Scale for Mexican-Americans II."

20. R. H. Mendoza, "An Empirical Scale to Measure Type and Degree of Acculturation in Mexican-American Adolescents and Adults," *Journal of Cross-Cultural Psychology,* 20 (1989), 372–385; Cuellar, Arnold, and Maldonado, "Acculturation Rating Scale for Mexican-Americans II"; Coleman, "Strategies for Coping with Cultural Diversity."

21. H. Landrine and E. A. Klonoff, "The African-American Acculturation Scale II: Cross Validation and Short Form," *Journal of Black Psychology,* 21 (1995), 124–153.

22. B. DeLeon and S. Mendez, "Factorial Structure of a Measure of Acculturation in a Puerto Rican Population," *Educational and Psychological Measurement,* 56 (1996), 155–166.

23. Landrine and Klonoff, "The African-American Acculturation Scale II."

24. I. Cuellar, L. C. Harris, and R. Jasso, "An Acculturation Scale for Mexican-Americans: Normal and Clinical Populations," *Hispanic Journal of Behavioral Science,* 2 (1980), 199–217.

25. Cuellar, Arnold, and Maldonado, "Acculturation Rating Scale for Mexican-Americans II."

26. Landrine and Klonoff, "The African-American Acculturation Scale II."

27. M. Winkelman, "Cultural Shock and Adaptation," *Journal of Counseling and Development,* 73 (1994), 121–127.

28. K. Oberg, *Culture Shock,* Bobbs-Merrill Series in Social Science, A-329 (Indianapolis: Bobbs-Merrill, 1954); K. Oberg, "Culture Shock: Adjustments to New Cultural Environments," *Practical Anthropology,* 4 (1960), 177–182.

29. Winkelman, "Cultural Shock and Adaptation."

30. Oberg, *Culture Shock;* Oberg, "Culture Shock: Adjustments to New Cultural Environments."

31. These models are briefly reviewed in M. K. Zapf, "Remote Practice and Culture Shock: Social Workers Moving to Isolated Northern Regions," *Social Work,* 38 (1993), 694–705; see also W. A. Smalley, "Culture Shock, Language Shock, and the Shock of Self-Discovery," *Practical Anthropology,* 10 (1963), 49–56; A. Richardson, *British Immigrants and Australia: A Psycho-Social Inquiry* (Canberra: Australian National University Press, 1974); D. J. Kealey, "Adaptation to a New Environment," in *Pre-Departure Documentation Kit,* ed. Canadian International Development Agency (Hull, Quebec: CIDA Briefing Centre, 1978), pp. 48–55.

32. S. Lysgaard, "Adjustment in a Foreign Society: Norwegian Fulbright Grantees Visiting the United States," *International Social Science Bulletin,* 7 (1995), 45–51.

33. Zapf, "Remote Practice and Culture Shock."

34. Winkelman, "Cultural Shock and Adaptation."

35. Ibid.

36. S. Rhinesmith, *Bringing Home the World* (New York: Walsh and Co., 1985).

37. W. Lonner, "Foreword," in *Culture Shock: Psychological Reactions to Unfamiliar Environment,* ed. A. Furnham and S. Bochner (London: Methuen, 1986), pp. xv–xx; A. Churchman and M. Mitrani, "The Role of the Physical Environment in Culture Shock," *Environment and Behavior,* 29 (1997), 64–87.

38. Winkelman, "Cultural Shock and Adaptation."

39. Kim, "Adapting to a New Culture."

40. Winkelman, "Cultural Shock and Adaptation."

41. Zapf, "Remote Practice and Culture Shock."

Intercultural Competence

CHAPTER OBJECTIVES

After reading this chapter, you should be able to

- Identify the four fundamental components of intercultural communication competence.
- Identify and discuss the elements of the knowledge component of intercultural competence.
- Assess your general cultural awareness.
- Identify and discuss the elements of the affective component of intercultural competence.
- Assess your intercultural willingness to communicate.
- Identify and discuss the elements of the psychomotor component of intercultural competence.
- Identify and discuss the elements of the situational features that affect intercultural competence.

O ne of the fundamental goals of this book is to help you become a competent intercultural communicator. This final chapter is devoted to *intercultural communication competence,* which is defined as the degree to which you effectively adapt your verbal and nonverbal messages to the appropriate cultural context. When you communicate with someone from a different culture, in order to be interculturally competent, you will have to adjust and modify the kinds of verbal and nonverbal messages you send. This process requires that you have some *knowledge* about the person with whom you are communicating, that you are *motivated* to communicate with him or her, and that you have the appropriate verbal and nonverbal *skills* in order to encode and decode messages.

Intercultural Competence

Interculturally competent people successfully and effectively adapt their verbal and nonverbal messages to the appropriate cultural context. For the most part, competence is something that is perceived about another person, rather than something an individual inherently possesses. In other words, an individual may appear competent to one person but not to another. Moreover, intercultural competence varies from situation to situation. That is, a particular American may be quite competent while interacting with Chinese people and relatively incompetent when interacting with Germans.

Verbal and nonverbal appropriateness and effectiveness are two important qualities of intercultural competence. According to Brian Spitzberg, appropriate behaviors conform to the rules, norms, and expectancies of the cultural context.[2] For example, when greeting a Japanese person in Japan, you are expected to bow. The rules associated with bowing are determined by one's status (e.g., age, sex, occupation, education). The person of lower status bows lower and longer than the person with higher status and typically does not make direct eye contact. Effective behaviors are those that successfully perform and accomplish the rules and norms.[3] For example, to the extent to which you are able to bow correctly, your behavior will be perceived as effective and competent. As we have seen throughout this book, the appropriateness and effectiveness of verbal and nonverbal messages varies considerably across cultures. Behaviors considered appropriate in one culture may not be wholly appropriate in another culture. Consider the exchange between Arab businessman Hashim Abdu Hashim and his American counterpart Steve Jones in the box on p. 366.[4]

Do you think Mr. Hashim perceived Mr. Jones as competent? Do you think Mr. Hashim perceived Mr. Jones's behaviors as appropriate and effective? Probably not. Mr. Jones commits at least three cultural blunders that severely jeopardize any possible future contract with Hashim. First, he mentions that he's been waiting for two days to see Hashim. Jones has not recognized the polychronic nature of Saudi Arabia. Business gets done on its own time. Second, Jones refuses the tea that has been offered to him in hospitality. Then, in a gross error of etiquette, he inquires about Hashim's wife. In Saudi, a man's wife is for his eyes only. Continuing on his blundering way, Jones hands Hashim the contract with his left hand. In

Intercultural Conversation

Arab and U.S. Managers

The scene: Mr. Jones is sitting (on the floor) in the hallway of a building in Saudi Arabia, waiting to meet with his Saudi counterpart, Hashim Abdu Hashim. The hallway is noisy, cluttered with people moving quickly from room to room. Mr. Jones arrived in Saudi two days earlier for a scheduled meeting. Since then his meeting has been postponed and rescheduled several times. After several hours of waiting in the hallway, Mr. Jones is called into Hashim's office. The office has no chairs, but instead, elaborate and ornate pillows on the floor. The walls are draped with embellished afghans. Mr. Jones enters.

Jones: Hello, Hashim. Gosh, I finally get to see you. I've been waiting for two days!

Hashim: Ah hello, Mr. Jones. It is good to see you.

Jones: Thanks. It's good to see you also. How's Mrs. Hashim?

Hashim: Was your trip to our country all right?

Jones: Yes, everything is fine. *(At this point the two are interrupted by a servant pouring tea. Jones refuses . . . then reluctantly accepts)*

No . . . no . . . thanks, I've had enough tea. Well . . . OK, thanks. So . . . Hashim. I came all the way over here to see if I could get you to speed things up with our order. See, our supplies have been sitting at some dock along the coast for two weeks. I was wondering if you could sign this petition *(hands it to Hashim using his left hand)* to hurry up the process.

Hashim: Hmmm . . . this is a problem?

Jones: Yes. Gosh, Hashim, I understand that sometimes supplies sit on ships for weeks at a time! Your people could really use these computers you've ordered. I need to have them released to your custody as soon as possible.

Hashim: I see. Well . . . we have been without computers for thousands of years. Waiting is no problem.

SOURCE: Adapted from L. Copeland, *Managing the Overseas Assignment* (San Francisco-Copeland Griggs Productions, 1983.)

many Muslim cultures the left hand is the "dirty" hand—that is, used for cleaning the body and handling waste. Finally, Jones demonstrates the urgency of his mission and getting the computers off the supply ship. His emphasis on schedules and deadlines communicates to Hashim that he is either insane or irreligious. Many Arabs believe literally in the phrase "Insha Allah," meaning "God willing." To them, the nature of things, especially time, is controlled by God. Events, meetings, and happenings are completed only if God wills them. Mr. Jones's behavior was neither appropriate nor effective. Mr. Hashim was probably offended and may never do business with Mr. Jones again.[5]

A MODEL OF INTERCULTURAL COMPETENCE

Brian Spitzberg and his colleague Bill Cupach argue that there are three necessary and interdependent ingredients of communication competence: (1) knowledge, (2) motivation, and (3) behavior.[6] The model of *intercultural competence* pre-

FIGURE 12-1   A Model of Intercultural Competence

sented in this text includes these three dimensions along with a fourth component—that is, situational features (see Figure 12-1). In this model, *intercultural competence* is the potential outcome of four interdependent components of the intercultural communication encounter. Each component influences and is influenced by the other three.

THE KNOWLEDGE COMPONENT

The *knowledge component* of intercultural competence consists of how much one knows about the culture of the person with whom one is interacting. To the extent that people have knowledge about other cultures, they are more likely to be perceived as competent (although there is no guarantee!). Consider your own general cultural awareness. Below is a self-report instrument designed to assess your level of cultural awareness.[7]

In order to be perceived as culturally knowledgeable, minimally one should have

Self-Assessment 12-1

Cross-Cultural Awareness

The scale consists of 15 items about what you know or don't know about other cultures. Respond to each item on a scale of 1 to 5. 1 = definitely no, 2 = not likely, 3 = not sure, 4 = likely, and 5 = definitely yes. Be as honest with yourself as possible in completing the scale.

1. _____ I can accurately list three countries that are considered collectivistic.

2. _____ I can accurately identify three countries that have high power distance.

3. _____ I can conduct business in a language other than my own.

4. _____ I know the appropriate distance at which to stand when interacting with people in at least two other cultures.

5. _____ I know the appropriate touch rules in at least two other cultures.

6. _____ I know in what countries I can use first names when conducting business.

7. _____ I can name the (political/governmental) leaders of four other countries.

8. _____ I understand and can practice appropriate gift-giving in three other countries.

9. _____ I can identify some gestures appropriate in the U.S.A. that are considered obscene in other countries.

10. _____ I understand sex-role differences in at least two other countries.

11. _____ I can name three countries that are considered polychronic.

12. _____ I understand the proper protocol for exchanging business cards in at least two other countries.

13. _____ I understand the business philosophies of Japan and China.

14. _____ I can name the United States' top three trading partners.

15. _____ I can name the currencies in four other countries.

SCORING: Sum the 15 responses. Scores must range from 15 to 75. The higher your score, the more culturally aware you are. Scores at or above 50 indicate a relatively healthy degree of cultural awareness.

some comprehension of the other person's dominant cultural values and beliefs. In addition, one should know whether the person is from an individualistic or collectivistic, high- or low-context, high- or low-power-distance, or high- or low-uncertainty-avoidant culture. In the model of intercultural competence, *verbal and nonverbal scripts* are also a part of the knowledge component. Communication theorist Charles Berger argues that verbal and nonverbal scripts (or plans) guide communication action. Scripts are like blueprints for communication that provide people with expectations about future communicative encounters with others. Berger has argued that knowledgeable communicators develop and maintain a repertoire of scripts that enable them to comprehend and predict the actions of themselves and others. Berger has demonstrated that people store scripts in long-term memory. According to Berger, when anticipating interaction with others, communicators establish goals. They search their long-term memory for instances when they have tried to accomplish similar goals and then access a script or plan that was successful in achieving these goals in the past. The frequency and similarity with which a particular script has been used facilitates access to it. In never-before-encountered situations people may possess vicariously based scripts. Perhaps one witnessed a similar event by watching a film or by reading a comparable account.[8] The more plans one has, the better equipped one is to enact them.

Cognitive simplicity and rigidity refers to the degree to which individuals process information about persons from different cultures in a simplistic and rigid manner. Young Kim includes this dimension in her model of intercultural conflict. According to Kim, people with simplistic and rigid cognitive systems tend to engage in gross stereotyping. Moreover, such individuals may have very narrowly defined and inflexible categories. Narrow categorizers tend to make more negative and more confident judgments about other people, particularly those from other cultures. Such persons probably think dogmatically (are narrow minded). Metaphorically, a person with a simple and rigid cognitive system sees the world with blinders on, like a racehorse. Obviously, the competent communicator would possess an open and flexible cognitive system. The person with a simple and rigid system would not be perceived as competent.[9]

As discussed in Chapter 5, *ethnocentrism* is the extent to which one perceives one's own group as the center of everything and judges other groups with reference to it. Ethnocentrics tend to create and reinforce negative attitudes and behaviors toward out-groups. Judgments about in-groups and out-groups almost always are biased in favor of the in-group at the expense of the out-group. Furthermore, ethnocentric groups see themselves as righteous and exceptional and view their own standards as universal and moral. Out-groups are seen as immoral, subordinate, and impotent. Ethnocentrism is clearly an obstacle to intercultural communication competence. The ethnocentric person most likely possesses narrow categories and a simple and rigid cognitive system.[10] In his research, Rich Wiseman found that ethnocentrism was the strongest predictor of general cultural understanding. That is, higher levels of ethnocentrism were associated with less general cultural understanding. Higher levels of ethnocentrism were also related to less positive regard for other cultures.[11]

THE AFFECTIVE COMPONENT

The *affective component* of intercultural communication is the degree to which one approaches or avoids intercultural communication—that is, one's motivation to interact with others from different cultures. A central feature here is intercultural communication apprehension (ICA). ICA is defined by Neuliep and Mc-Croskey as the fear or anxiety associated with either real or anticipated interaction with persons from different cultures. Persons high in ICA tend to avoid interacting with others from different cultures.[12] As mentioned in Chapter 1, because they are seen as strangers, people from different cultures may seem unusual and novel. This difference can create tension and anxiety, which, in turn, can lead to avoidance. On the other hand, some people may be positively predisposed to initiate intercultural interactions even when they are completely free to choose whether or not to communicate. This predisposition, labeled by Jeffrey Kassing, is called *intercultural willingness to communicate.*[13] You can asses your individual level of intercultural willingness to communicate by completing the Intercultural Willingness to Communicate Scale in Self-Assessment 12-2.

Young Kim has argued that one's ability to cope with stress also affects one's approach/avoidance tendencies. Because of the potentially inordinate uncertainty of intercultural communication, anxiety levels may be high as well, leading to increased stress. Some people handle stress well, whereas others do not. Gudykunst and Kim maintain that to be an effective intercultural communicator, one needs to tolerate ambiguity to a certain degree. The more that one is able to manage stress and to endure ambivalence, the more likely one is to initiate intercultural communication and to be an effective and competent intercultural communicator.[14]

The knowledge component and the affective component of intercultural competence are interdependent in that the more knowledge one has, the more likely one is to approach situations involving intercultural communication. The increase in knowledge generally leads to an increase in motivation. Likewise, the more motivation one has, the more likely one is to pursue interaction with people from different cultures, thereby learning more about them and their culture and increasing one's knowledge.

THE PSYCHOMOTOR COMPONENT

The *psychomotor component* of intercultural communication is the actual enactment of the knowledge and affective components. The elements of the psychomotor component are (1) *verbal and nonverbal performance* and (2) *role enactment.* Verbal performance is how people use language. A person may know a great deal about the language of the host culture but not be able to engage in a conversation. Many foreign exchange students in the United States come here not to learn more about English but to practice using it in actual conversations. An American student who recently returned from a year's stay in Japan reported that she had been paid handsomely for hourly conversations with Japanese. People would come to

Self-Assessment 12-2

Intercultural Willingness to Communicate Scale

Below are six situations in which a person might choose to communicate or not to communicate. Assume that you have *completely free choice*. Indicate the percentages of times you would choose to communicate in each type of situation. Keep in mind that you are reporting not the likelihood that you would have an opportunity to talk in these instances, but rather the percentage of times you would talk when the opportunity presented itself. Indicate in the space to the left what percentage of time you would choose to communicate. 0 = never, 100 = always.

1. _____ Talk with someone I perceive to be different from me.

2. _____ Talk with someone from another country.

3. _____ Talk with someone from a culture I know very little about.

4. _____ Talk with someone from a different race than mine.

5. _____ Talk with someone from a different culture.

6. _____ Talk with someone who speaks English as a second language.

SCORING: Your score must range from 0 to 600. Scores below 300 indicate a general unwillingness to communicate interculturally. Scores above 350 indicate a slight willingness to communicate interculturally. Scores above 400 indicate a moderate level, and scores above 500 indicate a high willingness to communicate interculturally.

SOURCE: Adapted from J. W. Kassing, "Development of the Intercultural Willingness to Communicate Scale," *Communication Research Reports,* 14 (1997), 399–407.

her apartment and pay her simply to converse in English about trivial subjects for sixty minutes. These Japanese had all the knowledge they needed about English but wanted to sharpen their performance skills. Knowing and being able to use a second language certainly increases one's perceived competence when interacting interculturally. Language scripts and plans that reduce uncertainty are of particular importance. The psychomotor function is where one puts the scripts and plans into action. If one does not speak the language of the host culture, then at the very least one should know some of the basic greetings, requests, and routines used frequently in that language.

Nonverbal performance is also an important part of the psychomotor component. Here the individual needs to pay close attention to the nuances of the kinesic, paralinguistic, haptic, olfactsic, and proxemic codes of the other culture. As with verbal knowledge and performance, one may have knowledge of a particular culture's nonverbal mannerisms but may not be able to execute them. Hence, before traveling to a foreign country, it might be wise to polish and refine your repertoire of nonverbal skills. For example, before traveling to Japan, you might practice bowing with family members or friends. Keep in mind also that how you smell will affect how others perceive you. Many cultures feel that Americans tend to smell antiseptic because of our frequent use of soaps, perfumes, and so forth. As mentioned in Chapter 8, we have a tendency to mask the natural odor of the human body, and to many other cultures this custom seems strange and odd.

Role enactment refers to how well one executes the appropriate verbal and nonverbal messages according to one's relative position and role in the host culture. The behaviors that professors in the United States enact in the classroom may be misinterpreted or seen as improper in classrooms in other cultures. Managers must be particularly careful about the types of strategies they employ across cultures. Men and women should know how their sex roles vary across cultures. American women returning from abroad frequently comment on how badly they were treated. The freedoms U.S. women have gained throughout this century are not shared by women across the globe. A female student who had recently returned from a semester of study in southern Italy recounted her experience:

> I couldn't believe how the men acted toward me and my friends. When we would walk through town, they would whistle and hiss at us. They would try to touch us and acted like all we wanted to do was sleep with them. It was simply expected. Everyone told us that this was how they treated women and to just get used to it.

As we have seen throughout this text, the verbal and nonverbal behaviors expected for sex and occupation roles vary considerably across cultures. In particular, understanding these two role positions are keys to becoming interculturally competent.

SITUATIONAL FEATURES

The fourth component of intercultural competence is the actual situation in which intercultural communication occurs. Remember that a person may be perceived as competent in one situation and not in another. Perceived competence varies with the situation. Some of the situational features that may affect competence include, but are not limited to, the *environmental context, previous contact, status differential,* and *third-party interventions.* Recall from Chapter 4 the influence of the environment on communication. Some situations may have higher information loads than others, which may affect your motivation and ability to enact appropriate verbal and nonverbal behaviors. Highly loaded situations may increase anxiety and reduce your motivation to approach another. In addition, you should have some knowledge of the host culture's perception of time and space. If you are lucky enough to be invited into someone's home, keep in mind that the use of space in homes varies dramatically across cultures.

In some of her work, Young Kim discusses the importance of previous contact and status differences.[15] Because of the dynamic nature of competence, any previous contact you may have had with a person from another culture may enhance your perception of competence. Competence and trust take time to establish and build, and your competence will grow as you interact more with the people of your host culture. Conversations with persons from other cultures provide a particularly rich source of data for you. The more contact you can have with these people, the more likely you are to learn about them (knowledge) and feel comfortable (affective) interacting with them, thus being enabled to master your verbal and nonverbal skills (psychomotor).

Although you may have sufficient knowledge about another culture and be motivated to interact, status differences may require you to take on multiple modes of behavior. Certain verbal and nonverbal strategies may be more or less appropriate depending on whether you are interacting with someone of lower, equal, or higher status. In the United States, we have a tendency to minimize status differences. In other cultures, as we learned in Chapter 2, one's status determines the order of speakers and the types of codes to use in a given situation. Because your status may be high in one situation and low in another, you should be mindful in understanding how the communication will vary accordingly.[16]

The addition of a third party may noticeably change the dynamics of the situation, and hence your competence. All of a sudden your status may go up or down, as might the status of the person with whom you are interacting. The sex of the third party may also alter the situational features. Topics that were just a moment ago appropriate may now be unfit for discussion. The competent communicator keeps a sharp eye on the changing characteristics of the situation and adapts his or her verbal and nonverbal communication accordingly.

The model of intercultural competence given in Figure 12-1 depicts the knowledge, affective, psychomotor, and situational features as interdependent. This means that as one component changes, the others are affected as well. Generally, as knowledge increases, one's motivation to approach increases. As motivation increases, one is more likely to engage in behaviors. If the behaviors are successful, one learns more about intercultural communication, which further serves to increase motivation. And the cycle continues.

INTERCULTURAL TRAINING PROGRAMS

Throughout the United States communication practitioners offer workshops, seminars, and training programs designed to introduce people to culture and to assist them in becoming interculturally competent. Due to the near reality of the "global village" concept, people from all walks of life, including business owners, managers, teachers, government officials, and family members of expatriates (i.e., persons from the United States living and working abroad) need the knowledge and skills to interact with people from different cultures. Cross-cultural training programs vary in content, but are typically designed to accomplish four goals, including (1) assisting people in overcoming cultural obstacles that might interfere with their enjoyment of their intercultural experiences, (2) teaching people how to initiate and develop relationships with people from other cultures, (3) help people accomplish job-oriented tasks in intercultural assignments, and (4) assist people in how to deal with the stress that often accompanies intercultural communication.[17]

The content of cross-cultural training programs varies, of course, but most contain a combination of lecture/discussion, self-assessment instruments, case studies, simulation role-plays, videos, and a variety of homework assignments. The most traditional format of cross-cultural training workshops involves the lecture/discussion format. According to Gudykunst and his colleagues, in this type of format trainers assume that a cognitive understanding of a culture is necessary to be effective in communication. In the lecture/discussion format, the trainer presents and discusses the similarities and differences between cultures. This format is analogous to the college classroom context, where the primary mode of instruction is a professor lecturing to students. The lecture/discussion format is designed to strengthen the knowledge component of the intercultural competence model.[18] Brislin and Yoshida point out that many cross-cultural training programs contain self-assessment exercises.

Virtually every chapter in this textbook offers self-assessment instruments. In Chapter 1, for example, students can measure their level of ethnocentrism. In Chapter 2, scales designed to measure individualism/collectivism, high/low context, high/low power distance, and weak/strong uncertainty avoidance are presented. In this chapter, a cross-cultural awareness scale and an intercultural willingness to communicate scale are presented. Many of the same instruments presented throughout this book are used in cross-cultural training programs. These instruments, if completed honestly, present a reliable and valid index of the individual's relative position on the concept being measured.[19] Self-assessment instruments are useful because trainees can use them to discover dimensions of the knowledge component and the affective component of the intercultural competence model.

Case studies are stories or narratives that have an educational message. In cross-cultural training programs, case studies are either real or hypothetical stories dealing with people in intercultural situations where something has gone wrong or miscommunication occurs. The specific cases are chosen because they serve to illustrate general principles and practices of intercultural communication. They typically have correct answers. Case studies are useful because they tap into the knowledge and affective components of intercultural competence. Moreover, case studies allow trainees to indirectly observe intercultural communication and empathize with the people involved. Virtually every chapter in this text includes *intercultural conversations* depicting people in intercultural communication situations. These conversations are similar to case studies because they allow you to see how the concepts discussed in the text (e.g., individualism/collectivism) are evident in human intercultural communication. In cross-cultural training programs, trainees are presented with a case study, are asked to discuss it, and may be asked a series of questions. Consider the box on p. 375.

Some cross-cultural trainers will incorporate simulation role-play exercises into their workshops. This approach is based on experiential learning (i.e., learning from experience). Role-play exercises typically have trainees actually engage in intercultural communication. For example, trainees might be asked to interview

Intercultural Communication in Practice in the Real World

Jim Neuman works in the sales division of General Kitchen Appliances. Jim sells kitchen equipment to industrial-sized kitchens (e.g., for hotels, restaurants). In the United States, Jim has been very successful. Last year he was named General Kitchen's salesperson of the year, surpassing all of his sales goals. Jim has decided that he would like to expand into international markets. He has been granted a job interview by Sonado Corporation, a major kitchen equipment manufacturer in Japan. Sonado is about to expand into European markets. Here's part of Jim's interview with Mr. Kietaro, head of sales at Sonado.

Mr. Kietaro: Mr. Neuman, why would you like to work for Sonado?

Jim Neuman: I believe I have the necessary skills and experience for this position. I'm independent and I set very high goals for myself. I believe your company will give me the opportunity to pursue them.

Mr. Kietaro: I see. What kind of goals do you have?

Jim Neuman: I have very high sales objectives. I try to reach the top in whatever I do. One of my goals is to become your leading salesperson. For example, I had the highest percentage of sales of anyone at General Kitchen. I was salesperson of the year last year.

Mr. Kietaro: I see. That's very impressive.

Jim Neuman: I'm a self-starter and self-motivator. Now I'd like to expand into an international market, I'd like to bring my experience and motivation to your company. I can be the best at Sonado, too.

In the end, Jim Neuman was not offered a position at Sonada. In his letter to Jim, Mr. Kietaro was very complimentary about Jim's performance at General Kitchen and explained that although Jim certainly had experience, he was not sure Jim would fit into the Sonado corporate culture.

1. Did Jim make any mistakes in his interview?

2. Characterize Jim's answers to Mr. Kietaro's questions.

3. What did Mr. Kietaro mean when he said Jim might not "fit into" Sonada's corporate culture?

4. What dimension of cultural variability (as discussed in Chapter 2) might have played a role in Mr. Kietero's decision to not hire Jim?

someone from a different culture. Other role-playing exercises might have trainees engage in a communicative situation designed to simulate the types of situations they are likely to face in another culture. For instance, in many countries during shopping, bargaining and negotiation are expected. Shoppers are encouraged to bargain with shop owners. In some countries, bargaining may be intense and loud. To the uninitiated American, this may seem very unusual and could be misinterpreted. Role-playing exercises that simulate such bargaining behavior could be very useful. Role-play simulations are valuable because they tap into the knowledge, affective, and psychomotor components of intercultural competence. In addition, role-play simulations can be modified to reflect the various situational features that affect intercultural communication. Careful attention should be paid to the construction of role-plays because trainees can experience intense affective reactions (e.g., apprehension, anxiety) to them.

In addition to lecture/discussions, self-assessment instruments, case studies, and simulation role-plays, videos and homework assignments are often used in cross-cultural training programs. Videos allow the trainee to "witness" intercultural communication situations and perhaps empathize with the people in the video. Homework assignments often include some type of journaling, in which trainees are asked to write their thoughts and reactions to the knowledge, emotions, and skills they are learning.

Chapter Summary

One of the foremost goals of this book is to help you become a competent intercultural communicator. As defined in this chapter, _intercultural communication competence_ is the degree to which you effectively adapt your verbal and nonverbal messages to the appropriate cultural context. This chapter has presented a model of intercultural competence that includes knowledge, affective, psychomotor, and situational components. In order to be a competent communicator, you must have some _knowledge_ about the person with whom you are communicating. In order to be a competent intercultural communicator, you need to be _motivated_ to communicate with people who are different than you. You need to engage in appropriate and effective verbal and nonverbal _skills_ in order to encode and decode messages. And you need to be sensitive to the situational features that influence the verbal and nonverbal messages you send.

It is to be hoped that having read this text, you are more knowledgeable about culture, are more motivated to enter into new cultures and establish relationships with persons from different cultures, and have gained some communication skills. Although challenging, intercultural communication is one of the most rewarding life experiences you will ever have.

GLOSSARY OF TERMS

Affective component: Approach-avoidance tendencies during intercultural communication. The extent to which one experiences intercultural communication apprehension and one's willingness to communicate.

Intercultural competence: The ability to adapt one's verbal and nonverbal messages to the appropriate cultural context.

Intercultural willingness to communicate: Predisposition to initiate intercultural interaction with persons from different cultures even when completely free to choose whether or not to communicate.

Knowledge component: The extent of one's awareness of another culture's values, and so forth. Also the extent to which one is cognitively simple, rigid, and ethnocentric.

Psychomotor component: The extent to which one can translate cultural knowledge into verbal and nonverbal performance and role enactment.

Situational features: The extent to which the environmental context, previous contact, status differential, and third-party intervention affect one's competence during intercultural communication.

REFERENCES

1. E. T. Hall and E. Hall, "How Cultures Collide," *Psychology Today*, 10 (1976). (Quote on page 66.)
2. B. H. Spitzberg, "A Model of Intercultural Competence," in *Intercultural Communication: A Reader*, 8th ed., ed. L. A. Samovar and R. E. Porter (Belmont, Calif.: Wadsworth, 1997), pp. 379–391.
3. Spitzberg, "A Model of Intercultural Competence."
4. This dialogue is loosely adapted from a scene in L. Copeland, producer *Managing the Overseas Assignment* [videorecording] (San Francisco: Copeland Griggs Productions, 1983.)
5. P. R. Harris, and R. T. Moran, *Managing Cultural Differences*, (Houston: Gulf Publishing, 1991).
6. B. H. Spitzberg and W. R. Cupach, *Interpersonal Communication Competence* (Beverly Hills, Calif.: Sage, 1984).
7. This scale is loosely adapted from N. P. Goodman, "Cross-Cultural Training for the Global Executive," in *Improving Intercultural Interaction: Models for Cross-Cultural Training Programs*, ed. R. W. Brislin and T. Yoshida (Thousand Oaks, Calif.: Sage, 1994), pp. 34–54.
8. C. R. Berger and J. Jordan, "Planning Sources, Planning Difficulty, and Verbal Fluency," *Communication Monographs*, 59 (1992), 130–149.
9. Y. Y. Kim, "Explaining Interethnic Conflict: An Interdisciplinary Overview" (paper presented at the annual convention of the Speech Communication Association, Chicago, Ill., 1990).
10. See, for example, W. G. Sumner, *Folkways* (Boston: Ginn, 1906); M. H. Segall, *Cross-Cultural Psychology: Human Behavior in Global Perspective* (Monterey, Calif.: Brooks/Cole, 1979); M. Hewstone and C. X. Ward, "Ethnocentrism and Causal Attribution in Southeast Asia," *Journal of Personality and Social Psychology*, 48 (1985), 614–623; M. R. Islam and M. Hewstone, "Intergroup Attribution and Affective Consequences in Majority and Minority Groups," *Journal of Personality and Social Psychology*, 64 (1993) 936–950.
11. R. L. Wiseman, M. R. Hammer, and H. Nishida, "Predictors of Intercultural Communication Competence," *International Journal of Intercultural Relations*, 13, (1989), 349–370.
12. J. W. Neuliep and J. C. McCroskey, "The Development of Intercultural and Interethnic Communication Apprehension Scales," *Communication Research Reports*, 14 (1997), 145–156.
13. J. W. Kassing, "Development of the Intercultural Willingness to Communicate Scale," *Communication Research Reports*, 14 (1997), 399–407.
14. Y. Y. Kim, "Intercultural Communication Competence: A Systems-Theoretic View," in *Cross-Cultural Interpersonal Communication*, ed. S. Ting-Toomey and F. Korzenny (Newbury Park, Calif.: Sage, 1991), pp. 259–275, W. B. Gudykunst and Y. Y. Kim, *Communicating with Strangers: An Approach to Intercultural Communication* (New York: McGraw-Hill, 1997).
15. Kim, "Explaining Interethnic Conflict."
16. Ibid.; Gudykunst and Kim, *Communicating with Strangers*.
17. R. W. Brislin and T. Yoshida, "The Content of Cross-Cultural Training: An Introduction," in *Improving Intercultural Interactions: Modules of Cross-Cultural Training Programs*, ed. R. W. Brislin and T. Yoshida (Thousand Oaks, Calif.: 1994, Sage), 1–16.
18. W. B. Gudykunst, R. M. Guzley, and M. R. Hammer, "Designing Intercultural Training," in *Handbook of Intercultural Training*, ed. D. Landis and R. S. Bhagat (Thousand Oaks, Calif.: 1996, Sage), 61–80.
19. Brislin and Yoshida, "The Content of Cross-Cultural Training."